Lecture Notes in Computer Science   7622

Commenced Publication in 1973
Founding and Former Series Editors:
Gerhard Goos, Juris Hartmanis, and Jan van Leeuwen

Bruce Christianson   James Malcolm
Frank Stajano   Jonathan Anderson (Eds.)

Security
Protocols XX

20th International Workshop
Cambridge, UK, April 12-13, 2012
Revised Selected Papers

 Springer

Volume Editors

Bruce Christianson
James Malcolm
University of Hertfordshire
School of Computer Science
Hatfield, AL10 9AB, UK
E-mail: {b.christianson, j.a.malcolm}@herts.ac.uk

Frank Stajano
Jonathan Anderson
University of Cambridge
Computer Laboratory
15 JJ Thomson Avenue, Cambridge, CB3 0FD, UK
E-mail: {frank.stajano, jonathan.anderson}@cl.cam.ac.uk

ISSN 0302-9743   e-ISSN 1611-3349
ISBN 978-3-642-35693-3   e-ISBN 978-3-642-35694-0
DOI 10.1007/978-3-642-35694-0
Springer Heidelberg Dordrecht London New York

Library of Congress Control Number: 2012954009

CR Subject Classification (1998): C.2, K.6.5, E.3, D.4.6, H.3-4, J.1

LNCS Sublibrary: SL 4 – Security and Cryptology

Typesetting: Camera-ready by author, data conversion by Scientific Publishing Services, Chennai, India

Printed on acid-free paper

Springer is part of Springer Science+Business Media (www.springer.com)

Preface

This volume collects the revised proceedings of the 20th International Security Protocols Workshop, held in Sidney Sussex College, Cambridge, during April 12–13, 2012. The theme of the workshop was "Bringing Protocols to Life." We are getting steadily better at specifying security protocols, but can we reason about their subtle interactions with the real world: with the environment, the application, and the system resources?

As with previous workshops in this series, each paper was revised by the authors to incorporate ideas that emerged during the workshop. These revised papers are followed by an edited transcript of the presentation and ensuing discussion. As happened last year, thanks to the valiant effort of all the workshop participants, this proceedings volume is published in the same year as the workshop.

Our thanks to Lori Klimaszewska for the raw transcriptions of the audio, later revised by the speakers themselves, and to Vashek Matyas and Michael Roe for serving with us on the Program Committee. Thanks also to Microsoft Research for financial support.

This workshop being the 20th, we introduced the Roger Needham Award for the paper that provoked the most interesting discussion. Each speaker ranked the papers, and following a Single Transferable Vote protocol the award was won by Sandy Clark, Matt Blaze and Jonathan Smith, for their paper on "The Casino and the OODA Loop."

Participation in the Security Protocols Workshop is by personal invitation following submission of a position paper. If you would like your position paper to be considered for the next workshop, please get in touch.

As always, our hope in disseminating these papers, and the debates that they engendered, is to encourage you to engage with these issues yourselves.

September 2012

Bruce Christianson
James Malcolm
Frank Stajano
Jonathan Anderson

Previous Proceedings in This Series

The proceedings of previous International Security Protocols Workshops are also published by Springer as *Lecture Notes in Computer Science,* and are occasionally referred to in the text:

19th Workshop (2011)	LNCS 7114	ISBN 978-3-642-25866-4
18th Workshop (2010)	LNCS 7061	*in preparation*
17th Workshop (2009)	LNCS 7028	*in press*
16th Workshop (2008)	LNCS 6615	ISBN 978-3-642-22136-1
15th Workshop (2007)	LNCS 5964	ISBN 978-3-642-17772-9
14th Workshop (2006)	LNCS 5087	ISBN 978-3-642-04903-3
13th Workshop (2005)	LNCS 4631	ISBN 3-540-77155-7
12th Workshop (2004)	LNCS 3957	ISBN 3-540-40925-4
11th Workshop (2003)	LNCS 3364	ISBN 3-540-28389-7
10th Workshop (2002)	LNCS 2845	ISBN 3-540-20830-5
9th Workshop (2001)	LNCS 2467	ISBN 3-540-44263-4
8th Workshop (2000)	LNCS 2133	ISBN 3-540-42566-7
7th Workshop (1999)	LNCS 1796	ISBN 3-540-67381-4
6th Workshop (1998)	LNCS 1550	ISBN 3-540-65663-4
5th Workshop (1997)	LNCS 1361	ISBN 3-540-64040-1
4th Workshop (1996)	LNCS 1189	ISBN 3-540-63494-5

No published proceedings exist for the first three workshops.

Table of Contents

Introduction: Bringing Protocols to Life
(Transcript of Discussion)

Bruce Christianson

University of Hertfordshire

Our theme this year (which it's customary to mention once on the morning of the first day) is "Bringing Protocols to Life".

We've gotten a lot better at specifying protocols in increasing degrees of formality, but it's not clear that this is actually making it easier to implement them, nor that it's improving the quality of the finished products to the extent that is often claimed.

It certainly has made it a lot easier to specify and build model checkers, and I am astounded at the progress those guys have made, they're doing things now that ten years ago I wouldn't have thought could be done. So I don't want to discourage that side of the agenda.

But there's a danger of falling into the trap of thinking that because something has been proved correct, that means it's more likely to be right than it was before it was proven correct. Dijkstra famously said that testing can show the presence of bugs but never their absence, and unfortunately the same taunt can be levelled against formal methods.

Failed attempts to prove correctness automatically can construct a break to a protocol, but the most that a successful correctness proof can show is that a successful break requires breaking one of the assumptions that the prover made. And since anybody who's ever implemented a protocol will tell you that 90% of the implementation is actually not about the specification of the protocol at all, but about the management of the system resources, and the interaction with the environment (that's true for any protocol, not just security protocols), this tends to be where the breaks now occur, helped immensely in the case of security protocols by the fact that cryptographic abstractions really do not layer well.

What can we do about that? Can we somehow model the interaction with system resources, and the interactions with the environment, and at what level of abstraction can we do that? And can we somehow use that modelling process to capture the additional assumptions that we're making about what needs to be true in order for the protocol to work?

In the talks over the next two days, we've got some very fine real-world examples of protocols that have quite interesting and subtle interactions with the real world, the environment, the application, and the system resources.

It's the Turing centenary this year, and I think all cryptographers are a bit conferenced out, so we decided to settle for quality and limit the workshop to two days this year.

We've also decided to introduce a prize this year to liven things up. In memory of Roger Needham there will be an award for the position paper that provoked the most interesting discussion, voted for by the speakers on the basis of a single

B. Christianson et al. (Eds.): Security Protocols 2012, LNCS 7622, pp. 1–2, 2012.

transferable vote protocol (so you might want to think about your tactical voting strategy over the next couple of days). The prize is a free drink and glory[1].

I know that many of you have been to one of these events before, but I see a couple of people who haven't, so I'll just go quickly through the rules of engagement.

This is a workshop and not a conference, so please be prepared to lead a discussion rather than attempt to give the talk that you came planning to give. It's also intended to be a reasonably supportive environment in which to make an idiot of yourself, so if you feel the urge to fly a kite, please do. Don't worry if it turns out not to work, because although we record the sessions and the discussions, we edit the transcript fairly heavily afterwards.

So if it works out you have a chance to change your position paper before it's published, and if it doesn't work out you have a chance to change the transcript.

---

[1] The prize was won, on the fifth ballot, by Matt Blaze and Sandy Clark for the last position paper to be submitted.

Secure Internet Voting Protocol for Overseas Military Voters

Todd R. Andel and Alec Yasinsac

School of Computing, University of South Alabama, Mobile, AL, 36688 USA
{tandel,yasinsac}@usouthal.edu

Abstract. Overseas military members are known to be disenfranchised at a far higher rate than traditional voters. This fact stems from problems associated with the traditional vote-by-mail absentee process, which does not mesh well to the military member's frequent address changes, mail delivery in combat environments, and the simple delay in the two way mail system. Initiatives by the Federal Voting Assistance Program aim to improve voting capabilities for U.S. military members. Among these initiatives are the efforts to provide a complete system allowing the military voter the ability to receive and cast voted ballots directly over the Internet. This paper proposes a communication protocol to securely provide this voting option to our military voters while maintaining integrity in the U.S. election process.

Keywords: Internet Voting Systems, Electronic Voting Systems, Absentee Voting, Election Integrity.

1 Introduction

The Internet has significantly changed our lives in many facets, from leisure, information, business, and even functions within our own government. One area to yet fully realize the Internet's benefits is within the United States voting system. While there are many proponents and opponents to such a system, all would agree there are many issues that must be resolved before (and even if) Internet-based voting will be allowed as a whole in our general elections. However, federal law already mandates the development of Internet-based voting options for U.S. military members residing outside of the country.

In order to support overseas and military voters, the 2002 and 2005 National Defense Authorization Acts (NDAAs) charge the Department of Defense (DoD) to expand assistance to eligible voters under the Uniformed and Overseas Citizens Absentee Voting Act (UOCAVA). This effort falls under the responsibility of the Federal Voting Assistance Program (FVAP). Two primary tasks the FVAP is responsible for are to simplify and standardize the UOCAVA and absentee voting process and to demonstrate a secure electronic registration and voting system. While this system is termed a *demonstration*, U.S. law requires that it be used to cast legal ballots in a federal election. This electronic voting system must be implemented in the first federal election after guidelines are developed and

B. Christianson et al. (Eds.): Security Protocols 2012, LNCS 7622, pp. 3–14, 2012.

posted by the U. S. Election Assistance Commission (EAC), currently working in conjunction with the National Institute of Standards and Technology (NIST) [1].

So is military disenfranchisement really a problem? It is estimated that UO-CAVA voters entail approximately 6.5 million people, to include the U.S. military and their voting age dependents, as well as other American citizens residing abroad [2]. UOCAVA voters experience many more challenges than voters who can physically cast their votes at their local polling place on election day due to various reasons: long mail delay in the ballot request-delivery-vote cast process, frequent address changes, mail delivery in combat locations and hostile environments, etc.

Military voting access has improved little in the past fifty years. A myriad of studies on this topic repeatedly confirm that military voters are disenfranchised in dramatically disproportions relative to resident voters, and even to resident absentee voters. Within the past ten years, studies by the EAC [3, 4] and the Government Accounting Office (GAO) [5, 6] show that even raw data to quantify this problem is in itself difficult to collect. More recent studies by the Pew Center for the States [7], the Overseas Vote Foundation [8], and the Military Voter Protection Project [9] confirm that even the advanced technology that now exists has done very little to improve voting access for military members.

This research aims to support implementation of a secure electronic Internet-based voting system for UOCAVA voters without reducing the integrity of the U.S. election process. Initial research focuses on the active duty military personnel subset of UOCAVA voters (approximately 1.4 million [2]), allowing the system to utilize the DoD Public-Key Infrastructure (PKI) already in place. The driving factor behind our focus is due to FVAP guidance provided at the UOCAVA Working Group meetings held in San Francisco in August 2011.

This research offers an Internet-based voting protocol dependent on the DoD PKI system using the Common Access Card (CAC), but can be easily applied to any system reliant on a smart-card like system, such as requiring a national voter card.

2   Internet-Based Voting Systems

There has been a significant public attention on electronic voting systems as their implementation has skyrocketed since Florida's butterfly ballot and hanging chad saga in the 2000 presidential election. The current norm in voting precincts is the Direct Recording Electric (DRE) machines that, for the most part, have taken place of the traditional paper-based ballots. Many DRE voting anomalies and vulnerabilities have occurred as these systems have been introduced in our voting process [10]. While these issues remain critical to the integrity of the voting process, we focus on securing the next generation of Internet-based voting to allow UOCAVA voters to receive election ballots and directly cast those ballots via the Internet from their dispersed duty stations throughout the world.

2.1 Current Use

While many of us have probably used the Internet to cast votes in organizational elections, our favorite television superstar, etc, most would believe Internet-based voting in general elections is just as easy. However, the security requirements for such an election are quite different in general elections for public office. That being said, these security properties are not completely unobtainable and numerous countries are already using, or in development of, Internet-based voting options in their general elections. As of January 2010 (according to the ACE Electoral Knowledge Network)[1], Austria, Australia, Canada, Estonia, France, Japan, and Switzerland have some forms of legally binding Internet-based voting. Many more countries have plans for non-binding trials underway.

2.2 FVAP Voting System Pilot Projects

To meet their congressionally mandated requirements, the FVAP has been actively involved in researching and developing Internet-based electronic voting system projects. In the 2000 general election the FVAP demonstrated the Voting Over the Internet (VOI) project to cast actual ballots over the Internet. The VOI project served as a feasibility study, allowing 84 voters over four states to cast legal ballots [2, 11] using the authentication features supplied by the DoD Public Key Infrastructure. Stemming from the success of the VOI project, the Secure Electronic Registration and Voting Experiment (SERVE) was to provide an expanded UOCAVA voter participation over seven states for the 2004 general election. However, the security concerns raised in the SERVE Report [12, 13] led to the cancellation of the project before it was ever used in an election.

With system security now a visible public focus, the FVAP has been focused on providing incremental Internet-based features short of actual vote casting. The 2004 Interim Voting Assistance System (IVAS)[2] allows UOCAVA voters the ability to register and download blank ballots over the Internet, but requires the marked ballots to be delivered back to the states through normal absentee ballot mail return procedures [2, 11]. In 2011, the FVAP targeted blank-ballot delivery guidelines to allow states to directly provide Internet-based blank ballots without having to use the federal government IVAS system. Additionally, the FVAP continues to work towards a full Internet-based electronic voting system demonstration as still required by 2005 NDAA which ties back to the focus of this paper to provide an Internet-based voting protocol.

2.3 Related Work

Cryptographic voting approaches are well-established in the literature (e.g., [14]). Most of these techniques are constrained by complex requirements for cryptographically ensured receipt freeness and complex encryption schemes [15–17]

---

[1] http://aceproject.org/ace-en/focus/e-voting/countries (accessed 13 June 2011).
[2] Subsequently renamed to the Integrated Voting Alternative Site in 2006.

that extends well-beyond the capability of existing vote-by-mail systems with the aim to provide complete voting systems as opposed to our approach to provide an alternative option for UOCAVA voters to replace vote-by-mail, but still integrate into the current U.S. election process.

Polyas [18] and Helios [19] are two recent complete end-to-end Internet-based voting systems that have been successfully used for university and international organization elections.

Polyas [18] provides a system for registration, vote casting, and vote tabulation as a complete package. The system runs under one authority, requiring electronic concurrence of multiple committee members to perform election actions and attempts to maintain secrecy and anonymity by separating the server responsibilities for authentication and vote casting and tabulation. While Polyas offers some similarities, as far as separating server responsibilities, to the voting protocol developed in this paper, these servers do not fall under separate authorities and therefore risk exists with local potential collusion. Additionally, Polyas being a complete electronic registration, vote cast, and vote tabulation system may be susceptible to wholesale voter fraud over the entire election results if an attacker gets into either the registration or vote tabulation servers.

Helios [19] provides the similar functionality of electronic registration, vote cast, and vote tabulation and is therefore subjected to the same risks of wholesale voter fraud. What differentiates Helios is the use of mixnets and homomorphic encryption schemes to provide public open auditing of an election through ballot casting assurance and universal verifiability. These properties are provided without compromising vote secrecy and voter anonymity. The Helios authors noted some limitations in scaling vote tallying to more than a few dozen votes and themselves do not endorse Helios for large-high stake government elections.

Work in[20] provides the closest theoretical approach to our proposed protocol. The most similar concept is that of a double encryption system, akin to a double envelope in the vote-by-mail system. However, this system has a single encryption on the vote, followed by a single voter signature over that vote. The vote signature must then be removed from the encrypted ballots before being sent to a separate server with the election decryption key for all ballots.

3 Voting System Requirements

The requirements within the voting process is convoluted and even contradictory at times, resulting in a challenging problem in providing a secure system to meet these requirements. Any voting system for U.S. general elections must ensure the following requirements:

1. *Vote Integrity.* The results of cast votes must reflect the intent of the voter. Cast votes must be securely delivered and protected against changes once cast. Additionally, an eligible voter is limited to casting a single vote for a given election item.
2. *Voter Anonymity.* Cast votes must not be traceable back to the original voter, protecting the voter from potential retribution.

3. *Vote Secrecy.* A voter should not be able to prove what vote they cast, guarding against the potential to sell votes.

In addition to these core requirements, voting systems must also be *transparent* and *verifiable*. First, transparency into the voting process enables the voter the ability to view the election process. In a physical election process it is just that, viewable. That is, transparency allows the voter the right to view the voting process along with the voting tabulation process (recall televised vote counting during the 2000 Florida presidential race). Transparency for Internet voting systems is not readily evident as the ability for the voter to watch the balloting process as bits over a network is conceptually challenging. However, open research on protocols and processes as opposed to closed proprietary systems maintains a sense of transparency. The second additional property, verification, ensures the results accurately reflect the intent of the voter by examining relevant artifacts and election processes. That is, verification must ensure the three primary requirements above of vote integrity, anonymity, and secrecy have been met.

Verification is complicated in elections because there are generally mechanisms in place to prevent any cast vote from being attributed to a specific voter. Moving to an Internet-based voting system introduces more challenges in meeting these requirements. In general, people outside of the computer security and voting guidance communities don't fully appreciate the security problems faced by Internet-based voting systems. For instance, since online banking is the acceptable norm and viewed "secure", most people would not see the difference between online banking and online voting. However, as computer security expert Bruce Schneier points out [21], these two problems are quite different. Online banking systems are vulnerable and systems are routinely breached, but rarely do these breaches make news headlines. While the individual whose banking information was stolen may be inconvenienced, the problem is typically quickly resolved by the bank through system logs and digital forensics. But even with its vulnerabilities, online banking continues to thrive as the benefits and conveniences it provides by and large outweighs the risks. This same risk is not acceptable for Internet-based voting systems. To maintain anonymity and secrecy voters must be disassociated from their votes. Unlike the forensic ability that assists to remedy attacks on banking systems, this disassociation requirement virtually makes reconstructing and validating the votes cast by an individual user infeasible and results in the inability to forensically recreate the voter intent.

Verification can come at different points in the process, as we describe referring to Figure 1. The lowest level, *intent verification*, determines if the act of the voting mechanism captures the intent of the voter. For example, marking or punching a selection on a paper ballot must properly indicate the voter's intent. Likewise, in current DRE voting machines the voter's choice on the screen should match their intent; software in an Internet-based voting system should operate in the same fashion. *Casting verification* indicates if the vote has been properly delivered or stored. The canonical standard is placing a paper ballot into a ballot box. In DRE machines the vote must be properly stored locally or to storage on a stand-alone local DRE network. In an Internet-based voting system this criteria indicates that messages cast on remote hosts must be transmitted and stored to an Internet Voting Server, akin to an electronic ballot box. At upper levels of the voting process, verification focuses on the ability the voter can be assured their vote counted and even more stringent the concept of *universal verifiable* systems [22] in that voters are assured that their's, as well as all other voters, votes were count as cast. Assuring votes are actually counted as cast in an Internet-based voting system encompasses the overall end-to-end system.

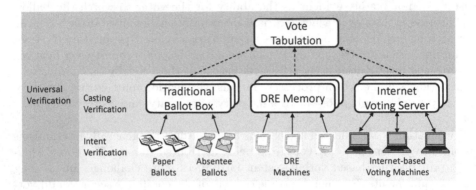

Fig. 1. Verifying Voting Processes

We contend and focus our Internet-based protocol not to eliminate current voting practices, but as a supplemental option to the current voting process. This approach provides an added, or potentially only, option for deployed military voters. That being said, Figure 1 indicates offline tabulation with dashed lines, thus integrating the Internet-based system with the current process for tabulating DRE machines and paper ballots. By forcing this offline restriction to the process, we can alleviate concerns of an attacker using the Internet to get into the vote tabulation process and potentially controlling an entire election. Therefore, our voting protocol must provide *casting verification* of the communicated messages, which we aim to show in this paper.

4   Proposed Internet-Based Voting Protocol

As our intent is to provide an alternative to UOCAVA voters, our protocol is intended to merge into the overall U.S. voting structure as indicated by Figure 1. As a result our protocol does not require the complexities of receipt-freeness or complete universal verifiable systems. The protocol we provide ensures communication security while maintaining our generalized voting security requirements to maintain the criteria for casting verifiability. In general, our protocol must be at least as secure as the current absentee vote-by-mail system used by our deployed military forces.

4.1 Assumptions

Our protocol relies on the following foundational assumptions:

- *Pre-Registration.* The voter has registered with their state prior to the election. We contend that the voting registration must be done outside of the voting system. If one could subvert an integrated registration system and maliciously receive validated credentials, the security of the voting system becomes irrelevant.
- *Physical CAC Issuance.* A military CAC with associated cryptographic signing and encryption keys is physically issued. This identity verification combined with the voter's pre-registration ensures we are dealing with a validated voter and not an automated or remote attacker being able to generate erroneous voting credentials.
- *Multiple Casts not Allowed.* While our protocol ensures one vote per voter, it is not intended to support multiple casts. Unlike the system proposed in [23], once a voter elects to be an Internet-voter during their pre-registration the state will not accept a paper absentee ballot from the voter and once a voter submits an electronic ballot the system will not support additional submissions as opposed to accepting only the latest submission. Therefore, we do not require precision time-stamps or the ability to remove prior votes from the same voter.
- *Controlled Environment.* While voting over the Internet is essentially voting over an uncontrolled environment, we assume that the voting endpoints as well as the voting application are secured. The security of these items is beyond the scope of our protocol but must be addressed prior to any full system development.

4.2 Protocol Description

The voting protocol shown in Figure 2 consists of three distinct parties: the voter, the vote token generator (VTG), and the state voting system (SVS). It is assumed the SVS and VTG are separate systems and fall under separate authorities. For the purposes of this discussion, the SVS, which is equivalent to the Internet Voting Server in Figure 1, is a system operated by the individual state(s) and the VTG is part of the DoD infrastructure. Assuming the voter is registered with their state of record, each state will generate a list of registered military voters, blank ballots for each voting district in which they have voters, and n unique key pairs, where n is the total number of registered military voters. This material is provided to the VTG prior to the election as indicated. Note that each of these unique keys is not tied directly to an individual registered voter. The key pairs are generated as public/private keys, consisting of K and K^{-1}; however, they are not *public* in the traditional sense as the public portions of the keys are provided to the VTG and subsequent voter only. We utilize public/private key pairs to allow for a unique per-vote signed acknowledgment at the end of the protocol.

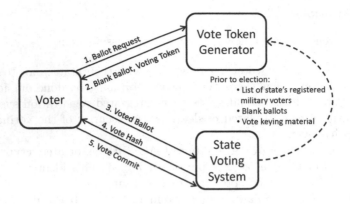

Fig. 2. 3-Party Internet Voting Protocol

Table 1. SVS Master Key List

KeyPair Number	SVS Key	State District	Vote Complete (Y/N)
KP_1	K_1^{-1}	ST_d	
KP_2	K_2^{-1}	ST_d	
...	...	...	...
KP_n	K_n^{-1}	ST_d	

The SVS stores and maintains a master key list as shown in Table 1.

The VTG maintains the following data based on the pre-election material sent from the states: blank ballots by state and voting district (ST_d), a list of registered military voters and their assigned ST_d as shown in Table 2, and a list of voting tokens (VT) as shown in Table 3.

Table 2. VTG Voter List

Voters	State District	Issued (Y/N)
Vid_1	ST_d	
Vid_2	ST_d	
...	...	...
Vid_n	ST_d	

Figure 3 provides a closer examination of the protocol messages, where [ ] indicates encryption and { } indicates a signature operation. All traditional public keys used by the SVS, VTG, and voter are generated and certified by the DoD PKI system. The voting process starts with the voter initiating a ballot request (BR), signed with their CAC-issued secret key (SK_{Vid}). The VTG authenticates the voter, looks up the voter's state and district information (ST_d). Using the

Table 3. VTG Token List

State District	KeyPair Number	Voter Key	Issued (Y/N)
ST_d	KP_1	K_1	
ST_d	KP_2	K_2	
...	...	...	...
ST_d	KP_n	K_n	

ST_d, the VTG randomly selects a key for that ST_d. A voting token is created with the ST_d, key pair number (KP_x) and key (K_x) for that unique key pair. The VTG marks both the KP_x and current voter (Vid) as issued. No further voting credentials will be issued to the voter and no other voters will be issued this unique per-vote key. The voting token along with the blank ballot associated with the ST_d for the voter (BB_{ST_d}) is sent in message 2 encrypted with the voter's CAC-issued public key (PK_{Vid}) and signed by the VTG's secret key (SK_{VTG}). At this point the voter casts the voted ballot (VB) along with the ST_d and encrypts it with the unique per-vote key (K_x) for the issued key pair number. That information is then tagged with the key pair number (KP_x) and encrypted a second time with the openly known public key for the SVS (PK_{SVS}) and sent in message 3. At this point message 3 is akin to the double envelope vote-by-mail ballot. The SVS decrypts the first layer using its traditional secret key (SK_{SVS}) and uses KP_x to identify the unique secret key (K_x^{-1}) to use for decrypting the voted ballot. The SVS generates a hash on the VB resulting in *(h(VB))*. This hash is sent in message 4 back to the voter using the unique K_x^{-1}, the voter verifies the hash value using K_x and the original copy of VB. While this hash could violate the receipt-freeness property, the SVS only records the vote once the voter returns the commit in message 5. Once the SVS receives the commit message it stores the vote and marks the the per-vote KP_x as used.

Message 1:	Voter→VTG	$\{Vid,BR\}SK_{Vid}$
Message 2:	VTG→Voter	$\{[BB_{ST_d},VT]PK_{Vid}\}SK_{VTG}$
		$VT = (ST_d, KP_x, K_x)$
Message 3:	Voter→SVS	$[[VB, ST_d]K_x, KP_x]PK_{SVS}$
Message 4:	SVS→Voter	$\{(h(VB)\}K_x^{-1}$
		voter verifies hash
Message 5:	Voter→SVS	$\{Vote\ Commit\}K_x$

Fig. 3. Protocol Execution

5   Security Discussion

As previously stated, our voting protocol is intended to provide *casting verification* of the communicated messages with respect to the defined properties of vote integrity, voter anonymity, and vote secrecy. Since our focus is to provide an option for UOCAVA voters, we compare security aspects of our protocol against the traditional vote-by-mail (VBM) absentee process routinely used by UOCAVA voters. Therefore, our protocol must maintain security properties >= that of the VBM process. If this criteria is met, our protocol can be used to meet the FVAP goal to reduce UOCAVA voter disenfranchisement.

We provide a general analysis of our protocol according to these general security requirements in-turn.

Integrity. The primary goal of integrity is to ensure the cast vote is not tampered with once cast. Our protocol provides integrity through the use of public-key encryption. Encryption is performed by using the traditional public key for the SVS (PK_{SVS}) and a per-vote key pair (namely K_x/K_x^{-1}). While the outer key is sufficient for general encryption, the second inner key protects against over votes as once the key pair is used, the SVS will not accept additional votes with that key. This protection exceeds VBM as a voter cannot be guaranteed their absentee ballot is not tampered with in transit nor can a voting authority perform detailed hand-signature analysis on VBM ballots.

Anonymity. The goal of anonymity is to ensure the voter cannot be tied to a particular voted ballot. Our protocol provides this property since the SVS gets no voter information from the voter. This assumes that the SVS and VTG are separate systems and fall under separate authorities. The VTG authenticates the user and provides the per-vote K_x. When the SVS decrypts with K_x^{-1} it can ensure it is from a validated and authenticated voter. This protection exceeds VBM as a voter has no guarantee that an election official has not looked at their name and signature on the exterior absentee authentication envelope and looked at their interior marked ballot at the same time. Also if a VBM ballot is intercepted in transit, anyone could look at the voter identity along with who they voted for (whether they then re-seal it and send it on or not).

Secrecy. The goal of secrecy is to ensure the voter does not use proof of their vote in order for personal gain (vote-selling). The protection of our protocol is equal to that of a VBM in that a print screen of a voting system ballot is no different than a photocopied absentee ballot. Neither of these documents show proof as they are not validated by the state as the cast choices; i.e., a voter has no proof that the copied document is what they actually submitted as their actual vote. Neither process stops a third party from physically observing (i.e., coercion) a vote while watching a voter; however, that is the risk U.S. election law accepts for the absentee process. The hash value returned in message 4 does not violate secrecy as the voter has not yet committed their vote so it cannot be used as proof of the submitted vote.

What our protocol does provide as far as a type of receipt, in message 4 from Figure 3, is an acknowledgment from the SVS that the vote was received. This step actually exceeds many states VBM process as it is not common for states to even acknowledge receipt of absentee ballots leaving the voter not knowing if their ballot was even received.

6   Conclusion

Even in the face of the complexities of Internet-based voting, it is difficult to reconcile how our society continues to allow the present state of disenfranchisement of our military members that are in harm's way to protect our right to vote, or even the acceptance of disenfranchising citizens who are not able to cast polling place ballots on election day. In this paper, we propose a secure Internet voting protocol that can dramatically reduce the latency that is inherent in existing vote-by-mail systems to fully enfranchise military members by using the capabilities embedded in military identification cards.

Our goal is to provide a system as an option to traditional vote-by-mail absentee ballots while maintaining the same security properties of the vote by mail system. We have shown that we have met, and even exceeded in some cases, this goal.

It is important to note that our proposed system is not replacing the current U.S. election process, just providing an option for UOCAVA voters. It is vital this system have separate off line registration based on the physical security provided by the authentication credentials in the military CAC-PKI system and the online portion of this system terminate at the electronic ballot box and not directly connected to a full election tabulation system.

This protocol provides the basis for a communication standard recommendation for the FVAP's goal to provide Internet-based voting for UOCAVA voters and is realizable today with the current DoD PKI system.

References

1. U. S. Election Assistance Commission: Report to congress on EAC's efforts to establish, guidelines for remote electronic absentee voting systems. Technical report (April 2010)
2. Stewart, D.B.: Elections: DOD expands voting assistance to military absentee voters, but challenges remain. Testimony before the Committee on Armed Services, United States Senate, GAO-06-1134T (September 2006)
3. U. S. Election Assistance Commission: Best practices for facilitating voting by U.S. citizens covered by the Uniformed and Overseas Citizens Absentee Voting Act. Technical report (September 2004)
4. U. S. Elections Assistance Commission: UOCAVA survey report findings 2006. Technical report (March 2006)
5. GAO: Elections: Voting assistance to military and overseas citizens should be improved. Report to congressional requesters, GAO-01-1026 (September 2001)
6. Walker, D.M.: Issues affecting military and overseas absentee voters. Testimony before the Subcommittee on Military Personnel, Committee on Armed Services, House of Representatives, GAO-01-704T (May 2001)

7. The Pew Center on the States: No time to vote: Challenges facing america's overseas military voters. Technical report (January 2009)
8. Overseas Vote Foundation: 2008 OVF post election UOCAVA survey report and analysis: A detailed look at how overseas and military voters and election officials fared in the 2008 general election and what to do about it. Technical report (February 2009)
9. Eversole, E.: Military voting in 2010: A step forward, but a long way to go. Technical report, Military Voter Protection Project (2011)
10. Harris, B.: Black Box Voting: Ballot Tampering in the 21st Century. Talion Publishing (2004)
11. FVAP: Department of defense: Expanding the use of electronic voting technology for UOCAVA citizens. Technical report, FVAP (2007)
12. Jefferson, D., Rubin, A.D., Simons, B., Wagner, D.: A security analysis of the secure electronic registration and voting experiment (SERVE). Technical report (January 2004), http://www.servesecurityreport.org/
13. Jefferson, D., Rubin, A.D., Simons, B., Wagner, D.: Analyzing internet voting security. Communications of the ACM 47, 59–64 (2004)
14. Fujioka, A., Okamoto, T., Ohta, K.: A Practical Secret Voting Scheme for Large Scale Elections. In: Zheng, Y., Seberry, J. (eds.) AUSCRYPT 1992. LNCS, vol. 718, pp. 244–251. Springer, Heidelberg (1993)
15. Adida, B., Neff, C.A.: Efficient receipt-free ballot casting resistant to covert channels. In: Proceedings of the 2009 Conference on Electronic Voting Technology/Workshop on Trustworthy Elections, EVT/WOTE 2009, p. 11. USENIX Association, Berkeley (2009)
16. Magkos, E., Burmester, M., Chrissikopoulos, V.: Receipt-freeness in large-scale elections without untappable channels. In: Proceedings of the IFIP Conference on Towards The E-Society: E-Commerce, E-Business, E-Government, I3E 2001, Deventer, The Netherlands, The Netherlands, pp. 683–694. Kluwer, B.V (2001)
17. Hirt, M., Sako, K.: Efficient Receipt-Free Voting Based on Homomorphic Encryption. In: Preneel, B. (ed.) EUROCRYPT 2000. LNCS, vol. 1807, pp. 539–556. Springer, Heidelberg (2000)
18. Menke, N., Reinhard, K.: Compliance of POLYAS with the common criteria protection profile - a 2010 outlook on certified remote electronic voting. In: Krimmer, R., Grimm, R. (eds.) Electronic Voting. LNI, vol. 167, pp. 109–118. GI (2010)
19. Adida, B., De Marneffe, O., Pereira, O., Quisquater, J.J.: Electing a university president using open-audit voting: analysis of real-world use of Helios. In: Proceedings of the 2009 Conference on Electronic Voting Technology/Workshop on Trustworthy Elections, p. 10. USENIX Association, Berkeley (2009)
20. Skagestein, G., Haug, A.V., Nodtvedt, E., Rossebo, J.: How to create trust in electronic voting over an untrusted platform. In: Krimmer, R. (ed.) Electronic Voting 2006. LNI, vol. 86, pp. 107–116. GI (2006)
21. Schneier, B.: Crypto-gram newsletter: Internet voting vs. large-value e-commerce, Februrary 15 (2001), http://www.schneier.com/crypto-gram-0102.html
22. Adida, B., Neff, C.A.: Ballot casting assurance. In: EVT 2006, Proceedings of the First Usenix/ACCURATE Electronic Voting Technology Workshop, August 1 (2006)
23. Volkamer, M., Grimm, R.: Multiple casts in online voting: Analyzing chances. In: Krimmer, R. (ed.) Electronic Voting 2006. LNI, vol. 86, pp. 97–106. GI (2006)

Secure Internet Voting Protocol
for Overseas Military Voters
(Transcript of Discussion)

Todd R. Andel

School of Computing, University of South Alabama

Our intent is to develop a system to allow deployed military voters to vote via the Internet. The system is to be *equivalent* to the absentee vote by mail system, without the problems that arise with physical mail. Therefore, the security of our system needs to be evaluated against the absentee process to ensure we meet current absentee security.

Our goal is not to replace the current U.S. voting system, but to provide and online option for our deployed military. In this discussion we focus solely on the communication protocol with respect to the three requirements for voting security:

1. Vote Integrity: a vote should be protected against change, plus only one vote per validated voter.

2. Voter Anonymity: votes must be dissociated from the voter so no one can prove who you voted for.

3. Vote Secrecy: a voter must not be able to prove whom they voted for.

To start our protocol, we assume that the voter has already pre-registered with their state/county and have indicated they wanted to use Internet based voting.

Joseph Bonneau: You keep saying state but it's local, right, I mean, I have to register with my county to vote. Are you aiming to support only state elections here, not local ones?

Reply: Well I do register with my county, but to keep it simple in the protocol design we focused on the state level. The protocol could be further broken down into county and district, but the votes then count as one state election. Your county and district dictates your local elections, and what might be in the ballot.

Matt Blaze: But the vote, the recipient of the ballot is the county registrar, right. Once I vote with this protocol that vote gets transmitted to the particular county.

Reply: It could be either the county or the state, whoever runs that system.

Matt Blaze: In the US, most elections are run by counties.

Reply: That's correct. So we could break this down to whatever local elections you like.

Bruce Christianson: We just think "county" every time we the word "state".

Jonathan Anderson: So that's brings up an interesting question which maybe you address on your next slide, but there could very well only be one voter from a particular county who's deployed to a particular place, and using this online system at the time.

B. Christianson et al. (Eds.): Security Protocols 2012, LNCS 7622, pp. 15–22, 2012.
© Springer-Verlag Berlin Heidelberg 2012

Reply: Yes if only one voter from a particular county is registered the anonymity is broken. That's why it may be potentially be good to run this system as a state process so we don't have a small voting pool. Typically though if it's someone from a place that has a military base, you have a lot of registered military voters in that county.

Paul Syverson: Yes, you can't be anonymous by yourself, so this point is well taken, but I would assume that your goal is that this is going to be entering the state, county, whatever system, and then there's nothing that sets it apart. If things are arriving basically in the same format as input into that system, I would think you're preserving this even if you're the only military voter in that jurisdiction.

Reply: Correct. For instance, if it's a county or a precinct that does DRE I would assume that the electronic votes would be in the same data format. We haven't looked at the application, but are focusing on the the transmission protocol at this point. Really any end voting application could be over this protocol, so if that a common format helps as far as this process is concerned that would be most beneficial, and we'd probably keep that.

Matt Blaze: When you say equivalent in security to an absentee ballot as the requirement, have you formalized that in any way beyond that statement, or has that been formalized anywhere beyond that statement?

Reply: There's been a lot of meetings with the Federal Voting Assistance Program (FVAP) and the UOCAVA workshops, but I still think that they don't even know the security of a vote by mail system. I think most people would agree to that. So formalizing, what we want to show is maybe some equivalences. A lot of that discussion goes back to, what is the security of a vote by mail system versus voting in-person, because both systems have different risks, and I don't think either system's risks are fully understood and quantified.

Matt Blaze: So the answer is that this is no better formalized than the rest of election systems.

Reply: Correct. Moving back to our discussion, we indicate that I register before I go on a typical deployment. The one thing that we do have as a military member is we're all issued actual official cryptographic certificates for use on a common access card or CAC. This issued certificate can be used to identify we are dealing with the voter whom I claim to be. However if I use this identification to cast my vote we have the problem of broken anonymity. What we must do then is use this certificate for identification, and then dissociate from the identity after before casting the vote. We're only going to allow ourselves to do one cast, so we don't necessarily keep time-stamps, we could if we wanted to do last cast. The biggest assumption is that we have controlled endpoints in the applications. Again, we haven't looked at is the application secure, and is the computer that I'm running secure.

Now granted if you're in a controlled environment using a government computer, I won't say that it's less hackable than a non-government system, but at least it's a standard set of protocols or applications that are on that machine. Hopefully it is less vulnerable than a machine sitting in someone's home.

But again, we can't make that claim, so we're going to have to go with the assumption at this point that the endpoint itself and the application are secure.

So what do we have in the system? Other than the voter, we have two primary entities: the State Voting System (SVS) and the Vote Token Generator (VTG).

We first have the State Voting System, again it could be either the state or the local election official of a county. Prior to the election, the military voters have registered with the state and indicated they wanted to use Internet voting. The state voting system now sends information back to the vote token generator, which we assume at this point is run by the DoD. The information sent for each registered military voter is: who they are, the blank ballots that are associated with those voters, and some type of vote keying material. This keying material is a public/private key pair, but not in the traditional sense. When I refer to this public key, it's not necessarily provided freely to everyone[1], it's something that's been issued to me within the CAC public key infrastructure. In a state voting system, the only thing I store is the key number, and half of that key pair, and whatever potential district. The key pair can only be use once, so that's what's going to give our one vote per person requirement.

On the vote token generator side, we have two lists; the voter list and the token list. In the voter list we have voter IDs, which we can now initially validate through the issued CAC certificates and then determine what state the voter registered with. At that point we randomly select the key number and assign the second half of the key pair back to that voter. The voter is going to use the issued key pair half solely to cast their vote to the state voting system. As long as we can trust that these two systems will not collude together, as one is run by the state and the other by the federal government, and they are separated systems, then we maintain our anonymity.

Let's look at the actual message structure here, including the entity of the voter. In this first message we do a ballot request to the vote token generator using the PKI credentials on my CAC. This step authenticates who I am and initiates a blank ballot request. The vote token generator then authenticates the voter and looks up the voter ID, randomly selects a pre-generated token from the state the given voter ID maps to and sends it back to the voter using the voter's traditional public key.

Frank Stajano: SK is your notation for public key?

Reply: This is my secret key, or my private

Joseph Bonneau: You're not sending it, you're using it to sign here?

Reply: Sorry, in this case I'm signing, so it is private[2].

Feng Hao: How do you deduce that Alice sent the public key to end user? How does the end know what your correct public key is?

Reply: When I physically go in to get my card issued they keep one half of the key, the public portion.

---

[1] Cf LNCS 1796 p 208.

[2] In the final paper we change our notation for the token key-pairs to K and K^{-1} to reduce confusion between the token key pair and the traditional CAC PKI keys used in the original authentication.

Paul Syverson: There is an established public key infrastructure that uses these, that is pre-existing.

Reply: Since we already have this CAC based PKI system in place, let's try to design something around it to allow us not to have to reinvent the wheel but rather utilize this already existing authentication system.

At this point when our blank ballot and voting token are sent back, the VTG is going to encrypt it with the voters original credentials that we know through our PKI, and then we're going to go ahead and sign that. Alright, so this is the initial authentication process of saying this is who I am, they know it's me, now I can go and do the vote.

Now let's get to the voting stage, what do we do? I mark my ballot with whatever software we're going to use, hopefully something very similar to DRE so the inputs and in particular the outputs are the same. We then encrypt the voted ballot using using the key issued in the voting token. So this key right here is not my traditional public key that's part of the PKI infrastructure that says who I am. Instead, this is an independent key that basically one half of that key that is still sitting on that state voting server. We can think of this as a double encrypted ballot that we have in the absentee process, shove it in the inner envelope, put it in the outer envelope, so we really have two levels here. And that's what this portion is, the external envelope. Now in this case this is a traditional sense that this is the public key of that state voting system, so we would have to know a certificate authority in this case to verify the state's traditional public key for the outer envelope.

Once we get the vote we can decrypt this as the state voting system. The state voting system takes the corresponding half of that key, unlocks the vote, and we have no voter identification here. Again, that's assuming that these systems are not going to collude as we have distributed that process to the federal government and a local state government. We then do a hash on the vote and send it back with a signature. This signature isn't necessarily a signature that everybody can verify, this is a signature that only that person that was issued that key can verify, because it's not a traditional public key. While some people might think that this is a receipt that I could potentially sell, we haven't committed that vote yet. So if we look at this analogy back to the mail ballot, if I took a print screen of my vote, and I took a photocopy of my absentee ballot, that doesn't necessarily mean that that's what I submitted. Now this doesn't protect against coercion if somebody was sitting behind me while I vote, but in the absentee ballot system we've accepted that risk in the US. So someone could physically fill my ballot out with me and put it in the mail.

Feng Hao: Are you going to publish the hash back?

Reply: No, this would not be verifiable for other individuals.

Jonathan Anderson: Is there another message then after the commit to say, I got your message?

Reply: I'm sure we could add another message, but we could get into an infinite regress loop here. As an absentee voter, I never get anything back from my local election official that they even got my ballot. So this is one extra item that lets me know my vote was at least received.

Frank Stajano: What is the benefit for the voter receiving message 4?

Reply: Just to ensure that we do get some type of response back. We wouldn't have to necessarily put that in there, but it does provide us that extra information, as if it were a return receipt. Also, because the hash value is on the vote, we know that everything got there correctly in transmission.

Phil Brooke: So the analogy with the absentee vote actually finishes that message 3 proof where you sent in votes for ballot.

Reply: Yes, the doubly encrypted vote represents putting the vote inside the inner envelope, and then the outer envelope.

Jonathan Anderson: But of course you don't necessarily need message 5.

Reply: Yes, so you wouldn't necessarily need really 4 or 5 to be fully analogous to just a vote by mail system.

Jonathan Anderson: Well I think 4 is very nice, and if you're allowed to send 3 again you get a different 4, you still have the property that you can't prove that you voted for X or Y?

Reply: Correct. Which I think is very similar to systems out there where you could vote multiple times and they will just take the last one. Since we didn't actually want to track time-stamps, especially globally, we didn't necessarily put that in.

Sandy Clark: Oslo, Norway is using that system where the last vote counts.

Reply: Yes, I know there's quite a few systems out there that will do something like this.

Omar Chaudary: I was just wondering, what happens if you don't send the last message and the receipt. So is that message saying that the user is happy with the hash. If I don't send that what happens, it's like I change my mind, do I start over?

Reply: If you didn't send commit, then the key would never be marked as used in the state voting system. At this point the voter can restart the voting process.

Omar Chaudary: In the table where you're choosing the key at the end, is that key 1 or key 2?

Reply: At this point, I wouldn't get another set of credentials. The system wouldn't mark the key as used until the commit. Once I make that commit, I know that I never could accept another vote that had that key pair pair as it is only issued once.

Omar Chaudary: I'm just wondering, one possible issue to look at is also the possibility of someone messing up with that last message and what happened there.

Reply: Like a denial of service on that last message?

Bruce Christianson: That applies to any protocol whatsoever.

Matt Blaze: I guess the concern that I have is that there are three thousand counties in the United States, but there are only four to six, depending on how you count, vendors of voting systems that those counties are using that are properly certified today. It seems to me that we may be analyzing the wrong problem. The cryptographic literature has anonymous, oblivious delivery of things, and so on, and we can quibble with whether this is the right protocol, and you can prove some properties of it. But in fact it's not actually looking at the end-to-end problem of casting a ballot that's been defined by one of these three thousand counties, and delivering that ballot to that county's voting system with some integrity about whether it's going to be delivered. This is introducing a mid-point that in fact doesn't exist in these counties systems as it is now. So it seems to me that in order to have any confidence in this system we need to look at the somewhere between the three thousand counties and four different back end voting systems used by these counties, and understand how this interacts with them. It seems pretty early to be talking about the cryptography going between this brand new mid-point that's being invented for the purpose of the system, and voters being deployed to wherever-istan.

Reply: I've talked with some of these vendors, but we were trying not to tie anything to the vendors; this would be a completely new system.

Matt Blaze: But ultimately it has to be tied to the vendors, because that's where these votes get counted; the software of these vendors' voting systems is what's counting the ballots, and defining the ballots.

Paul Syverson: You did this under the auspices of, with cognizance of FVAP, right?

Reply: Oh absolutely.

Paul Syverson: The Federal Voting Assistance Program is the DoD's attempt to deal with this. So by creating this artificial mid-point in some sense what you're doing is providing the potential for a standardized interface, and then if the DoD says we will buy this stuff if this becomes part of the standard. So this doesn't have to just be, you know, some cryptographer said this is an interesting idea. This can basically be a federal standard for a voting system, and they will rush to adopt.

Matt Blaze: Yes, it's worked out so well with HAVA.

Paul Syverson: But I think this actually has a bit more potential. I mean, HAVA for one thing they did roll something out. But here you have a little bit more assumptions that you can make about the environment, and you could actually potentially drive the system development.

Matt Blaze: My argument is not that this is impossible, my argument is only that aspect of it is essential for the analysis.

Paul Syverson: In the end, but you can always do the usual security analysis thing where we say, OK, we're secure up to this boundary, and then we assume that it's solved outside. And then of course you make it look like it's a reasonable boundary.

Reply: We've been discussing this all along. With this inner double encrypted message we do have it protected with better integrity than I do in my vote by mail system. In a vote by mail system someone can take my physical envelope and open it up and change my vote. Additionally, when my vote actually gets to the local election official, I really doubt that they can do hand analysis to ensure my signature. So through this system I've actually shown that I am a validated person, and that no-one tampered with the vote in transit. Additionally someone could open up my envelope in transit and look at it, and open my outer and my inner envelope, because they are not enciphered, and put me along with my vote. Not even just someone in transit, but actually a local election official that I mail it to. So I'm able to provide the voter with this system properties that I cannot provide in the vote by mail system. Also we already talked about the secrecy thing, if I photocopy my ballot, and I print my screen of my ballot, that doesn't necessarily mean that is my cast vote, so we feel that we've matched secrecy. Coercion potentially is still there if someone is there with me but that matches the current risk in the vote by mail system.

Joseph Bonneau: I guess my biggest concern is that, really long-term concern anyway, biggest concern is that there would be demands for a standard system if it was actually successful.

Reply: This is a big issue at the UOCAVA workshops. Literally you've got lawyers in the room, you've got academics, voting vendors and the slippery slope idea comes up a lot as an argument not to proceed. The FVAP says that's a Congress issue and its a Congress responsibility to decide what they want to do long-term. However, for the current time they mandated that we proceed to do this one time demonstration project for military voters. Now we all see the writing on the wall if something is successful the decision-makers might go down that path.

Joseph Bonneau: Yes, it makes sense.

Jonathan Anderson: It's actually worse than that. It falls on the Federal Voting Assistance Program to make sure how they phrase it, this is only for military, it requires the assumptions that you have this in place. Because you just know that people are going to say, look, if this is secure enough for the U.S. military surely it's secure enough for the rest of us, and that would be a disaster.

Reply: And that's why when we go back to this system we want to be very clear that we are not tied in any way whatsoever into the overall system. Because that is one thing that is different, I would say that we're more vulnerable in this case if someone gets into any system we have the potential for wholesale voter fraud, many votes being changed as opposed to, did somebody change my one vote. One vote is still bad to change in the mail, but the impact of that one vote versus a million and half military voters is much different.

Jonathan Anderson: Although as a counter argument, if you say this system is secure enough for the military, so it should be good enough for our absentee voters, and you take all the people who are filling out pieces of paper and stuffing them in envelopes, and you replace that with some kind of PKI thing, that's probably not making things worse.

Sandy Clark: Yes, but in the US (I don't know whether this applies to the military or not), most absentee votes are counted only in a case of a close race.

Reply: Oregon does a 100 percent absentee election, so they're opening theirs I hope.

Sandy Clark: And it's so completely random and distributed that you don't know what's going on in one state or one county from another.

Reply: Yes, that is a problem too. Every state has their own process because the federal government does not want to dictate that.

Joseph Bonneau: Another problem is that then you've mandated an extra system that every county has to support forever, and this can basically only increase complexity for what they have to support.

Reply: Well there are parts of any system that they must develop. For instance the FVAP developed IVAS a few years ago along with the Elections Assistance Commission. However, the FVAP can only recommend best practice to the state.

Self-enforcing Electronic Voting

Feng Hao, Brian Randell, and Dylan Clarke

School of Computing Science
Newcastle University, UK

Abstract. Verifiable electronic voting has been extensively researched for over twenty years, but few protocols have achieved real-life deployment. A key impediment, we argue, is caused by the existing protocols' universal reliance on the probity of the tallying authorities. This might seem surprising to many people as dependence on tallying authorities has been a de facto standard in the field. However, this dependence is actually a legacy inherited from traditional physical voting, one that has proved problematic in the electronic context. In this paper, we propose a radically new concept called "self-enforcing electronic voting", which refers to voting systems that are free from reliance on any tallying authority. This proposal goes significantly further than all existing or proposed e-voting systems. We explain the feasibility of this new approach, with a theoretical definition of the system properties, a concrete engineering design, a practical implementation, and real-world trial experiments. We also highlight some open issues for further research.

1 Introduction

Self-enforcing security protocols are powerful, as they do not depend on any external authorities, and thus are much more secure and deployable than those that do. Similarly, we define "self-enforcing electronic voting" as a voting system that does not depend on any external tallying authorities. By this definition, existing e-voting protocols such as Helios [1] are not self-enforcing, as they universally rely on tallying authorities.

The idea of depending on tallying authorities is a historic legacy. From the beginning of voting, the perceived trustworthiness of the authorities has been an important factor in persuading the general public to trust the vote tallying process, at least when buttressed by the use of effective independent observers. This tradition also carries over to e-voting, where existing voting protocols all involve tallying authorities.

But, the theoretical assumption of trustworthy tallying authorities in e-voting proves very tricky to implement. For example, in the recent deployment of the Helios e-voting system in the Université catholique de Louvain (UCL), two problems were reported [1]. The first is usability. For fairness and security, the UCL election committee appointed tallying authorities from diversified backgrounds. But, the chosen tallying authorities knew little about cryptography. They were incapable of understanding and performing complex cryptographic operations,

B. Christianson et al. (Eds.): Security Protocols 2012, LNCS 7622, pp. 23–31, 2012.

and in reality had to rely on external crypto experts to perform the authorization tasks. The second related problem is security. It was assumed that the authorities were subject to a threshold control: each of them was responsible for safeguarding a private key, and it took a quorum of authorities to be able to tally the votes. However, it is possible that authorities might lose their private keys, which could lead to a catastrophic result (the inability to complete the tallying would in effect act as a Denial of Service attack to the entire election). Hence, the election committee decided to centrally back up all of the tallying authorities' private keys and entrust the copies to a notary public. Obviously, the notary public was able to view all the secret votes, which completely defeats the assumed threshold control.

2   Proposal

Our proposal is to eliminate the reliance on (allegedly) trustworthy tallying authorities altogether. We call the resultant voting system "self-enforcing electronic voting".

Figure 1 portrays the evolution of voting technologies. From the beginning of voting, central authority has been playing a pivotal role in instilling trust in the tallying process (an issue which is neatly captured by a famous saying attributed to Joseph Stalin: "It's not the people who vote that count; it's the people who count the votes"). In the current e-voting deployment around the world (US, India, Brazil, etc.), voters have to trust their e-voting machine completely, and transitively have to trust the authority that certifies the machine. Researchers have been trying to apply cryptography to make these e-voting systems more verifiable. The current state of the art in the field involves distributing trust among several authorities using some cryptographic threshold scheme. This is an improvement over relying on a single authority, but not a clean solution. Voters have to trust the authorities do not collude but they cannot verify that this is indeed the case. The mere fear that the authorities might collude to compromise the election would have deterred many voters in the first place. Against this background, our vision of next generation e-voting is that the election will need to be self-enforcing: free from reliance on any tallying authorities.

We now give a slightly more formal definition of "self-enforcing e-voting". For simplicity of explanation, we discuss just the case of a single-candidate election. However, the definition can be easily generalized to multi-candidate elections.

Consider a machine that pre-computes a table of N electronic ballots before the election. As shown in Table 1, each ballot contains two cryptograms representing: "No" and "Yes" (which correspond to numeric values 0 and 1 respectively in our implementation). We thereby define a (single-candidate) self-enforcing e-voting system as one that satisfies the following properties.

1. *Well-formedness* – For each ballot, given n_i or y_i, it is easy for anyone to verify that the given cryptogram is an encryption of one of the two values: "No" and "Yes".

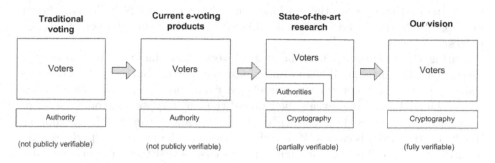

Fig. 1. Evolution of voting technologies

2. *Concealing* – For each ballot, given n_i without y_i, or given y_i without n_i, it is infeasible to compute whether the given cryptogram represents "No" or "Yes".
3. *Revealing* – For each ballot, given both n_i and y_i, it is easy for anyone to compute which cryptogram represents "No" and which represents "Yes".
4. *Self-tallying* – Given a set of choices of one arbitrary cryptogram from the two on each of the N ballots, it is easy for anyone to compute the tally of "Yes".

Table 1. Pre-computed electronic ballots

Ballot no	No_Cryptogram	Yes_Cryptogram
i	n_i	y_i
1	n_1	y_1
...	...	...
N	n_N	y_N

3 Feasibility

In this section, we show the proposed system is feasible by addressing the following three questions: 1) is it possible? 2) how does it work? 3) is it practical?

The first question is whether "self-enforcing e-voting" is theoretically possible. We answer this question affirmatively. In particular, the DRE-i protocol (Hao, Kreeger, 2011) as described in [2] fulfils all of the above properties. However, the DRE-i protocol is only one specific embodiment; there may be other methods to realize "self-enforcing e-voting". Hence, in this paper, we will only discuss the abstraction of system, focusing on the essence of the new proposal.

The second question is how does such a system work in practice. Given a cryptosystem that satisfies the four properties, it is straightforward to apply it to e-voting. As an example, let us consider an on-site voting system that employs a touch-screen Direct Recording Electronic (DRE) machine to records votes. Before the election, the machine generates a table of N ballots as shown in Table 1 (N should be significantly bigger than the total number of eligible voters).

During the election, each authenticated voter casts her vote in two stages. First, the DRE machine displays an unused ballot with both cryptograms initially hidden. The voter touches one choice from the screen - say she chooses "No". The DRE machine reveals the value of the No_Cryptogram on the screen. In stage two, the voter should either "confirm" or "cancel" the vote. If she chooses "confirm", the ballot is casted. If she selects "cancel", she essentially performs the auditing function. The machine must in this case reveal the other cryptogram. With both cryptograms revealed, the ballot is counted as a dummy vote. Dummy votes will not add to the tally. The voter will be assigned another unused ballot and repeat the same two-stage process to vote.

In the above procedure, all the revealed cryptograms (including valid as well as dummy votes) will be published on a public bulletin board and also printed on the receipt. Based on the *Well-formedness* Property, anyone can verify that the confirmed vote is either "No" or "Yes". Based on the *Concealing* Property, the single revealed cryptogram does not disclose the voter's choice, so the receipt does not show how the voter had voted (this is to prevent coercion). However, the same *Concealing* Property also implies that the DRE machine might cheat – when one selects "No", the machine may display Yes_Cryptogram, and the voter would not be able to tell the difference (i.e., knowing that his vote had been subverted). This is where the *Revealing* Property becomes useful. If the machine cheats by switching the cryptograms, this will be caught when the voter chooses to cancel (i.e., audit) the vote. Finally, the *Self-tallying* Property ensures that when the election finishes, any member of the public is able to tally the "Yes" votes without involving any tallying authorities. (Satisfying the *Self-tallying* Property is the most difficult part in the design of a self-enforcing voting system. The way that is achieved in [2] is based on a technique proposed six years ago at SPW'06 [3].)

The third question – perhaps the most important and most difficult – is whether the proposed system is practical. We answer this question positively by presenting two real-world trial elections based on the self-enforcing e-voting technology, as we detail in the following section.

4   Trial Elections

Based on the DRE-i protocol specification in [2], we have developed a fully functional self-enforcing e-voting system, and conducted two (admittedly rather small scale) trial elections among members of the School of Computing Science at the Newcastle University to elect the "favorite chocolate" and "favorite cheese" in October, and November, 2011 respectively. (The two winners were "Quality Street" and "Wensleydale".) In total, 74 people participated our trials.

In both election trials, all participants were the staff and PhD students of the Computing Science department of Newcastle University. The first election involved participants trying three types of chocolate and then voting for their favourite flavour. The second election involved participants trying three types of cheese and then voting for their favourite type.

In both cases, participants were able to try the items on offer and then take a random paper slip from a box placed next to the food. The food and the paper slips were put in a room that was only accessible to the department staff and PhD students. The slip contained a web address for on-line voting and a random passcode. Each participant was free to take a random passcode, so voting was anonymous. When participants had finished voting on-line, they were asked to complete a questionnaire.

4.1   Chocolate Election

This trial was based on an implementation of the DRE-i protocol using a multiplicative cyclic group – the same underlying group as the Digital Signing Algorithm (DSA). The voting trial had 39 participants. All participants casted a confirmed vote. Four of them audited a ballot once (i.e., casted a dummy vote) before confirming their votes. No voter audited more than once.

The feedback questionnaire consisted of 6 statements and respondents were asked to indicate their agreement or disagreement on a Likert scale from 1 to 5 (i.e., "strongly agree", "agree", "neural", "disagree", "strongly disagree"). The statements were as follows:

1. I understood how to vote.
2. Voting was easy.
3. I understood how to check my ballot had been recorded correctly.
4. Checking that my ballot had been correctly recorded was easy.
5. I understood why I was being asked to check ballots.
6. I felt confident that my vote had been recorded correctly.

The feedback questionnaire was answered by 23 voters. One respondent did not give an answer for statement 2; other than this, every respondent gave an answer for every statement. The results are shown in Table 2.

4.2   Cheese Election

The subsequent cheese election trial was conducted one month after the chocolate election. For this trial, we changed the implementation to using an additive cyclic group – the same underlying group as the Elliptic Curve Digital Signing Algorithm (ECDSA). The basic DRE-i protocol remained the same, but the implementation became more efficient and the size of the receipt significantly shorter.

The voting trial had 35 participants. All participants casted a confirmed vote, and one voter audited a ballot once before confirming the final vote. No voter audited more than once.

Table 2. Feedback Questionnaire on the chocolate election

Question	Strongly Agree	Agree	Neutral	Disagree	Strongly Disagree	Average score (nearest option)
1	13	7	3	0	0	1.57 (Agree)
2	10	7	3	2	0	1.86 (Agree)
3	7	6	5	4	1	2.39 (Agree)
4	4	2	7	7	3	3.13 (Neutral)
5	5	6	0	9	2	2.86 (Neutral)
6	7	7	3	4	2	2.43 (Agree)

The feedback questionnaire consisted of 7 statements and respondents were asked to indicate their agreement or disagreement on the same Likert scale as before. The statements were as follows:

1. I understood how to vote.
2. Voting was easy.
3. I understood how to check my ballot had been recorded correctly
4. Checking that my ballot had been correctly recorded was easy.
5. I understood why I was being asked to check ballots.
6. I felt confident that my vote had been recorded correctly.
7. I felt confident that my vote was anonymous.

The questionnaire was answered by 20 voters. Every respondent gave an answer to every statement.

Table 3. Feedback Questionnaire on the cheese election

Question	Strongly Agree	Agree	Neutral	Disagree	Strongly Disagree	Average score (nearest option)
1	15	2	2	1	0	1.45 (Strongly agree)
2	12	1	6	1	0	1.80 (Agree)
3	4	9	2	5	0	2.40 (Agree)
4	2	4	6	7	1	3.05 (Neutral)
5	4	6	4	5	1	2.65 (Neutral)
6	5	6	6	3	0	2.35 (Agree)
7	7	5	6	1	1	2.20 (Agree)

5   User Feedbacks and Open Issues

In the trials, we did not provide any manual to explain how to vote. The only thing that was available to the voter is a slip that contains a voting website URL and a random password. We wanted to see how far voters could go. The feedback shows that users generally found the system intuitive to use – overall 86% of users stated that they well understood how to vote even without any manual or prior training; 71% rated the voting procedure as "easy"/"very easy"; 58% expressed their "confidence"/"strong confidence" that their votes had been recorded correctly. Clearly, there is still a lot of room for improvement, but we found the initial user feedbacks broadly encouraging.

So far our pioneering investigation on self-enforcing e-voting has increased our belief that it has great potential. However, we have also identified a number of open issues. (In fact, most of these issues are generally applicable to all e-voting protocols, not specifically to ours.)

1. *Zero Knowledge Proofs* – The *Well-formedness* Property requires using the ZKPs to ensure the correct format of the ciphertext. Existing ZKPs techniques can well support the first-past-the-post type of voting (using the 1-of-n ZKP), but not the ranked choice voting. More research in this aspect is much needed.

2. *Receipts* – Voters need to verify the receipt against the public bulletin board to ensure the data match. However, the cryptographic data printed on the receipt is essentially random. Comparing random data is trivial to a computer, but tedious to a human. In our first trial, about 43% users expressed difficulties in comparing receipts against the data on public bulletin board. In the subsequent trial, we improved the implementation using Elliptic Curve Cryptography to make the receipt significantly shorter. But still 40% users found it difficult to visually compare the receipt with the bulletin board. This highlights a serious usability problem that has been generally ignored in the past. An often-suggested solution is to apply some visual hashing technique to transform the random data to a visual pattern. However, we have not found a really good visual hashing algorithm that is suitable for practical use. An alternative solution, as we propose, is to print the receipt on a transparency, that the user can overlay on the computer screen to verify that the data match identically.

3. *Re-voting* – Re-voting permits a voter to vote multiple times but ensures that only the last vote counts. Although it appears to be a useful feature, re-voting should be implemented with caution. This is because re-voting essentially overwrites the previous vote, and thus invalidates the previous receipt. Disputes may arise if the re-voting requests are not handled in a publicly evident manner. We know it is possible to implement re-voting at a polling station (as explained in [2]), but currently we do not know how to do it securely in an entirely remote setting. (We notice that Helios allows re-voting in an Internet election [1], but we have not seen detailed analysis on how this was securely achieved.)

4. *Anonymity* – In our implementation, anonymity is achieved through physical means: each voter takes a random password to vote. Of course, this solution will not work in an entirely remote setting. The Helios system claims to protect user's anonymity over the Internet by using pseudonyms [1]. But we think that claim is incorrect – the server can still work out the matching between the real user and the pseudonym. The problem of how to achieve

real anonymity in remote e-voting – without any physical means – is still unsolved. In fact, we do not even know if the problem is solvable.

5. *Auditing* – If we allow voters to audit the system (i.e., voter-initiated auditing), how many of them would actually endeavor to do that? This is an important question, but has been generally neglected in the past. For example, we did not find concrete data in the Helios paper [1]. Our own trials indicated that – without any incentive scheme – only a very small percentage of our voters had bothered to audit the system: only 7%. (And these were all computer scientists, many of whom were particularly interested in security and dependability.) This shows the necessity of employing dedicated auditors (possibly from the representatives of different parties) for national-scale elections. But still, we consider it important to set up incentive schemes to encourage voters to audit the system. One specific example of the scheme is suggested here as follows: if the voter chooses to audit the system, he will get a charity token, and he will be free to donate it to one of the charities near the exit of the polling station. We regard this simple solution as an especially ethical form of so-called "ethical bribery" – we term it the "Waitrose scheme" to acknowledge a similar charity program run by Waitrose food stores in the UK.

6. *Understandability* – How does one get the general public to trust a system that they know they do not understand, especially one whose use/reliance on cryptography is all too invisible and mysterious to them? We do not yet have a good answer to that, but the same question applies to all e-voting schemes that involve cryptography.

7. *Dependability* – In conventional e-voting schemes, tallying authorities have some error-correction capability: if some ballots are lost, the authorities may decide to exclude the missing ballots and only tally the rest (of course, this capability may be misused). By contrast, self-enforcing e-voting schemes are free from tallying authorities (and hence free from any potential misuse), but they naturally lose the external error-correction capability. As a result, all electronic data on the public bulletin board must be precise and complete; otherwise, the public verification of the integrity of the tally will fail. In the extreme disastrous situation where electronic data on the bulletin board is corrupted, the system will degenerate to the current e-voting products, where the e-voting machine announces a tally at the end of election, but the public are unable to verify it. In summary, self-enforcing e-voting has bought its property of self-tallying at a cost of much higher dependability requirements. We believe this is achievable, but further research is needed.

6 Conclusion

In this paper, we have outlined a new design called "self-enforcing electronic voting". This addresses a critical problem in e-voting: ensuring the integrity of the election tallying result when the e-voting machine is totally corrupted. And this goal is achieved without any tallying authority involvement, which greatly simplifies the election management and organisation.

Our proposal is only the first step in exploring a new direction in e-voting and there are still a number of open issues to resolve, but we believe it has promising potential of becoming the next-generation e-voting.

References

1. Adida, B., Marneffe, O., Pereira, O., Quisquater, J.J.: Electing a University President Using Open-Audit Voting: Analysis of Real-World Use of Helios. In: Proceedings of the Electronic Voting Technology Workshop / Workshop on Trustworthy Elections (2009)
2. Hao. F., Kreeger, M.N.: Every vote counts: ensuring integrity in DRE-based voting system. Newcastle University technical report No. 1268 (2011)
3. Hao, F., Zieliński, P.: A 2-Round Anonymous Veto Protocol. In: Christianson, B., Crispo, B., Malcolm, J.A., Roe, M. (eds.) Security Protocols 2006. LNCS, vol. 5087, pp. 202–211. Springer, Heidelberg (2009)

Self-enforcing Electronic Voting
(Transcript of Discussion)

Feng Hao

Newcastle University, UK

Good morning everyone. In the past six months I have been doing some preliminary investigation on what the future e-voting will look like. We have made some progress and I would like to share with you our findings, and also highlight some open problems. I would appreciate your comments and critics. For this presentation I have prepared an election. All you need to do is take one pass code. You will need a laptop with Internet access to vote. I will just pass around the pass codes now. Voting is anonymous, and feel free to take one pass code. Of course you may ask, what is this election about? I'm not going to tell you yet (laughter from the audience) but near the end of my talk I will reveal the results of the election.

In general there are two types of e-voting implementations. One is to use a touch screen DRE machine to record the voter's choice directly. And such DRE machines have been widely used around the world. In particular in India and Brazil, all the national elections have been using DRE machines. The second type is remote e-voting using a web browser. If you see the picture on the right, the man in the picture is the Prime Minister of Estonia casting his vote from his office. In 2007 Estonia became the first country in the world that allowed Internet voting for national elections.

But e-voting is controversial, as you often read from newspaper. This is a diagram from USA Today newspaper, and this shows the usage of the DRE in the country. As you can see, from 2000 to 2006, there is a rapid increase of the DRE usage in the country. But during this time researchers also found many security problems with the deployed DRE machines, and that greatly affected people's confidence. As a result, in 2006 several States in the US abandoned DRE, which caused a big decline of DRE usage. Similar controversy can also be observed in other countries, such as Germany, Netherlands and Ireland. Those countries suspended e-voting around 2008-2009. All this leads us to the question about the future of e-voting: will e-voting be more widely used, or should it be completely abandoned? These are important questions, and are the questions we aim to address in the research.

First of all we need to understand where it went wrong in the past. A basic problem with many deployed e-voting systems is that they're not verifiable, so the system works like a black box. At the end of the election the black box tells you who is the winner, but you can't verify it. If the public can't verify the tallying result, how can you make the pubic trust that the result is actually accurate? In many countries the governments try to solve this problem by certification – if the machine is certified you should trust it. But this doesn't really solve the fundamental problem, because a certified black box is still a black box,

B. Christianson et al. (Eds.): Security Protocols 2012, LNCS 7622, pp. 32–40, 2012.

and you still can't verify it. In the past few years researchers have repeatedly demonstrated that they could hack into certified machines, and change election results without being detected. That greatly reduces the public confidence on the integrity of a black box voting system. Therefore, the lesson here is that for e-voting to succeed in the future it must be verifiable.

However, that leads to a bigger question. The concept of verifiable e-voting is not anything new. In fact, it has been researched for over 20 years. Why hasn't it really caught on? So many protocols have been proposed in the previous 20 years, but in reality, few of them have actually been implemented, and almost none of them have been widely used in real world elections. So there is something wrong.

The state-of-the-art in the e-voting field, which is basically the same as 20 years ago, is follows: the voter casts a vote and gets a receipt. The receipt is encrypted to protect the voter's privacy. At the end of the election the system publishes all the receipts on an official website. Some people call it a public bulletin board. Basically it is a mirrored public website. Every voter can compare the receipt with the website which ensures that the vote has been captured. All the data published are encrypted, so you need another decryption system to do the decryption, and that will involve a set of tallying authorities with each authority holding a share of the decryption key. A lot of voting protocols focus on designing this decryption system, because this system by itself is a complex technology.

However, there is a fundamental problem with this architecture, as we argue. The problem is the very reliance on the tallying authorities who are humans. Why do tallying authorities become a problem here? By assumption, tallying authorities need to satisfy all of the following expectations. First, they don't collude with each other. But that is unverifiable. If they did collude, you would not know. Second, they need to be cryptographers. The technical skills for the authorities are very demanding. Third, they need to be expert in computer science. They need to write their own software (and probably their own compiler), because they don't trust anyone else. Finally, they have to be extremely careful not to lose the key. If you lose the key the entire election will be aborted because all the data is encrypted, and it would be impossible to decrypt data once the key is lost. As you can see, the practical implementation of these tallying authorities is not that easy.

Let's look at one real world example. Among so many authority-based voting protocols only a few are actually implemented. Helios is probably one of the most famous, and it was used in 2009 to elect the University President of UCL at Belgium. In the paper the authors acknowledged that the tallying authority presented one particularly difficult issue. Why is that? As we know, authorities need to be selected from different voting parties to be representative of different interests so that they don't collude. In the University election you can't select all authorities from computer science, because that's not fair to other departments. So in the UCL election, the authorities were selected from students and staff of different departments. That's good, but now you have a problem. The selected authorities didn't know crypto and they didn't know how to write their own software. And then there's a process you need to generate private keys; you need to do the secret sharing; you need to store the private keys. These things are often taken for granted as being easy, but in reality, they are not that easy. Finally, you need to do the backup of the private keys. Again, authorities were not capable to do that properly. This is real life. What can we do?

So the solution used by Helios is that since the authorities don't know how to do these operations, let's find another group of experts to do these cryptographic operations. Who are they? The paper doesn't explain. It just says, authorities need to trust these experts. Basically, the experts wrote their own python scripts, and did some crypto operations. At the end of the operation, they saved the generated private keys on the USB sticks, and gave the USB stick to each of the authorities. This is a key they need to keep, and they need to keep it securely. But still, there is a danger. If one authority happens to lose the stick, or damage it, the whole election would be aborted. That is because of the way they set up their secret sharing, and some people may argue why not to have a more error-tolerant secret sharing scheme, so that it takes cracking a few tokens to ruin the election. But actually this is a complex issue. In the Helios implementation, they chose the most straightforward way to implement threshold cryptography. It provides the highest level of resistance against collusion by corrupt authorities. The downside is that if one authority loses his USB stick the whole election will be aborted. Therefore, in the actual implementation, all the private keys were essentially backed up by one single trusted authority. So one can naturally ask: what's the point of distributed trust, and what's the point of secret sharing, when everything comes back to the centralised single point of failure?

This is just one problem, and there are more problems. First of all, in Helios, everyone is required to enable JavaScript, but some people choose to disable JavaScript in the browser for some security reasons. In addition, everyone is required to install a Java plug-in but some people don't do that. Voters are also required to use relatively fast client computers because you need to do extensive encryptions in your browser; if you use a slow computer it just doesn't work. Finally, everyone is required to accept and execute download code from the Helios server. What exactly does the code do? Ordinary users cannot know, and even for many experts, they cannot tell. Some people may argue, OK never mind, these are just practical implementation issues, and there's nothing wrong with the theory. But I disagree. I think theory and practice always come together. The fact that you have so many practical problems indicates there's probably a problem in the theory.

Indeed all these problems are actually rooted in the reliance on tallying authorities. Because you have tallying authorities, you need to do encryption in the real time under the tallying authorities' public key. How can you actually do the encryption in the browser? You need to install a Java plug-in. Right, and for the Java plug-in to work, you need to enable JavaScript. In addition, the Java plug-in needs to execute some code. Where does it come from? You need to download the code in real-time from the Internet. So all these problems can actually be traced back to the fundamental problem, which is the reliance on tallying authorities.

Here is our proposal. We propose to completely get rid of tallying authorities, and replace them with one public algorithm, and see what will happen. Because the algorithm here is public so it is fully verifiable. No one has proposed this before, partly because the idea is very counter-intuitive. As we know by convention in cryptography, you have encryption and then decryption. The decryption always involves some secret keys. But here we don't involve any secret keys. We have all the encrypted data, and then we have one public algorithm to do the decryption. It may seem impossible, but it is actually possible. The basic intuition is that when we do the encryption here it always involves some random factors. And in fact you can encrypt in some clever way so that at the output when you multiply all the encrypted data together, you can cancel out all of the random factors. Then you will be able to get the decrypted tallying output. So that is the basic idea; it is based on a protocol that I presented six years ago in this workshop together with Piotr Zielinski[1].

So here is an overview of this system. It's just one example to demonstrate that such self-enforcing e-voting is actually feasible. You can read more in our technical report. Of course there may be other ways to construct self-enforcing e-voting protocols. This is a whole new paradigm of designing e-voting. Our protocol is the first example, but we expect there will be more. In this talk we will try not to dive too deep into the mathematical details, but keep it at a higher level of abstraction. You may construct self-enforcing e-voting in several ways, but in general, for all methods, the protocol should have three stages: setup, voting, and tallying. I will briefly explain what each stage is expected to do.

So the first stage. This is probably the most important stage. In all other voting protocols, heavyweight cryptographic operations are done on the election day, but we do it differently here. We do all the heavyweight, complex encryptions before the election. This is one example of how to achieve self-enforcing e-voting. Basically you pre-compute, for example, 10,000 ballots, electronic ballot. In this example, it is a single candidate election, so you just have two choices, either "no" or "yes". For each ballot you generate a random public key. You will compute one cryptogram for "no", and another cryptogram for "yes". There are some technical reasons why the formula is defined in such a way. I'm not going to get into the details of that, but you can read the paper. What is important on this slide are these four properties, which are summarized in this table. You can design self-enforcing e-voting in other ways as long as you satisfy these four properties.

The first one is called "well-formedness". In other words, given any single cryptogram, you can verify that it is either "yes" or "no". This is because of the use of the zero-knowledge proof. The second property is called "concealing". If you just have one cryptogram, for example for ballot one you only know one single cryptogram, it doesn't tell you whether the cryptogram is "no" or "yes".

You cannot tell because it is indistinguishable from random. Our third property is called "revealing". If you have a pair of cryptograms, that becomes interesting. It will be obvious which is "yes" and which is "no", because of the correlation between the two cryptograms. As you can see, the cryptograms for "no" and "yes" have clear correlation because the latter is the former multiply by a g. If you have both, that is a pair of cryptograms, then it becomes trivial – you can tell which is "yes" and which is "no".

Bruce Christianson: Is that a useful property?

Reply: Yes, it will be useful for auditing.

The last property is probably the most interesting property. It's called "self-tallying". In other words, you have these 10,000 ballots. Now you take an arbitrary selection of any single cryptogram from each of the ballots. If you have that selection, what this property gives you is that you can easily compute how many "yes" in your selection. This is an important property, which makes the whole system self-enforcing. So you don't rely on any tallying authorities. Is that clear to everyone?

Bruce Christianson: Does it require everyone to put a vote in?

Reply: Yes.

George Danezis: That's exactly what I was about to say. If I take one of these ballots and I eat it, as my house-mate did in the Canadian elections, then you cannot count anything, should the information be theoretically secure, well secured down to those security of the Diffie-Hellman?

Reply: If you ate your ballot, you cannot verify your own vote. But it does not affect the integrity of the whole system. All these data are published by the voting system. You keep the receipt so that you can compare it with what is published by the voting system. If someone tampers with the voting system by deleting data on the website, the integrity of the system will be lost.

George Danezis: But this is not about the data on the website, this is about the ballots that have been issued, even if it was not cast. So you have to be very careful to create the group of ten that exactly matches the voter number that will vote.

Reply: That's a good point. What we need is a maximum number of possible voters, and then we multiply that by a safety factor. This is all for auditing, which I will explain later.

The next slide is voting. If we have a cryptosystem that satisfies the four properties as I explained in the previous slide, we can easily apply this for voting. The voting basically has two stages. In the first stage, you select a choice: vote for Alice, yes or no? You pick one choice, and the machine will make a commitment by printing a cryptogram. So you can imagine behind each choice, there hides some crypto data. Once you touch the choice, it flips to reveal the hidden crypto data. Meanwhile, the machine makes a commitment by printing the data on the paper. This cryptogram doesn't reveal any information because of the concealing property. But then you have an issue: how do you know this cryptogram is the encryption of your first choice?

At this point the voter has an option, which is the second step: whether you want to confirm or cancel. If you cancel this vote then the machine has to reveal the other cryptogram. As I explained earlier, because of the revealing property you have two cryptograms, then you can verify whether this machine has cheated. If the machine wants to cheat then it has 50% probability to get caught for each single challenge. Of course, the voter is free to cancel the selection at this stage, and the voter can cancel as many times as he likes. When he is satisfied with that, he can make a selection and cast his vote. This selected cryptogram will be published on the voting website as the confirmed cryptogram. And all the cancelled cryptograms will also be published on the website. Since they are cancelled votes, they will not add any value to the tally, and they are useless to the coercer. As for the tallying process, this is usually the most complex part in the voting protocols, but in our case it is really simple. Since we have all the cryptograms on the official website, and the DRE machine tells you the tally, so anyone can verify whether the tally is accurate by checking the cryptograms. Because of the self-tallying property we don't need any tallying authority. That is key in the system.

George Danezis: So can I ask you another question, I assume it is still allowed to ask questions in the middle of the talk.

Reply: Yes.

George Danezis: So you have no tallying authorities as a central point of trust, but someone has to generate the ballots, right, so the ballots just appeared out of nowhere?

Reply: No, the ballots are pre-generated by the system. If that computation process is corrupted, it doesn't affect the tallying integrity.

George Danezis: But it affects privacy right.

Reply: It affects privacy. I will come to the privacy issue later, because with existing voting systems, privacy is one confusing point. Most people think that privacy is protected by encryption, but I will argue that privacy is actually a chain of security, and encryption is just part of this chain. There are other ways to compromise privacy, for example, if you stand in front of a touch-screen machine, and put your finger on the screen, do you think you have privacy?

George Danezis: I'm with you, I don't care about privacy either. It is the case though that if you relax that you might actually say that the tallying authorities at the end as well are just taking care of privacy because you can run a protocol that does very clever decryptions, and none of them can actually cheat.

Reply: Exactly, if we are able to achieve the same as with the tallying authorities, why we need the authorities? The traditional view is that we have to have tallying authorities, but we are arguing tallying authorities are not that as compelling as many people have thought.

Joseph Bonneau: So when you said that if the ballot generation system gets compromised it can't affect the integrity of the election, do you mean after it's already generated everything, or before?

Reply: At any stage, during the whole generation process you can corrupt this pre-computation as much as you like. Because after you do the pre-computation, you need to publish commitment such as random public keys before the election starts.

The protocol is applicable to both local and remote voting; there's really no difference between the two types of e-voting, just difference in the implementation.

We did some preliminary prototyping and experiments. Last year we did one "favourite chocolate" voting at Newcastle University. I bought three boxes of chocolates, and a box of passcode slips next to the box. Everyone is free to try a taste of chocolate, and then vote. We got very good feedback, but here I just want to focus on the issues we found. One issue is that, we know it's important to let voters audit their votes, but the question is: how many of them actually did audit? By audit I mean canceling a vote, and checking the receipt. Less than 10% of the voters did that. And another problem is that about 44% of the voters found checking receipt was difficult. This is a real problem that has largely been ignored by researchers in the field. Everyone assumes you have a receipt, and you check the receipt with the website. But this is not as easy as people may think. Data on the receipt is random. Comparing random data is easy for a computer, but not so easy for a human. Since we are talking about real-life voting, so we have to take human into consideration. So in the following trial election we improved our prototype by changing to elliptic curve cryptography, so that the receipt got shorter. This time we had a cheese election. Still we had the same issues: only one actually did the auditing, and still many people expressed that it was difficult to check the receipt.

Phil Brooke: Does that represent that a lot of people are just indifferent to the accuracy of an election?

Reply: That's probably part of the reason.

Bruce Christianson: Or just people feeling that it's somebody else's job to do that? It's the scrutineer's job; this is the returning officer's job; it's not my job.

Phil Brooke: It's not my problem.

Matt Blaze: Wensleydale's success in the election may be related to the fact that it was the default choice?

Reply: Yes, this was pointed out by some other people as well. You are very right.

Now I want to tell you the result of this election. Has everyone tried to vote? Yes, OK. Let's just see what's the result. I have one pass code here, and I will also cast my vote. This is the voting interface, and you need a pass code to vote. I will just enter my pass code. Now, I have this voting interface. So choose one of the four, and I choose the "dead parrot", then I submit. This is the data published on the voting website. Of course you can see all the data here is encrypted. How do I know this is encrypting my choice? I have the chance to cancel the vote. If I cancel the vote I see cancelled vote for "dead parrot". This is all I need to check. The "dead parrot" is in plaintext, and then the whole receipt is published on the public website. You don't have to understand what this cryptogram is about. You just need to make sure that the same data appears on the official website. That's all you need to do. You don't need to know any cryptography and you don't need to be any computer expert.

Joseph Bonneau: So my concern is that, supposing Y is to claim an election was fraudulent that wasn't, why couldn't you mock up that webpage and change all the numbers around, and go to the press and say, look this election was fraudulent, the voting server gave me these numbers that weren't on the website.

Reply: That's a good point. This number contains the voting machine's signature, so you can't actually falsify that.

Omar Chaudary: It's like the phishing website. How do you know that they are changing what I've seen compared to what they show me on the next page.

Reply: I get your point. You could print these pages if you have a printer, or save the page.

So you have up to five chances to vote. And let's try another one and see if it works. Again the data is encrypted. I don't know what's in the data, so I audit. OK, it's actually cancelled for the "silly walks" vote. And now if I'm comfortable with that I will choose my vote, and I will vote for the "spam" here. I submit, and now I can confirm. You can print this page, and there is a link to the public bulletin board where you can compare the data. You only need to ensure the data match. Anyone with a computer will be able to verify all the ballots in a batch, and in theory if you have at least one person in the world to do this verification, that should be fine.

Now we can get the results. The results are actually the day after tomorrow, but I will to do some cheating here (laughter from the audience). Sorry about that. By cheating, I mean I will prematurely end the election. When we end the election the system has to reveal all the cryptograms and publish on the board. Oh, we've got a tie here (the two candidates "dead parrot" and "spam" got the same highest number of votes). We have a high percentage of the cancelled vote, which is very good. There's also Open Source software to help you verify all the data. That's all for the voting.

So so far we've got some good feedback from the users, 80% of users found this simple to vote, and 74% agrees it's quite easy. Some people may ask why you can't get 100%. That is room for improvement, and there are other issues. Some of these issues are largely ignored in the past papers, but I think they are important issues that we have to address.

Joseph Bonneau: Sorry, what's fundamentally impossible for the visually impaired? I mean, this should be accessible to people who have screen readers and things.

Reply: It should be, but on the other hand, because of the requirement of verifiability, every voter needs to verify the receipt. For normal ordinary voters it's easy, but if you have visual impairment, how do you actually verify the receipt?

Joseph Bonneau: Well, I mean, how you use the web, if you're visually impaired? You have to have accessibility software.

Reply: Yes, it depends on the level of vision impairment I guess. But it can be difficult for a certain population.

Dylan Clarke: Problems to do with actually comparing random strings of letters using the screen reader are that you're having to sit and listen to each letter individually, and comparing one by one.

Reply: Finally, we have some blue sky ideas about how to encourage people to audit. So this is one. We know bribery is bad, but we have another "ethical bribery". What does that mean? If you vote, and if you audit the system, then you will be able to get a token, and when you leave the polling station you can drop the token to one of the charity organisations. So this is bribery, but it is ethical, at least we believe.

George Danezis: You can make the vote count more (laughter from the audience).

Reply: That's a good point.

We can also make a receipt as a transparency. Basically we propose one new design of the e-voting protocol, and we believe that in the future we shouldn't rely on tallying authorities in e-voting, and if we can get rid of tallying authorities, we should do that. That's for the conclusion. Thanks for your attention.

Approaches to Modelling Security Scenarios with Domain-Specific Languages

Phillip J. Brooke[1], Richard F. Paige[2], and Christopher Power[2]

[1] School of Computing, Teesside University, Middlesbrough, TS1 3BA, UK
pjb@scm.tees.ac.uk
[2] Department of Computer Science, University of York, York, YO10 5GH, UK
{richard.paige,christopher.power}@york.ac.uk

Abstract. Many security scenarios involve both network and crypto-graphic protocols and the interactions of different human participants in a real-world environment. Modelling these scenarios is complex, in part due to the imprecision and under-specification of the tasks and properties involved. We present work-in-progress on a domain-specific modelling approach for such scenarios; the approach is intended to support coarse-grained state exploration, and incorporates a classification of elements complementary to computer protocols, such as the creation, personalisation, modification and transport of identity tokens. We propose the construction of a domain-specific language for capturing these elements, which will in turn support domain-specific analyses related to the reliability and modifiability of said scenarios.

1 Introduction

We present a work-in-progress report on modelling security scenarios beyond the level of the network and cryptographic protocols to the level of human inter-actions with the security components. This work is an application of a coarse-grained state exploration approach that incorporates a classification of elements that are complementary computer protocols, such as the creation, personalisa-tion, modification and transport of identity tokens. The present conceptual work for these attributes is currently being implemented as a domain-specific language (DSL) in a modelling and simulation framework.

Current research has looked at security scenarios in detail regarding the com-puting aspects; however, there has been low focus on the types of attacks that can happen in a physical environment involving human users. The following scenario demonstrates one such case:

> Alice applies for, and is issued, an identification card from her local municipality. The card is couriered to Alice's home address. This card will be used by Alice in various businesses and services in the community. With many of the transactions, such as applying for a tax certificate for her car, a clerk, Bob, will take Alice's card, and check it for various pieces of information. Bob the clerk at the tax office uses card as a means of verifying Alice's claims of things about herself (e.g., name, age).

B. Christianson et al. (Eds.): Security Protocols 2012, LNCS 7622, pp. 41–54, 2012.

In this scenario, it is insufficient to consider only attacks on the cryptographic and networking components. For instance, there are potential problems with physical consistency throughout the system. If Alice has an identification card, it must have been created and sent to her. There are points along that value chain where attacks of opportunity can happen. The person issuing the card could make an error about Alice's age, or a courier taking the card to Alice could lose it. It is also possible that the courier could actively try to take and use Alice's card to obtain a service to which he is not entitled.

Within such scenarios, *beliefs* also play a role; this is because in some of the activities within the scenario, two or more actors are involved, and each may have a different set of behaviours *in that context*. For example, while Bob might believe the information on the identification card when Alice uses it, he may be less likely to believe it when the courier is using the card.

All of these situations lead to a complex set of properties that must be represented in any system hoping to model security risks that may arise from execution of a scenario.

This line of work was originally motivated by the UK's Identity Cards Act 2006 (now repealed). The type of question we were interested in trying to answer was: Given a scenario, what difference do particular configurations of that scenario make to the outcome? More concretely, in our example above, does the existence and use of an identification card make enough of a difference to the identification decisions the clerk, Bob, has to make to justify its additional cost?

To help to answer such questions, we would benefit from an infrastructure that can describe and test assertions about identification scenarios. This paper contributes our work-in-progress to modelling the elements of scenarios beyond the network and cryptographic protocols.

2   Modelling Security Scenarios

We outline the overall approach taken to modelling scenarios like the identification example presented earlier. In general, these are scenarios with (informally) some element of *fuzziness* to them — specifically, scenarios which can be configured and where the decisions within are taken based on probability distributions. We present a high-level overview of the model, starting with its requirements and then presenting its key entities.

2.1   Requirements for the Modelling Approach

The requirements for our modelling approach are as follows. They are expressed assuming that we wish to exploit, as much as possible, model checking approaches, so as to use proven technology. We have three simulation or exploration requirements concerning automated exploration, probabilistic evaluation and simulation of individual paths through the scenario, as well as a need for a DSL.

Automated Exploration. We want to analyse every possible path through the scenario. This is akin to model checking (using tools such as FDR2 [8] or SPIN [25]), and is necessary for completeness.

Probabilistic Evaluation. When exploring every path, we want to assess how likely it is to occur. It is very unlikely that an agent will sell alcohol (under jurisdictional restrictions) to a 5 year old, yet someone who appears to be over 21 is unlikely to be challenged. This makes the scenarios fuzzy, requiring parameterisation. Such parameters might include

- a probability density function of the age of a subject;
- a probability density function giving an agent's perception of the subject's age, given her actual age.

Individual Path Simulation. For validation and understanding of the model, we would like to be able to step through particular paths. We anticipate increasingly complex scenarios, and individual path simulations are a useful counterpoint to the complete automated exploration.

Domain-Specific. We could build a simulation in any computer language. To make it understandable and usable, we require something specific to the problem domain. It has to understand that there are actors and objects, that actors can show objects (*e.g.*, identity cards) to other actors, *etc.*

Additionally, the set up of a scenario is a distinct and complicated step. Concretely, does the subject remember to take her identity card with her? How were they issued? We could take this a step further and simulate the issue and delivery of such credentials. This bootstrap has to be included in the scenario, as it gives opportunities for people to make mistakes, others to intercept credentials, and so on.

One approach to better enable the construction and validation of scenarios is to provide a domain-specific language, specifically defined and constrained to support exactly and only the concepts and logic for describing scenarios. If we are able to define such a DSL, capturing *just* the concepts of scenarios (and their semantics), we ideally make it easier for end-users (who may be security experts) to specify relevant and meaningful scenarios of interest, and provide greater confidence that said scenarios are acceptable and valid. Moreover, if the DSL is specified and implemented in an appropriate way (*e.g.*, using Eclipse EMF or other similar modelling technologies), automated tools can be developed, such as editors, that end-users can apply in constructing and checking their scenarios. Such *convenience facilities*, while not essential, can add further confidence that well-formed scenarios have been constructed.

2.2   Concepts and Definitions

The model we present has been adapted from scenario based design proposed by Carroll and Rosson [24] for the design of interactive systems. Essentially, we are simulating actors (the subject, the agent) interacting with different components of the system, and the events that occur in response to those interactions. These concepts were identified by sketching use cases of a series of scenarios.

People and actors can be classified within a scenario thus

Subject. An individual that initiates or triggers a scenario; often a user or customer (*e.g.*, a person being identified). In police or immigration-related scenarios, the subject is a person being identified.

Imposter. A person masquerading as a subject (whether the subject actually exists or not).

Cheat. A subject who is attempting to convince an agent that they hold a property that in fact they do not. For example, a cheat may try to convince an agent that they are of a particular age when they are not. We distinguish a cheat from an Imposter, who attempts to impersonate a different subject.

Agent. A representative (*e.g.*, sales assistant, police officer) of an organisation that interacts with the subject.

Actor. A generic term covering all the roles above, as well as others not explicitly noted. For example, in an identification scenario, a particular subject could be using another actor's identification tokens.

We need to model a *memory* for all actors. This represents their prior beliefs, current impressions, their understanding of an encounter so far, and so on. In section 4, we fold these into properties, *i.e.*, the memory of an actor is a property of the actor, simply to reduce the amount of terminology and different fields in the formal definitions. A further possibility is to consider *forgetfulness* as another source of errors or protocol problems.

Agents may act on behalf of an organisation:

Organisations. An organisation owns artefacts of values, and has representatives (agents) that engage in scenarios. Organisations wish to ascertain whether subjects hold properties related to artefacts of value. Some of these organisations will issue identity cards; others may courier or deliver items, cards, *etc.*

Some scenarios involve identity cards, *e.g.*, national identity cards, passports, driving licences, PASScards, which involve the following entity types:

Genuine Card. A genuine (non-forged) identity card: it may be held by the subject, or by an imposter. Additionally, it may be a card that an imposter has persuaded the issuer to wrongly issue. Genuine cards may be faulty in some sense, *e.g.*, smartcard chips may have been damaged (deliberately/maliciously or accidentally) and not operate.

Forged Card. An identity card that has not been issued by the issuer.

Tampered Card. A genuine card that has been tampered with, *e.g.*, to modify the photograph. (Both forging and tampering with credentials is well-known in practice.)

Card Terminal. A card reader, that incorporates a slot or interface for the genuine or forged card, a key pad for entering PINs and a display to direct the user. Some terminals may be able to take biometric readings.

We could further address the issue of corrupted terminals in this work — such terminals could skim the card, attempt to retain other data such as the subject's PIN or biometric reading, or give misleading information on a display. There are other problems that can be investigated here, many similar to ATMs, such as whether subjects have good cause to trust terminals. How can they know the terminal is not corrupt? What stops someone 'shoulder-surfing' to obtain a PIN?

Objects. A generic term covering all the items above, as well as any others required in a particular scenario. Other services (the two examples immediately below) are encoded into the objects that provide access to those services.

Verification and CRL Services. Cards can be verified via terminals. These may be on- or off-line, and thus network and cryptographic protocols are required. Some services could perhaps be used for the identification of subjects who are not carrying credentials.

Communication Links. Terminals must be able to communicate with both an organisation's computers and verification services. In the same way that we need to model the couriering of cards from issuer to subject, communication between computers is mediated by these links.

Within a scenario, actors (*e.g.*, subjects, agents) interact, sometimes using particular artefacts (*e.g.*, items of value such as ID cards). Some interactions are constrained by location: for example, a subject cannot show an identity card to an agent if they are not both in the same location. As such, the model has to support constraints in scenarios.

The sketch use cases that produced the concepts above also produced possible *operations* applicable to concepts and configurations. Operations are interpreted as events resulting in state changes. Specifically, the operations identified are: **pick up** and **drop** an object from or into a location; **give** an object to another actor (presumably in the same location, *e.g.*, a courier); **say** to another actor (*e.g.*, to trigger some transaction); **show** an object to another actor; **set** a property or belief; and, **move** between locations. Many of these are relatively simple in terms of state change and modelling. **say** and **set** are substantially more complicated, as they can be used as "escape hatches" to implement relatively complicated interactions.

There is one further class of entity that we need to describe: attackers.

2.3 Attackers

We have used Casper [15] as an inspiration for some of this work; so we require an analogue of the most general intruder. In one sense, this is partially covered in the Actors described above (*e.g.*, Imposter and Cheat).

A more specialised treatment may allow our analysis to produce emergent, unanticipated results. So an attacker may be involved in

- the interception of credentials in transit, similar to the missing-in-post problem for delivery of credit cards;
- theft and robbery: simply taking items from a location or another actor;

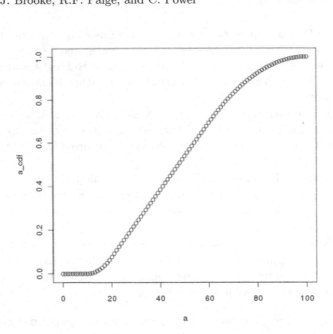

Fig. 1. Example cumulative density function for an off-licence subject's age

- interacting with other attackers. There may be multiple actors behaving as attackers. This interaction could involve cooperation or even competition between attackers. Indeed, some systems may not trust their expected subjects (such as e-cash services, where the system has to prevent the subjects adding extra value without payment).

3   Fuzziness and Probabilities

Nondeterminism is inherent in this work. When an actor sees another actor, they both form impressions about the other. In scenarios where ages are important, an actor will assess another's age as being approximately the correct age, but we assert that this is likely to be a normal distribution. When close to a legal boundary, this can be important. As an example, we might use a simple trapezoid to describe the probability distribution of the *actual* age of subjects attending an off-licence, as illustrated in figure 1. The agent who has to determine the subject's age will have a probability density function giving her *estimate* of the subject's age given the actual age, for example, figure 2. This particular example illustrates the need for different configurations of a scenarios —the likely distributions may vary according to the particular deployment— and the need for validation.

Similarly, when confronted with a photographic credential and an actor asserting to be the person in the photograph, the likelihood of the verifier accepting that identification depends on the quality of the credential, the difference in time, changes in appearance, the diligence of the verifier and the skill of the verifier. Alternatively, an automated device may be involved, such as in the current

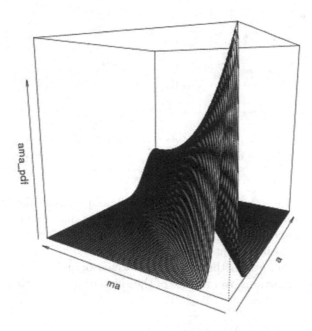

Fig. 2. Example probability density function for an off-licence scenario. a denotes the subject's actual age, ma is the perceived age and ama_pdf is the probability.

generation of some eGates at national borders and services such as `face.com`. Such matters can be modelled as nondeterminism.

A final source of nondeterminism in our scenarios is *mistakes*. Humans make errors. Some may simply not care or be less diligent than other actors. But we cannot guarantee that the actors in our scenarios will follow protocols faithfully; indeed, the point of our work is that actors cannot always follow protocols perfectly.

4   Formal Definitions

Given the concepts, configurations, notions of constraints, and operations, a formalisation of the model (in, e.g., Z) is straightforward. We now give a more formal description of scenario, state and event.

A *scenario* is a tuple $(A, B, O, L, P, E, s, e_e, e_a)$ where

- A is a set of actors;
- B is a set of (passive) objects;
- O is a set of organisations;
- L is a set of locations;

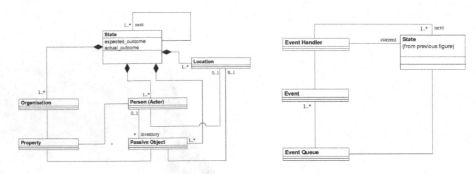

Fig. 3. States model   **Fig. 4.** Events model

- P is a set of properties (which include, for example, if an identity document has been modified and the beliefs that an actor may form about another actor or their memories);
- E is a set of possible events;
- s is a sequence of events that set up the scenario; and
- e_e and e_a are functions over a state of the simulation evaluating the expected and actual outcomes.

We illustrate this in figures 3 and 4.

A *state* is a tuple (l, i, r, q) where

- $l : A \nrightarrow L$ gives the locations of the actors;
- $i : B \nrightarrow L \cup A$ gives the location containing or actor holding each object;
- $r : A \cup B \cup O \cup L \nrightarrow P$ gives the properties associated with the actors, objects, organisations and locations; and
- q is a priority queue of pending events. They are prioritised as
  immediate contains events that should happen as soon as possible, such as an actor's reaction to another actor's action;
  delayed contains events with a natural delay, such as movement, or posting an item. These happen after all immediate events; and
  deferred contains events relating to the simulation management.

l, i and r are partial functions, which allows for an actor or object to not be present at all and for only desired properties to be selected.

Finally, an *event* is a conventional transition on a state (l, i, r, q) resulting in one or more new states (l', i', r', q'). The operational view of an event is that the head of q is processed according to its definition. The processing of an event may add additional events to the queue; some of these additional events are implicit in the design, for example, the arrival of an actor might cause a second actor to carry out some action, which itself is represented by enqueuing further events. Where more than one state results, the *transition* is associated with either a fixed probability (*e.g.*, 0.6) or an abstraction of a random variable to handle nondeterminism; again this is defined by the event.

Given a scenario $(A, B, O, L, P, E, s, e_e, e_a)$, we create an initial state $(\emptyset, \emptyset, \emptyset, s)$. Configuration may slightly adjust initial events or probability distributions (e.g., in our running example, identity cards may not be available at all). From the initial state, we select the first event and this results in a subsequent state or subsequent states: thus our model may end up with multiple current states if we are attempting an exhaustive exploration instead of concentrating on only one successor at a time. We repeat this for each subsequent state until the queue of pending events is empty in each current state, at which point we evaluate e_e and e_a to determine the outcome of each terminal state.

One particular issue is that the rich state, in part resulting from modelling actors' memories, turns what might have been a fairly large digraph into a tree for all but the most trivial scenarios. Thus traditional model checking approaches are problematic.

5   Domain-Specific Language

We aim to refine and implement this model using a domain-specific language; this will allow us to capture scenarios (involving actors, etc) and will support end-users —who may be identification specialists, security experts, software engineers or business specialists— in expressing scenarios and validating them. Building a suitable DSL is therefore a way of *implementing* our scenario-based approach. Our rationale for constructing a DSL as opposed to simply implementing the model in, e.g., an object-oriented programming language, is that a DSL-based approach allows us to capture only essential concepts, thus making it easier to validate the scenarios (and underlying model) that we produce.

As is the case with the design of any language, we want our scenario DSL to be sufficiently expressive while practical: it should allow end-users to capture the full scope of a scenario without the underlying model being too large to meaningfully analyse.

The DSL has to capture the actors, objects, etc. It must also deal with constraints, such as an actor can only **give** an object to another actor if they are both in the same location; and responses, such as an actor responding to another **saying** something. Some of these should be implicit to the simulation and are generic (e.g., **give**) whereas others are likely to be specific to each scenario.

We could consider the separate phases of a scenario. For example, we might view bootstrap and an encounter of a subject and agent as being two phases. Complex scenarios may have more than two phases. Splitting them into distinct phases allows more reusability. Similarly, the configuration must be captured, for example, is a particular type of identify credential available in this run?

We need to describe the outcomes we are testing. At its simplest, the simulation knows what the correct outcome is: it knows whether or not the subject should be able to carry out whatever transaction they are requesting. Thus we can simple enumerate possible outcomes and compare true/false positive/negative outcomes for different configurations. However, there are further characteristics we might wish to check: a significant one relates to privacy and information leakage. Does a particular configuration make it easier for one actor to obtain (unnecessary) information about another?

Some form of overloading is desirable: some behaviours of actors will be generic, yet the actors will also need scenario-specific and even configuration-specific behaviours and responses.

Lastly, we must describe the attacker(s) behaviour. Can someone misbehave in this scenario? What emergent behaviours might we see?

6   Related Work

Much of the motivation for this work concerns simulation or model checking of scenarios involving humans and identity, where identity is a property of entities that allows entities to be distinguished from each other. Sometimes humans are attempting to identify another individual, or are instead carrying out the task of verification. Sometimes a computer or network is involved, perhaps as an intermediary between two humans, or in place of one of the parties.

Precise definitions of 'identity' can be controversial [3]. In this case, it is recognising an individual which degenerates (in our examples) to unique naming. Identification is the process of establishing an entity's identity via a particular mechanism (or set of mechanisms), *e.g.*, comparison to a trusted repository of identities. Of course, different actors will have different assessments of the trust of any particular repository.

Current identification practices are varied, and can involve a vendor making a judgement as to age, or accepting other documents that may never have been intended for this purpose. The notorious example here is the use of utility bills for identification. Government-issue ID such as driving licences (particularly photo-card variants) and passports are popular, as are third-party schemes such as the Proof of Age Standards Scheme.

The systematic approach proposed is similar to the use of Casper [15] but involves other aspects such as the actors in the scenario, the physical movement of credentials, and so on. Interruptions and modifications can occur, involving such behaviours as intercepting a document so that a third party can use it, or the intended recipient modifying it to support different claims such as a different age.

At a high level, this work has some relation to what are sometimes called "serious games", such as military simulations and wargames, public order models and fire/evacuation models (as exemplified by Galea's group at Greenwich). Looking more closely at actors, there are classic belief-desire-intention models and competency models (in the context of training, learning, assessment and development) which could have influence on development of our work.

The most closely related work we are aware of is due to Martina and Carlos [16], where they describe the same type of issue, *i.e.*, that security protocols need to take into account the environment. This necessarily includes the interaction of humans. Subsequent work [6] presents first steps to an Isabelle/HOL model, which distinguishes the work from our attempts at a simulational and model-checking model.

Ideally, we would like to exploit domain-specific validation and analysis toolsets such as Lowe's Casper [15], which is itself based on FDR2 [8]. However we also desire a way to simulate individual runs of a scenario. This is to allow us to explain and further understand how individual results might come about. Thus, our current prototype simply enumerates every possible run (every trace in process algebra terms) by brute force, but also allows us to run this in an interactive mode (as in FDR2 *vs.* Probe [21]). Other notations and tools could also be considered. We could enhance our CSPsim [5], but this will likely involve a significant amount of effort for proof-of-concept, as it would require us to extend the formal model and the model checker, when we are at a stage of evaluating whether the approach to scenario modelling provides benefit.

Tools such as PRISM [13] potentially can be applied to such problems. It has a rich language capturing a range of probabilistic features (from simple probabilities for nondeterministic choice to variants of Markov chains), with a tool that allows exhaustive calculation and path simulation. However, it does not allow potentially expensive exhaustive exploration to be performed and then repeatedly re-calculated for the probabilistic calculations (as in our current prototype). Confusingly, there is another tool called PRISM [1] based on Prolog. Programs for this tool are logic programs in which facts have a parameterised probability distribution: this is very similar to the mechanics of the approach we have adopted in our work. A difference is that it does not support exhaustive exploration of the scenarios. Similar reasoning applies to considerations of tools such as SPIN [25]. However, state-rich formalisms such as Event-B [2] or Alloy [12] may provide a sensible basis for supporting rich simulations, but these require extensions to associate probability distributions with events (and hence interactions). Other more simulation-oriented tools include Anylogic [28] and Demos2k [17]. A useful list of such tools is available from Rizzoli [22]. Monahan's DXM [17] is notable for using a Monte Carlo style of modelling. Lanotte *et al.* [14] outline an analytical approach using probabilistic transition systems. These tools and approaches, with suitable extensions, could support analysis of probabilistic models as described in this paper, but we would then lose the benefit of using model checking infrastructure to support analysis outside of exhaustive state exploration.

The model used in this paper is inspired by fuzzy logic [29] and probabilistic logics. Significant tool support for modelling fuzzy logic-based scenarios was provided by XFuzzy [18], which included a specification language as well as rules for manipulating linguistic variables. XFuzzy focused on analysing block diagrams rather than scenarios, making it unsuitable for problems like those considered in this paper. There has also been extension to logics for reasoning about probability; besides the state machine models underpinning PRISM, extensions to refinement calculi [20] and formal specification languages (*e.g.*, Event-B [19]) have been proposed.

The work in this paper is related to that of reasoning in the presence of uncertainty, *e.g.*, as exemplified by research on analysis incomplete or inconsistent requirements specifications. Most noteworthy here is work on the XCheck model checker [7] which provides a multi-valued symbolic model checker; such a model checker provides probabilistic support but not support for reasoning with probability distributions and for manipulating configurations of scenarios.

Substantial work has been carried out on the design and implementation of DSLs; [26] is a comprehensive reference, and many of the important design principles and technical patterns for implementing DSLs are discussed in [9]. DSLs are typically defined to support modelling of a particular problem domain, to address a particular engineering tasks (*e.g.*, a form of analysis), or to enable particular stakeholder groups to more easily express their concerns. DSLs have been constructed in a number of ways, including via embedding of a DSL in another, more general-purpose language, and through abstraction of other languages.

A significant example of the latter approach is MetaBorg [4], which is a transformation-based approach for the definition of embedded textual DSLs implemented based on the Stratego framework. The MetaBorg approach defines new concepts by mapping them to expansions in the host language. MetaBorg was designed for textual languages. This means that the transformations involved can be expressed by means of transformations on abstract syntax trees rather than abstract syntax graphs. Stratego is also used in [10] to develop an external DSL for web development.

The underlying notion of an embedded DSL seems to have been discussed first by Hudak [11]. The idea of *forwarding* that is now a standard technique for defining embedded textual DSLs using attribute grammars was introduced in [27].

7   Preliminary Conclusions

We claim that it is possible to construct scenarios involving our desired properties in such as way that they can be explored and produce useful results, at least for comparing different configurations. A major difficulty of the work is to properly set the scope: too small and it's not expressive enough; too large and we can perform no analysis. A research question here is: Can we find a viable scope for interesting scenarios? Routine scenarios are easy: they involve all the actors behaving "correctly" and no attackers. Yet the interesting scenarios are where people make mistakes and others are actively attacking the system.

The DSL is currently being elaborated to provide more detail. Our next step is to present a more elaborate and rigorous definition of the DSL, perhaps using Eclipse-based EMF tools, and implement a suitable model-to-text transformation that enables compilation, analysis and simulation via state-of-the-art simulation tools. A prototype implementation in Python (with unvalidated parameters) suggests a one or two percentage point difference in true/false positive/negative outcomes between different configurations of an age-related scenario that might have used ID cards. As a result, we suspect that the actors' behaviour will swamp technical aspects of protocols, hence it is valuable to pursue this line of work.

This work is closely related to the model checking of protocols. There are necessarily assumptions about the protocol that the actors follow in particular scenario. Additionally, we have to consider the probabilities associated with some decisions. As well as the general scenario correctness problem —however we formulate a model, it will always be an abstraction of a real system— this inclusion of probabilities adds additional validation problems. One approach is to test the stability of any results under perturbation. If the results are unstable under perturbation of the parameters, the validity of the model is questionable. Automating this perturbation analysis would result in greater computational demands.

Rich state gives us less scope to reduce the size of the state space because the actors know their own history. As this history is part of the state, it is less likely that there will be a significant number of identical states following transitions. Classical model checking approaches (*e.g.*, FDR2 [8], SPIN [25]) or even lazy approaches such as CSPsim [5] each have a restricted set of data types. A richer simulation worsens this problem.

As an alternative, describing the scenario in an interactive fiction environment such as TADS3 [23] would certainly satisfy the domain-specific and individual path simulation requirements, as well as adding rich simulation capabilities. Automated exploration would require some work (*e.g.*, a driver program), along with a way to abstract the probability distributions. Canonicalisation is also harder due to the opaque state within the interactive fiction interpreter.

Acknowledgements. The authors thank the delegates to the Twentieth International Workshop on Security Protocols for their constructive comments on this work.

References

1. PRISM: PRogramming in Statistical Modeling (February 2012), http://sato-www.cs.titech.ac.jp/prism/
2. Abrial, J.-R.: Modeling in Event-B: System and Software Engineering. Cambridge University Press (2010)
3. Anderson, R.J.: Security Engineering: A Guide to Building Dependable Distributed Systems, 2nd edn. Wiley (2008)
4. Bravenboer, M., Visser, E.: Concrete syntax for objects: Domain-specific language embedding and assimilation without restrictions. In: Proc. 19th Annual ACM SIGPLAN Conf. on Object-Oriented Programming, Systems, Languages, and Applications (OOPSLA 2004), pp. 365–383. ACM Press (2004)
5. Brooke, P.J., Paige, R.F.: Lazy exploration and checking of CSP models with CSPsim. In: McEwan, A.A., Ifill, W., Welch, P.H. (eds.) Communicating Process Architectures 2007, pp. 33–50 (February 2007)
6. Carlos, M.C., Martina, J.E., Price, G., Custódio, R.F.: A proposed framework for analysing security ceremonies. In: Proc. SECRYPT (2012)
7. Easterbrook, S.M., Chechik, M.: A framework for multi-valued reasoning over inconsistent viewpoints. In: ICSE, pp. 411–420 (2001)
8. FDR2 model checker, http://www.fsel.com/software.html. (last visited January 12, 2012)
9. Fowler, M.: Domain-Specific Languages. Addison-Wesley (2010)

10. Hemel, Z., Kats, L.C.L., Visser, E.: Code Generation by Model Transformation: A Case Study in Transformation Modularity. In: Vallecillo, A., Gray, J., Pierantonio, A. (eds.) ICMT 2008. LNCS, vol. 5063, pp. 183–198. Springer, Heidelberg (2008)
11. Hudak, P.: Modular domain specific languages and tools. In: Proc. 5th Int'l Conf. on Software Reuse, pp. 134–142. IEEE Computer Society Press (1998)
12. Jackson, D.: Software Abstractions. MIT Press (2008)
13. Kwiatkowska, M., Norman, G., Parker, D.: PRISM: Probabilistic Symbolic Model Checker. In: Field, T., Harrison, P.G., Bradley, J., Harder, U. (eds.) TOOLS 2002. LNCS, vol. 2324, pp. 200–204. Springer, Heidelberg (2002)
14. Lanotte, R., Maggiolo-Schettini, A., Troina, A.: Parametric probabilistic transition systems for system design and analysis. Formal Aspects of Computing 19, 93–109 (2006)
15. Lowe, G., Roscoe, B.: Using CSP to detect errors in the TMN protocol. IEEE Transactions on Software Engineering 23(10), 659–669 (1997)
16. Martina, J.E., Carlos, M.C.: Why should we analyse security ceremonies. In: Proc. CryptoForma Workshop (May 2010)
17. Monahan, B.: DXM — Demo2k eXperiments Manager. Technical Report HPL-2008-173, HP Laboratories (2008)
18. Moreno-Velo, F.J., Baturone, I., Sánchez-Solano, S., Barros, A.B.: Xfuzzy 3.0: a development environment for fuzzy systems. In: EUSFLAT Conf., pp. 93–96 (2001)
19. Morgan, C., Hoang, T.S., Abrial, J.-R.: The Challenge of Probabilistic *Event B* —*Extended Abstract*—. In: Treharne, H., King, S., C. Henson, M., Schneider, S. (eds.) ZB 2005. LNCS, vol. 3455, pp. 162–171. Springer, Heidelberg (2005)
20. Morgan, C., McIver, A., Seidel, K.: Probabilistic predicate transformers. ACM Trans. Program. Lang. Syst. 18(3), 325–353 (1996)
21. ProBE — CSP animator, http://www.fsel.com/software.html (last visited February 2, 2011)
22. Rizzoli, A.E.: A collection of modelling and simulation resources on the internet, http://www.idsia.ch/~andrea/sim/simtools.html (last accessed January 6, 2012)
23. Roberts, M.J.: TADS 3 downloads, http://www.tads.org/tads3.htm (last visited January 4, 2012)
24. Rosson, M.B., Carroll, J.: Scenario-based design. In: The Human-Computer Interaction Handbook, ch. 53, pp. 1032–1050. Lawrence Earlbaum Associates (2002)
25. SPIN — model checker, http://spinroot.com/spin/whatispin.html (last visited January 4, 2012)
26. van Deursen, A., Klint, P., Visser, J.: Domain-specific languages: an annotated bibliography. SIGPLAN Not. 35(6), 26–36 (2000)
27. Van Wyk, E., de Moor, O., Backhouse, K., Kwiatkowski, P.: Forwarding in Attribute Grammars for Modular Language Design. In: Nigel Horspool, R. (ed.) CC 2002. LNCS, vol. 2304, pp. 128–142. Springer, Heidelberg (2002)
28. XJ Technologies. Anylogic, http://www.xjtek.com/anylogic/why_anylogic/ (last accessed January 6, 2012)
29. Zadeh, L.: Fuzzy sets. Information and Control 8(3) (1965)

Approaches to Modelling Security Scenarios with Domain-Specific Languages (Transcript of Discussion)

Phillip J. Brooke

Teesside University

Good morning, I'm Phil Brooke. My co-authors hail from York, and I'm based at Teesside. For a couple of years we've been looking at how people interact with protocols, and the implicit protocols in how people carry out transactions. What we want to do is get some answers in terms of: if I change a process for how I run a particular transaction, do I get a benefit from it? The motivation for this came originally from the Identity Card Act, which has since been repealed in the UK. So our scenarios involve somebody trying to buy some age restricted goods. Rather than just eyeballing the person and saying, "I think you're over 18", or asking for some other identification which may or may not be easily forged, you would have this gold standard ID card, and they'd be able to look at it and say, "yes, of course you are old enough," and on we go. Our question wasn't so much are these good or bad things, but how much difference would it make to us and can I measure that? Can I model it?

Protocols are part of scenarios. We're generalising beyond identity scenarios: a big question is, what do I actually need to represent? We've come up with a long, long shopping list, and it comes down to being a scoping problem. We can look at the main specification languages. York has a lovely toolkit, called Epsilon, in which you can invent languages, and Epsilon does a lot of the work of dealing with the syntax and related tools. This is better than lex and yacc, which I would otherwise still play with.

We need to capture what actors do and their roles: they might be a subject in a scenario. Perhaps I'm going somewhere and I need to prove my identity, or I need to prove some property about myself. They might be someone who is pretending to be someone else, and this is where the scenarios become interesting. Routine scenarios where everybody plays nice are easy. It's more interesting when somebody who is trying to break the system turns up: "I really want that bottle of cider, and I'm only 15, can I get it at the off-licence?" People are well-known to tamper with identification: there are dodgy ID cards and they have been a mini industry for many years, and I'm sure that'll continue. We have abstract tokens which are meant to convey some properties, or have some information which may be linked to someone, and those tokens as well as the people can have properties.

There is an infrastructure. We don't have to use it: we might simply have two people in a transaction. In higher value scenarios, say bank transactions (picking on one of the Identity and Passport Service's old scenarios), you might take a card, and put the card into a reader, do the biometric checking, and the

B. Christianson et al. (Eds.): Security Protocols 2012, LNCS 7622, pp. 55–59, 2012.
© Springer-Verlag Berlin Heidelberg 2012

infrastructure does some online checking including a blacklist — has this card been reported stolen?

Can I model all this stuff? I want to explicitly include locations, because some of the ways to break the scenarios involve how I set them up. The scenario doesn't start when the person is at the location trying to carry out that transaction. The scenario starts at the very beginning when they want to get hold of this credential in the first place. If you're going to present a credential, I've got to issue that credential, so if I'm going to issue, say, a passport, somebody has got to fill in a form. Somebody has got to receive that form, somebody has got to process that form and decide, "am I going to accept it?" I can lie on the form. Somebody's got to send the passport back. There are cases where credentials or financial instruments are intercepted in the post and misused, so things can go wrong before I even start the main scenario. I've got to think about what I would do with the post and couriers. At this point I can make my scenarios a bit too big.

I come from a formal methods background, so a natural way for me is to follow Gavin Lowe's Casper approach. I want to build a monstrous CSP-like model of one of these scenarios, then feed it to the FDR model checker or SPIN, let that grind away and say, "I didn't find any problems", or "here's a list of problems I found". The problem is that any way that I build these actors, they look like agents in AI-type programming. They've got to carry a memory and impressions. People form an impression in these scenarios and you end up with probabilistic bits of data in here. They've got to carry this memory, this information forwards, and it completely ruins any form of model checking. Instead of a digraph with some cycles in it which might reduce the overall problem size, I end up with a very large tree. I don't have a good answer to that yet.

The agents have some very simple operations. They'll be presenting tokens and identity cards. They're going to pick them up, and they're going to give them and show them to other agents. There are messier operations. How they interact with people, for example: "I have seen someone come in — how old do I think they are? Am I going to follow the rules?" We know that humans are fallible, they make mistakes. We're not sure how often they make mistakes in any given scenario, and I don't know to measure that. But these messier operations are escape hatches to embed more special behaviour into my models.

Our DSL is essentially event driven. In the example, something is delivered to a location, and an actor can come and pick it up. So if the actor has posted a form, the passport or ID card is sent back to them: it gets delivered to them, they can accept it, and they can try to present it to do something else. This is the sort of operational level that we're trying to model. The actors have got to make decisions which are based on their memory. All this is essentially implementing some form of protocol in the sense of it being a conversation between all the actors, and all the other objects, but with the added complication that I'm trying to do a bit of a simulation underneath it.

I have to enforce some constraints otherwise it gets far too big. Now the title mentions DSLs. We've got attempts using m4 macros and CSP to try and build these models. The program I'm working on is Python-based, and we're moving into Epsilon that I mentioned before. The essential aim of all the DSLs is to only capture the information that is important. What I'm after here is: what's important in the scenarios? The bit which is expensive so far is describing the rules of behaviour. What are the actors allowed to do? Something happens; what do they do then? When I've got my great big simulation, I want to explore all possible paths through it. Once I can explore all the paths through it I can ask, what happens if they used that token? What happens if that system wasn't there? or that token wasn't available at all? Does it make a difference? When we've thrown some (not even remotely validated) numbers into a scenario, it mightn't make more than one or two percentage points difference. From there, we can ask: if it doesn't make much difference to the outcome, why am I rolling out all the infrastructure? That takes us back to our original motivation: why am I spending all this money on a large infrastructure, why am I spending money on card terminals, and a big database? It doesn't actually make any difference, because the actors' behaviour, or the actors' failure to follow the rules, or the actor saying, "I'm not going to check your card, because I can clearly see you're OK, whoops, I made a mistake" — those errors swamp any of the gains that I get by implementing all this technology with all these nice crypto protocols, because somebody else didn't follow the human protocol that was implicit in it.

We need lots of generic roles: what a "person" does. We need a model of a person and we're part way through that. I need to consider the interaction with cryptographic protocols because a lot of these scenarios involve a technical system with a crypto protocol. We assume that the cryptography all works for now. Overall, we're trying to build something which is large enough to express the concepts I've described, but is minimal otherwise. Our feeling at the moment is that it's too big. I'll come back to that in a moment.

We have an analogue of Casper's most general intruder. I assume that people here are at least vaguely familiar with Casper. Casper has descriptions of crypto protocols: it re-writes them into FDR input, you run the model checker over it, the model checker says, "I didn't find any problems," or it says, "here's a counter-example," and you can reverse it see how the protocol failed. Part of the model has an intruder who can listen to everything. They can inject messages. They're not allowed to manipulate secret data unless they've already managed to find it in some other way.

As well as our general actors, things like our subjects, and our shopkeepers, we need to have this idea of what it means for someone to do a "bad thing". People look over other people's shoulders and get PIN numbers. Everyone can stand in the supermarket queue and you watch somebody type and we can read off the PIN trivially. Do I need to represent that? Obviously some scenarios involve something which has a PIN with it, but if it involves you typing in a PIN, does my intruder need to have some way of modelling this?

I mentioned probabilities: I said people make mistakes, so how do I represent people making mistakes? The crudest way is to have a non-deterministic choice buried in the model. At a decision point, it's a roll of the dice: did they make a mistake? You can also have fuzzier examples such as trying to say how old someone is.

Scenario correctness: I can build this DSL and I can say I want to build a minimal DSL. But can I build something that looks correct enough given that I'm effectively trying to build a real world simulation here? Does it actually sufficiently represent the world that I can say it was useful? Rule capture is the most complex aspect, so this is back to this issue of our actor having a model of what they're trying to do. If I want to take money out of a cash point, I have to have a card, I have to have a PIN number because it's going to ask me for that, I've got to go to a cash machine. There are all these entities I have to model, and I have to write some rules to capture them. What the syntax looks like doesn't matter. We can build a UML diagram of it, but ultimately it comes down to some very detailed rules. One question is, has anyone here ever come across something like this before outside of games? Because the only other place we've seen this is in serious games, such as milsim, public order simulation, where you've got models of what you think is human behaviour, or like the Galea fire simulation work.

Sandy Clark: Have you looked at military modelling?

Reply: Yes, we've seen some of the military modelling stuff. There you have behaviours of your pixeltruppen and some low-level tactical simulators.

Sandy Clark: There are also competency models for people as well.

Reply: Yes, like decision-making models. So we have things like traditional gold-silver-bronze or strategic-and-tactical level simulations, where you're trying to say what is the likely reaction of your simulated world to doing something. I could throw away all the slides and write, I am trying to build a simulation of people doing things with identity documents, and how they interact, and is that safe? If I can do that can I measure something? If I measure something it's dependent on the original numbers I put into it. If I change some numbers a little bit does it drastically change my result? If it changes the result drastically it's clearly unstable and I've got a problem. If it looks reasonably stable my problem is a little bit easier now. I still have a question of the overall validity. If I took the whole room and worked my way through everyone, getting everybody to guess someone's age, that would probably end up with a normal distribution around a true age, but with quite a big wide range I suspect, because people aren't very good at it.

Matt Blaze: So the scenario of correctness in your last point there, you reminded me with your example of how hard it is to model the correct requirements. You gave an example of, is this person old enough to buy a book on cryptographic protocols? And I want to ensure that the requirements of that protocol are actually quite subtle because I might want to ensure, for example, that in proving my age I'm not also revealing my identity. And it's easy to design a protocol that needs some set of requirements. It's harder to design a protocol where we're confident that we've chosen the right set of requirements.

Reply: Yes, for instance, in the age restricted scenario. We're choosing that one because it's the smallest example we can find, and we're finding it difficult enough. We can model that in terms of safety and liveness. Now, the simulator knows their true age as well as the age they're masquerading as. The safety requirement is clearly if their true age is below the limit then they shouldn't be allowed to succeed by buying alcohol or the crypto protocols book. So I can do a comparison of what their real age is versus what the simulation result is, and say how many pathways through are giving me a true negative. I can write a liveness requirement: if you are over that age limit you shouldn't be denied the transaction, because that's clearly bad as well. But then there's those additional requirements, such as does it leak information that we don't want them to have? In that sense it still looks like the Casper analogue: does the environment, or does another actor get extra information? Does their memory, the model in their head, now have more information about the person than they actually need?

Bruce Christianson: How do you model the constraints on actors' beliefs or do you need to do that?

Reply: The actors' belief model at the moment: for a generic actor, say Alice, you'd want to have her walk in to the shop and she's got a property such as what her real age is. She has additional sets of beliefs which at the moment we tend to randomise, such as is she going to borrow somebody else's card off them? If she gets someone else's card then you now have another set of randomisations: is that card going to plausibly look like her? You can ask if someone looks the same as in a picture, as well as does someone look a particular age. How many people are good at looking at photo IDs? In practice it's not that easy, especially when they're worn or they're of low quality.

So this actor might arrive in a location. Her arrival is going to trigger a change in the other actors' mental model, who adds "There is this person, I'm estimating her age as whatever" to his beliefs. Or he adds whatever properties you care about in this scenario. If she presents a card, I make an estimate of "do I think that this card matches that person". That's obviously got to be skewed by the simulation of the real world saying, this is really her card. Because if it's really her card with her real picture then it should be more likely that he agrees it is. If it's somebody else's picture, he should have a lower chance of accepting it, but this is more affected by the fuzziness of the scenario. Do I believe that these probabilities are even remotely correct and meaningful? Are they correct enough to give me a sensible answer, because clearly I'm not going to get answers to n decimal places. But am I going to get some answers which I can use to make an argument that changing my process is valuable? I'm not interested in just one run of it and saying, "here are some numbers that fell out" because that's got no value at all really. My interest is, if I change how I carry out this transaction, if I change how this protocol runs, does it give me different answers to the safety and liveness characteristics that I mentioned a moment ago?

Sandy Clark: The stuff that I mentioned, it's Face.com that's advertising age recognition.

Reply: Thank you.

The Casino and the OODA Loop
Why Our Protocols Always Eventually Fail

Sandy Clark, Matt Blaze, and Jonathan M. Smith

University of Pennsylvania, Philadelphia, PA 19104, USA
{saender,blaze,jms}@cis.upenn.edu

Abstract. Security protocols are almost always part of an iterated game, but existing abstractions don't model this behavior. Models for such systems have been developed in other contexts, and we propose the use of one, John Boyd's Observe-Orient-Decide-Act (OODA) Loop, as appropriate for the security context.

1 Introduction

Information security can be characterized as getting the right information to the right people at the right place and time, while at the same time keeping it from the wrong people. Security protocols are intended to meet these requirements in the face of of a more formalized (but static) *threat model*. The protocol designer tries to outwit adversaries, whose behavior is characterized by a set of assumptions based on the threat model. Unfortunately, real adversaries are both dynamic and learn over time; the smarter ones seek to violate assumptions, either explicit or implicit, made by the security protocol designers.

2 The OODA Loop

John Boyd's "OODA Loop" [1], illustrated in Figure 1, provides a principled basis for a design intended to overcome an adversary, using automation to accelerate responses, control the battlespace, and confuse the adversary, "getting inside" their OODA cycles. Boyd's analysis militates for agility and rapid adaptation, and was used to great practical effect in the design of the F-16 aircraft. This strategic model identifies opportunities for automation intended to improve the integration between human and system. In Boyd's theory, both attacker and defenders are running an OODA Loop. The winner is the one who gets "inside" the enemy's loop, reacting quicker than his opponent, getting ahead of his opponent's decision process and changing conditions so his opponent's actions mismatch those conditions. To do this, the winner must cycle through his own OODA loop faster than the enemy can cycle through his.

So, what is in a "Protocol OODA Loop"? There are several examples from the attacker's side:

B. Christianson et al. (Eds.): Security Protocols 2012, LNCS 7622, pp. 60–63, 2012.
© Springer-Verlag Berlin Heidelberg 2012

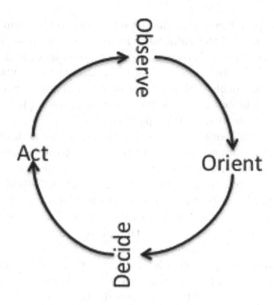

Fig. 1. Observe, Orient, Decide, Act: Boyd's OODA Loop

- New attack technologies (buffer overflows, fuzzing, *etc.*)
- Controlling the environment (clocks, *etc.*)
- Controlling the naming infrastructure
- Violating tamper resistance assumptions.

But few, if any, from the defender's side. Once a protocol is accepted, there is no loop, no changes, it is rarely, if ever altered. It is as if one side of this game refuses to learn.

3   The Casino

Casino gambling game protection measures are a surprisingly rich source of examples of continually evolving security protocols. Since "winning" (even if unfairly) can have significant financial impact, casinos (and gambling more generally) have found their game offerings under constant attack since the first bets were made. Casinos must provide an attractive, pleasurable and accessible environment to their patrons, while at the same time guarding carefully against every possible type of cheating (something which differs for every game they have available). They guard against attackers who may be smart amateurs or highly skilled professionals, working alone or in teams, outsider or employee, using sleight of hand or complicated tools and they may expect to be attacked 24 hours a day, 7 days a week, every day of the year.

Over the years casino game protection has evolved sets of specialized procedures for each area of concern, *e.g.,* handling money, dealing cards, control of dice, changing cheques (chips), *etc.* As with other security protocols, these procedures act to limit the access the attacker has to the vulnerable areas, or limit the attack surface of the vulnerable items that (because of the game) are sometimes under the attacker's control. Because casinos recognize that cheating will always be possible, and expect that it is always being attempted, unlike computer security protocols, Casino game protection protocols are continually being updated and adapted as new attacks are discovered [4,3].

Examples include blackjack and craps/dice.

Blackjack is the only game where the house has a disadvantage. Card counting is addressed with multiple decks, and by limiting the betting range, as well as watching betting patterns. Card counting teams are addressed by forbidding late entry. Advantage play more generally can result in "blacklisting", *e.g.*, via http://www.nj.gov/oag/ge/exclude_home.htm. Collusion w/ dealer & staff (dealer's hole-carding) are addressed with monitoring and surveillance.

Dice/Craps is the only game where the player controls the source of randomness. Switching dice is addressed by elaborate protocols. Controlled/skilled throwing are addressed by protocols and equipment, for example, does the shooter display empty hands at end of throw and do the dice hit the bumper. Late / switched betting are addressed through surveillance, *e.g.*, capping chips is a term for placing more chips on a stack used for a bet while the dealer is distracted.

4   Discussion: Why Our Protocols Fail

We see the essential issue as defining the problem. The problem we worry about is that the designer wasn't as smart as the attacker. Protocol designers try to develop the perfect protocol, or at least the best possible. The protocol development methodology is such that protocols converge on becoming considered stronger. This methodology depends on static properties of the protocol, and when a protocol is accepted and put into general use, it is 'finished'.

The reason most protocols actually fail is that *the attacker finds a way to violate our assumptions*. There are dynamic properties - of application/environment outside the control of the developer that affect security. Strong protocols ultimately converge on failure.

Three lessons we can learn from casinos and the OODA Loop:

1. Do not seek to design "perfect" protocols, instead design *adaptable* protocols. A static protocol cannot anticipate or pre-emptively respond to potential threats and therefore must wait for attacks to occur. Static protocols cannot counter attacks in any meaningful way, frequently they cannot be patched and must be discarded.
2. Security protocol design (and implementation) is an iterated game The formal properties of the protocol might not change, but everything else involves an "arms race". Attacker capability / understanding is constantly evolving, so must we [2,5].
3. Protocol design is inherently a zero-sum tradeoff space trading off factors such as resources, usability, complexity, interoperability, *etc.*

Acknowledgments. Sandy Clark's work was partially supported by DARPA Contract No. N66001-11-C-4020, Matt Blaze's work was partially supported by DARPA Contract No. N66001-11-C-4020 and NSF CNS-0905434. Jonathan M. Smith's work was partially supported by NSF CNS-1040672 and ONR N00014-09-1-0770.

References

1. Boyd, J.: Boyd bibliography, `http://danford.net/boyd/`
2. Cellini: The Card Counter's Guide to Casino Surveillance. Huntington Press Pub. (2003)
3. Boss, A.Z.D.: Casino Security and Gaming Surveillance. Auerback Publications (2010)
4. Forte, S.L.: Casino Game Protection: A Comprehensive Guide. SLF Publishing LLC (2004)
5. Powell, L.F.G., Tyska, L.: Casino Surveillance and Security: 150 Things You Should Know. Asis International (2003)

The Casino and the OODA Loop:
Why Our Protocols Always Eventually Fail
(Transcript of Discussion)

Matt Blaze

University of Pennsylvania

This is joint work with Sandy, who is here, and Jonathan Smith, who's not. The title of my talk, which is a moving target, is the Casino and OODA loop, and why we are converging on failure. I want to start with a disclaimer that this talk is going to be all questions and no answers or new protocols, so I apologize for that. But I'm going to add a claimer which is that at least this year we are on the theme I think maybe more than anyone else here is, so that's enough for me.

I'm going to talk about four points. The first is that security protocols are in practice, when applied to systems, part of an iterated game. The flip-side of that is that our abstractions almost always fail to capture the fact that we are part of an iterated game in the applications that we are writing our protocols for, and I'll talk about that a bit more. I'm going to suggest a model for understanding the game that we are playing, stolen from military and competitive strategy, called the OODA loop that I think is relevant to us, and that our community deserves to consider and learn from. And finally, rather than looking inward at our own examples of protocols which converge on failure, we should look to successful examples rather than failed examples for inspiration, and I'm going to suggest that we look at casinos, particularly casinos that are still in business.

Bruce Christianson: What's the five letter acronym, sorry?

Reply: The five-letter acronym is: "too long and did not lead"

So why do our protocols fail? We know that our protocols fail. Ross told us that our protocols fail longer ago than perhaps either of us would care to admit[1]. I was in the audience when he said it, and we appear to have all agreed with Ross' points, and learned nothing from them over the years because our protocols continue to fail. Now I'm going to argue that the reason for this is that we are worried about the problem that academics and smart people always worry about, which is, are we smart enough? That is, when we design our protocol we worry about whether our protocol is correct, and what that really means is that we worry that we aren't as smart as the attacker. Or conversely, when we analyze protocols we are looking for an opportunity to point out that we are smarter than the person who designed the protocol by finding a weakness or a flaw in the protocol. An implicit constraint on the game is that we are required to analyze the protocol in the terms that the protocol designer chose to present it to us, and we win if we say, well your protocol as described has some internal inconsistency or some problem with it, and so on. And we subject our protocols

---

[1] Why Cryptosystems Fail: in Proceedings of the 1st ACM conference on Computer and Communications Security, 1993.

B. Christianson et al. (Eds.): Security Protocols 2012, LNCS 7622, pp. 64–75, 2012.
© Springer-Verlag Berlin Heidelberg 2012

to the scrutiny of the community. If we're doing a good job, we're trying to build a successful protocol, and in principle we iterate this process and throw darts and, and our protocols converge on becoming stronger, they converge to the point at which we, we reach a point at which we have very, very high confidence that this protocol is correct and works.

But of course that's not what attackers do, that's not actually the game that *they're* playing. The attackers generally realise that protocol designers are very good at what they do, and the game the attackers play is to violate the designers' assumptions in some way, in the application in which the protocol is provided. We violate the assumption that this key is going to be secret, we violate the assumption that this is what is protected, we violate the assumption that this is the correct security protocol for this application, or what have you. That is, rather than static properties of the protocol, attackers are looking at the properties of the application and environment in which the protocol is running, which are constantly changing, and in fact which the protocol designer probably didn't know about, by the time the system is being considered for attack. That is, the application in the environment in any successful protocol will change because this is a successful protocol and people want to use it in their application and apply it.

So if we are lucky, applications that we didn't anticipate will use our designs, and our cryptography, and our cryptographic protocols, and our security protocols. So the number of assumptions, and what those assumptions are, by definition, the stronger the protocol is, the more often those underlying assumptions are going to change, and the more opportunities that the attacker has to violate those assumptions in one way or another. So we have this process that converges on success, but in a scenario that ultimately converges on failure because when this is running the protocol designers are not participating anymore, this protocol has been set in stone. So this is a really strange way of doing security, right, we are arguably the only people who do security like this, hey, here's our protocol, bye, and perhaps we might look at environments in which that isn't how things are done.

So if we fail to adapt we are guaranteed that at some point the attacker capability is going to change, the thing that is being protected is going to change, and so on, even if the properties of the security, and the protocol, and the cryptography, have been proven in some way, they've been proven with respect to a specific environment. And I think this is largely something we understand, but it's also something we haven't actually allowed to influence us. Certainly I still think about the things that I've been trained to think about, which is, you know, cryptography, and security, and so on. And I don't think about applications because I get to claim that that's someone else's problem. But it in fact isn't a reasonable guarantee of any kind of success in the long term. So let me admit that I am not going to provide any helpful advice about how we might change, but only point to communities that understand this better than we do, that perhaps are worth looking at.

One way to think about this is security as a game, and by game I don't mean the things that are fun, I mean games as in game theory, although some people think that's fun, an iterated game in which we have payoffs and actions that we can take, and in which we are moving from one part of this space to another with each move, and trading advantage and disadvantage with our adversary in some way. And if we are lucky, it may have some equilibrium state, but in practice it probably has to be adapted, and we have to keep playing the game with an adaptive strategy over and over again. Ron Rivest is perhaps the most prominent example of applying this to protocol and security protocol design, particularly his keynote at the Crypto Conference last year where he proposed the Flip It game as a more rich model for understanding security as a zero sum possibility game, in which our adversary and I have to play this game in which we have to commit resources that weaken us in other ways. It looks like a very interesting approach, but it's a very preliminary work, and it hasn't yet really been applied to a point where it can influence what we do in what we design.

The military has been at this for longer than us, they understand security protocols as an arms race, and I'm going to describe a modelling technique called the OODA loop that may be relevant, and I'm then going to point out that casinos are a rich source of examples of security protocols that in fact are very highly adaptive in a way that I think we can learn from. So what's the OODA loop? The OODA loop was proposed around 1976, or at least named around 1976, by a fellow by the name of John Boyd, who is I will argue the most important security meta-engineer that you have probably never heard of. He was a fighter pilot in the US Air Force, later a military theorist, he was for a while best known as the father of the F16, now he's perhaps best known as the father of the F16 and of the OODA loop. The OODA loop stands for observe, orient, decide, act, and the basic ideas that these are the steps that any two sides in a conflict are performing, and they're constantly doing this, both sides, in any environment, whether they are defensive or offensive, performing a loop in which they are observing the situation; they are orienting, evaluating what they have observed, they're making some sense of their situation; they are making decisions based on this; they're then adapting their behaviour, and then going back to observing. And this is a way of modeling that is simplifying a conflict in terms of the OODA loop to understand where advantage and disadvantage might lie.

Virgil Gligor: The second part of the OODA loop is that whoever executes a loop ...

Reply: No, wait, you're not allowed to look at that yet. So essentially both the attacker and the defender are constantly running an OODA loop whether you know it or not. The winner, according to Boyd's theory of the OODA loop, is the player with the faster loop. His theory is informed originally by flying fighter planes, in which this OODA loop is running very, very fast, but he ultimately understood this in very broad terms ranging from competition in business to almost any kind of game environment, where you can simply understand this. You can model the OODA loop in a particular situation more correctly. You can figure out who will win by understanding who is able to perform it faster. Executing your OODA loop faster than your adversary is more important than whether you've got better resources than your adversary, whether you are stronger than your adversary, whether you are flying a better aeroplane from your adversary, or have faster computers from your adversary, the essential determining factor of advantage is who is performing their OODA loop faster. That is each side's goal is to dip inside their adversary's OODA loop such that they are able to change the situation faster than the other side is able to comprehend that the change has taken place.

Frank Stajano: The goal to make the OODA loop as fast as possible reminded me of some random colleagues who are in London doing financial transactions as fast as possible. Why is success not affected by the resources you have, by the biggest computer and so on?

Reply: Well that may affect how fast you can perform it, but the important thing when modeling it this way is that merely having the resources, being stronger, or better, or what have you, in various ways, is not what you are attempting to achieve.

Frank Stajano: No, but in order to be the fastest don't you have to buy the biggest computer?

Sandy Clark: Your adversary's OODA loop may depend on other resources that you don't have and that you're not taking into consideration.

Reply: Your ability to execute your OODA loop may be improved by having more resources. I mean, this doesn't say we defund the military and simply explain to them about the OODA loop and they'll win all of the wars.

Omar Chaudary: I guess you may have all the resources in the world, but you if get the worst army you're never going to win.

Reply: That's right, and in particular if you're only reacting you are by definition executing your OODA loop slower than your adversary. And so if you're only, for example, patching when a failure in your protocol has been detected, you are executing your OODA loop slower than the adversary.

Jonathan Anderson: So presumably where resources come into it is that each of these four things has to be done effectively, like if the action is throwing a spear at an F16, it's not actually really performing?

Reply: That's right, that's not an action that actually has any effect, your OODA loop needs to actually enable you to exercise your advantage.

Bruce Christianson: But it's like the two different approaches to a project getting behind schedule. One is to say, well it needs more resources, put more people on, the other approach is to find out who is slowing it down and transfer them to a rival project.

Reply: That's right, as Brooks pointed out[2], adding more programmers to a problem is not usually the solution,

Jonathan Anderson: It makes for a nice bigger problem.

---

[2] The Mythical Man-Month: Addison-Wesley, 1975.

Reply: But it does make for a nice bigger problem, one Ken Thompson is worth a hundred Matt Blazes, but fifty Matt Blazes is worth more than a hundred Matt Blazes.

Virgil Gligor: An interesting observation about the OODA loop, this is the exercise under a different name by the Japanese quality improvement, actually in the 60s. That's precisely what they did, they observed, they measured, oriented themselves, they decided what to do, what to improve, and they acted, and they did that faster than anyone else in several industries, almost wiped out their adversaries, namely their competitors.

Reply: Right, and this tells you, get more resources when it will help you run your OODA loop faster, right, and otherwise you don't really know why you're getting them. But I think for us the relevant point here is to look at what we do, we try to design the best protocol that we can design, and then we stop, until we discover that we're wrong, and then we really design the best protocol that we can design by patching the one that we had before, and then we declare, well we had victory before, but now we really have victory, and now we can stop. So we act in a way that the OODA loop theory of security protocols would predict *a priori* that we are going to fail, because we are acting in this strictly reactive way, we are playing a different game from the adversary.

So getting inside the OODA loop, let's observe how attackers get inside the OODA loop in security protocols. Well they do a number of things. They've invented new attack technologies, buffer overflows, brand new attack technologies, fuzzing is a sort of updated version of finding things like buffer overflows without the need to understand what's actually going on in the application, or even knowing what protocol it runs. Controlling the environment, because the assumptions have changed, in which the attacker may have control over something that originally when the protocol was designed was assumed to be secure, and not changeable. The naming infrastructure is another example, violating tamper resistant assumptions, and so on. A protocol designed for a computer that the adversary can't control suddenly is placed in an environment in which the adversary can control it. And this is simply a short list that ties back to examples from famous attacks over the last, small amount of time, there are hundreds and hundreds.

How do we try to get inside the OODA loop of the adversary? Well I don't really have any examples.

Michael Roe: Windows updates is an example where you're trying to reduce the time it takes when discovering someone's using new exploits to getting the security patch deployed on people's desktops.

Reply: Well there is that, but if we're using as the source for our attacks what the attackers have told us by attacking us, then all we're doing is allowing them to be inside our OODA loop a little less efficiently, but they're still in it.

But, if we start attacking our own protocols, and as a matter of course, and try to do that faster, then we are now playing at least the same game that the adversary is. And I think, you know, Microsoft presumably is doing that.

Omar Chaudary: Are we doing that all the time, because you obviously you want us to attack someone?

Reply: Well we attack protocols, but we don't currently attack the environment that the protocols are in, because we start abrogating our responsibility and saying, well, you know, that aspect is someone else's problem.

Bruce Christianson: The person who implemented it.

Reply: Yes, those silly implementers have misused our protocol, of course it didn't work, well we could have told them that if they'd have asked us.

Joseph Bonneau: Then somebody else who you haven't met publishes, at a different conference, this real world break where they actually hack the OS server. So it does happen, it's just not usually a better person who designed the system.

Reply: And in particular, we devote far less energy to that, the culture that we're in takes it far less seriously than when it's part of a really deployed attack in the real world. The thing that gets our attention is the zero-day that's got an exploit in the wild, which is inherently a reactive strategy once the protocol has been designed.

Sandy Clark: One other point that we're trying to make here is that when we design protocols we're not designing them as part of an eco-system that they're going to run in, and we should be. All we're doing is designing this protocol, and it's almost isolated by itself, and everything else is up to somebody else. But security involves an entire system and that's what we should be paying attention to. So our protocols need to be adaptive, as well as originally designed with security in mind.

Phil Brooke: So make it be the best it has to be in sort of equal environments.

Sandy Clark: Whatever we need to do.

Reply: I said in advance that we're only pointing out problems and raising questions, not answers, only to observe that what we are doing is not the same game that the adversary is doing.

Jonathan Anderson: There are some positive examples on the defenders' side, but they tend to be much longer term where we can't fundamentally change the environment, because eventually people got sick of all these buffer overflows and stuff. And somebody said, alright, fine, from now on within Microsoft, or whatever, people who don't know anything about security are not allowed to use unsafe languages, for instance, they must use managed languages. And there are various ways in which you can actually change the environment where you say, from now on all applications that run on phones will run inside a sandbox. You can change the environment, but it sometimes takes a very long time to do, and sometimes we only have the opportunity to do that when we are having a shift to a new kind of technology.

Sandy Clark: And there are new ways to do things.

Phil Brooke: But isn't that just a better defence?

Jonathan Anderson: Well it is sort of a meta thing where you're changing the rules of the game to say, we seem to be losing at this game, so we're going to play a new game, we're going to play inside a different kind of a box.

Sandy Clark: Another good example for that is ASLR, but there are numerous examples that show that the other side is still running a faster OODA loop, because while HD Moore (the author of Metasploit) said that ASLR made going from vulnerability to successful to exploit change from a matter hours to weeks, yet it has not slowed down the rate of discovery of vulnerabilities and exploits.

Jonathan Anderson: But the thing where you say from now on you're going to use these much more constrained languages is a fundamental change in the game.

Reply: Oh absolutely.

Jonathan Anderson: But it takes fifteen years to take effect.

Reply: And it was done in reaction to real attacks, right, we knew about the possibility of buffer overflows long before Robert Morris Jr first exploited one in the wild, and people still said no-one would be able to do it, in practice.

Omar Chaudary: Sometimes you need to be quite quantifying about this sort of playing the game. Perhaps different academic institutions are part of the same side, and then the other attackers, people like the Mafia or something like that, are trying to get money by looking at the security protocol, or the security proof, and then someone goes to develop an attack. And then the academic institutions come again through the loop, and to their part of the game once the attack has been implemented.

Sandy Clark: Yes, possibly, but our loop is certainly pretty slow if we model in that way. There is no-one whose job is to break real systems, or analyse entire systems end to end, as efficiently as people who are trying to actually steal things are trying to do it. And, if we understand things in that way, we at least identify that we have a fundamental problem in the game we're playing.

Reply: Yes, and it's interesting. Red Teaming, which is applied in the military and in some high value environments commercially is itself a fairly static process. We red team it and then we say, ah, the red team found this, we fixed their problems, perfectly secure, pat ourselves on the back. So you know, even when we do attack systems we're still playing the static game rather than the adaptive game.

So I'm going to suggest as a source of inspiration we might look at the casino gaming world. There is a field within the casino world, what they call game protection, that sounds very sinister, that is the anti-cheating world that analyses games and methods of cheating in the games, particularly table games, played in casinos. There's money at stake, which means that the results are measurable. We're succeeding to the extent that the house is winning. Interestingly as a result they don't attempt to design perfect security protocols, games in which cheating is not possible, they try to design games in which there is this well understood probabilistic model that works in the long run.

Sandy Clark: And also the game designs revolve around making cheating discoverable.

Reply: So the interesting thing about this world that makes it particularly worthwhile is they understand everything precisely the same way we do.

There is remarkably little security through obscurity in this world, they understand the value of an open literature, in fact they have an almost academic style of maintaining credit for discovery and countermeasures like we do. There's a well documented history when new attacks are discovered, when they're detected, when countermeasures are deployed, and measuring their success of those countermeasures against the loss of income because some of these countermeasures decrease usability. I have an example of a standard checklist for the surveillance in a casino from the craps game, which is the dice game in a casino. It includes, what the surveillance is supposed to look at, it has 18 steps including, is the stick man changing the dice after they land, are the box man and stick men watching the correct ends of the table during play. Some of these patch specific forms of cheating, some insider, some outsider, others are aimed at preventing classes of cheating, and in general they're always trying to orient themselves as to whether they are winning and making money, when they reconcile at the end of the evening. The most fascinating thing I discovered, and by the way, I can heartily recommend, is this out of print and expensive, but entirely worthwhile book. It can be self-financing research because it describes all of the ways of cheating: Casino Game Protection, by Steve Forte, it's a wonderful and very academically styled book.

Sandy Clark: The book is an example of attack and defense, new attack, new patch, it's a wonderful history of the entire arms race in casino security.

By the way, the cheapest place to get this book is from Gambling Incorporated, and they have a limited number of copies. But if you're going to buy this then don't buy the other one he has, because it's just on Poker, and it's a chapter of this book.

Reply: What I found particularly fascinating is the standard in a casino for setting up every game that they have. We've all seen movies in which everyone is watching everyone else, but the standard roles in all the games invariably include three times, or a little more than three times the number of participants that you would expect would be required to perform the protocol. So apparently they have discovered Byzantine agreement compound, and the requirements for Byzantine agreement protocols, completely independently from our theoretical ability to model it. So it's very interesting that they understand the division of roles, and how much insider cheating they can tolerate before they start actually losing. And we can look at examples, I'm focused on blackjack and craps, because they have interesting properties in which they are constantly looking for potential advantages.

Blackjack is interesting because it's the only game where the house has a disadvantage, it's vulnerable to card-counting which is not a form of cheating, but it is a way of causing the house to lose. They counter card-counting with things like multiple decks, and limiting the range of betting, and card-counting teams, they forbid people from entering games late in the deck, advantage playing, the introduction of shuffling machines, which was intended as a countermeasure, can also leak information in different ways, there are protocols for shuffling. Dice is interesting because it's the only game in which the player influences the random number generator, and controls and touches the source of randomness in the game, so there are a variety of attacks that are unique to that class of game they have to worry about, and watching the players and limiting their actions without chasing away potential suckers. So there's a very interesting tension going on there that we can learn from I think.

So again, my point is not that I have any suggestion about how we should do things differently. One of the strengths of academia is that we get to publish, we get to specialise, and because we get to specialise we get to be smarter. But arguably specialization is also preventing us from looking at the context in which these protocols are performed, and forces us to play this much more static game in which we eventually declare victory until we are defeated.

In respect of the game that we are demonstrably playing in security, I think the OODA loop model is deserving of our attention, and I think that casinos are a good source of inspiration, and if we understand it well enough, funding, so thanks.

Joseph Bonneau: Are you claiming that attackers aren't playing a reactive game?

Reply: Well they're playing a game in which they are certainly inside our OODA loop, so in that sense they're not as reactive as we are.

Joseph Bonneau: So can you define that a little bit more, because I guess I missed that, I mean, it seems like, defenders for the protocol, and attackers having to pre-attack.

Reply: The theory of the OODA loop in the military environment is that the way you can tell whether you are outside or inside of the two OODA loops is, if you have the ability to change the situation faster than the adversary is able to understand your changes then you are on the inside loop. That is, by the time they have understood what they need to do to attack you, or to counter your attack, the game has changed before they can act. And, you know, we don't do that, we actually almost have an ethic against doing it, that I think I subscribe to at some level. So we should design something, make sure everyone understands the design, if there's any problem with it let's fix it, and eventually it becomes so good that the fact that the adversary understands it isn't a disadvantage.

Bruce Christianson: But when we say, if it isn't broke don't fix it, we're actually saying, wait for the attacker. We're deliberately putting ourselves on the outside OODA loop.

Reply: That's right.

Omar Chaudary: For example, the attacker, in a similar attack in mind, he has an exploit already, but he has already five more just in case the system gets fixed, he does apply zero day for the new attack. On the defenders side, it is hard to say what the attacker has in mind, so what should I do to fix?

Reply: Well certainly right now, that's a reasonable thing for an attacker research lab. Somewhere, probably in a basement, there is an attacker conference — just like this one but with bad guys — who are looking for attacks that they can bank, and use, and keep on the shelf, for when whatever attack they're exploiting today isn't working because we notice they're using it and we fix it. They are inside our OODA loop if they're able to do the next attack by just pulling it off the shelf. If they can't afford to bank and put these attacks on the shelf, because they'll be irrelevant by the time it's time to deploy them, then we're inside their OODA loop, assuming that we are defenders.

Bruce Christianson: I have a horrible feeling that their meeting is actually in a penthouse.

Reply: Yes, OK, that's a good point.

Bruce Christianson: But the other difficulty we have is that security is often seen as a defensive game, in other words, we are in a siege situation, and there isn't the same incentive to break out and attack the enemy camp, and indeed there's sort of laws that almost discourage us from doing that. There was a talk here a few years ago[3] about this idea of whether it was ethical or not to take the battle to the enemy, is it ethical to distribute stuff that looks like viruses that have the effect of inoculating people against colonization, and so forth. One of the things we need to do apart from just thinking about our interaction with the environment is to think about what the legitimate moves are on our side of the game.

Reply: Yes, can we play an offensive game as well.

Paul Syverson: What are the public health interests?

Bruce Christianson: Yes, do they justify us to play an offensive security game.

Sandy Clark: But the CDC does something like that, right? When they develop this year's flu shot.

Bruce Christianson: Yes, precisely. But in other sectors there isn't nearly the same preactive process.

Ross Anderson: But casinos are different, and the reason is that attacks that are successful are instantly evident. If you leave a casino with $20,000 more than when you arrive, they will follow you home, and they will have extracts from the CCTV, and they will figure out what you did, and they will ban you. So you are in a position where the casino is very much more able to react quickly and decisively, and to spread the knowledge to other casinos, than is generally the case for example with banking protocols, or any of the other things we usually look at.

Jonathan Anderson: Because the casino makes rules. If the banks had made similar rules for the way that transaction protocols worked, when they had the chance, then they would probably be in the same position as the casinos. Once it gets captured by consultants who like to pad the EMB spec because it's a good living, or whatever, maybe then you'd lose.

Bruce Christianson: Ross' point is a very good one, but to some extent it's because of the design constraints we put ourselves under. We're currently trying to design a protocol which prevents, rather than saying there should be an equal emphasis on detection. Instead of saying, oh somebody broke our protocol, that's really bad, we must fix the protocol, perhaps we should be trying to get to a position where we are saying, OK, we know who's going home with the money,

---

[3] Dan Cvrcek and George Danezis, *Fighting the 'Good' Internet War*, Security Protocols XVI, LNCS 6615 pp 3–11. The transcript was not published for legal reasons.

because it was an objective of the protocol to tell us that, now we just have to work out exactly how they're doing it.

Phil Brooke: Prevention detection reaction type loops, so some prevention stuff, and some detection.

Bruce Christianson: Yes, and particularly where the game is integrity, as it is with us, at least more than half the time, that's good enough.

Reply: Yes I think I agree with the first part of Ross' observation that the casino environment *is* certainly different from say the banking environment, but I'm not sure that that's *inherently* true.

Ross Anderson: I think it is. To give similar detection in the banking environment, then whenever somebody spends money in a shop you have to phone them up to check that he really spent it, and then you would instantly detect card fraud.

Paul Syverson: I think it has to do with the feedback. In order to allow certain pieces of the economy to work at all, there are things where we have to run risks that transactions are non-atomic, and that you're not going to find out for three weeks whether all these things balance up and stuff, and that's why we have accounts. With the casino, on some level that's also true, but in the end, with the game, as Ross said, when somebody walks out with $50,000, you know about it, that's a flag.

Sandy Clark: This argument is based upon the misassumption that casinos do this really well, because you must do this instantaneously, and they don't. One of the things that really surprised me at these casino protection conferences is how much effort after the fact they have to go to. It's very costly to them and, the myth of Oceans 11, that they're tracking you, they've got your credit rating, and they know exactly how much money is in your pocket the minute you walk into the casino, is just a myth. And that they catch you with high-tech media.

Reply: That's actually part of the game, right, the fact that you believe that casino security is good discourages you from cheating, and in fact it's not very good. If people, if the adversary understood the ways in which it's not very good in particular environments, there would be more cheating.

Sandy Clark: Many casinos still use videotape. They don't even have digital surveillance cameras.

Ross Anderson: That may be your US environment. My information is from people who have worked in casinos in the UK, where you must join as a member, so they know who you are, they've got a copy of your passport, you can't play unless you're a member, and you must play with plants or with chips, you cannot play with banknotes. So they know exactly and instantly if you walk out with 20K more than you went in with.

Sandy Clark: Are they RFID?

Ross Anderson: No idea.

Sandy Clark: By the way, I have some reference materials for you on, one on the Hidden and Visible Features of the Checks, and another on all of the protocols for the games.

Bruce Christianson: I think the analogy is with the phone call you get from your credit card company about a very old transaction where they're not trying to prevent fraud, they're trying to ...

Reply: Right, they're trying to manage it.

Bruce Christianson: They're trying to work out whether their fraud protection system needs work.

Jonathan Anderson: And they're training new classifiers.

Bruce Christianson: That's right, and we don't have anything analogous to that.

Feng Hao: I just wonder if you lose at the casino games online in which case ...

Sandy Clark: This is happening.

Reply: Yes, I think that's certainly a good way of getting them to inherit all of our problems.

Sandy Clark: They're going to wifi gaming, they want to give you a pad when you walk in, and that you play while you're in the restaurant or walking around, and they have not pen-tested the networks.

Reply: So I think what's interesting about the casino environment is not that it tells us exactly what to do, but that at the meta-level they understand that they are in an OODA loop, and they adapt their protocols and their environments in ways that are quite precisely what we don't do. So, there is something to be learned there.

Bruce Christianson: If only they had our expertise.

Reply: If only they had our expertise we could all clean up in the casino, yes.

Statistical Metrics
for Individual Password Strength

Joseph Bonneau

University of Cambridge
jcb82@cl.cam.ac.uk

Abstract. We propose several possible metrics for measuring the
strength of an individual password or any other secret drawn from a
known, skewed distribution. In contrast to previous ad hoc approaches
which rely on textual properties of passwords, we consider the problem
without any knowledge of password structure. This enables rating the
strength of a password given a large sample distribution without assuming anything about password semantics. We compare the results of
our generic metrics against those of the NIST metrics and other previous "entropy-based" metrics for a large password dataset, which suggest
over-fitting in previous metrics.

1 Introduction

It is often desirable to estimate the resistance to guessing provided by a specific password. This can be useful both for research purposes to compare password choices between two groups with insufficient data to construct full distributions [9,11,14]. It can also be used to make a proactive password checker which
indicates to a user the strength of a particular password during enrolment. [1].
Current practice usually relies on rules-of-thumb based on entropy estimates of
English such as those standardised by NIST [3]. These have been argued to be
inaccurate estimators of a password's vulnerability to cracking attacks [15].

Instead, we advocate using probability estimates based on an approximation of
the distribution $\mathcal{X}$ which a password x was drawn from. We'll call such a measure
the *estimated strength* and denote it as $S_{\mathcal{X}}(x)$. It is important to recognise that
any estimated strength is only as accurate as our approximation for $\mathcal{X}$ is accurate for a target population. For example, the password tequiero (which roughly
translates to iloveyou) is much weaker within a distribution of passwords chosen
by Spanish speakers than by English speakers.[1] We'll assume initially that the
purposes of this paper that the population-wide distribution of passwords $\mathcal{X}$ is
completely known before exploring the implications of relaxing this assumption.

---

[1] This problem was illustrated by the research of Dell'Amico et al. [7], who found
vastly different guessing efficiency based on the language of a password dictionary
and the users who chose passwords in a dataset.

B. Christianson et al. (Eds.): Security Protocols 2012, LNCS 7622, pp. 76–86, 2012.

2   Desired Properties

We can describe two important properties that we would like for a strength metric:

1. **Consistency for Uniform Distributions:** For a discrete uniform distribution $\mathcal{U}_N$ in which each of N events is equally likely, such as randomly-chosen 64-bit keys, we want any strength metric to indicate that each value has 2^N bits of strength. Specifically:

$$\forall_{x \in \mathcal{U}_N} \quad S_{\mathcal{U}_N}(x) = \lg N \tag{1}$$

2. **Monotonicity:** A strength metric should rate any event more weakly than events which are less common in the underlying distribution $\mathcal{X}$:

$$\forall_{x,x' \in \mathcal{X}} \quad p_x \geq p_{x'} \iff S_{\mathcal{X}}(x) \leq S_{\mathcal{X}}(x') \tag{2}$$

3   Strength Metrics

We formalise several purely statistical techniques for estimate a password's strength in this way, which require no general assumptions about human tendencies in password selection. In all cases, we convert our strength estimates into units of bits to satisfy our desired consistency property.

3.1   Probability Metric

The simplest approach is to take the estimated probability p_x from $\mathcal{X}$ and estimate the size of a uniform distribution in which all elements have probability p_x:

$$S_{\mathcal{X}}^{P}(x) = -\lg p_x \tag{3}$$

This is, in fact, the classic definition of the *self-information* of x (also called the *surprisal*), which is the underlying basis for Shannon entropy H_1 [13]. It is easy to see that for a randomly drawn value $x \xleftarrow{R} \mathcal{X}$, the expected value of this metric is:

$$E\left[S_{\mathcal{X}}^{P}(x) \,\middle|\, x \xleftarrow{R} \mathcal{X}\right] = \sum_{i=1}^{|\mathcal{X}|} p_x \cdot -\lg p_x = H_1(\mathcal{X}) \tag{4}$$

Previous metrics which attempt to measure the probability of a password, for example using Markov models [6,12,4] or probabilistic context-free grammars [16], can be seen as attempts to approximate $S_{\mathcal{X}}^{P}(x)$.

Applied to guessing, this model measures the (logarithmic) expected number of guesses before x is tried by an attacker who is guessing random values $x \xleftarrow{R} \mathcal{X}$ with no memory. This attack model might apply if an attacker is guessing randomly according to the distribution to evade an intrusion-detection system. For optimal sequential guessing attacks however, this metric has no direct relation.

3.2 Index Metric

To estimate the strength of an individual event against an optimal guessing attack, the only relevant fact is the index i_x of x, that is, the number of items in $\mathcal{X}$ of greater probability than p_x. We can convert this to an effective key-length by considering the size of a uniform distribution which would, on average, require i_x guesses. This gives us a strength metric of:

$$S_{\mathcal{X}}^{\mathrm{I}}(x) = \lg\left(2 \cdot i_x - 1\right) \tag{5}$$

Intuitively, this metric is related to real-world attempts to measure the strength of an individual password by estimating when it would be guessed by password-cracking software [10].

A practical problem with this metric is that many events may have the same estimated probability. If we break ties arbitrarily then in the case of the uniform distribution $\mathcal{U}_N$ the formula won't give $\lg N$ for all events. In fact, it won't even give $\lg N$ on average for all events, but instead $\approx \lg N - (\lg e - 1)$ (proved in Appendix B).

A better approach for a sequence of j equiprobable events $x_i \cdots x_{i+j}$ where $p_i = \ldots = p_{i+j}$ is to assign index $\frac{i+j}{2}$ to all events when computing the index strength metric. This is equivalent to assuming an attacker will choose randomly given a set of remaining candidates with similar probabilities and it does give a value of $\lg N$ to all events in the uniform distribution.

This is slightly unsatisfactory however, as it means for a distribution $\mathcal{X} \approx \mathcal{U}_N$ which is "close" to uniform but with a definable ordering of the events, the average strength will appear to jump down by $(\lg e - 1) \approx 0.44$ bits.

A second problem is that the most probable event in $\mathcal{X}$ is assigned a strength of $\lg 1 = 0$. To satisfy our consistency requirement is a necessary limitation, since for $\mathcal{U}_1$ we must assign the single possible event a strength of $\lg 1 = 0$.

3.3 Partial Guessing Metric

The probability metric doesn't model a sequential guessing attack, while the index approach has a number of peculiarities. A better approach is to consider the minimum amount of work done per account by an optimal partial guessing attack which will compromise accounts using x. The α-guesswork $\tilde{G}_\alpha$, defined in [2], reflects exactly the (logarithmic) expected amount of work per account required of an attacker desiring to break a proportion α of accounts. We provide the full definition for computing $\tilde{G}_\alpha$ in Appendix A.

For example, if a user chooses the password encryption, an optimal attacker performing a sequential attack against the RockYou distribution will have broken 51.8% of accounts before guessing encryption. Thus, a user choosing the password encryption can expect to be safe from attackers who aren't aiming to compromise at least this many accounts, which takes $\tilde{G}_{0.518}$ work on average per account. We can turn this into a strength metric as follows:

$$S_{\mathcal{X}}^{G}(x') = \tilde{G}_{\alpha_x}(\mathcal{X}) : \alpha_x = \sum_{i=1}^{i_x} p_i \qquad (6)$$

Because $\tilde{G}_{\alpha}(\mathcal{U}_N) = \lg N$ for all α, the consistency property is trivially satisfied. Moreover, for "close" distributions $\mathcal{X} \approx \mathcal{U}_N$ where $|p_i - \frac{1}{N}| < \varepsilon$ for all i, we'll have $S_{\mathcal{X}}^{G}(x_i) \to \lg N$ for all i as $\varepsilon \to 0$, unlike for S^I where strength will vary as long as there is any defined ordering.

As with $S_{\mathcal{X}}^I$ though, we encounter the problem of of ordering for events with statistically indistinguishable probabilities. We'll apply the same tweak and give each event in a sequence of equiprobable events $x_i \cdots x_{i+j}$ the index $\frac{i+j}{2}$.

4   Estimation from a Sample

Just like for distribution-wide metrics [2], there are several issues when estimating strength metrics using an approximation for $\mathcal{X}$ obtained from a sample.

4.1   Estimation for Unseen Events

All of the above metrics are undefined for a previously unobserved event $x' \notin \mathcal{X}$. This is a result of our assumption that we have perfect information about $\mathcal{X}$. If not, we inherently need to rely on some approximation. As a consequence of the monotonicity requirement, $S(x' \notin \mathcal{X})$ must be $\geq \max(S(x \in \mathcal{X}))$. The naive formula for $S_{\mathcal{X}}^{P}(x')$ assigns a strength estimate of ∞ though, which is not desirable.

We should therefore smooth our calculation of strength metrics by using some estimate $p(x') > 0$ even when $x' \notin \mathcal{X}$. Good-Turing techniques [8] do not address this problem as they provide an estimate for the total probability of seeing a new event, but not the probability of a specific new event. A conservative approach is to add x' to $\mathcal{X}$ with a probability $\frac{1}{N+1}$, on the basis that if it is seen in practice in a distribution we're assuming is close to our reference $\mathcal{X}$, then we can treat x' as one additional observation about $\mathcal{X}$. This is analogous to the common heuristic of "add-one smoothing" in word frequency estimation [8]. This correction gives an estimate of $S_{\mathcal{X}}^{P}(x) = \lg(N+1)$ for unobserved events.

For the index metric, this correction produces the smoothed estimate $S_{\mathcal{X}}^{I}(x') = \lg 2N + 1$, an increase of roughly 1 bit, due to the aforementioned instability for a distribution $\mathcal{X} \approx \mathcal{U}_N$. For the partial guessing strength metric we have $S_{\mathcal{X}}^{G}(x') \approx \tilde{G}_1(\mathcal{X})$, representing that guessing an unseen value requires at least an attacker willing to guess all known values.

All of these estimates are somewhat unsatisfactory because they don't allow us to distinguish between the estimated security of a new observation encryption1 compared to e5703572ae3c, the latter of which intuitively seems much more difficult to guess. Solving this problem inherently relies on semantic evaluation of the newly-seen event, which is out of scope.

4.2 Stability of Metrics

All of the proposed metrics will produce variable results for low-frequency events in a sample. The logarithmic nature of the estimators damps this problem to a large extent: if the hapax legomenon password sapo26 occurred two more times in the RockYou data set, tripling its observed frequency, its strength estimate would decrease by only 1.59, 2.22 and 2.55 bits for S_{RY}^{P}, S_{RY}^{I}, and S_{RY}^{G}, respectively.

It is straightforward to establish bounds on the worst case error when changing an event's observed probability from $p \to p' = p + \Delta p$. For S^{P}, the estimate can change from $\lg p$ to $\lg p'$, a difference of at most abs $\left(\lg \frac{p'}{p} \right)$ bits.

For the index metric the worst-case scenario is that changing from $p \to p' = p + \Delta p$ changes the index by N, the total number of events in the distribution, if all other events have probability $p \le p^{*} \le p + \Delta p$. In this case, the maximum number of events in the distribution is $N = \frac{1}{\min(p,p')}$. This gives a worst-case change of $\lg(2N - 1) - \lg 0 \approx \lg \frac{2}{\min(p,p')}$.

The worst-case change for S^{G} occurs in the same situation but is just $\lg N - \lg \frac{1}{p'} = \lg \frac{1}{p} - \lg \frac{1}{p'} = $ abs $\left(\lg \frac{p'}{p} \right)$, exactly as the case was for S^{P}. This is an attractive property of S^{G}: it offers worst-case stability equivalent to S^{P} while having a better connection to real guessing attacks.

However, in the special case where $\mathcal{X}$ is a Zipf distribution For a Zipf distribution each event's probability is roughly proportional to the inverse of its index in the distribution raised to a constant s:

$$p_x \propto \left(\frac{1}{i_x} \right)^{s}$$

Thus, if an event's probability increases by a constant factor k, its index should decrease by a factor of $k^{\frac{-1}{s}}$. This will decrease S^{P} by $\lg k$ bits and decrease S^{I} by $\frac{\lg k}{s}$ bits. For the classic Zipf distribution with $s \approx 1$, this means that changing an event's probability by k will affect $S_{\mathcal{X}}^{I}$ and $S_{\mathcal{X}}^{P}$ by exactly the same amount. While we reject the hypothesis that passwords are produced by a simple Zipfian distribution [5], this is a rough justification for why we don't expect $S_{\mathcal{X}}^{I}$ to be highly unstable in practice.

5 Example Estimates for Individual Passwords

Example values for the proposed strength metrics are given in Table 1 for passwords in the RockYou data set. Overall, the differences between S^{P}, S^{I}, and S^{G} are moderate with the exception of very common passwords, which receive significantly lower strength estimates by S^{I}. For much of the distribution, S^{G} provides estimates in between those of S^{P} and S^{I}, until the region of less-common passwords for which S^{G} is lower as it incorporates an attacker's ability to stop early upon success.

The fact that $S^{I} < S^{P}$ holds in every row is not a coincidence. Because the elements are ordered by probability, an event's index will always be lower in a

Table 1. Example strength estimates for a selection of passwords from the RockYou data set. The estimator S^{NIST} is calculated using the NIST entropy estimation formula [3].

x	$\lg(i_x)$	f_x	S^{P}_{RY}	S^{I}_{RY}	S^{G}_{RY}	S^{NIST}
123456	0	290729	6.81	0.00	6.81	14.0
12345	1	79076	8.69	1.58	7.46	12.0
password	2	59462	9.10	2.81	8.01	18.0
rockyou	3	20901	10.61	3.91	8.68	16.0
jessica	4	14103	11.17	4.95	9.42	16.0
butterfly	5	10560	11.59	5.98	10.08	19.5
charlie	6	7735	12.04	6.99	10.71	16.0
diamond	7	5167	12.62	7.99	11.30	16.0
freedom	8	3505	13.18	9.00	11.88	16.0
letmein	9	2134	13.90	10.00	12.48	16.0
bethany	10	1321	14.59	11.00	13.09	16.0
lovers1	11	739	15.43	12.00	13.74	22.0
samanta	12	389	16.35	13.00	14.42	16.0
123456p	13	207	17.27	14.00	15.13	22.0
diving	14	111	18.16	15.00	15.87	14.0
flower23	15	63	18.98	16.00	16.62	24.0
scotty2hotty	16	34	19.87	17.02	17.38	30.0
lilballa	17	18	20.79	18.01	18.13	18.0
robbies	18	9	21.79	19.06	18.93	16.0
DANELLE	19	5	22.64	19.96	19.62	22.0
antanddeck06	20	3	23.37	20.84	20.30	30.0
babies8	21	2	23.96	21.78	21.00	22.0
sapo26	22	1	24.96	24.00	22.44	20.0
jcb82	23	0	23.77	24.00	22.65	18.0

skewed distribution than in a uniform distribution with identical events, so we will always have $S^{\text{I}} \leq S^{\text{P}}$.

The entropy estimation formula proposed by NIST [3] is shown for comparison as S^{NIST} (though note that S^{NIST} doesn't meet either of our desired mathematical criteria for a strength metric). It fails for a few passwords which demonstrate the challenges of semantic evaluation: both scotty2hotty and antanddeck06 score highly by S^{NIST} for being long and including digits. Neither is particularly strong, however: scotty2hotty is a professional wrestler, while antanddeck06 is based on the name of a British comedy show. In contrast sapo26 is much shorter and rated 10 bits lower by S^{NIST}, but doesn't have a well-known real-world meaning.

Because we listed passwords in order of exponentially increasing index, we can test the Zipfian relationship on the difference between S^{P} and S^{I} using the data by comparing the ratio of differences for successive passwords x_2, x_1 in Table 1:

$$s \approx \frac{S^{\text{P}}_{\text{RY}}(x_{i+1}) - S^{\text{P}}_{\text{RY}}(x_i)}{S^{\text{I}}_{\text{RY}}(x_{i+1}) - S^{\text{I}}_{\text{RY}}(x_i)}$$

For successive rows of the table, we get estimates for s ranging from 0.34 to 1.37. The average estimate, however, is $s = 0.76$, almost identical to the estimate we would get by computing s using only the first and last row of the table. Using the equivalence between the power-law and Zipf formulation that $a = 1 + \frac{1}{s}$, we would estimate $a = 2.31$ given $s = 0.76$. This is not a sound way of computing a Zipfian fit for the data set s in general, but the fact that it is plausible supports our hypothesis that S^I will be stable for realistic distributions which follow a (very rough) power-law approximation.

6 Application to Small Data Sets

A second application of strength metrics is to estimate the average strength given only a very small sample for which distribution-wide statistics [2] can't be computed. This method can only be accurate for data sets which are approximately drawn from the same population as the base distribution, though this limitation is equally true of evaluation by password cracking [10] or semantic evaluation [14].

If we interpret the small set of passwords as a sample from some larger distribution, we need to reason about the expected value of each strength metric. We've already shown in Equation 4 that $E\left[S_{\mathcal{X}}^P(x)\middle|\, x \overset{R}{\leftarrow} \mathcal{X}\right] = H_1(\mathcal{X})$. The expected value of S^I was too complicated to compute directly even for a uniform distribution. Similarly, the expected value of S^G is:

$$E\left[S_{\mathcal{X}}^G(x)\middle|\, x \overset{R}{\leftarrow} \mathcal{X}\right] = \int_0^1 \tilde{G}_\alpha(\mathcal{X})\mathrm{d}\alpha \tag{7}$$

which doesn't appear to admit a simple analytic formula. Instead, we can only compute $E\left[S_{\mathcal{X}}^I(x)\middle|\, x \overset{R}{\leftarrow} \mathcal{X}\right]$ and $E\left[S_{\mathcal{X}}^G(x)\middle|\, x \overset{R}{\leftarrow} \mathcal{X}\right]$ directly for our reference distribution $\mathcal{X}$ and use this as a benchmark for comparison against a smaller distribution.

In Table 2 a variety of small password data sets for which clear-text passwords are available are evaluated using the RockYou data set as a baseline. None of the statistical metrics are obviously superior, though S^G is typically in between the values produced by the other two.

The NIST formula produces more plausible results when averaged than for individual passwords, correctly ranking the 2011 Twitter blacklist as much weaker than the other lists (though not as weak as the statistical estimates). The NIST formula also plausibly rates the foreign-language Hebrew data set lower than the statistical estimates, as it doesn't assume the passwords are in English like using RockYou as a baseline implicitly does.

In the myBart data set about two-thirds of users retained site-assigned random passwords. This set was rated highly by all of the metrics, being recognised inadvertently by the NIST formula because the site-assigned passwords always contained a number.

Table 2. Average strength estimates for small lists of leaked passwords. The NIST entropy estimation formula [3] is listed as S^{NIST}.

Dataset	M	% seen	S^{P}_{RY}	S^{I}_{RY}	S^{G}_{RY}	S^{NIST}
RockYou (baseline)	—	100.0%	21.15	18.79	18.75	19.82
small password sets						
70yx (sampled)	1000	34.0%	22.28	21.24	21.52	20.21
Fox	369	68.8%	20.95	18.99	19.33	19.28
Hebrew	1307	50.3%	21.25	19.63	20.14	17.46
Hotmail	11576	57.6%	21.82	20.29	20.43	18.21
myBart	2007	19.0%	22.93	22.37	22.54	23.53
MySpace	50546	59.5%	21.64	20.02	20.19	22.53
NATO-Books	11822	50.9%	21.66	20.17	20.47	19.35
Sony-BMG	41024	61.3%	20.93	19.10	19.53	19.87
malware dictionaries						
Conficker	190	96.8%	16.99	13.60	15.07	16.51
Morris	445	94.4%	18.62	15.68	16.56	15.27
blacklists						
Twitter-2010	404	7.9%	23.16	22.86	23.02	15.30
Twitter-2011	429	99.8%	15.11	11.31	13.46	15.27

The largest difference in the rankings occurred for the Hotmail and MySpace data sets, which produced indistinguishable statistical estimates but differed by over 4 bits by the NIST formula. Examining the passwords, it appears that a good portion of the MySpace data was collected under a policy mandating non-alphabetic characters: password1 is the most popular password, over twice as popular as password, and most of the other top passwords include a number. Popular numeric passwords such as 123456 appear to have been banned under some of the collection rules, as they are less common than variants like 123456a. The Hotmail data set, on the other hand, appears to have had no restrictions. Because the NIST formula awards a constant 6 points to passwords with a mix of numbers and letters, the MySpace complexity policy significantly raises S^{NIST}. However, the statistical estimators suggest these passwords may not actually be much stronger by this policy as a large number of users simply append a digit (usually a 1 or 0) to a weak password. In this case, statistical strength metrics are less influenced by the effects of complexity requirements.

The NIST formula also struggled to recognise datasets of explicitly weak passwords. For example, it considers the Conficker password dictionary to contain stronger passwords than the the Morris password dictionary, though the Conficker list is a more modern, better attack dictionary (containing much weaker passwords). Similarly, the two versions of the Twitter blacklist are rated similarly by the NIST formula, but the statistical metrics identify the 2011 version as a vast improvement (again in that it contains weaker passwords).

References

1. Bishop, M., Klein, D.V.: Improving System Security via Proactive Password Checking. Computers & Security 14(3), 233–249 (1995)
2. Bonneau, J.: The science of guessing: analyzing an anonymized corpus of 70 million passwords. In: SP 2012: Proceedings of the 2012 IEEE Symposium on Security and Privacy (2012)
3. Burr, W.E., Dodson, D.F., Timothy Polk, W.: Electronic Authentication Guideline. NIST Special Publication 800-63 (2006)
4. Castelluccia, C., Dürmuth, M., Perito, D.: Adaptive Password-Strength Meters from Markov Models. In: NDSS 2012: Proceedings of the Network and Distributed System Security Symposium (2012)
5. Clauset, A., Shalizi, C.R., Newman, M.E.J.: Power-Law Distributions in Empirical Data. SIAM Review 51, 661–703 (2009)
6. Davies, C., Ganesan, C.: BApasswd: A New Proactive Password Checker. In: Proceedings of the 16th National Computer Security Conference (1993)
7. Dell'Amico, M., Michiardi, P., Roudier, Y.: Password Strength: An Empirical Analysis. In: INFOCOM 2010: Proceedings of the 29th Conference on Information Communications, pp. 983–991. IEEE (2010)
8. Gale, W.A., Sampson, G.: Good-Turing Frequency Estimation Without Tears. Journal of Quantitative Linguistics 2(3), 217–237 (1995)
9. Just, M., Aspinall, D.: Personal Choice and Challenge Questions: A Security and Usability Assessment. In: SOUPS 2009: Proceedings of the 5th Symposium on Usable Privacy and Security (2009)
10. Kelley, P.G., Komanduri, S., Mazurek, M.L., Shay, R., Vidas, T., Bauer, L., Christin, N., Cranor, L.F., Lopez, J.: Guess again (and again and again): Measuring password strength by simulating password-cracking algorithms. Technical Report CMU-CyLab-11-008, Carnegie Mellon University (2011)
11. Kelley, P.G., Mazurek, M.L., Shay, R., Bauer, L., Christin, N., Cranor, L.F., Komanduri, S., Egelman, S.: Of Passwords and People: Measuring the Effect of Password-Composition Policies. In: CHI 2011: Proceedings of the 29th ACM SIGCHI Conference on Human Factors in Computing Systems (2011)
12. Narayanan, A., Shmatikov, V.: Fast Dictionary Attacks on Passwords Using Time-Space Tradeoff. In: CCS 2005: Proceedings of the 12th ACM Conference on Computer and Communications Security, pp. 364–372. ACM (2005)
13. Shannon, C.E.: A Mathematical Theory of Communication. Bell System Technical Journal 7, 379–423 (1948)
14. Shay, R., Komanduri, S., Kelley, P.G., Leon, P.G., Mazurek, M.L., Bauer, L., Christin, N., Cranor, L.F.: Encountering Stronger Password Requirements: User Attitudes and Behaviors. In: SOUPS 2010: Proceedings of the 6th Symposium on Usable Privacy and Security. ACM (2010)
15. Weir, M., Aggarwal, S., Collins, M., Stern, H.: Testing Metrics for Password Creation Policies by Attacking Large Sets of Revealed Passwords. In: CCS 2010: Proceedings of the 17th ACM Conference on Computer and Communications Security, pp. 162–175. ACM (2010)
16. Weir, M., Aggarwal, S., de Medeiros, B., Glodek, B.: Password Cracking Using Probabilistic Context-Free Grammars. In: SP 2009: Proceedings of the 2009 IEEE Symposium on Security and Privacy, pp. 391–405. IEEE (2009)

A   Definition of α-guesswork G_α

Taken directly from the derivation in [2], the definition of $\tilde{G}_\alpha$ requires several parts. The α-work-factor μ_α reflects the required size μ of a dictionary needed to have a cumulative probability α of success in an optimal guessing attack:

$$\mu_\alpha(\mathcal{X}) = \min \left\{ \mu \left| \sum_{i=1}^{\mu} p_i \geq \alpha \right. \right\} \tag{8}$$

This metric doesn't account for the average number of guesses per account, which will be lower since the attacker is able to stop early after correct guesses. The α-guesswork G_α reflects the average number of guesses per account:

$$G_\alpha(\mathcal{X}) = (1 - \lceil\!\lceil \alpha \rceil\!\rceil) \cdot \mu_\alpha(\mathcal{X}) + \sum_{i=1}^{\mu_\alpha(\mathcal{X})} p_i \cdot i \tag{9}$$

Note that a rounded-up $\lceil\!\lceil \alpha \rceil\!\rceil$ is used to reflect that the actual probability of success after μ_{alpha} guesses may be more than α:

$$\lceil\!\lceil \alpha \rceil\!\rceil = \sum_{i=1}^{\mu_\alpha(\mathcal{X})} p_i \tag{10}$$

Finally, G_α is converted to bits by finding the size of a uniform distribution which would have an equivalent value of G_α and taking a logarithm:

$$\tilde{G}_\alpha(\mathcal{X}) = \lg \left[\frac{2 \cdot G_\alpha(\mathcal{X})}{\lceil\!\lceil \alpha \rceil\!\rceil} - 1 \right] - \lg(2 - \lceil\!\lceil \alpha \rceil\!\rceil) \tag{11}$$

B   Proof of Expected Sum for Naive Index Strength Metric $S^{\mathrm{I}}(x)$ for the Uniform Distribution

As claimed in Section 3.2, using the definition from Equation 5:

$$S_{\mathcal{X}}^{\mathrm{I}}(x) = \lg \left(2 \cdot i_x - 1 \right)$$

and randomly assigning an ordering to the uniform distribution does not produce an expected value of $\lg N$, but $\approx \lg N - (\lg e - 1)$.

Proof. We first take the expectation:

$$E\left[S_{\mathcal{X}}^{I}(x)\,\middle|\, x \xleftarrow{\text{R}} \mathcal{U}_N\right] = \sum_{i=1}^{N} \frac{1}{N} \cdot \lg\left(2 \cdot i - 1\right)$$

$$= \frac{1}{N} \cdot (\lg 1 + \lg 3 + \lg 5 + \ldots + \lg(2N - 1))$$

$$= \frac{1}{N} \cdot \lg(1 \cdot 3 \cdot 5 \cdot \ldots \cdot (2N - 1))$$

$$= \frac{1}{N} \cdot \lg\left(\frac{(2N)!}{2 \cdot 4 \cdot 6 \cdot \ldots \cdot 2N}\right)$$

$$= \frac{1}{N} \cdot \lg\left(\frac{(2N)!}{2^N \cdot N!}\right)$$

We can use Stirling's approximation $\ln N! \sim N \ln N - N$, converting the base to get $\lg N! \sim N \lg N - N \lg e$:

$$E\left[S_{\mathcal{X}}^{I}(x)\,\middle|\, x \xleftarrow{\text{R}} \mathcal{U}_N\right] = \frac{1}{N} \cdot \lg\left(\frac{(2N)!}{2^N \cdot N!}\right)$$

$$= \frac{1}{N} \cdot \left(\lg(2N)! - \lg N! - \lg 2^N\right)$$

$$\approx \frac{1}{N} \cdot (2N \lg 2N - 2N \lg e - N \lg N + N \lg e - N)$$

$$= \frac{1}{N} \cdot (2N \lg N + 2N - 2N \lg e - N \lg N + N \lg e - N)$$

$$= \frac{1}{N} \cdot (N \lg N + N - N \lg e)$$

$$= \lg N - (\lg e - 1)$$

Statistical Metrics for Individual Password Strength (Transcript of Discussion)

Joseph Bonneau

University of Cambridge

I'm not proposing any protocols here, I'm talking about passwords, which is what I've spent the last year or so doing now. An interesting problem, which came up in my thesis, is how to tell how strong an individual password is. There's a growing body of publications on how to assess the strength of a big pile of passwords. So if a bunch of passwords leak from a new website there are some measures that I've developed, and some things other people have worked on, to try and compare this new body of passwords to all of the passwords at a different website. But the world of analysing a single password is still in the dark ages I would say. Obviously the difference is that with a group of passwords you can start to do statistics, and you can look at how many passwords are repeated within that set, whereas if you just have one password you have to reason about what set it came from.

The first approach for doing this is to assume some probability distribution that this password was drawn from, then try and figure out roughly what the probability was within that distribution. The traditional way of doing this, the entropy-based method, is that you start looking at the different character classes in the password and the length of it. And then you say, OK, well a password like this, we're going to assume the probability distribution is strings of length 10, which include lower case letters and digits, in which all passwords that are equally likely. Then you can go ahead and do a lot of calculations. This is a screen-shot from a website actually which does this, and it's quite simple. They basically say, we're assuming this comes from an alphabet size of 36 characters, that's 10 characters randomly drawn from that alphabet, so we estimate that this password has a probability 3.76 x 10 to the minus 15, and that's basically the strength of this password.

Matt Blaze: And then they add it to their database of passwords.

Reply: Yes. Right, so trusting what goes on over the web, this one actually is in JavaScript ...

Unknown: JavaScript?

Reply: Yes, so nothing could possibly go wrong. You can run it if you're really paranoid disconnected from the Internet, not that I recommend this site, I can put my cards on the table now and say I think this is really misleading, it doesn't get us very far. In 2005 I believe NIST published some guidelines, the document is called Electronic Authentication Guidelines, and they included this table in the back for how to calculate how strong an individual password is. And this is very simple, you just look at the length of the password, though for some reason they decided to start going by 2s after a while, and then how it was composed, different types of alphabets, whether or not there was a dictionary

B. Christianson et al. (Eds.): Security Protocols 2012, LNCS 7622, pp. 87–95, 2012.
© Springer-Verlag Berlin Heidelberg 2012

check, whether or not it's a member of some known dictionary. And then they give you a quite accurate, with decimal points, estimate for how strong this password is, and this is supposed to be in bits somehow. So we'll come back to this, but the reason I bring this up is that a lot of websites actually base their password strength meter on this table now, and also publications where people look at, say how people choose passwords in different scenarios will actually use this to try and do research on usability.

Frank Stajano: So what are the numbers, when it says 10 characters out of those two columns what do they mean?

Reply: Good question. I'm sure it's in the spec. This table is a little bit confusing.

Frank Stajano: But suddenly when you go to white background you get decimals, and before you get ...

Reply: Yes. If I'm remembering correctly, this is actually what this space is if you do it randomly, because if it's a ten character alphabet, and you have one character, and it was truly random, then you would have 3.3 bits exactly, right. So these two columns are if the password is drawn completely at random, and these are assuming human choice in different scenarios. So these two columns basically have no information.

Matt Blaze: Well they are made up and the other has guesses.

Reply: Yes, they could be summed up just by one logarithm I guess.

Michael Roe: Going from your previous paper[1], entropy is the wrong measure to be using anyway.

Reply: Yes, right, we'll get to that, but entropy is actually the wrong terminology if you're talking about single events in any case. Entropy is defined over distributions, and if it's a single event you're supposed to say either surprisal or self information, but that has too many syllables so the word entropy gets used in the publication, and sadly it's become a second definition for entropy that people that want to assign to an individual password.

Paul Syverson: Surprisal has the same number of syllables as hedgehog.

Reply: Anyway, there are some interesting proposals for how to model probability distribution of passwords. People have tried to make a Markov model, given the previous N characters, what's the probability distribution of the next character, and you can train this on big datasets. The one that's actually been the most successful when used for training cracking libraries is to model passwords as a probabilistic context-free grammar, so there's some probability that people choose the rule of only use digits, and some other people only use letters, and of course it's recursive because it's a context-free grammar, so it can be a bunch of letters followed by a bunch of digits followed by some more letters, and then you can evaluate all these probabilities on data and get something that's sort of reasonable.

The other approach for trying to assess how strong an individual password is, is to just run some cracking algorithm that you think might actually simulate

---

[1] The science of guessing: analyzing an anonymized corpus of 70 million passwords, IEEE Symposium on Security and Privacy, Oakland 2012.

your adversary, and see how long it takes to get to the password in question. You could say if the password you're reasoning about is the first thing that the cracking library tries, it's not very good, and if it takes billions and billions of guesses then it starts to seem pretty good. Of course there isn't any standard cracking algorithm, the closest thing now is John the Ripper, which is open source, and people can download it and play with it, but it's still not really standard because it depends on how you configure it. There are different word lists, and there are different mangling rules, which is a problem for research because people will say, we ran John the Ripper and it took this long to crack the password, but you never really know exactly what they ran, so it's actually pretty hard to get precisely the same outcome. And then there's a whole sub universe of proprietary cracking algorithms that you can spend up to $14,000 on, you can read the text right here, but that's discounted by $5,000.

Matt Blaze: So there's a standard edition, a forensic edition, and an organised crime edition.

Reply: Yes.

Sandy Clark: I think the organised crime one is the cheapest.

Reply: No, it's the most expensive?

Paul Syverson: You only get to sell it once.

Reply: It's a pretty crazy world. It seems like the main customers for this are actually people who want to spy on their spouse or their teenage kid, or businesses who want to crack their employees' passwords.

Omar Chaudary: What's the main difference between the free version the and the $14,000 version?

Reply: I don't know.

Paul Syverson: About $14,000.

Omar Chaudary: Is it 14,000 times faster, or something like that?

Reply: Well actually it's not any faster because it's just software, I mean, it's only as fast as the hardware.

Omar Chaudary: I don't know, perhaps you get a fast implementation?

Reply: To be honest, they don't really provide that much when you go to their website, but maybe they have a slightly more tuned wordlist.

Jonathan Anderson: It seems like the pricing might be meant to target low-information purchases.

Reply: Yes, I don't think that it's dramatically different.

Matt Blaze: How much does their customer list cost?

Reply: I also haven't asked. But there hasn't been any good research that's actually compared them, there's one or two research papers where people have been given the expensive cracking library to try out, but there hasn't been a good comparison yet that actually evaluates this as any better than the thing you can get for free.

Sandy Clark: And standard tools, not the password cracking in particular, but in general, the purchase of the $3,000 core impact version is much better than the Black Cat 5 which is excellent, but is an order of magnitude better.

Reply: The answer to that is that I really don't know. What I do know is that there are now big datasets of passwords that are fairly easy to come by on the Internet. The RockYou Leak is still the most famous, there were 32 million passwords that got leaked about two years ago. There's a whole basket of others now, nothing as big, but there's a bunch of different datasets with a million passwords or so floating around.

So my approach, particularly for measuring the difficulty of entire distribution against guessing, is to assume that the attacker knows the distribution completely, and then we can reason about this purely as a probability distribution, not have to rely on some complicated model, and not have to rely on cracking software. So, really simply, for this talk the only question I want to address is, if we have a probability distribution that is known completely, and I ask how you evaluate the strength of an individual event against guessing, what's the right way to do this? And I claim that there's two basic properties of any measure for evaluating strength in this model should have, one of which is just that the measure should be uniform for a normal uniform distribution. So if you have a uniform distribution, say random 128-bit strings, every event in that distribution should have the same strength, which should be a log of the space of the distribution. I think that's pretty straightforward, and should at least give us the property that if we do our strength metric on crypto keys it will give the strength. And the other property is also pretty straightforward, just that the strength should be monotonically increasing with less likely events, so the most likely event in the distribution has to be the one that we say is the weakest, and we can only get stronger from there.

Metric number 1, the first thing you might think of, is basically what the entropy metrics I showed you at the beginning are an approximation for, because you just look at the probability of the event you're trying to assign some strength to, which I assume that we know exactly, and you take the logarithm of it. This is exactly the definition that Shannon came up with for surprisal. So the nice things, obviously this is a very simple metric, it does have the uniformity property, it's monotonic. The problem with it is that it really doesn't have anything to do with guessing, there's no direct correlation between this and how difficult something is to guess. It's conceptually nice, but it's not really valid for the problem we're trying to study.

What seems to make a lot more sense is to forget about the probability of the event and just look at what its index is within the distribution. So if it's the most likely event, no matter what its probability is, the fact that it's the most likely means that it's the first thing that an optimal attacker will guess, and we can assign some strength based on that. To get this to have a uniformity property, it's a little bit of a struggle actually, we have to apply a trick, which is to say that if we have a uniform distribution we don't randomly assign index 1 through N to everything in the distribution, but we give everything an index of $\frac{N}{2}$. Basically we don't break ties, if there's a bunch of events that are equally probable we give them all an average index, which is sort of sensible because it says that if there's a bunch of stuff that is equally likely, the adversary won't always pick the same thing to guess within that set, that the adversary will actually choose randomly, which starts to make it OK.

There's a problem that I get into more detail in my paper about, which isn't super interesting, which is that, if you have an approximately uniform distribution where you can no longer assign everything an average index, but you have some ordering, then all of a sudden the average strength of all the events in that distribution will jump down, so it becomes discontinuous there, which isn't great.

The other problem here is that the strength that you assign to the most likely event in the distribution ends up being zero, which, depending on your philosophy I guess, this is a question for debate, it should be. If you assume that the attacker will guess something first, does that mean that it is useless as a password then? The people who use 123456 which in the real world is almost always the most common password of any population of people, are we comfortable saying that the effective security they get is zero? I don't know.

Omar Chaudary: What is the basis for saying that if you have the set with the same probability you have to give it $\frac{N}{2}$ as a strength, compared to giving it N?

Reply: I'm not saying $\frac{N}{2}$ is the strength, I'm saying that's the index. If you have a uniform distribution where everything has the same probability, this metric requires that you assign an index to everything, so you have to say where does this rank in the distribution, and you can either break ties arbitrarily and just say we're going to randomly pick something to be the most probable event, and the second most probable, or you can say that everything is the $\frac{N}{2}$-th most probable event.

Omar Chaudary: Yes, but why $\frac{N}{2}$ and not N for example?

Reply: If you say everything is the least probable event in the distribution, that doesn't make sense either, right?

Omar Chaudary: I'm thinking about the situation where you have $N - 1$ events, all within the same distribution, and one thing which has the least probability. You say the last index is the strongest one, but all the other are just before that somehow?

Reply: Well I say the others should be averaged amongst how many there are.

Omar Chaudary: I'm just asking is there any theory saying that it is better to just say you have them in the middle rather than giving it the maximum strength?

Reply: Well the theory is that, if you don't put it in the middle then the expectation for the uniform distribution won't end up being $\log N$, the uniform distribution will start to look either really bad or really good, because you'll always get the most probable event, or the least probable event. Whereas if you put it in the middle and you say, well I always get an average event, this is basically what happens, right?

Michael Roe: And the intuition is the amount of guesses the attacker has to do before they find it.

Reply: Yes exactly. Right, so the third metric, the third approach I want to take comes out of my thesis work. For my thesis work I developed the philosophy which I think that works the best for assessing the strength of a whole distribution against guessing. You first determine what the adversary's goal is, and parameterize that as α, the proportion of accounts that an attacker is trying to break, and it turns out that an attacker trying to break 50% of accounts versus 10% of accounts, ends up being a really different attacker. There are two metrics you can develop from that, you can either say, well if they want to break 50% of accounts how big does my dictionary have to be, or if they want to break 50% of accounts how much work will I have to do per account. And these are these metrics μ and G, and this graph hopefully will make this make a lot more sense.

Plotted not in logarithmic space, these are some statistics for the distribution of PINs. For an attacker the success rate is increasing from 0 to 1. This blue line is how much bigger your dictionary needs to be. So a fairly small dictionary of under 500 different things will be enough to guess about half of people's PINs correctly. And then eventually to get all the way to 1 your dictionary has to go to size 10,000. That's the dictionary size metric, and the other way is the expected amount of work, which doesn't grow nearly as quickly. The expected amount of work per account if you're going to break every account doesn't get all the way up to 10,000, it gets up to a little over 1,000 guesses per account that you're trying to break.

I think it's a little bit hard to read this graph, in particular this black line, this is what random four-digit PINs would get you, and this is what random three-digit PINs would get you. But I have a trick, which is to convert it to logarithmic space, where it finally starts to make a lot more sense. In logarithmic space both of these metrics are uniform for an attacker with a different success rate. For a random three digit PIN or a random four digit PIN those are equivalent to the attacker, no matter what his desired success rate is. And these other two lines again are pretty close, and the expected number of guesses doesn't get all the way up to the full size of the space. To adapt this to an individual event in an interesting way, let's suppose that my password is 7r1596. If an optimal attacker will guess about 50% of other accounts before getting to that, this is the point in the attack at which the guesser will guess, 7r1596, and we'll say that the expected amount of work the attacker is doing *per account* at that point in the attack, that can be the strength of that password 7r1596.

Jonathan Anderson: Is there a place to plug in more information, such as an attacker who's been to the protocols workshop before, or knows Sydney Sussex, and how they do their codes?

Reply: Yes, so that would mean that the distribution has changed, right? And I guess that's why, for all of the strength metrics I proposed, I've been subscripting by this calligraphy $\mathcal{X}$, which is the distribution that the attacker has assumed. Or it's the distribution that we're assuming when assigning a strength to this password. But I think you fundamentally have to do that because, for 7r1596, there's some distributions in which that's a really, really weak password, like the distribution of wireless passwords in this room where it's on the white-board. But in some other distribution it might be a really good password, or at least a decent password.

If that transition made any sense of going from the distribution-wide guessing attack to the individual password and saying, at what point does that individual password get caught, this works out really smoothly as a strength metric. The normalisation that monotonicity has already taken care of, and unlike the index metric which assigned a strength of zero to the most probable event, the strength of the most probable event by this metric is the min entropy of the distribution, which to me is a little bit more defensible.

So those are the metrics, and I have some examples here for the RockYou distribution, which is the first place to start when you're evaluating passwords statistically now. Here I have taken, at equally spaced intervals logarithmically in a distribution, some example passwords, this is how many times they occurred in the RockYou distribution, and this is the strength that would get assigned to them by the three metrics I mentioned, probability, index, and this guessing attack metric. And then in this last column, this is the strength of the password you'll get by the NIST formula, which is the table I had at the beginning. I've colour-coded that to compare these four metrics, the red is the biggest overestimate, and the blue is the biggest underestimate of these. The high level trend comparing these, the index metric says that the really common stuff is extremely weak, obviously starting from 0 and then slowly building up. The guessing attack metric is nice, it's usually in-between the other two. Not surprisingly the NIST metric jumps around quite a lot, so it assigns 30 bits to this password, scotty2hotty. I didn't know what it meant, but it turns out it's a professional wrestler, so even though it's fairly long and it has a number in it, 34 people chose that password, and it's not particularly strong, but it does quite well by the NIST metric. Whereas diving, the word diving, looks very bad by the NIST metric because it's short and it just has lower case letters, actually is a dictionary word too, but it's not dramatically more popular than the wrestler's name. I think it's not surprising that the NIST metric doesn't do particularly well head to head against the other ones.

As a slightly more interesting experiment, I took a bunch of datasets of passwords that are too small to actually do statistics on. If you only have 200 passwords you can't start to reason about the distribution, but what you can do is you can look at how strong each of those passwords would be if you assume that they were drawn from the RockYou distribution, and try and assign a strength to that set of passwords by averaging. One reason people really want to do this is to do usability experiments where you bring in sets of users and you add two different conditions, maybe one set of users you give a really strong policy to, the other users you just say, you can choose passwords however you want. Maybe you can only do 100 users this way, but you want to ask the question of which group of users actually picked better passwords, and how did it change.

Matt Blaze: RockYou was from a single service, right, that was compromised.

Reply: Yes.

Matt Blaze: Not from multiple services? So it was fairly homogeneous?

Reply: Yes and no. It's a company that develops a bunch of different social applications They have a couple of different Facebook games, some photo sharing applications, and they run one sign-on service for all the different applications they develop. But essentially, yes, it's mostly Facebook users, most of the passwords are English speakers, though there are a lot of Spanish speakers too. But it's not like when I collected some data at Yahoo, which is really nice, as they run a little bit of everything.

Right, so that's really a scenario where you would want to apply the individual strength metrics to a whole group of passwords, if you have a small sample and you're trying to figure out how two different groups compare, and this is what the NIST metric gets used quite a lot for in the password usability research now. I wanted to see if these statistical metrics I proposed look any better or worse.

I think that there's actually definitely some cases where the NIST formula produces more plausible results. I had one dataset of passwords chosen by Chinese speakers, and one dataset of passwords chosen by Hebrew speakers, which look relatively much stronger by the statistical metrics if you use RockYou as the baseline, because RockYou didn't have very many Chinese or Hebrew speakers, so the stuff that they pick looks relatively strong if you put it into the RockYou distribution. But by the NIST formula those passwords get scored much more weakly because the NIST formula doesn't have any concept of language or semantics, and so if they're short and they don't have numbers then they're rated weakly.

Frank Stajano: When you're doing Chinese does it mean Chinese with Chinese characters?

Reply: Well in practice no, because Chinese users almost never actually use Chinese characters in their passwords.

Frank Stajano: But if you did wouldn't the NIST formula have to be modified so each letter doesn't account for 26?

Reply: Yes, the NIST formula is really only defined for ASCII, but at least in the datasets that Rubin and I have been looking at, Chinese speakers essentially never use Chinese characters in passwords, which is partly an artefact of the way that they input the characters.

Frank Stajano: I was just wondering if this thing could be even plugged into the NIST formula if it contained Chinese characters?

Reply: I suppose, if you treated each Chinese character as one letter. But then, it would produce strange results because the alphabet is so much bigger. The NIST algorithm doesn't have instructions on how to deal with that problem.

Hannan Xiao: I use Pinyin for the Chinese characters.

Reply: Yes, exactly. I think that the cases where the NIST formula does pretty poorly, down here I have dictionaries which are sort of cheating because they're chosen to be very weak passwords, either the passwords that are contained in different Malware that tries to do guessing attacks, or the blacklist that Twitter uses, which they for a long time now have implemented client-side in JavaScript. I check it every month or so and see how they update the blacklisted passwords that they don't allow. It was actually a terrible blacklist too up until about a year ago, it had a bunch of really uncommon names in it, and it didn't have 123456 for a long time, which is kind of amazing because it's always the most common password. I think that actually the statistical metrics capture this really well, they say that the passwords on the 2010 blacklist were actually quite strong, which is a bad thing if you're developing a blacklist. And then in 2011 they finally did a more sensible one, and the average strength of these passwords went way down, but by the NIST formula there was basically no difference. So that was the case where the NIST formula really struggled.

OK, there's a lot more about the math and how to estimate these things from samples, and deal with unseen events and things like that in my paper and my thesis, but at a high level this covers what I wanted to propose today.

Street-Level Trust Semantics
for Attribute Authentication

Tiffany Hyun-Jin Kim, Virgil Gligor, and Adrian Perrig

Carnegie Mellon University
Pittsburgh, PA 15213
{hyunjin1,virgil,adrian}@ece.cmu.edu

Abstract. The problem of determining whether a receiver may safely *accept attributes* (e.g., identity, credentials, location) of *unknown senders* in various online social protocols is a special instance of a more general problem of establishing trust in interactive protocols. We introduce the notion of *interactive trust protocols* to illustrate the usefulness of *social collateral* in reducing the inherent trust asymmetry in large classes of online user interactions. We define a social collateral model that allows receivers to accept attributes from unknown senders based on explicit recommendations received from social relations. We use social collateral as a measure of both social relations and "tie strength" among individuals to provide different degrees of accountability when accepting attribute information from unknown senders. Our model is robust in the face of several specific attacks, such as impersonation and tie-strength-amplification attacks. Preliminary experiments with visualization of measured tie strength among users of a social network indicate that the model is usable by ordinary protocol participants.

1 Introduction

In many real-world social interactions, the authentication of someone's attributes is a crucial requirement. For example, accepting an invitation to a social event from an unknown person often requires an introduction that establishes that person's identity, and possibly credentials. If verified, that person's social connections may be sufficient to establish an identity that is suitable for the invitation protocol. In short, many social interactions in the physical world rely on one's ability to authenticate others' attributes. In these interactions, a receiver's friends, family members, or professional colleagues are often able to authenticate the attributes of a sender with whom they are acquainted but who may be unknown to the receiver. Typically a receiver accepts the attribute authentication of an unknown sender from his/her social relations conditionally, depending upon affirmative answers to the following two questions. First, is the receiver's social relation sufficiently strong (e.g., close friend, immediate-family member, colleague of long standing) to warrant the receiver's trust for the particular protocol? And second, does the receiver's social relation know the sender well enough to competently vouch for the authenticity of a particular attribute?

As social interactions migrate from the physical to the online world, it would be desirable that the authentication of an unknown sender's attributes would

B. Christianson et al. (Eds.): Security Protocols 2012, LNCS 7622, pp. 96–115, 2012.

proceed along the same lines as in a physical-world protocol and match a receiver's natural expectations. Users are less likely to make costly mistakes and accept unauthentic inputs, disclose private information, and fall victims of online scams if protection measures with which they are familiar in the physical world are supported in the online world. However, current online social networks do not use any form of social authentication from the physical world, and as a consequence they cannot guarantee the correspondence between an online and a physical-world identity. A typical example is a Facebook invitation, which cannot guarantee the physical identity of the issuer or even that the issuer exists in the physical world. Authenticating an individual's identity by examining a list of mutual Facebook "friends" provides inadequate identity authentication in practice [1,2,13], even for security-conscious individuals [23]. Furthermore, associations between an online identity and a public key, which is typically provided by identity certificates, are becoming more and more uncertain [3] – not just cumbersome to obtain. Online protocols prompting users to accept an unknown identity's certificate i) for a single protocol session, ii) forever, or iii) never, offload certificate-authenticity determination to a certificate receiver who cannot possibly make that determination in an informed manner; i.e., the certificate receiver often may not know the real owner of that certificate.

In this paper, we argue that the problem of determining whether a receiver may safely accept attributes (e.g., identity; credentials, such as certificates, groups, roles; and locations such IP addresses, or URLs, physical coordinates) of unknown senders is a special instance of a more general problem of establishing trust in interactive protocols. We define the salient properties of interactive trust protocols and use them to illustrate the usefulness of social collateral in reducing the inherent trust asymmetry in these protocols (Section 2). Then we present a social-collateral model in which receivers are able to accept attributes from *unknown senders* in a safe manner based on explicit recommendations made by social relations; e.g., by their friends, relatives, collaborators (Section 3). We use the notion of the *social collateral* as a measure of both social relations and of "tie strength[1]" among individuals to provide different degrees of accountability for accepting attributes of unknown senders on an *ad hoc* basis (Section 4). Our model is robust in the face of several specific attacks, such as impersonation and tie-strength-amplification attacks (Section 5). The key feature of our model is that a user only needs to perform a single informal measurement of the tie strength between his/her friend and an unknown sender, which is represented by a simple visual diagram. Preliminary experiments with visualization of measured tie strength in a social network indicate that the model is usable by ordinary protocol participants (Section 6).

---

[1] *Tie strength* is the technical term that refers to the closeness, social proximity, or propinquity of two individuals.

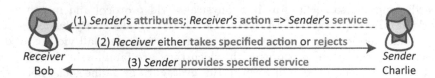

Fig. 1. An interactive trust protocol. When both parties are honest (i.e., complying with the protocol specifications), both are better off after protocol execution.

2 Interactive Trust Protocols

A receiver's decision of whether to accept a sender's attributes is an instance of the more general problem of input trust. In fact, one can show that a receiver's decision to accept input from an unknown sender, where (1) the sender and receiver cooperation benefits both and (2) lack of cooperation benefits the sender and causes the receiver to incur a loss, is an instance of a classic trust problem of behavioral economics [9]. This problem also manifests itself in interactive trust protocols often found in online social applications. The following three generic steps, which are illustrated in Figure 1, characterize these protocols:

1. A sender invites a receiver to participate in a social protocol. (The invitation can be implemented by an explicit protocol message sent to a specific receiver, or by an open invitation posted on a website to any receiver). The sender's invitation comprises the sender's attributes and protocol specification; i.e., if the receiver takes a specified action, the sender will provide a service that will benefit the receiver. For example, the action required of the receiver may be to click on a link provided by the sender, disclose personal information (e.g., personal identification, bank account, credit card number), pay for a forthcoming answer to a query or a solution to a problem, or invest in a specified enterprise. The invitation message itself is assumed to be a benign input to the receiver; e.g., it can be verified to be free of malware.

2. The receiver verifies the unknown sender's attributes and follows the protocol specification: he either takes the specified action or rejects. If the receiver rejects, the protocol ends.

3. The protocol specification allows the sender to verify whether the receiver took the specified action. The sender performs the verification and if the verification passes, the sender follows the protocol and provides the specified service. Otherwise, the sender terminates the protocol. The sender can always give the receiver another chance in the future.

4. If the receiver determines that the sender is non-compliant, it never runs this protocol with the sender again. Non-compliance may manifest itself whenever the unknown sender uses spoofed identity, credentials, or location; and provides corrupt service (e.g., incorrect results, messages containing malware) or no service at all.

Interactive trust protocols have three properties: a value promise, asymmetric trust, and expected execution safety.

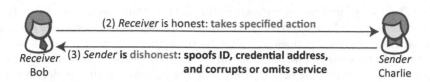

Fig. 2. Asymmetry of an interaction trust protocol. When the sender is dishonest, the sender is better off and the honest receiver is worse off after protocol execution.

Value Promise. If both parties are honest, namely they both follow the protocol specification, then both parties are better off after protocol execution. Clearly, the protocol specification must imply that both the sender and the receiver would derive some positive value; i.e., there must be a net benefit in executing the protocol honestly to both parties. We denote the value derived by receiver from honest protocol execution by $HV_R > 0$, and by the sender by $HV_S > 0$. If a positive value does not materialize for either the sender or receiver, the protocol would never be advertised or executed [9].

Asymmetric Trust. To obtain the value promised, the sender can always verify and never needs to trust a receiver's honesty. In contrast, a receiver can never verify the sender's honesty before the protocol ends and hence must trust that the sender is honest to obtain the value promised.

The asymmetric trust property implies that the protocol has *asymmetric outcomes* whenever participants are dishonest. If the sender is dishonest, he is better off than when he is honest, since he receives the value promised without having to deliver any service (i.e., any value) to an honest receiver. Specifically, if we denote the sender's positive benefit from dishonesty (i.e., from protocol non-compliance) by DV_S, then the dishonest sender's ill-gotten gain is $Gain_S = DV_S - HV_S > 0$. This means that the sender has an incentive to be dishonest. Furthermore, an honest receiver is worse off whenever the sender is dishonest, since he has to deliver the value promised without obtaining anything in return. Hence, the protocol implies that $Gain_S > 0 \Rightarrow HV_R < 0$. However, if the receiver is dishonest, and claims to have taken the action required by the protocol without actually doing so, the sender terminates the protocol. (Recall that the sender can always discover whether the receiver took the required action.) In this case, $DV_R = 0$ and $HV_S = 0$. Hence, $Gain_R = DV_R - HV_R = -HV_R < 0$, which implies that the receiver has no incentive to be dishonest.

Note that an honest receiver might not even be able to discern a sender's dishonesty until far beyond the end of the protocol. For example, the service provided by a dishonest sender may comprise an arbitrary program whose output behavior cannot always be verified by the receiver. (Verifiability of the output behavior of an arbitrary program is undecidable.) Or, the verification cost may exceed the value of the sender's service to the receiver; e.g., the receiver may have to verify the solution to a co-NP complete problem, which is very unlikely to be possible in polynomial time [9]. Figure 2 illustrates this protocol state.

The trust and outcome asymmetry in interactive trust protocols is inherent: the honest receiver benefits only if the receiver trusts the sender in all protocol runs, whereas the sender does not have to trust the receiver to benefit in any protocol run. Of course, one could modify the protocol specification so that the balance shifts in the favor of the receiver at the expense of the sender, but the inherent trust and outcome asymmetry that characterize these protocols cannot be eliminated. The reasons for this are apparent.

First, in an interactive trust protocol, the *receiver cannot isolate himself from sender's* misbehavior. To receive any value, the receiver has to respond to the server's invitation first, and hence the receiver becomes exposed to a sender's misbehavior, which includes no response at all.

Second, the *receiver may be unable to recover* from sender misbehavior after the protocol ends. Recovery may be expensive or impractical, as it may have complex dependencies on other users' actions, which may be impossible to undo such as recovering a leaked secret or private information. More importantly, the receiver may not even be aware that recovery is necessary. As noted above, he might not be able to detect the effect of a sender's corrupt service until long after recovery becomes impractical; e.g., whether the sender's response message contains malware that damages the receiver may not be an efficiently answered question, if at all.

Third, the *receiver may not have any evidence* of the sender's trustworthiness. Of course, the type of evidence needed depends on whether the sender is a computer or a human using a computer. If the service is a computer, checking trustworthiness evidence reduces to an assessment of correctness evidence in a computational setting. Such evidence, however, is hard to come by: very few systems or services exist that have ever been evaluated at high levels of assurance by most accepted criteria, from the Orange Book (1983) to Common Criteria (2011), and none of these are commodity systems available to all users. Only few commercially available systems, all designed for special applications, have been evaluated at high levels of assurance for the past three decades. If a sender is a human, or a human operating a computer, the notion of trustworthiness becomes strictly stronger than that of computational correctness, as it must encompass evidence of trustworthy human behavior, which is much more difficult to obtain and evaluate. Furthermore, trustworthiness evidence is always about past behavior and hence, even if available, it cannot be a guarantee of sender's present or future behavior in an interactive trust protocol.

Fourth, the *receiver may be unable to deter* a sender's misbehavior. Although intuition suggests that deterrence requires punishment, and punishment requires accountability, it is unknown what punishment and accountability are sufficient for deterrence. Even if sufficient punishment becomes available to deter a dishonest sender, such punishment may be impractical because the sender may be located in a different network jurisdiction than the receiver.

Although asymmetry elimination may not be possible without intervention by other external trusted entities (e.g., trusted third parties), asymmetry reduction may be possible in specific protocol instances. Recent research [9] shows that the four areas of asymmetry reduction mentioned above, namely isolation, recovery, trustworthiness-evidence evaluation, and deterrence represent the closure of countermeasure types a receiver can employ using both computational and behavioral trust. For interactive trust protocols, all that computational trust suggests can be classified as isolation-, recovery-, and correctness-evidence-based countermeasures for receivers. All that behavioral trust suggests is enhanced receiver preferences (i.e., diminished risk and betrayal aversion) and beliefs in the trustworthiness of the sender. Both preferences and beliefs can be enhanced whenever sender's dishonesty triggers sender's punishment; i.e., it seems natural that betrayal aversion can be decreased and belief in trustworthiness increased by punishment that would deter. Similarly, it seems natural that risk aversion can be decreased and trustworthiness increased by assuring feasible recovery from sender's dishonesty.

Safety. The question faced by a receiver is this: given the inherent asymmetry of interactive trust protocols, is it ever safe for a receiver to accept a sender's invitation and take the required protocol action? The answer to the safety question is unequivocal, if somewhat surprising: under well-defined conditions, a receiver can trust a sender despite the inherent asymmetry of the interactive trust protocols. These conditions are:

1. The protocol is repeated indefinitely in the future, and hence the promise of future value exists;
2. The sender is rational, and hence can compute the present value of future honest behavior; and
3. The present value of future honest behavior exceeds the value of the sender's dishonest behavior (i.e., of DV_S). Hence, the sender has no incentive to cheat.

The questions that need to be answered are how the receiver can compute (i) present value of a sender's future behavior, and (ii) the value of the sender's dishonest behavior. To compute the present value, the receiver must know the sender's discount rate, $r > 0$. Informally, since rational users prefer value in hand over future value, they discount the future value. Discounting future value accounts, among other things, for the uncertainty in obtaining it from a business partner, and interest rates. Since an interactive trust protocol is executed in multiple future sessions (by Condition 1), and the sender's discount rate is $r > 0$ (by Condition 2), at each round, t, of the protocol the value obtained by the sender by executing the protocol honestly is:

$$\frac{HV_S}{(1+r)^t} \quad \text{where} \quad t = 0, 1, 2, \ldots$$

Hence, the present value of all future protocol sessions is

$$HV_S + \frac{HV_S}{1+r} + \frac{HV_S}{(1+r)^2} + \frac{HV_S}{(1+r)^3} + \cdots = \frac{HV_S \cdot (1+r)}{r},$$

and Condition 3 above becomes

$$\frac{HV_S \cdot (1+r)}{r} > DV_S \quad \text{or} \quad r < \frac{HV_S}{DV_S - HV_S} = \frac{HV_S}{Gain_S}.$$

Thus, if $r \geq \frac{HV_S}{Gain_S}$, the sender may not be trusted.

Note, however, that a receiver cannot possibly know the value of the sender's precise discount rate, r, except in very general terms, and hence even if the receiver could compute the ratio $\frac{HV_S}{Gain_S}$, he could not figure out whether r is less than $\frac{HV_S}{Gain_S}$. However, the receiver knows that if $\frac{HV_S}{Gain_S} \to 0$, then $r > \frac{HV_S}{Gain_S}$ and the sender cannot be trusted. In this case, $Gain_S \gg HV_S$, which implies that $\frac{DV_S}{HV_S} \gg 2$. This means that the protocol will have very few sessions before the receiver has to end it. Conversely, if it is a priori known that the protocol will only have a few sessions, say 2, then the receiver should not ever start since the sender has all the incentives to cheat. This implies that all interactive trust protocols that have very only few sessions (e.g., one), may in fact be scams, or deception attempts. Similarly, if previously honest senders discover that they have lost the receivers' trust, they have strong incentives to cheat during the (last) session of the protocol.[2]

Now suppose that, $\frac{HV_S}{Gain_S} \to +\infty$ or that $Gain_S \to 0$. In this case, $r < \frac{HV_S}{Gain_S}$ and the rational sender can be trusted since he has no incentive to cheat during any session of the protocol. Hence, protocol asymmetry would eliminated. However, by the arguments presented above, this is ruled out in interactive trust protocols where, by the definition, $Gain_S > 0$.

3   The Role of Social Collateral

Collateral and Trusted Third Parties. One way to ensure that $Gain_S \to 0$ is to modify the protocol and introduce a third party that is trusted by *both* sender and receiver. The role of the trusted third party (TTP) is simple: the TTP computes $Gain_S$, establishes a collateral value that exceeds $Gain_S$, and collects it from the sender before the first protocol session. If the sender does not comply with the protocol in some session, the TTP uses the sender's collateral and compensates the receiver for his losses. This effectively eliminates a sender's incentive to be dishonest and thus the protocol asymmetry. Of course, for a receiver to accept a sender's invitation to engage in the protocol, the receiver's potential loss must be less than the collateral value. In this case, even if a sender cheats, the receiver never loses anything. In short, two conditions must be satisfied to eliminate protocol asymmetry:

- **Sender's Deterrence:** TTP Collateral > $Gain_S$; and
- **Receiver's Acceptability:** TTP Collateral > Receiver's Loss.

Although this modification of the interactive trust protocols resolves the asymmetry problem, it is impractical for two reasons:

---

[2] This fact is also consistent with the observation that insiders, who are trusted to provide honest services to their organizations, are likely to attack their own organization when they suspect that they are about to be fired [21,22].

1. The modification assumes that an external TTP can be found that is trusted by both sender and receiver. This may be challenging and less than satisfactory: the protocol between a sender who deposits collateral and the TTP who received the collateral is an interactive trust protocol itself and so is that between a receiver and the TTP. In effect, by using a TTP, we have simply removed the asymmetry from the original trust protocol and moved it to the sender and receiver protocols with their common TTP. Hence, we have not completely eliminated trust asymmetry.

2. More importantly, the modified trust protocol is unlikely to start whenever the sender invites multiple receivers, since it does not scale: the sender may be unable to post separate collateral for every receiver who might accept the sender's invitation to engage.

Social Collateral, Deterrence, and Acceptability. We now show that it is possible to reduce the asymmetry of an interactive trust protocol between a receiver and an unknown sender *without relying on a TTP* to collect, hold collateral, and compensate the receiver for his loses when needed. Let us assume that a social relation exists between the receiver and a third party who also has a social tie to the unknown sender. That is, the third party may be a close friend, immediate-family member, or colleague of long standing of the receiver. In the social collateral model [15], this implies that the third party has social collateral with the receiver and any misbehavior by the third party would cause loss of the collateral. In particular, the third party would be deterred from providing false inputs to the receiver by the loss of the social collateral. Thus, all recommendations made to the receiver are likely to be correct, or at least not intentionally deceitful. Also, the existence of a social relationship implies that any trust protocol between the receiver and the third party could be repeated indefinitely and the present value of future honest protocol sessions is high. Furthermore, it implies that any trust protocol between the receiver and the third party can always be initiated.

The role of the third party in interactive trust protocols is *not* that of a TTP. First, the third party need not be trusted by *both* the receiver and sender. In fact, the sender and the third party need not trust each other at all. They only need to have a social tie that is sufficiently strong so that the third party's recommendation to the receiver regarding the sender is, in fact, accepted by the receiver. Furthermore, the trust between the receiver and the third party is already fully captured by existing social collateral and need not be established by yet another trust protocol. In short, the trust asymmetry between the receiver and the unknown sender is reduced without requiring a TTP.

The remaining questions are whether (1) the present value of future honest protocol sessions implied by social collateral exceeds the third party's value of dishonest behavior (i.e., false recommendations) in any future protocol session, and (2) the receiver considers the social collateral acceptable. The answer to the first question would determine whether the loss of a third party's social collateral with the receiver is sufficient to deter any misbehavior (i.e., bad recommendation) by the third party. The answer to the second question would determine whether the third party's social collateral exceeds the receiver's loss resulting from potential misbehavior of the third party. While these questions cannot be answered without taking into account the specifics of an interactive trust protocol, evidence indicates that loss of social collateral has non-negligible deterrent value, and that the reduction of asymmetry between the third party and receiver has a direct relationship to loss exposure by the receiver [15]. Hence, in our model for attribute authentication we rely on the following hypothesis and asymmetry-reduction criterion.

Deterrence Hypothesis: *The loss of a social relation deters misbehavior.*[3]
Asymmetry-Reduction Criterion: *The greater a receiver's exposure to loss is, the more social collateral is required.*

4   A Social Collateral Model for Attribute Authentication

All characteristics of an interactive trust protocol are found in the online social network problem of accepting an invitation from an unknown sender. In online social networks, the receiver can materialize the *value promise* only by accepting the sender's attributes, even when attribute authentication may be impractical in the absence of an identification and authentication infrastructure. For example, when the receiver accepts the sender's attributes, the receiver's potential benefits are as follows: (1) build new social, professional, or business connections with the sender and his friends; (2) use sender's services with the assurance that the sender is accountable, since his identity and social connections are known; and (3) develop his/her own social network connections by building future strong ties with the sender and be recommend by the sender to others. *Asymmetry* is also evident: the receiver knows nothing about the sender attributes' authenticity whereas the sender knows everything about them. The *safety problem* also arises here: is it ever safe to accept the attributes of an unknown sender in the absence of an identification, authentication, and accountability infrastructure?

A receiver's decision to accept a third-party's authentication of an unknown sender's attributes presented in Section 1 can now be framed as a trust decision to be made in an interactive protocol where a third party has (1) a *social relation* with the receiver and (2) a *social tie* with the invitation sender and the receiver. This scenario is illustrated in Figure 3, where $SC(A)@B$ denotes the social collateral which third party A *has* with receiver B as the result of their friendship, whereas $SC(C)@A$ denotes the social collateral *assigned* by receiver B to the signed recommendation made by third party A for an attribute of the unknown sender C.

Social Ties. Unlike social relations, which imply the existence of social collateral, we use social ties only as a measure of the *social distance* between two parties. Although they do not necessarily imply existence of collateral, social ties

---

[3] Recent evidence shows that loss of social relations deters more than the law, even when both law and loss of social collateral fail to provide sufficient deterrence for specific forms of misbehavior (e.g., insider misuse of permissions) [14].

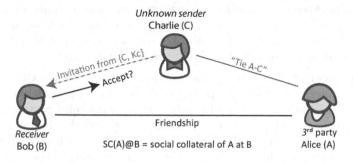

Fig. 3. An interactive trust protocol with a social relation. In this figure, 3rd party A has a social relation with receiver B and a social tie with sender C. K_C stands for the public key of C.

serve as an indication of the knowledge one party has about the other. Stronger ties imply more accurate knowledge, and this in turn serves as the basis for more credible recommendations. Hence, being able to measure the strength of a tie between receiver B's friend A and unknown sender C in a manner that can be easily evaluated by B becomes important, particularly since our model requires B to assign a social collateral value to the strength of a tie between A and C (discussed below).

Social science research has studied a variety of parameters that capture the strength of ties between individuals. Gilbert and Karahalios [6] have recently showed that four relatively simple parameters are sufficient for determining tie strength in practice: communication reciprocity [5,11,19], existence of at least one mutual friend [24], recency of communication [20], and interaction frequency [7,11]. Our model relies on the ease of measurement, display, and understanding of these parameters by humans since it requires assessment of tie strength values and assignment of social collateral to them. In addition to these four parameters, we use length of the relationship as an additional tie-strength indicator. We do this because the length of a relationship increases accountability by adding a significant degree of moral responsibility to reporting authentic attributes of unknown senders. Shneiderman's work on the rich feedback about content quality provided by patterns of past performance online [25] supports the inclusion of this additional parameter.

The tie strength parameters are collected from a variety of online sources; e.g., online social networks, email, peer-to-peer (P2P) communication, physical-encounter evidence provided by GPS-enabled phones, accounts of phone communications. Some of these (required) parameters could be deliberately manipulated by a single individual; e.g., communication recency may be inflated by spurious emails and P2P messages. However, not *all* parameters can be manipulated *simultaneously* unilaterally to generate consistent false tie-strength measurements, since not all parameters are under the control of a single individual. For example, physical encounters, accounts of reciprocity in phone calls require both individuals to act. Nevertheless these parameters could be *artificially inflated* by collusion between two individuals. Furthermore, some parameters under user control could be *decreased* whenever individuals collude to hide the strength of their social tie. Hiding the strength of a social tie may not necessarily be a malicious act designed to misinform an unsuspecting receiver.

Privacy Concerns. While the privacy of his tie to the unknown sender may be less of a concern for the third party with respect to his friend the receiver, revealing the strength of his social ties which the the the third party may violate the privacy concerns of the unknown sender. However, this is not a surprise: very often, protocols that establish authenticity conflict with privacy in an unavoidable manner [16]. However, in interactive trust protocols, the potential loss of privacy is under the control of the parties who are affected by it. That is, the sender and the third party can decide how much, if any, of their social tie strength to reveal to a receiver. Furthermore, this decision can be unilaterally taken or negotiated; e.g., the third party may refuse to sign the strong tie evidence requested by a sender, and the sender may selectively remove or decrease the values of some revealing parameters under individual control. However, not all parameter values can be simultaneously decreased, as some values may be provided by network services outside individual user control; e.g., phone and e-mail account information. The use of these parameters is required by the receiver so that he could assign social collateral to the social tie in an reasonably accurate manner for deterrence purposes.

Social Collateral Assignment. In our model, a recommendation for the authenticity of an unknown sender's attributes comprises (1) the specification of the attribute whose authenticity is vouched by the third-party recommender, (2) the evidence of the social tie between the unknown sender and recommender, and (3) the recommender's signature. In contrast with $SC(A)@B$, which is a direct measure of the friendship between A and B, to assign collateral value $SC(C)@A$ to third party A's recommendation, receiver B verifies A's signature, using A's public key which we assume B already has, and evaluates the social-tie evidence included in the recommendation.

In assigning social collateral to the third party A's recommendations for unknown sender C's attributes, higher collateral values correspond to stronger evidence of the social tie between C and the recommender A. Since some of C's attributes may require more knowledge about C for authentication, a stronger tie between A and C becomes necessary. This is the case because receiver B's risk of security exposure caused by accepting a false attribute as authentic for a particular application may be higher for some attributes than for others. Hence, that risk must be offset by recommender A's better knowledge of, and stronger tie to, the unknown third party C. For example, accepting C's identity as authentic would require lower tie strength than accepting C's public key, since the public key may be used to set up a secure channel for the later transmission of sensitive data, whereas C's identity may be used merely for granting C read access to low-sensitivity objects. Similarly, accepting a set of attributes would require higher strength of tie than accepting a proper subset of those attributes.

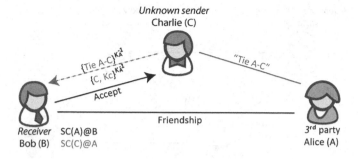

Fig. 4. Accepting a certificate from an unknown sender signed by a friend

Acceptability and Deterrence. The above discussion indicates that receiver B has a particular collateral threshold for accepting an attribute of an unknown sender C in his application. Let $T_B(app, attr)$ denote that threshold. Hence, receiver B verifies that

$$Acceptability: \quad SC(C)@A \geq T_B(app, attr)$$

where $T_B(app, attr) \geq 0$ is a measure of the loss incurred by B's application, app, if attribute, $attr$, is unauthentic.

In our model, recommender A looses her social collateral with friend B, namely $SC(A)@B$, if the recommendation to accept an attribute, $attr$, as authentic in B's application, app, turns out to be false. Our deterrence hypothesis suggests that loss of this social collateral would prevent A from making false recommendations to B. However, A faces a clear case of moral hazard. That is, if the social tie between recommender A and the unknown sender C is stronger than the friendship between A and receiver B, C could conceivably bribe A to make a false recommendation to B. This fact has been pointed out in the social collateral model of Karlan et al. [15]. Hence, B has to verify that his/her friendship with A is stronger than A's social tie to C.

$$Deterrence: \quad SC(A)@B - SC(C)@A \geq P_B(app, attr)$$

where $P_B(app, attr) \geq 0$ is a measure of the net loss of social collateral incurred by A if A's recommendation attribute, $attr$, for B's application, app, is unauthentic.

Figure 4 illustrates B's acceptance of a public-key certificate recommendation for unknown sender C from his friend A.

Second Independent Opinion. Suppose that receiver B's acceptability check for unknown sender C's attribute, $attr$, does not pass for application, app, because the tie strength between A and C is too low. To ensure that his rejection of C's invitation is justified, B can seek a second, independent third-party's recommendation. To do so, B searches sender C's social graph to determine whether C has a social tie with any other of B's friends. If this search returns a non-empty list of B's friends who have a social tie with C, then B selects, at random,

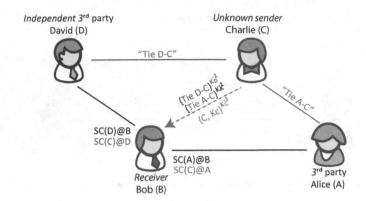

Fig. 5. Accepting a self-signed certificate from an unknown sender C. Receiver B seeks second opinion from 3rd party friend D who is independent from friend A.

another possible recommender for C's attribute, from the list, say friend D. Then B informs C of the need to obtain a signed recommendation from D and provides it along with C's invitation. When this second recommendation is made available, receiver B's acceptability and deterrence checks become:

$$Acceptability : SC(C)@A + SC(C)@D \geq T_B(app, attr)$$
$$Deterrence :\quad SC(A)@B - SC(C)@A \geq P_B(app, attr)\ and$$
$$SC(D)@B - SC(C)@D \geq P_B(app, attr)$$

Note that, in the social collateral model of Karlan et al. (2009), the social collateral available on two separate paths between a source and destination is unconditionally additive. In contrast, in our model, additivity is conditioned on B's random selection of a second recommender friend, D, who has a social tie with unknown sender C. The random choice of D implies that C's chances of bribing both of B's independent friends, A and D, to deliberately reduce their tie strength evidence simply to pass B's deterrence checks and vouch for unauthentic C attributes, are significantly diminished.

Figure 5 illustrates B's acceptance of a public-key certificate for unknown sender C based on the independent recommendations of his friends A and D.

Forwarded Recommendations. Suppose that a social tie between unknown sender C and any one of receiver B's friends does not exist. Instead, a social tie between C and a friend of A, namely E, exists. This case is illustrated in Figure 6. Furthermore, suppose that B's friend A has accepted a recommendation from her friend E regarding the authenticity of unknown sender C's attribute (i.e., public key certificate $\{C, K_C\}^{K_E^{-1}}$, and that A is willing to forward E's recommendation to B along with E's public key.

In this case, unknown sender C can present two pieces of evidence to receiver B to justify the authenticity of C's attribute: i.e., certificate $\{C, K_C\}^{K_E^{-1}}$. The first is the evidence of E's tie to C signed by A, namely $\{Tie(C - E)\}^{K_A^{-1}}$. The second is A's assessment of E's social collateral at A (i.e., E's friendship with A) signed

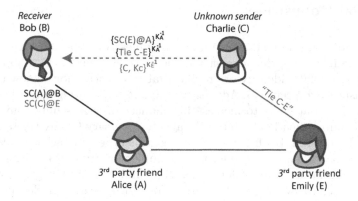

Fig. 6. Accepting an unknown sender C's attribute signed by a friend (E) of a friend (A)

by A, namely $\{SC(E)@A\}^{K_A^{-1}}$. Given these pieces of evidence, should receiver B accept the forwarded authentication of C's attribute, $\{C, K_C\}^{K_E^{-1}}$? To accept, B has to evaluate both the recommendation itself and whether A's forwarding of E's recommendation is warranted by B's social relation (friendship) with A.

To evaluate E's recommendation of C's attribute, B asks the following question: are A's deterrence and acceptability criteria for E's recommendation at least as strong as mine (B's)? To answer this question, B has to apply the two criteria using his own parameters, namely $T_B(app, \{C, K_C\})$, $P_B(app, \{C, K_C\})$, and his assignment of social collateral to the tie $\{Tie(C - E)\}$, namely $SC(C)@E$, after verifying signatures appropriately. B's criteria are:

$$Acceptability : SC(C)@E \geq T_B(app, \{C, K_C\})$$
$$Deterrence :\quad SC(E)@A - SC(C)@E \geq P_B(app, \{C, K_C\})$$

To determine whether A's forwarding of E's recommendation is warranted, receiver B again applies his criteria to friend A's and social tie between A and E. To do so B uses A's assignment of social collateral to her friendship with E, namely $SC(E)@A$, as follows:

$$Acceptability : SC(E)@A \geq T_B(app, \{C, K_C\})$$
$$Deterrence :\quad SC(A)@B - SC(E)@A \geq P_B(app, \{C, K_C\})$$

In short, when these two pieces of evidence are made available to receiver B by unknown sender C, receiver B's acceptability and deterrence checks become:

$$Acceptability : min\{SC(E)@A, SC(C)@E\} \geq T_B(app, \{C, K_C\})$$
$$Deterrence :\quad min\{SC(A)@B - SC(E)@A, SC(E)@A - SC(C)@E\}$$
$$\geq P_B(app, \{C, K_C\})$$

We note that these two checks are applicable to other attributes of C, not just certificate $\{C, K_C\}$.

5   Model Robustness

The social collateral model defined above assumes two types of adversarial attacks. In the first type, the adversary is the unknown sender, C, who attempts to impersonate a false identity or provide a false certificate for a known identity to an unsuspecting receiver B. Adversary C *unilaterally manipulates* tie strength parameters in an attempt to increase his chances of successfully convincing B to accept his unauthentic attributes. In affect, adversary C may try to inflate a recommendation from B's friend A. However, this type of attack cannot succeed in the protocols proposed above for three complementary reasons. First, recommender A will not agree to endorse (i.e., sign) inflated tie strength parameters since he is deterred by the social collateral loss with receiver B. Second, the inflation of all social tie parameters will fail because, as discussed in the previous section, some parameters may not be controllable by the user and others may require collusion with the recommender. Third, our model offers no incentive to recommender A to collude with sender C and endorse tie strength parameters inflated by C. The deterrence check performed by B would reject very strong ties between C and A. Hence, the moral hazard to which A might be exposed by refusing to endorse C's inflated social tie parameters (e.g., the distrust revelation problem [17]) does not materialize in our model.

In the second type of adversarial attack, the unknown sender C colludes with receiver B's friend A to *conceal and diminish* the real strength of their tie and induce B to accept C's false credentials. (Recall that collusion between A and C to inflate their tie strength is countered by B's deterrence check, as discussed above.) A particular instance of this attack may materialize when unknown sender C is in fact a secret Sybil of B's friend A. Our model addresses this type of attack in three distinct ways.

Independent Second Opinion. If the social-tie strength is too low and does not pass receiver B's acceptability threshold, B would automatically request an independent second opinion from friend D (viz., in Figure 5). Should a second independent opinion not be available, B's acceptability test would fail. It is rather unlikely that C could anticipate and "bribe" a randomly chosen independent provider by a second opinion. Furthermore, note that the independence of the second opinion could not be easily manipulated by sender C since the the the choice of the second-opinion provider, D, is exclusively receiver B's. Sender C has no say in it. Furthermore, unknown sender C has no clue of the amount of collateral receiver B's friends A and D have with B. All C sees in the social graph are "friend" connections. C would have to bribe *all* of B's "friends" he knows since he does not know B's future second-opinion provider. Thus, it seems unlikely that *both* Bob's friends A and D would collude with their acquaintance C against receiver B. Also note that whether A and D are (not) connected on the social graph is irrelevant to our notion of recommendation independence.

Deterrence against Threshold Probing. Receiver B can also detect whether recommender friend A and unknown sender C probe his acceptability threshold in a particular application by repeatedly including different tie-strength parameter values. First, repeated recommendations for the same identity C issued by A within a given time interval would automatically cause a second-opinion request by B. Second, repeated recommendations for different identities corresponding to real C, would require that all identities be related to B's other friends since a second opinion request would fail otherwise. Furthermore, low tie strength evidence for any of C's identities would have to be maintained by A for all C's recommendations in the social network over an interval of time. Otherwise. B's false recommendations of C could be detected. Third, a couple of failed recommendation attempts by A would cause A to lose his collateral with B.

Mandated Tie Strength Parameters. If the colluding parties, namely A and C, could control *all* tie strength parameters simultaneously, they might still be able to discover a (narrow) range of parameter values that are both acceptable to B and pass his deterrence check. Our model also addresses this type of attack that not all recording mechanisms for measurable tie strength parameters be under users' control. Hence, not all parameters could be decreased simultaneously to create consistent false evidence of weak social ties. We require that some parameters that could not be manipulated by any colluding parties be used in all recommendations. These parameters would be routinely provided and endorsed by third parties such as phone, e-mail, and other service providers.

6   Usability

We have conducted an extensive set of user studies to verify real users' ability to display, understand, and evaluate the tie strength between parties. We stress that this is the only parameter of our model that needs to be explicitly measured and displayed to users. In contrast, the collateral values of social relations of a user can be reasonably accurately estimated by the user himself/herself. Our usability studies are reported in detail elsewhere [18]. In this section we summarize those findings.

6.1   Visualization of "Tie Strength" Evidence

Tie strength can be visualized to help authenticate online identities. For example, based on the social relationship as depicted in Figure 5, receiver Bob can decide to accept an online "friend" invitation from unknown sender Charlie as follows: if the invitation contains visual tie strength evidence endorsed by their mutual friends (Alice and David in this case), Bob accepts Charlie's invitation based on the social collateral he assigns to the tie strength between Charlie and his two mutual friends.

We have formulated the details of visualizing tie strength, and Figure 7 is an example of tie strength visualization. This visualization displays six parameters:

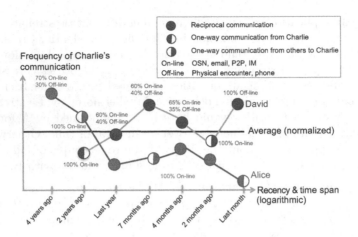

Fig. 7. Visualization of tie strength between Charlie and Bob's friends (Alice and David). This diagram displays how frequently Charlie has been interacting with Alice (red graph) and David (blue graph).

- **Frequency of Communication:** This parameter is represented on the y-axis. Bob can compare how frequently Charlie has interacted with Alice by comparing Alice's graph with the *average* interaction frequency line which represents the interaction frequency that Bob had with all his other friends (i.e., 4 years ago, Charlie interacted more frequently with Alice than with all his other friends).
- **Length of Relationship:** As represented on the x-axis, this parameter shows how long Charlie has known Alice and David.
- **Reciprocity of Communication:** The variations of coloring schemes on a circle represent the reciprocity information. A fully-colored circle represents that two people communicate reciprocally, and a half-colored circle represents one-way communication where one party attempts to interact but the other party does not respond.
- **Selected Mutual Friends:** The individual graphs in visualization correspond to selected mutual friends between the invitation sender and the receiver. Figure 7 displays Alice and David as Bob's selected mutual friends.
- **Recency of Interaction:** The rightmost point on the graph represents how recent the interaction was between the sender and the mutual friend. In Figure 7, Charlie's most recent interaction with David was last month.
- **Communication Type:** People can communicate using (1) on-line channels (e.g., Online Social Networks (OSNs), emails, Instant Messengers), or (2) off-line channels (e.g., physical encounter, phone conversations). Labeling the communication type empowers the receiver to judge the approximate strength of ties. For example, a "100% on-line" label for the entire length of relationship may indicate individuals who have only established a relationship through purely on-line means.

6.2   Usability Evaluation: A Facebook Application

In order to test whether the tie strength visualization help users make correct authentication decisions, we have developed a Facebook application that plots interaction frequencies. After querying the Facebook database according to the user's policy, this application retrieves a stream of wall posts between the sender and mutual friends, and plots interaction frequencies on a graph.

Procedure. We designed an online user study and recruited 93 participants using Amazon Mechanical Turk. All our participants were living in the U.S.

We asked each participant to download our Facebook application and run it to check the tie strength visualization of their pending Facebook invitation senders or their friends (if they did not have any pending invitations). We asked each participant to run the application at least 3 times.

We then asked them to provide feedback on our tie strength visualization. More specifically, we asked questions related to (1) how understandable is the visualization, (2) how easy is the application to use, and (3) whether they would accept an invitation even if this application displays below-average interaction frequency with the participant's friend(s).

Results. Overall, participants provided promising feedback.

- **Understandability:** 85% of the participants indicated that they understood tie strength of people as shown on the visualization, and 85% indicated that Figure 7 was a good way of displaying tie strength.
- **Robustness:** 90% indicated that they would not accept an invitation if the graph were placed below the average interaction frequency.
- **Usability:** 83% indicated that the visualization was easy to use, and 88% mentioned that our authentication application was easy to use. When we asked for possible future use, 84% expressed likeliness to use our application before accepting invitations.

The study results confirm that providing tie strength visualization to users is a promising direction to help users authenticate online identities.

7   Conclusions and Future Work

This paper introduces the notion of interactive trust protocols and illustrates how to establish attribute-authentication trust between two untrusting parties (e.g., between service providers and service receivers) who do not share a common trusted third party (TTP) or trust infrastructure (e.g., a public-key infrastructure). While helpful in many cases, TTPs create additional complexity and uncertainty, and sometimes become an attractive attack target. More fundamentally, the need for TTPs would beg the very question we want to answer, namely how can we establish trust between two previously untrusting parties. To remove the need for a TTP, we used a social collateral model inspired by those found in behavioral economics [15].

Interactive trust protocols could also be used in modeling the basic steps of online scams and/or deceptions. Most such protocols include a value proposition, asymmetric trust/outcomes, and an unsatisfied, or unsatisfiable, safety condition. Hence, the use of these protocols to model scams and deceptions would offer a way to detect patterns of possible scams and alert unsuspecting users. A good starting point would be to use these protocols for the few real-life cases of scams described by Stajano and Wilson [26].

Another extension of this work would be to develop social collateral models for *trust networks* [8], perhaps along the lines of those studied in behavioral economics. For example, the modeling of "agency problems" using Greif's well-known model [12] may in fact work better in 21st century's computer networks than in 11th century's coalitions of Maghribi traders [4,10].

Acknowledgments. This research was supported in part by NSF under awards CCF-0424422 and CNS-1050224. The views and conclusions contained here are those of the authors and should not be interpreted as necessarily representing the official policies or endorsements, either expressed or implied, of CMU, NSF or the U.S. Government or any of its agencies.

References

1. Sophos Facebook ID Probe, http://www.sophos.com/pressoffice/news/articles/2007/08/facebook.html
2. Bilge, L., Strufe, T., Balzarotti, D., Kirda, E.: All Your Contacts Are Belong to Us: Automated Identity Theft Attacks on Social Networks. In: Proceedings of WWW (2009)
3. Economist. Duly notarised (September 2011), http://www.economist.com/blogs/babbage/2011/09/internet-security
4. Edwards, J., Ogilvie, S.: Contract Enforcement, Institutions and Social Capital: the Maghribi Traders Reappraised. CSEIFO Working Paper (March 2008)
5. Friedkin, N.E.: A Test of Structural Features of Granovetter's Strength of Weak Ties Theory. Social Networks (1980)
6. Gilbert, E., Karahalios, K.: Predicting Tie Strength With Social Media. In: Proceedings of the 27th ACM SIGCHI Conference on Human Factors in Computing Systems, CHI (2009)
7. Gilbert, E., Karahalios, K., Sandvig, C.: The Network in the Garden: An Empirical Analysis of Social Media in Rural Life. In: Proceedings of the 26th ACM SIGCHI Conference on Human Factors in Computing Systems, CHI (2008)
8. Gligor, V., Perrig, A., Zhao, J.: Brief Encounters with a Randomkey Graph. In: Proceedings of the 17th Security Protocols Workshop (April 2009)
9. Gligor, V.: Towards a Theory of Trust in Networks of Humans and Computers (Transcript of Discussion). In: Christianson, B., Crispo, B., Malcolm, J., Stajano, F. (eds.) Security Protocols 2011. LNCS, vol. 7114, pp. 243–257. Springer, Heidelberg (2011)
10. Goldberg, J.: Making reputation work: re-examining law, labor and enforcement among Geniza businessmen. Before and Beyond Europe: Economic Change in Historical Perspective (Yale University) (February 2011)
11. Granovetter, M.S.: The Strength of Weak Ties. The American Journal of Sociology (1973)

12. Grief, A.: Contract Enforceability and Economic Institutions in Early Trade: the Maghribi Traders Coalition. American Economic Review (June 1993)
13. Hamiel, N., Moyer, S.: Satan Is On My Friends List: Attacking Social Networks. In: Black Hat Conference (2008)
14. Hu, Q., Xu, Z., Dinev, T., Ling, H.: Does Deterrence Work in Reducing Information Security Policy Abuse by Employees? Communications of the ACM (2011)
15. Karlan, D., Mobius, M., Rosenblat, T., Szeidl, A.: Trust and Social Collateral. The Quarterly Journal of Economics (August 2009)
16. Kent, S.T., Millett, L.I. (eds.): Who Goes There? Authentication Through the Lens of Privacy. National Academies Press (2003)
17. Kim, T.H.-J., Bauer, L., Newsome, J., Perrig, A., Walker, J.: Challenges in access right assignment for secure home networks. In: Proceedings of the 5th USENIX Workshop on Hot Topics in Security, HotSec 2010 (2010)
18. Kim, T.H.-J., Yamada, A., Gligor, V., Hong, J.I., Perrig, A.: RelationGrams: Tie-Strength Visualization for User-Controlled Online Identity Authentication. Technical Report CMU-CyLab-11-014, Carnegie Mellon University (2011)
19. Krackhardt, D.: The Strength of Strong Ties: The Importance of *Philos* in Organizations. In: Nohria, N., Eccles, R. (eds.) Networks and Organizations: Structure, Form, and Action (1992)
20. Lin, N., Dayton, P.W., Greenwald, P.: Analyizing the Instrumental Use of Relations in the Context of Social Structure. Sociological Methods Research
21. Moore, A.P., Cappelli, D.M., Caron, T.C., Shaw, E., Spooner, D., Trzeciak, R.F.: A Preliminary Model of Insider Theft of Intellectual Property. Journal of Wireless Mobile Networks, Ubiquitous Computing, and Dependable Applications (2011)
22. Moore, A.P., Cappelli, D.M., Trzeciak, R.F.: The "Big Picture" of Insider IT Sabotage Across U.S. Critical Infrastructures. Technical Report CMU/SEI-2008-TR-009, Carnegie Mellon University (2008)
23. Ryan, T.: Getting in Bed with Robin Sage. In: Black Hat Conference (2010)
24. Shi, X., Adamic, L.A., Strauss, M.J.: Networks of Strong Ties. Physica A: Statistical Mechanics and its Applications
25. Shneiderman, B.: Designing Trust into Online Experiences. Communications of the ACM (2000)
26. Stajano, F., Wilson, P.: Understanding Scam Victims: Seven Principles for Systems Security. Communications of the ACM (2011)

Street-Level Trust Semantics
for Attribute Authentication
(Transcript of Discussion)

Virgil Gligor

Carnegie Mellon University

In keeping up with the idea of bringing security protocols to life, I'm going to talk about the act of trusting in interactive send-receive protocols. This class of protocols is similar to the "trust game" I presented last year, except that it does not require the existence of a dealer.[1] Specifically, I am going to ask the question of whether it is *ever* safe to trust input received from an unknown sender. In the class of protocol discussed,

1. there is a value proposition, which tempts the receiver to accept the input,
2. the protocol outcomes are asymmetric in terms of who benefits from (un)trustworthy behavior, and
3. the question of whether it is *ever* safe for the receiver to accept the unknown sender's input does not have an obvious answer.

To provide a practical answer to this question, one could introduce the notion of *collateral*, which unfortunately requires a third party who is trusted by *both* the receiver and *unknown* sender, and hence not easy to come by.

In this presentation I will argue that a different form of collateral, namely *social collateral*, which is almost always available and does *not* require a trusted third party, and which can be used to reduce the asymmetry inherent in the class of protocols presented. In particular, social collateral can almost always be used in protocols that require authentication trust; e.g., in protocols where a receiver is supposed to accept an identity or a self-signed certificate from an unknown sender in the absence of a trusted certification authority. In short, I will present an interpretation of the social collateral model for accepting attribute authentication, which requires visualization of social ties between users, and the results of some preliminary user studies, which indicate that real users find the proposed visualization to be helpful.

In interactive trust protocols, receivers communicate with unknown (e.g., anonymous) senders because they realize some positive benefit. However, the outcomes of these protocols are asymmetric: the receiver needs to trust that the input received from the sender is not corrupt (i.e., does not contain spoofed identity, certificates, and malware) whereas the sender does not need to trust the receiver since it can always verify the receiver's messages. In analyzing the trust invested in these protocols and their outcomes, we assume that we have

---

[1] V. Gligor and J. M. Wing. Towards a Theory of Trust in Networks of Humans and Computers. In Proceedings of the 19th International Workshop on Security Protocols, March 2011, LNCS 7114, Springer Verlag, pp. 223 - 242.

B. Christianson et al. (Eds.): Security Protocols 2012, LNCS 7622, pp. 116–125, 2012.

a *trusted path* between senders and receivers and malicious third parties cannot interfere with sender-receiver communication.

To reduce the asymmetry between the sender and receiver trust, the receiver may try to *isolate himself* from sender's (mis)behavior. In other words, whenever the receiver can check the validity of all the inputs he receives from the unknown sender, the receiver does not need to trust that the sender complies with the protocol and the asymmetry is eliminated. Clearly, receiver isolation is not always possible. In fact, receiver isolation is often impractical. Second, short of isolation, the receiver might try to figure out if *the sender is trustworthy*, meaning that the sender's code is correct and the sender's behavior complies with the protocol specifications; i.e., the unknown sender is honest. Of course, it is not always possible to come up with evidence of sender trustworthiness and to evaluate this evidence completely and correctly. The third possibility is to have the *receiver recover from corrupt sender inputs*. Suppose that this is practical. If so, the receiver does not need to trust the unknown sender, since the receiver can always recover if the input is bad. Unfortunately, recovery is not always possible. In fact, it's seldom practical to recover from accepting input that contains malware, since the receiver might not even know that he has to recover. And finally, the receiver might try to avoid trusting an unknown sender by *deterring the sender* from sending bad inputs. That is, the receiver can identity the sender, the receiver can hold the sender accountable, and then punish him for providing corrupt input. And, of course, this is not always possible, since deterrence is seldom available to interactive protocol participants.

So given that a receiver cannot isolate himself from sender misbehavior, has no evidence of sender's trustworthiness, no possibility to recover from a sender's corrupt inputs, and no ability to deter a sender from sending such inputs, how can the receiver realize the value promised by the protocol specifications? The real question is: is it ever safe for the receiver to trust that an unknown sender is not providing corrupt input? In other words, it is possible that asymmetry reduction is not a necessary condition for trust in these protocols?

Omar Chaudary: I have a question: is it true that one can never trust the results of a computation performed by the sender? For example, what about the notion of verifiable computation? Doesn't it apply here?

Reply: Of course, there are cases where the receiver can actually verify the results of a computation performed by an unknown sender. Suppose that the receiver outsources the execution of a program to the sender. Theoretically, the receiver can always verify that the execution of that program by the sender has produced correct results. However, this seems to require use of fully homomorphic encryption of the outsourced program, as illustrated in Bryan Parno's PhD thesis at Carnegie Mellon University.[2] If homomorphic encryption were available at a reasonable performance cost, then the receiver wouldn't have to trust that the sender has executed the receiver's computation correctly; i.e., he does not even have to trust the unknown sender's hardware – not just the oper-

---

[2] Parno, B., Trust Extension a a Mechanism for Secure Code Execution on Commodity Computers. Ph.D. Thesis, Carnegie Mellon University, 2010.

ating system, and the administrators. In fact, the receiver does not need to trust anything about the sender except that the sender will return results. However, let me give you another example where it's highly unlikely that the receiver can verify the results of a sender's computation. Suppose that the receiver does not outsource a program's execution to the sender. Instead, assume the receiver asks the unknown sender to solve a computational problem, and the sender can pick the algorithm needed for that computation. For a large class of computational problems, namely for co-NP complete problems, the sender's execution is efficient but the receiver's verification of the sender's execution is inefficient. Of course, it is highly unlikely that any receiver would attempt to verify such results, in general.

Omar Chaudary: But this assumption is just for some cases, not every case...

Reply: Absolutely. However, we should recall that the class of interactive trust protocols we are discussing here, whereby a receiver gets an invitation from an unknown sender to participate in a protocol, is inherently asymmetric in the sense that, while the sender can always verify the receiver's protocol compliance, the receiver can never do that. By the definition of this class, the receiver can never verify the sender's input; e.g., received results of a computation. The protocol discussed in last year's presentation[3] contains a simple example for what I call a one-round "interactive trust protocol."

Now suppose that the interactive trust protocol iterates for many rounds, as Matt Blaze suggested last year, and in each round, the sender tries to decide whether to cheat the receiver; and conversely, the receiver tries to anticipate the sender's cheating. It turns out that this is fairly easy to do for the sender and difficult for the receiver. Specifically, a *rational* sender can compute the *present value of future honest protocol executions* and check whether it exceeds the value of his gain by cheating at a particular round. If yes, he is better off if he cheats; otherwise, he has no incentive to cheat. To compute the present value of future honest executions, the sender uses his *discount rate*, $r > 0$. That rate captures the interest rate, the sender's assessment of the receiver's reliability in engaging in future protocol rounds, etc. Of course, the receiver could not perform this computation and hence cannot anticipate whether the server will cheat. Even if the receiver could determine a sender's ill-gotten gain by cheating in a round, the receiver could not determine the sender's discount rate, r. As in last year's example, suppose that the sender and receiver net \$15 per round if they execute a trust protocol honestly, and the sender nets \$25 in the round he decides to cheat, in which case the receiver loses his initial \$10 investment to the sender. Using the standard computation for the present value of future honest protocol executions, the sender can decide whether to cheat at a round by the following comparison:

$$\$15 \cdot \frac{1+r}{r} > \$25$$

---

[3] Gligor and Wing, *op. cit.*

It follows that, if $r < 60\%$, the rational sender will behave honestly; otherwise, he has an obvious incentive to cheat.

An immediate question arises: how can the sender be punished if he cheats? Or, in other words, how can one deter an unknown sender from cheating, or remove his obvious incentive to cheat? Clearly, if a dishonest sender is punished by removal of his ill-gotten gain of $25, he will not have any incentive to cheat. The above inequality will hold independent of the sender's discount rate, r. We can modify last year's one-round trust protocol so that the sender places $25 as collateral with a trusted third party (TTP), namely the Dealer. Hence, if the trust protocol ends normally, both sender and receiver net $15, and if the sender cheats he loses his collateral. The receiver is made whole by the TTP using the collateral. In this protocol, the trust asymmetry is eliminated.[4] Although this solution appears to eliminate asymmetry, it would not work in practice. If the sender could post collateral for every receiver he would engage, the sender would be rich. Obviously, a collateral-based solution does not scale very well for the sender.

One form of collateral which is widely available is *social collateral*. Let us assume that a third party exists who has a "social relationship" with the receiver and a "social tie" with the sender. That is, the third party may be a close friend, immediate family member, or colleague of long standing of the receiver's, and may also know the sender quite well; i.e., the sender is *no longer anonymous*. The existence of a social relationship has immediate benefits. One can informally compute the net present value of interacting with a social relation, and thus confer some long-term value to that relationship. Of course, the third party values the social relation with the receiver; e.g., the third party may value the receiver's social connections, which means that he would want to use these relations in the future. This implies that the third party can be trusted by the receiver as the third party would have no incentive to cheat the receiver in a trust protocol. This means that the third party has social collateral deposited with the receiver; i.e., the value of their friendship. And if he cheats the receiver, he loses that collateral. Hence, he is deterred.

Recent studies show that social collateral acts as a deterrent from cheating and forms the basis for trust protocols, such as financial lending in Third World countries; e.g., Peru.[5] Furthermore, same studies show that social collateral is the basis for job search recommendations; e.g., a third-party friend recommends acceptance of an unknown sender's services to a receiver. Other studies suggest that even when loss of social relations and the law cannot fully deter insider attacks, the potential loss of social relations deters more than the law.[6] Although the results of these studies may be culturally influenced (e.g., they were conducted in China), there is a reason to believe the hypothesis that loss of social

---

[4] Trust asymmetry is not completely eliminated since both parties need to trust the TTP, each in an asymmetric way.

[5] D. Karlan, M. Mobius, T. Rosenblat, and A. Szeidl. Trust and Social Collateral. *The Quarterly Journal of Economics*, August 2009.

[6] Q. Hu, Z. Xu, T. Dinev, and H. Ling. Does Deterrence Work in Reducing Information Security Policy Abuse by Employees? Communications of The ACM, 2011.

relations deters misbehavior holds universally. In short, the use of social collateral is two-fold. First, we hypothesize that social collateral *deters cheating* in trust protocols, and thus it can remove trust asymmetry *without requiring a TTP*. Second, the amount of social collateral available in a protocol has to be acceptable to the receiver; i.e., the greater the receiver's exposure is in a trust protocol, the higher the collateral he requires. This gives us a *collateral acceptability* criterion.

The question that we explore here is how one can use the notion of the social collateral between a receiver and a third-party friend, and the strong ties between the third-party friend and an unknown sender, in trust protocols where the receiver can safely accept authentication information from an unknown sender; e.g., identity, certificates—either self-signed by the sender or signed by others. In short, explore whether social collateral and strong ties can be used to *reduce asymmetry* between the sender and the receiver in an interractive trust protocol. Of course, in our setting, trusted public-key infrastructures are unavailable. Specifically, I will use an interpretation of the social collateral model of Karlan *et al.*, for recommendation trust.[7] Recalling the example that I gave in last year's presentation, suppose that Frank Stajano is a friend of mine and he sends a certificate by which he introduces Matt Blaze to me. The question is: do I believe this introduction? That is, do I believe that this certificate is authentic?

Matt Blaze: So the question is whether that person is Matt Blaze, or whether Matt Blaze is going to harm you?

Reply: The question is whether that person is Matt Blaze. In other words, is the certificate authentic, as opposed to being a *compelled certificate*, forged by some unknown government agency for some spy masquerading as Matt Blaze. The question is whether Frank sent me a false certificate for a spy who calls himself Matt Blaze in my interactions with him?

Matt Blaze: So we're starting with naming?

Reply: Yes, we're starting with naming. In fact, we restricted this discussion to naming and authentication attributes, basically identities and certificates. It may very well be that Frank only needs to help me authenticate Matt's identity. It is possible that I already received Matt's public key via a "Seeing-Is-Believing" type of protocol[8] or by touching my phone and Matt's in a "Resurrecting Duckling" style.[9] That is, I have this individual's public key but I have no idea who he is until Frank tells me that what I've got is really Matt's key. In effect, Frank's recommendation enables me to create a public key certificate for Matt so that I do not need to use a public-key infrastructure. This could be extended to other kinds of inputs.

[7] D. Karlan, M. Mobius, T. Rosenblat, and A. Szeidl. Trust and Social Collateral. The Quarterly Journal of Economics, August 2009.

[8] McCune, J., Perrig, A., and Reiter, M., Seeing-Is-Believing: using camera phones for human-verifiable authentication. In *Int. J. Security and Networks*, vol. 4, nos. 1/2, 2009, pp. 43 - 56.

[9] Stajano, F., and Anderson, R. J., The Resurrecting Duckling: Security Issues for Ad-hoc Wireless Net- works. In Security Protocols Workshop, Cambridge, April 1999.

Bruce Christianson: It could equally be an attribute certificate. It could say: "at the end of that phone is someone who knows a lot about cryptography."

Reply: Right. It could be another of Matt Blaze's attributes. Of course, there is a further step in terms of the degree of risk involved here. Frank might recommend that I accept *any input* from *this* Matt Blaze because he considers Matt to be trustworthy, which I might decline since such a recommendation might exceed Frank's knowledge of Matt. However, I am accepting Frank's recommendation of Matt's authentication attributes including his identity and certificates, since I expect Frank to produce evidence of his social tie to Matt.

Here is a simple example of how this would work. Let Bob be a friend of Alice. Hence, Alice has social collateral with Bob, so she can make recommendations to Bob about the attributes of other parties who are unknown to Bob. If Alice makes false recommendations, she loses her social collateral with Bob, so she's deterred from deliberately doing so. At the same time, Alice has a social tie with Charlie, and the strength of that tie can be measured and presented as evidence to Bob. Social science has established parameters that measure the strength of social ties. Recent studies suggest that four key parameters can provide an accurate measure of tie strength between two parties; i.e., the frequency of communication between the two parties, recency of communication, reciprocity, and the existence of a third party who knows both. We might add other measurable parameters, such as the length of the relationship. Now suppose that we can measure the tie strength between Alice and Charlie and can visually display it so that receiver Bob can assign a social collateral value to it in the trust protocol.

In an interactive trust protocol, sender Charlie, who is unknown to receiver Bob, wants Bob to accept his certificate. Charlie presents Alice's recommendation to Bob, namely a signed record containing evidence of their social tie. The record may include evidence of how often Alice and Charlie bumped into each other last year, which may be produced by their GPS-enabled phones, evidence of how much they talked to each other recently, who called whom and when, evidence of their Facebook "friend" relationship, and evidence of Google email exchanged. Before Alice signs such evidence, she examines it to ensure that it is consistent with her own records. Bob verifies Alice's signature on the social-evidence presented by Charlie, and then checks whether the tie between Alice and Charlie is strong enough for his risk taken when accepting Charlie's certificate. Obviously a strong tie implies that Alice knows Charlie sufficiently well to authenticate his certificate. However, an extremely strong tie also suggests that Charlie could actually bribe Alice to sign anything, so that he could impersonate somebody else. Thus, Bob has to verify that Alice's collateral with Bob exceeds the collateral value Bob assigns to the Alice-endorsed tie strength evidence presented by Charlie. This verification is a necessary deterrence condition.

Jonathan Anderson: I'm not really clear on why it actually matters to Bob whether or not the red circle corresponds to a global absolute name C? I mean, why instead of having "do I believe that C is actually C," it is not enough to have Bob refer to C as "the guy who Alice calls C," for instance?

Reply: It doesn't matter at all, in this case. I didn't mean to imply that C is a universal name. Charlie could be an attribute given by Alice to this particular red circle C.

Jonathan Anderson: Because it seems to me that the only time this matters is when you're trying to evaluate, based on this information, whether C can do me some harm; or if I ask C to fix my car, will C do a good job? And C's name is kind of a secondary argument.

Reply: Yes, of course. However, I do not argue that one needs a global name for C, but only that one (e.g., Bob in this case) has to have some identification that *makes C accountable*, for example in cases when one plans to set up a channel with C later. This is basically an accountability matter: Alice's recommendation makes C accountable to Bob.

Alice's recommendation for C's identity has to be accountable to Bob in terms of the risk Bob is taking by accepting an unauthentic identity for C in a particular application. Hence, the social collateral Bob assigns to the strength of Alice's tie with C has to exceed Bob's risk threshold for his application. Also, Alice's social collateral with Bob has to exceed the collateral assigned to that tie strength. These two checks, which Bob performs before accepting C's identity, imply that the trust between Bob and C (aka Charlie) is the minimum of the social collateral values of the Bob-Alice and Alice-Charlie links. This is consistent with the original social collateral model.[10]

Frank Stajano: If we are going back to the example you had earlier with us, if you are to trust my recommendation of Matt, then you have to be more friends with me than I am friends with Matt, because otherwise I could be playing a game on you.

Reply: That's correct. I accept your recommendation if you are more of a friend of mine than you are of Matt's. However, if your knowledge of Matt is too superficial, as displayed in the diagram of your tie strength with Matt (shown later), then I won't accept it.

Frank Stajano: I have a slight problem with that, which is that you know how much we are friends between us, and as far as how friends I am with Matt you only have this evidence that I'm presenting, but I could be hiding something.

Reply: He presents the evidence not you.

Frank Stajano: He presents it, but if we are very much more friendly between us than I am with you, we could say, let's just disclose to Virgil that we are one tenth of a friend, one tenth of how much we really are friends, so that we can still cheat him later. And you have no other way to assess how much friends we really are.

Reply: But if you do that, you may not pass my acceptability threshold. So if you lower your tie strength to Matt too much, and I have a high threshold value for the particular application, I will not accept your recommendation, so you have an optimization to make here.

---

[10] D. Karlan, M. Mobius, T. Rosenblat, and A. Szeidl. Trust and Social Collateral. *The Quarterly Journal of Economics*, August 2009.

Frank Stajano: But I still have scope for cheating you by not disclosing my real strength of tie with the guy I'm introducing, right?

Reply: Yes, but the cheating in that sense is countered by these checks, because I set the acceptability threshold for my application and you have no control over it. It is my local decision to accept your recommendation or not.

Matt Blaze: Well, first Frank is going to introduce me, Matt1, with his 10% certificate, and then I present this 10% certificate from Frank to you. And then I'm going be Matt2 with my 15% certificate from Frank.

Reply: Yes, you can attempt to find my threshold that way, except that whenever Frank's recommendation fails my acceptability test, I am going to ask for a second *independent* opinion. And if I cannot find it, Frank's recommendation fails. And if it fails multiple times (e.g., for Matt1, Matt2) for a sensitive application, then his social collateral with me is gone.

In my current example, suppose that Alice's recommendation for Charlie fails Bob's acceptability test. If Bob can find another individual, say David (i.e., D in my diagram), who is a friend of Bob's and also knows Charlie, then Bob can ask for a second independent recommendation for Charlie.

Frank Stajano: One of those is what happens in the PGP web of trust, right, you can add together independent parts to evaluate?

Reply: Not quite, this is actually quite different. This model could also model the PGP notion of trust, but this does a lot more than the PGP. A PGP case will be presented on the next slide where you have an indirection (i.e., friend-of-a-friend recommendation) check. Anyway, the point is that in the original social collateral model, if you have two independent paths of trust, the overall level of trust is determined additively. In our model, this happens in cases where one recommendation is too weak, or the receiver's threshold of recommendation acceptance for an application is too high. This may happen when an application is too sensitive to accept casual friends' recommendations.

Jonathan Anderson: But your notion of independence depends on the relationship between A (Alice) and D (David).

Joseph Bonneau: Well, I was just going to ask about independence; does that mean that David and Alice have no relationship?

Reply: The only relationship that they could have that matters in this case would be through receiver Bob; i.e., their *social collateral* with Bob and *social ties* with unknown sender Charlie.

Jonathan Anderson: But how would you know that? Because it's only if Alice and David would have to be unrelated?

Reply: Well because, for example, in a social network one can tell whether Alice and David have a relationship by looking at the graph. However, they could always have an "illicit" relationship, which is not represented in the graph.

Joseph Bonneau: I mean, just sociologically it's sort of unlikely that David and Alice would both know you (nb., Bob) and both know Charlie, and yet have never crossed paths.

Reply: Unclear...

Joseph Bonneau: Yes, it's unlikely.

Reply: Remember *all trust is local* to Bob, and he picks David among his good friends who know Charlie. This is exclusively Bob's decision and Charlie has no say in it.

Joseph Bonneau: I mean, sociologists have done this kind of stuff, and for different small sub graphs like this, like a square without the cross lines, that's pretty unusual.

Reply: Well, if you look at the average user of Facebook, he has about 600 "friend" connections out of which only about 30 are actual friends in reality; i.e., friends who have social collateral with Bob. If Bob has a few choices of *real friends* who know Charlie, Bob can determine who can offer an opinion that is likely to be independent of Charlie's potential collusion with Alice. Of course, one can modify one's criterion for selecting the second opinion provider in any way one wants; e.g., one may add a requirement that Alice and David should not have crossed paths, but that is less relevant here. What makes a difference here is the fact that Bob has a second opinion from someone who is *unlikely to collude* with Charlie, and this is what David's collateral adds here.

The last example that I would like to present is that of *forwarded recommendations*. In this example, Bob receives a recommendation for Charlie made not by Alice but by Alice's friend. The acceptance and deterrence criteria for this case is related to the calculation of trust (collateral) paths in the original social collateral model; i.e., trust along a multi-link path should be determined by the minimum for all social collateral values on the path. In our interpretation, receiver Bob has to evaluate both the recommendation made by Emily and whether Alice's forwarding of Emily's recommendation is warranted by B's social relation (friendship) with Alice. For the first evaluation, Bob uses his own assessment of the social tie strength between Emily and unknown sender Charlie, and his own acceptability and deterrence thresholds. For the second evaluation, Bob uses his deterrence and accountability checks for Alice, and Alice's assignment of social collateral to her friendship with Emily.

Finally, the key question is how usable this model is in real life, "on the street." Of course, we all have a mental measure of the social collateral value of our friendships, and hence we do not need to visualize these values in a system. In contrast, we do need to visualize the tie strength between a recommender and the unknown sender of an invitation to us. The reason for this is simple: we need to assign a social collateral value to tie strength evidence and for that, we need to display and evaluate that evidence.

To illustrate how the tie strength evidence is displayed visually, let us revisit the case where Bob receives two independent recommendations from his friends for Charlie, one from Alice and the other one from David. The display of the measured parameters that characterize Alice and Bob's tie strengths with Charlie are plotted on a two-dimensional graph easily displayed on a small screen. The graph captures the frequency of communication on the Y-axis, the length of the relationship on the X-axis, and the recency of communication on the X-axis. Reciprocity, namely whether both parties initiate communication with each other, or lack thereof, namely when only one party initiates communication, is also displayed on the graph. One-party initiation is represented by a half-filled circle, and a fully filled circle is used to denote communication initiation by both parties in any time period.

In our example of tie strength visualization, we notice that Alice's tie to Charlie has been fairly weak. The tie strength curve is well below the (normalized) average. Hence, Bob needs to solicit an independent second opinion from his friend David. We notice that David's tie to Charlie is stronger and perhaps the collateral assigned by Bob to both tie strength graphs adds up to an acceptable value.

We performed user studies on Facebook with this type of tie strength visualization, and collected Mechanical Turk data to investigate the acceptability of this visual representation. Specifically, we asked questions related to (1) how understandable this type of visualization is, (2) how easy the recommendation system is to use for identity authentication in an on-line invitation, and (3) whether participants would accept an invitation even if this application displays below-average interaction frequency with the participant's friend(s). Participants provided the following useful feedback. About 85% of the participants indicated that they understood the notion of tie strength between people using our visualizations, and 85% indicated that our visualization was a good representation of tie strength. 90% indicated that they would not accept an invitation if the graphs were placed below the average interaction frequency. 83% indicated that the visualization was easy to use, and 88% mentioned that our identity authentication application was easy to use. When we asked for possible future use, 84% expressed likeliness to use our application before accepting invitations. We did not study the authentication decisions involving other attributes, second-opinion based authentication, or authentication based on forwarded recommendations. The study results confirm that providing tie strength visualizations to users is a promising direction to help users authenticate on-line identities.

Sandy Clark: So Virgil, I think I've actually seen this sort of social validation in action. The old peppercorn socialization where everyone still used handles and didn't have the real names on anything, would have these key-signing meet-ups where they would basically go and get people's keys, and get them to sign your keys based on who introduced you to someone, and whether or not they could vouch for you, and you trusted them.

Reply: Yes, that's great, I'd like to see the reference to that.

Sandy Clark: Let me see if I can find it.

Reply: That would be wonderful, that could bolster the case for "street level trust."

Jonathan Anderson: And apparently the social collateral model is how empires used to function before the industrial age: the reason why you bought commissions and things was because your livelihood depended on the king, and the king knew he could trust you because he could take your livelihood away like that.

Reply: We not only have the compelled trust hierarchies in real life, but we also have a social-collateral model interpretation for them, which is quite an interesting topic in itself.

Analysis of Issues and Challenges
of E-Voting in the UK

Dylan Clarke, Feng Hao, and Brian Randell

School of Computing Science
Newcastle University, UK

Abstract. Official trials were conducted of a number of e-voting systems in the UK in 2002/3 and 2007 during local government elections, yet none of these test systems were subsequently used in any further elections, and all trials were suspended in 2008. We describe these trials, concentrating on the second more extensive 2007 trial, and how their results were received. Based on these events, we consider the key challenges involved in introducing current e-voting systems into the present system of UK national and local elections, and what general implications this may have for achieving practical take-up of e-voting within the UK.

1 Introduction

E-voting systems were trialled in the UK in 2002/3 and 2007, yet none of these systems were ultimately used, and all trials were suspended in 2008.

We consider the key challenges in bringing e-voting algorithms to life within the system of UK general and local elections, and what implications this may have for the implementation of practical systems. This begins with a description of the system of national and local elections used in the UK, and the underlying principles that have led to it. Next we look at key pilot studies that were performed in 2007 and how they were received by the Electoral Commission. (National and local elections are conducted in a very similar fashion, so the presumption is that trials performed as part of a local election will be of equal relevance to national elections.) We follow this with an analysis of the issues which led to the perceived failure of these pilots, and indicate what issues would need to be resolved to meet the challenges of producing an e-voting system that could be successfully introduced into the UK's electoral process. Finally, we conclude by examining the insights that this analysis provides us towards the issue of bringing algorithms to life in general.

2 Voting in the UK

UK elections, both national and local, are centered around the principle of each voter being entitled to one vote that is cast purely based on their own conscience, without any possibility of coercion from others. One of the cornerstones of this freedom from coercion is the Secret Ballot Act of 1872, which initiated

B. Christianson et al. (Eds.): Security Protocols 2012, LNCS 7622, pp. 126–135, 2012.

the requirement for ballots to be cast secretly, rather than votes being publicly stated.

Simply requiring that ballots be cast secretly was not considered to be enough for an election to be coercion free however, and a variety of legislation grew to help provide fair elections, centering around three key themes.

Firstly, regulations and monitoring are used to ensure the integrity of elections. This includes measures to ensure that ballots are counted correctly, having been stored securely until they are counted, procedures to allow the result of an election to be challenged, and regulations to prevent voting being conducted in a way that is discriminatory to some categories of voters. A key part of this theme is that the integrity of the election is observable. Ballots are cast on paper, and independent observers (typically representing the various rival parties) as well as officials are able to observe that each stage of the election is carried out correctly [13].

Secondly, regulations and monitoring are used to ensure the anonymity of voting, as a secret ballot is not sufficient if there is a way for third parties to deduce a link between voters and their vote. This anonymity however is not an intrinsic property of UK elections and is partly provided by legal protections [3]. A sealed list linking voters to ballots is kept for a prescribed time after each election (to facilitate investigation in the event of complaints), and this list, and the ballots it refers to, can be opened only at the order of an election court, or the House of Commons, as specified in the Representation of the People Act 1983.

Thirdly, election expenses are monitored and limited, along with the content of promotional materials [14].

UK elections centre around polling stations, physical locations in which voters are allowed to vote for the candidates for their area on a given election day. (Voters are allocated to a particular polling station, and in principle their identity is checked against that polling station's list of voters before they are handed a ballot paper and proceed to cast their vote. The ballot papers each carry a distinct but unobtrusive number, and a record is made of this number before a ballot is given to the voter, the list of such numbers being retained in case there is a subsequent need to investigate any voting irregularities.) Generally, between 1000 and 2000 voters are registered to vote at each polling station, although the numbers can be lower in areas with a low population density.

Two possible solutions are allowed for voters unable to attend a polling station to vote; the postal vote and the proxy vote. The postal vote involves the voter registering in advance for a postal vote, receiving a ballot paper and posting this ballot paper to the returning officer by the day of the election. The proxy vote involves the voter registering in advance for a proxy vote, and then a specified person attending the polling station to vote on their behalf. (Most concerns about the UK's present scheme of voting have in fact centered on fraudulent postal voting [20]. The accuracy and privacy of the actual paper-based voting system are widely trusted.)

3   The 2007 E-Voting Pilots

Five pilot studies were performed during the 2007 local government elections. In each pilot, individual voters were allowed to choose whether to use an e-voting system to cast their ballot or one of the traditional voting methods. These pilots were run by Rushmoor Borough Council [4], Sheffield City Council [5], Shrewsbury and Atcham Borough Council [6], South Bucks District Council [6] and Swindon Borough Council [7]. Each of these local authorities independently formulated a set of objectives before beginning the pilot and evaluated the success of the pilot. Further evaluation was performed by the Electoral Commission.

There were differences between the objectives for each authority and many of the objectives related to the pilot study itself rather than the possible benefits of an e-voting system (e.g. "pave the way for the expansion of future e-voting innovations in Sheffield" [5]). However, three key themes were found to feature in all of the councils' objectives and evaluations. Firstly, a desire to improve the turnout; the number of people who vote at the election. Secondly, a desire to reduce the cost of the election. Thirdly, a desire to improve the accessibility of the election, both to the public in general and to minority groups and those with disabilities.

Security was an issue that was mentioned among the objectives and evaluation criteria but none of the councils expressed an aim to increase security beyond that of the current paper based system. Instead, the Electoral Commission considered whether election offences had increased during the pilots, and local authorities considered whether the system was sufficiently free of security risks before using it, and attempted to assess whether it was sufficiently secure during the election.

Issues like increased verifiability, guaranteed anonymity, and provable security properties were not mentioned among the objectives or evaluations. This is in direct contrast to the strong emphasis placed on these properties by many researchers in the field of e-voting algorithms.

The e-voting systems that were trialled in 2007 were largely remote e-voting systems using the Internet and in some cases the telephone network. The one exception to this was the pilot run by Shrewsbury and Atcham Borough Council, where voting kiosk based advance e-voting was trialled alongside remote e-voting. This advance voting involved voters attending one of two locations, and using the remote voting system through hardware provided for that purpose. A member of staff was present at each location, allowing voters who had not registered for remote e-voting to register immediately before voting.

The e-voting systems used were from three suppliers, resulting in three underlying sets of algorithms being used. The first of these was Scytl's Pnyx.core system, used by Rushmoor Borough Council and South Bucks District Council [15,11] .

This system centered around the use of public key cryptography. Each voter would complete an electronic ballot, which involved using a unique ballot number chosen by the user. This ballot would then be encrypted with a public key for the election administrators and signed with a private key for the voter. The election adminstrators' private key was stored using a threshold cryptography scheme to ensure that a majority of administrators had to be present before any ballots could be decrypted.

The digital signatures would be used, along with voter ID numbers, to verify who had voted and prevent multiple ballots being cast by one voter. However, these digital signatures were stripped away and the ballots were mixed before decryption.

The second system, used by Sheffield City Council and Shrewsbury and Atcham Borough Council [9,10], was provided by Opt2Vote. With this system, a voter ID and password were used to authenticate each voter and the voting information was received via an HTTPS connection as plaintext (from the point of view of the election system). The information received was stored in two databases, with each entry encrypted using the RSA public key algorithm. One database contained the information that, upon decryption, could be used to determine which candidate had been voted for. The other database contained the information that, upon decryption, could be used to link a particular voter to a particular ballot.

The third system, used by Swindon Borough Council [12], was provided by the TCS consortium. With this system, a voter ID and password were used to authenticate each voter; the voting information was then encrypted using the election administrators' public key at the client side and then sent to the election server via HTTPS. The election administrators' private key was stored using a threshold cryptography scheme to ensure that a majority of administrators had to be present at decryption. The decryption software used this private key to decrypt all ballots and provide a count for each candidate. Information linking each voter to their voter identification number was stored separately.

These three systems can be seen to centre around two key sets of algorithms; public key cryptography algorithms and threshold schemes. Both of these sets of algorithms are well understood and have been widely implemented in the past.

No serious failures were reported during any of the trials. There was no request for a recount in any of the areas performing a trial. However, it is noted that the system used by Rushmoor Borough Council had the facility for a recount [4], and that the system used by Sheffield City Council did not [5].

Despite this use of well understood algorithms, and the availability of algorithms that provide a variety of other desirable properties for elections, the Electoral Commission subsequently suspended all further e-voting pilots until further notice. We now look at the issues that contributed to this decision.

4   Analysis of Issues

We begin by considering the three themes that were identified as drivers for the trialling of e-voting; increasing turnout, decreasing cost and improving accessibility. We then look at other issues that arose from the pilots; project issues, security concerns and public trust. This analysis concentrates on issues from the 2007 trials as these trials aimed to build upon knowledge gained from the 2002/3 trials (South Bucks District Council was the only local authority performing a pilot in 2007 that had not previously performed one in 2003) and were the trials that ultimately led to the suspension of further e-voting pilots.

Our decision to concentrate on the 2007 trials is strengthened by the observations in [1] that the 2002 trials had similar turnout and cost issues to those we identify. Further, the desire to increase turnout and the possibility of improving accessibility were identified in [18] when considering why some local authorities chose to run e-voting pilots and others did not during 2002/3.

4.1   Driving Themes

Turnout. General election turnout has fallen from 78.8% in February 1974 to 59% (the lowest figure since 1918) in 2001 [21]. It rose to 61.4% in 2005 [2], but was still considerably lower than the turnout between 1945 and 1992. Local election turnout is usually significantly lower then general election turnout.

Election turnout was increased in four of the areas running trials, but was slightly decreased for Rushmoor Borough Council who had a turnout of 35.2% in 2007 and a turnout of 36% in 2006. Three of the four local authorities that saw an increase in turnout had an increase of 1.5% or less, with only South Bucks District Council seeing an increase of 5.9%.

The percentages of voters who chose to use e-voting systems were 16.3% (equivalent to 5.7% of the total electorate) in South Bucks, 10.2% (equivalent to 4.3% of the total electorate) in Shrewsbury and Atcham, 3.4% (equivalent to 1.2% of the total electorate) in Sheffield, 24.1% (equivalent to 8.5% of the electorate) in Swindon and 18% in Rushmoor (equivalent to 6.3% of the electorate). Further, opinion polls conducted at South Bucks and Shrewsbury and Atcham suggested that only 29% of electronic voters would not have voted if the electronic channel had not been available. (An opinion poll conducted at Swindon gave a figure of 25%.)

These figures did not lead to confidence among the local authorities or the Electoral Commission that these e-voting trials had significantly increased turnout.

Cost. Analysis of the cost of each trial showed a high cost relative to the number of voters who used e-voting. For example, the cost per e-vote cast in Rushmoor was £137, whereas the average cost of casting a vote of any type was £27.26. Similarly, the cost per elector in Swindon of the pilot was £8.33 whereas the cost per elector of a conventional election was £2.30.

It is suggested in [8] however that this high cost may be partly due to the nature of the trials, including a number of one-off costs and expensive short term hosting solutions, and partly due to the low usage of e-voting systems relative to traditional voting methods.

While these results do not necessarily indicate that e-voting would increase costs, they also do not provide any evidence that costs would be reduced if e-voting was adopted. In [8] the Electoral commission state that "despite the high costs of these pilots, it is not possible to conclude that e-voting is inherently or inevitably expensive".

Accessibility. The accessibility theme includes both making voting easier for electors who have difficulty attending a polling station, and making voting easier for electors who have difficulty using the current paper-based voting methods. The first category can be seen to be currently addressed by postal and proxy voting, although there are a number of concerns about postal and proxy voting fraud. This suggests that e-voting is only likely to provide advantages if it is more convenient than postal and proxy voting, or addresses some of the current concerns with these methods.

Postal voting fraud is generally possible because genuine voters can be coerced into voting for a particular candidate. This stems from the removal of the guarantee of privacy when voting, as there is no control over where the voter will fill in the ballot, or who may be with them. While e-voting can do nothing about this possibility, there is some potential to mitigate against it through re-voting. This involves voters being allowed to vote multiple times, and only the last vote being counted as a valid vote. Hence a voter may be coerced into casting a ballot for a particular candidate, and then secretly cast another ballot for their own choice of candidate. Such a system would be hard to implement with physical ballot papers.

Postal, and proxy, voting fraud is also possible through the registration of non-existent voters whose ballots are then cast by the fraudsters. This is an attack on the registration system rather than the voting system, and would not be addressed by e-voting systems.

The second category is one that e-voting has a large potential for. A wide range of software and hardware is already available to assist people with visual or motion impairments in using computers. E-voting systems that are designed to follow compatibly guidelines for this software and hardware provide the potential for electors to leverage solutions that they already use for other online activities.

One major barrier to accessibility in both of these categories during the 2007 trials was the use of postal based registration for e-voting. Electors were required to use a postal channel to register and receive voting credentials. This immediately removed any advantage to electors who have difficulty with paper based communication, and gave the system many of the characteristics of postal voting.

User studies also showed that voting sites were not entirely compatible with software for those with visual impairments, and that the complexity involved in authentication made the system less accessible for some voters [16]. The main issues arising with authentication were the use of different terminology on registration paperwork from that in the actual voting system, and a lack of instructions to advise voters to keep a note of the password that they chose when they filled in the registration paperwork.

Overall Analysis. Examining these three key themes shows a key factor in the failure to date of e-voting in the UK. Trials did not demonstrate that any of the three key drivers for implementing e-voting that had been identified by the local councils beforehand would be achieved.

4.2   Project Issues

The audits performed by and on behalf of the Electoral Commission showed a number of project issues affecting all five of the 2007 trials. Generally, too short a period of time was allowed for the implementation and testing of systems; suppliers generally agreed that six months was required, but each project began around ten weeks before the election date. Key documentation was not produced, or was not thorough enough and quality assurance was only performed around security.

One key risk that was identified across the pilots was that user acceptance testing was scheduled for a time when, if a major fault had been detected, there may not have been sufficient time to resolve the fault before the system was due to be used. There was also a concern that the deletion of data after the election was not witnessed by election officials and hence there was no assurance that the secrecy of the ballot had been maintained [8].

4.3   Security Concerns and Public Trust

Traditionally, public trust in UK elections has been heavily based on the use of independent observers at every stage of the election. Many possible attacks against the integrity of an election are prevented mainly by the fact that observers would notice them taking place.

This provides a large challenge for e-voting systems, where security is largely based on the difficulty of certain mathematical operations and trust in certain pieces of hardware and software, generally perceived to only be understood by a small group of experts. For example, an observer can easily see whether all ballots in a ballot box are emptied onto a table, or several are removed. Observing a piece of computer software failing to count certain ballots is not possible in the same way. Furthermore, there is no guarantee that an observer will be able to detect an error in a cryptographic system even if they should happen to observe some evidence of it.

One possible way of ensuring that there are observers who can understand the underlying security mechanisms of an e-voting system is to employ election officials with the necessary understanding. However, this does not allow any member of the public to verify for themself that the election has been performed fairly; it merely adds a small group of officials who can claim that it has been.

During the 2007 trials, there was confusion among local authorities and election software providers about what should and shouldn't be observable. Some observers were prevented from seeing what was happening on the screens of computers used to tally ballots in the count. Some operations were performed without observers present and system changes were made by election staff to resolve technical problems [17].

A further safeguard in traditional elections is provided by the number of people who would have to collaborate to compromise the result. Guaranteeing a fraudulent result in a large election is likely to involve the changing or miscounting of a large number of paper based ballots, a very difficult task without collaboration between a large number of people in specific positions.

The concept of insubvertibility was introduced in [19] as a measure of "how much trust the voter is expected to place in how few people". Insubvertibility is estimated by dividing the number of people who would have to collaborate to commit a specific fraud by the number of votes that could be subverted by this fraud.

Insubvertibility is likely to be low in any electronic voting system where it is possible for a small number of people to collaborate to make changes to the system, unless the results are independently verifiable, as, without verifiability, system changes can completely change the numbers of votes cast for each candidate.

5   Implications for Bringing Algorithms to Life in General

This analysis of the trialling of e-voting in the UK leads us to two key observations about the process of moving from an established algorithm to a real-world system.

Firstly, all the requirements of the real-world system must be explicitly modelled, rather than assuming that they will proceed from the system. It is our belief that e-voting systems do have the potential to increase the accessibility and hence the turnout of elections, while reducing the cost through the automation of time consuming tasks. However, none of these properties are inherent in any of the algorithms on which the systems used in the 2007 e-voting trials were based.

We also note a clear example of a requirements conflict in the systems changes during a live election described in [17]. Here, an emergency solution to the requirement for availability of the system during the count conflicted with the requirement for observers to be able to verify the fairness of the election by observing that the system had not been tampered with. Explicit modelling of the verification requirements would have identified that the system must not reach any state needing this emergency solution.

Secondly, explicit or implicit assumptions must not be relied upon unless it can be shown that practical concerns do not invalidate them. A prime example of this from the e-voting trials is the use of public key cryptography to allow voters to digitally sign votes in the trials run by Rushmoor Borough Council and South Bucks District Council. Public key signing algorithms have been shown to be secure if certain mathematical assumptions hold, and if the private key is known only to the individual it belongs to. However, for accessibility reasons, the system used during the Rushmoor pilot generated each voter's private key at the server and then sent it to the client via HTTPS. This immediately invalidates the assumption that the private key will only be known to the voter.

We believe that these two principles are not unique to e-voting in the UK, and are likely to be relevant whenever an attempt is made to move from an algorithm with a proven set of properties to a real world system designed to solve a particular set of problems.

References

1. The Electoral Commission. Modernising elections a strategic evaluation of the 2002 pilot schemes (2002), http://www.electoralcommission.org.uk/files/dms/Modernising_elections_6574-6170__E__N__S__W__.pdf
2. The Electoral Commission. General elections - 2005 election results (2005)
3. The Electoral Commission. Ballot secrecy factsheet (2006)
4. The Electoral Commission. Electoral pilot scheme evaluation: Rushmoor borough council (2007),
http://www.electoralcommission.org.uk/__data/assets/electoral_commission_pdf_file/0008/13211/Rushmoorstatutoryevaluationreport_27184-20104__E__N__S__W__.pdf
5. The Electoral Commission. Electoral pilot scheme evaluation: Sheffield city council (2007), http://www.electoralcommission.org.uk/__data/assets/electoral_commission_pdf_file/0009/13212/Sheffieldstatutoryevaluationreport_27185-20105__E__N__S__W__.pdf
6. The Electoral Commission. Electoral pilot scheme evaluation: Shrewsbury and atcham borough council (2007),
http://www.electoralcommission.org.uk/__data/assets/electoral_commission_pdf_file/0010/13213/Shrewsburystatutoryevaluationreport_27212-20106__E__N__S__W__.pdf
7. The Electoral Commission. Electoral pilot scheme evaluation: Swindon borough council (2007),
http://www.electoralcommission.org.uk/__data/assets/electoral_commission_pdf_file/0014/13217/Swindonstatutoryevaluationreport_27190-20110__E__N__S__W__.pdf
8. The Electoral Commission. Electronic voting:may 2007 electoral pilot schemes (2007), http://www.electoralcommission.org.uk/__data/assets/electoral_commission_pdf_file/0008/13220/Electronicvotingsummarypaper_27194-20114__E__N__S__W__.pdf
9. The Electoral Commission. Technical evaluation of sheffield city council e-voting pilot (2007), http://www.electoralcommission.org.uk/__data/assets/electoral_commission_pdf_file/0020/16193/Actica_Sheffield_27247-20138__E__N__S__W__.pdf
10. The Electoral Commission. Technical evaluation of shrewsbury and atcham borough council e-voting pilot (2007), http://www.electoralcommission.org.uk/__data/assets/electoral_commission_pdf_file/0003/16194/Actica_SABC_27246-20139__E__N__S__W__.pdf
11. The Electoral Commission. Technical evaluation of south bucks district council e-voting pilot (2007), http://www.electoralcommission.org.uk/__data/assets/electoral_commission_pdf_file/0004/16195/Actica_South_Bucks_27243-20140__E__N__S__W__.pdf
12. The Electoral Commission. Technical evaluation of swindon borough council e-voting pilot (2007), http://www.electoralcommission.org.uk/__data/assets/electoral_commission_pdf_file/0005/16196/Actica_Swindon_27245-20141__E__N__S__W__.pdf
13. The Electoral Commission. Managing a uk parliamentary general election guidance for (acting) returning officers (2009)
14. The Electoral Commission. Local elections in england and wales: Guidance for candidates and agents (2012)

15. Actica Consulting. Technical evaluation of rushmoor borough council e-voting pilot (2007), http://www.electoralcommission.org.uk/__data/assets/electoral_commission_pdf_file/0019/16192/Actica_Rushmoor_27248-20137__E__N__S__W__.pdf

16. PA Consulting. Connected2voting an evaluation of accessibility of the local election pilots (2007), http://www.electoralcommission.org.uk/__data/assets/electoral_commission_pdf_file/0006/16197/MainReportAugust2007_27281-20157__E__N__S__W__.pdf

17. Kitcat, J., Brown, I.: Observing the english and scottish 2007 e-elections. Parliamentary Affairs 61, 380–395 (2008)

18. Liptrott, M.: e-voting in the uk: A work in progress. Electronic Journal of E-Government 4(2), 55–62 (2006)

19. Randell, B., Ryan, P.Y.A.: Voting technologies and trust. IEEE Security & Privacy 4(5), 50–56 (2006)

20. White, I., Coleman, C.: Postal voting and electoral fraud - commons library standard note. House of Commons Library (2011)

21. Wilks-Heeg, S.: Treating voters as an afterthought? the legacies of a decade of electoral modernisation in the united kingdom. The Political Quarterly 80, 101–110 (2009)

Analysis of Issues and Challenges
of E-Voting in the UK
(Transcript of Discussion)

Dylan Clarke

University of Newcastle

My name is Dylan Clarke and I'm from Newcastle University. I've been working with Feng Hao on the self-enforcing e-voting system that you saw earlier, and this is another piece of work that is connected to that project. When we started off, we weren't just looking at what desirable properties can that system provide, and what can it do for elections. We also started looking at the fact that we don't have e-voting in the UK, despite it having been trialled before, and we wanted to investigate why don't we have it, and what's stopped us from having it.

So to introduce the subject, e-voting was trialled in the UK in 2002, 2003 and 2007. In 2008 the Electoral Commission recommended all further trials be suspended; they were, and as of now e-voting isn't in use. We're looking at why isn't it in use and I'm going to consider four areas.

First I'll examine issues to do with the UK election system that are relevant to e-voting. Then I'll look at the 2007 trials; I won't be particularly covering the 2002 and 2003 trials, because the 2007 trials were supposed to build on them, and a lot of the issues are similar between the two sets of trials. Then I'll be analysing some of the issues that came out of the trials, and finally looking at some insights from the analysis.

The basic principles behind voting in the UK, putting things together from a few different sources, are that each voter is entitled to one vote that's cast purely based on their own conscience without any possibility of coercion from others. Now historically this hasn't always been the case, for example, before secret ballots were introduced in 1872 we had open elections where each person would tell the returning officer who they wanted to vote for. This was considered a good thing in that it was very hard for the integrity to be compromised in an election in terms of your vote being recorded incorrectly, because everybody present could hear who you asked to vote for. However, one of the big problems was that a lot of working class people ended up voting for whoever either their employer or their landlord, which in some cases was the same person, wanted them to. This was because if you didn't vote for who your employer wanted you to you could lose your job, and if you didn't vote for who your landlord wanted you to you could lose your home. So, to combat this, the Ballot Act was introduced; Secret ballots were brought in, and then you could safely vote for whoever you wanted, then go and tell your employer, "yes, I voted for who you said," when actually you'd voted for whoever you wanted to.

B. Christianson et al. (Eds.): Security Protocols 2012, LNCS 7622, pp. 136–144, 2012.
© Springer-Verlag Berlin Heidelberg 2012

Now that wasn't the only thing that was needed to make elections coercion free, and there's been a lot of other legislation over the years.

There are three key themes that arise from the legislation. First of all is integrity; things that have been done to make sure that elections can't be fixed, and the main way that's done in the UK system is making every step other than actually writing on the ballot paper observable. For example, there's a picture here of ballot counting at the Brighton and Hove election in 2007, and as you can see there are independent observers watching the counting taking place. Now obviously this doesn't make it impossible for somebody to change some ballot papers, but it gives a high chance that they will be detected. Also, if somebody was going to change some ballot papers at this stage, they might be able to feasibly get away with changing a couple of ballot papers, but they're not going to be able to take a thousand ballot papers and change them. And at all stages of the election, other than when you actually mark your ballot, independent observers are allowed to be present.

The second theme is anonymity and privacy, the idea that nobody can know who you voted for. But one interesting thing about the UK system, especially compared to what tends to be done in e-voting systems, is that, in the UK system this is a legal protection, it's not intrinsic to the system, and in fact the legislation says that it can't be intrinsic to the system. At present, each ballot paper has to be numbered, and a list has to be kept of which ballot paper corresponds to which person. The two lists are kept sealed separately, and an Election Court or the House of Commons can order them to be opened if an election is challenged. So, to somebody with the right degree of power in the right circumstances there is no anonymity, but in practice there is because of the way that the lists are kept and the legal controls on opening them.

The third theme is that expenses and what promotional materials can be used are controlled to stop somebody influencing the election because of personal wealth, or because of things that they said about other candidates.

When it comes to actual voting we use polling stations (the actual election terminology allows several polling stations to be located in one polling place, but the phrase polling station tends to be used in everyday speech to mean polling place) and typically there's about one to two thousand people per polling station. To avoid any sort of influence due to people not being able to get to vote, there has to be a polling station sufficiently local to each voter so that they're not inconvenienced. But a consequence of this, and the need to verify people and stop them voting twice, is that each voter can only use the polling station they're allocated to. This could be inconvenient in some cases; For example, normally you would go to the polling station closest to where you live, but if you are working away then on that day you will still be expected to go back to that polling station. Now as a solution for voters who are unable to attend a polling station there are postal and proxy votes. A postal vote is a fairly simple idea, you fill in a ballot paper and you send it in through the post with safeguards such as using a signature, and having two envelopes for anonymity. A proxy vote is where somebody else attends and votes for your with your permission, supposedly voting for the candidate you've told them to, although you have no way of checking this.

Most concerns around elections in the UK centre around postal voting fraud. One way that postal voting fraud has happened in the past is that somebody has registered non-existent people for postal votes, which is harder to check than if they were voting in person. For example, a candidate was caught having suddenly had a large number of people move into his small house just before an election and all registering for postal votes, and then not being able to produce them. The other possibility with postal voting fraud is people getting hold of other people's postal votes, or coercing them into filling them in in a particular way because, as has been mentioned previously, you've not got the protection of the election booth.

Now we'll look at the 2007 e-voting trials. There were five trials performed; these weren't the only trials performed in that year's elections, these were five trials of e-voting, run at the same time as trials of electronic counting and various other schemes. The trials were performed during live local elections of councillors. In each case people were allowed to choose either to vote electronically, or get a postal vote, or just vote at the polling station. The five areas were Rushmoor, Sheffield, Shrewsbury and Atcham, South Bucks and Swindon, and there's a map here showing their locations. They were fairly well distributed around the mainland UK, although there seems a bit of an absence of them in the north.

Each local authority was allowed to set its own objectives for the trial and its own criteria for evaluating the trial, as well the Electoral Commission evaluating them. Across these objectives and evaluation criteria there were three key themes that we identified. The first was to improve the turnout, the second was to reduce cost, and the third was to improve accessibility. Improving turnout is desirable because there's been such a decline in the number of people voting over about the last sixty years, and this has been thought to be a problem for democracy, so they'd like to get more people voting, and one theory was that inconvenience was one of the things stopping people. Reducing costs is always a factor for local authorities, they would like to be able to do more with the money that they've got, or to charge less tax. The final theme was to improve accessibility both for people who couldn't attend on the day and for people with physical impairments.

Now it's interesting that increasing security above that of paper-based elections wasn't given as an objective. There was mention of not reducing the security, and not wanting fraud to occur, but nowhere was there an objective of making it more secure, or making it verifiable, or putting in systemic anonymity, or putting in any sort of provable security properties, which I think is quite interesting because these are the kind of things we tend to look at from a research perspective.

The trials mainly used remote e-voting. Shrewsbury and Atcham also had advance voting, which was basically e-voting on some computers provided by the local authority in several locations of theirs with staff to help voters use them. This was offered for a certain length of time before the paper based election started.

The local authorities trialling e-voting used systems that came from three suppliers. All of these systems centered around public key and threshold cryptography schemes. They generally weren't verifiable. The idea in all of them was that a member of the public would vote (in one case they would sign their vote by using a public key scheme, in the others they would just send it to the authority via HTTPS without a signature), the vote would be stored in a database (encrypted with a public key from the local authority), and then later a tallying system would get these ballots from the database, mix them, and then perform the tallying. To do this they would need keys from three out of five administrators for the election.

No major failures occurred in any of the trials, and yet all further trials were suspended, and to date

Matt Blaze: No, detected rather than occurred.

Reply: Yes, that's true definitely, there were none detected. As far as the trials were concerned, they said no failures occurred, because a lot of their criteria were things like, no security breach will be detected.

Matt Blaze: I know how to meet that requirement.

Reply: I suspect some of the local authorities did as well.

Now, if we go back to the systems themselves, they were based around public key cryptography and threshold cryptography, which are fairly well tested, and not things that have just been invented five minutes ago, and yet still the trials failed. That's what I want to look at next: what were the problems?

So first of all we looked at the trials in light of the three criteria we saw earlier: Did they improve the turnout, did they reduce costs, and did they improve accessibility. Then we looked at project issues, security concerns and public trust.

Now, on the turnout side, there were small increases in turnout, except in Rushmoor where the turnout decreased. In South Bucks it increased by 5.9%, in the others by 1.5% or less. However, the percentage of voters who chose to use e-voting varied from 10.2% to 24.1%, and of those people, opinion polls suggested that only 25% to 29% of them wouldn't have voted if e-voting wasn't available. There was also some suggestion at the time that some people who said they wouldn't have voted without e-voting possibly would have voted anyway, it was just that they found e-voting a lot more convenient. So, this certainly doesn't show that e-voting wouldn't improve turnout, but from these trials we just can't tell. It certainly didn't give local authorities or the Electoral Commission confidence that e-voting increased turnout. There was also some sociological analysis with suggestions that the issues causing low turnout weren't about convenience anyway; If somebody doesn't think that the democratic process makes a difference to their life, no matter how convenient you make it for them to vote then they're probably not going to.

The next thing we looked at was cost. Each trial showed there was a high cost relative to the number of voters who used e-voting. First of all we'll look at the cost per vote cast: For each e-vote, the cost was £137, whereas, if you just average all the votes, including the e-voting ones, it was £27.26 per vote.

Now partly this is because of the low numbers of people who voted, so if you actually look at it across all the people who could choose to vote, as is done here in Swindon, e-voting cost per person who could vote was £8.33, whereas the cost in a conventional election was £2.30 per person who could vote. So even then you're talking a big increase. However, the high level of costs were affected by large one-off development costs. Also, the trials were quite short-term, and as a result the hosting costs were very expensive, and the low usage pushed up the average cost. Although of course it didn't when it came to the cost per elector, that's only when we're looking at the cost for e-votes cast.

The trials don't prove that e-voting is more expensive, but they also don't prove that it's less expensive. I think the Electoral Commission said something along the lines of, "these trials have shown that it is not inevitable that e-voting will push up the cost of elections". Now this is a problem when you're looking to reduce the cost of the elections. Also there were suggestions that it would be possible to make things a lot cheaper by having it set up once, and then using one supplier for every local authority. But then you've got the problem that you don't have diversity across the systems, and a break in the systems is a break everywhere, rather than it being a break at one local authority. There's also been the argument put forward that e-voting at present

Jonathan Anderson: I was just going to ask how much of the labour that goes into running an election counting paper ballots and stuff is volunteer versus professional?

Reply: It's all paid.

Jonathan Anderson: Really, everybody who sits in a polling station and watches is paid to be there?

Reply: Yes, though a lot of them are actually local authority staff who get the day off from their ordinary job and get paid to do that as well.

Joseph Bonneau: So they're getting double pay?

Reply: I think so. I knew people who worked for a local authority who would be off for the day to do a polling session, and they had to get permission to have the day for it.

James Malcolm: And other people from the community, they're all paid, but they don't have to be local authority staff, it's just a convenient source.

Sandy Clark: What about training costs, do you have to train the polling staff?

Reply: Yes, there are training courses as well.

Jonathan Anderson: It's £2.30 per vote when everybody involved in the system is being paid to be there.

Reply: That was £2.30 per person who could have voted.

Paul Syverson: They could be paid like juries are in the US, it's not at the minimum wage, but you are paid a per diem.

Jonathan Anderson: Yes, so is this the wage or is it, "thanks for coming, here's £10 to buy lunch"?

Reply: It depends whether you're a polling clerk or a presiding officer, I can't remember exactly what the amount is, but I know it was considered worth doing for local authority staff, it was a nice bonus.

Bruce Christianson: The only people who aren't paid are the representatives of the political parties who act as scrutineers.

Jonathan Anderson: They're paid in other ways.

Bruce Christianson: They are paid in other ways.

Reply: So the other issue then of cost is that in all the trials, and in any possibilities suggested for the future, people who want to vote at a polling station will still be allowed to. This means that we have to have polling stations local to everybody who might want to vote, so the question then becomes, which staff can you actually get rid of if you've got e-voting? Admittedly, when it comes to counting the ballots then if there are fewer ballots being cast you need fewer staff to count them, but then again, if you don't know how many are going to be cast you still need the staff to handle the maximum number, so there are a lot of questions about cost there.

The third criteria is accessibility. There are two categories of people who accessibility is an issue for. First are people who can't attend the polling station, and the second are people who have difficulty using paper ballots. The first category is already addressed by postal and proxy voting, but as I said earlier, there are concerns about fraud. Postal vote fraud could be coercion or it could be the registration of fake voters.

E-voting does have a partial solution for coercion where postal voting doesn't: allowing people to change their vote. For example, you could allow yourself to be coerced into casting a vote online for a particular candidate, and then two days later you could change your vote, and the person who coerced you wouldn't know. Admittedly, in some cases they might do if you live with them and they control your access to the computer. This of course doesn't do anything about vote selling. The registration system is a separate issue, e-voting doesn't solve that at all, and it would have to be addressed separately.

Now when it comes to people who have difficulty using paper-based ballots, e-voting obviously can offer a lot of benefits because you can use standard screen readers and other accessibility devices on your computer. However, in the trials people were required to fill in a paper-based form and post it in to get their access credentials, which meant anybody who has trouble filling in a paper-based form will have exactly the same problems. Also, in the trials a lot of the software wasn't entirely compatible with all screen readers.

Then we come to project issues. There was a lot said about too short a period of time being allowed for implementation. Most of the vendors said it would normally take them six months to produce an e-voting system, and they were given ten weeks for operational reasons. This was due to the system being approved at quite a late date, when there was already a fixed date set for the election. Also, there were a lot of problems with key documentation not being produced. These were things like the risk documents. Also quality assurance was only performed around security, not around accessibility or availability in a lot of cases, and that again was down to time constraints. User acceptance testing was performed so near to go-live dates that if the systems had failed the user acceptance testing, the trials wouldn't have been able to go ahead when they'd already been publicised, which was felt to have put some pressure on the people doing the testing to make sure that the system passed.

Finally, we'll look at security issues and public trust. Traditionally public trust is based on the use of independent observers at all stages of an election, whereas e-voting is making people rely on mathematics, hardware and software. The average member of the public can understand what a ballot box looks like, and can see if somebody is interfering with it, or if somebody's disappearing ballot papers up their sleeve while they're counting them. However, if you asked them to evaluate whether a cryptographic scheme is secure or not, they're not going to know. There are also issues when it comes to observability. There's a short video here of observers at the Brighton and Hove count, showing people walking around as the counting activity is happening. They can see roughly what's going on and check that nothing untoward is happening. Whereas next we have a simulation of what we could observe in the tallying of an e-voting system. The computer is sat there. We don't know whether this is correctly tallying ballots or doing nothing, or

Paul Syverson: Well you could still hire a watcher.

Jonathan Anderson: So they don't lose their jobs.

Matt Blaze: What is the historical threat in the UK of election related fraud? Is there a history of fraud, who commits it, is it for local council elections, or parliamentary elections?

Reply: Generally, looking historically, there isn't that much, however recently, especially in local authorities, there has been a lot of postal voting fraud occurring.

Matt Blaze: And chiefly in local elections?

Reply: Yes. There have also been a few instances of other irregularities to do with people making false allegations against other candidates in literature and things like that. And it has seemed to be candidates, or friends of candidates, behind it.

Now one possibility is to employ election staff with cryptographic and computer engineering knowledge, have them look at the system as it's running and look at the source code beforehand, but that doesn't quite give us what we've got now. It doesn't let any member of the public verify for themself that the election is fair to a reasonable degree by looking at it. Instead they have to trust that group of staff.

During the 2007 trials there was confusion amongst some authorities as to what observers should be allowed to see. For example, in one of the trials originally they told observers that they would be able to see the server room. They were then told on the day that they couldn't. Some observers were allowed to take photographs around computers, some weren't.

There was also confusion about what the analogues to observation in a traditional election were. For example, in a traditional election you can see the counting going on, but you obviously can't go and look at the numbers on the back of the ballot papers. One local authority took the equivalent to be that observers were not allowed to see anything that happened on the computer screen, which seems to be a bit of a problem if you're trying to verify e-voting is working properly.

Also there were some things that could be described as ridiculous in the trials. For example, one authority had given instructions that no member of the vendor staff was to talk to any observer, so if the observers had a question they had to ask a member of election staff, who had to then go over and ask the relevant person from the vendor, and then come back and tell them the answer that they'd been given. Also, system changes were seen to be made by election staff and by vendor staff to resolve technical problems during the elections. Now this was done when there were problems with computers doing the tallying, but it immediately adds some risk if you've got an election being run on a supposedly secure computer, that somebody's changing the software, putting in USB sticks, changing to another computer in the middle of the count.

Also, in traditional elections, you need a lot of people to collaborate to guarantee a fraudulent result. It would take a large number of the observers to get together to ignore fraud, and to block other observers from seeing it, or you'd need all the staff at a polling station to get together to change the ballot papers. Conversely, in electronic elections you only need a few people to collaborate to change the system, unless the results are publicly verifiable.

Finally we looked at a couple of implications of the trials. The first was that all the requirements of the real-world system need to be explicitly modelled, and this was illustrated by a requirements conflict in South Bucks. Availability in an election is vital, if the election doesn't go forward the local authority running it has big problems, and an election not going forward can even cause rioting.

During the trial in South Bucks the tallying computer stopped working. Now the solution if, for example, you were dealing with data relating to bins that hadn't been collected would be to bring someone in from the vendor, change things round a bit on the computer, sort the software out, and fix any bugs. Yet when you do that in a live election you've immediately got a huge trust problem.

The second big implication we saw from the trials was that explicit or implicit assumptions mustn't be relied upon unless it can be shown that practical concerns don't invalidate them. For example, Rushmoor were using public key cryptography for signatures to prove that the ballots came from the particular voters. This seemed like quite a good idea. However, there were usability concerns that a lot of voters might not be able to generate their own keys, so it was decided that the vendor would generate the keys for them, and then give them their keys online when they asked for the ballot. So, these keys that the vendors had all the time would be used to authenticate that the ballot definitely only came from the voter.

Another assumption that was made implicitly was cost reduction. It was assumed that if we put computers in there it will make it more efficient and it will cost less. In practice it didn't, and there are questions about whether it could.

Finally, there was accessibility. Again there was the implicit assumption that it will become accessible if you use computers, but then that assumption wasn't fed into the actual development as a requirement to make sure that the systems developed were accessible.

That pretty much concludes this presentation, are there any further questions?

Michael Roe: You didn't say much about the registration process and I wonder if also there's possible attacks on registration, for example, rather than coercing a voter to vote a particular way, you can coerce them either to not vote or not go to the polling booth, I just wondered if you saw any big difference in the spirit of that kind of front in the process of a change to e-voting?

Reply: There are some possible advantages in that. For example, if people go into the polling station obviously it's easier to see if somebody's attended a polling station if you told them not to, rather than to see if they've accessed a site on the Internet from any computer.

Just to say a bit more about registration in general, the registration system probably is where the biggest problems are at the moment. It's relatively easy to get fake voters registered, as well as to stop people from registering. And to give a personal example, I currently have a voting card at home which I'm going to have to return. It's addressed to my ex-girlfriend who moved out of the property around six months ago. She has a voting card at her new property as well. The two voting cards are for different polling stations so in theory I could send a female friend along with the voting card to vote in a local election.

The Electoral Commission has actually said one of the things that they want in place before e-voting is trialled again, is an individual registration system rather than a household one, which will improve a lot of those things.

Protocol Governance: The Elite, or the Mob?

Ross Anderson

University of Cambridge

My talk will be about the life that protocols acquire once they start evolving in a competitive environment. Why is the CA infrastructure so totally broken? Why are the APIs of hardware security modules almost unfixable? The answer, I will argue, is that the interface between the crypto layer and the comsec layer is becoming unmanageable because of conflicts of interest, governance failures at scale, asymmetric information and assorted externalities — in other words, a bundle of security-economics issues.

Worse, the evolution that happens under lobbying pressure may be good for the lobbyists, but it's bad for resilience. Suppose that there were some benevolent deity (say, the world-wide web consortium) that could respond to a failure by mandating changes. Suppose now that the infrastructure breaks because of a change sought by lobbyists — for example, the expansion of the number of CAs from half a dozen to 600 as firms either coveted a share of Verisign's monopoly rent, or just wished to avoid paying it. But if the lobbyists knew that W3C could deprive them of their gains, they would have made it a target too. So it's hard to design a governance structure to repair the security damage done by lobbying. I propose this as a crypto policy equivalent of the old adage that "power corrupts, while absolute power corrupts absolutely".

The implications for robust and sustainable crypto design are fascinating. Lobbyists tackle concentrations of power, and are less effective where power is spread — as when democracies elect new governments. Can we come up with governance structures in which crowdsourced bugfixes can prevail over special interests? We've seen one or two humorous examples in the past (such as Matt Blaze's "Angry Mob Cryptanalysis"); but what might a real implementation of democratic security look like?

B. Christianson et al. (Eds.): Security Protocols 2012, LNCS 7622, p. 145, 2012.
© Springer-Verlag Berlin Heidelberg 2012

Protocol Governance: The Elite, or the Mob? (Transcript of Discussion)

Ross Anderson

University of Cambridge

The topic that I suggested when we were asked for abstracts and talk titles back in January was "Protocol governance: the elite, or the mob?". And sustainability is very fashionable these days so let's ask ourselves whether protocols are sustainable. We've had one or two comments from previous speakers that all protocols tend towards failure because of environmental changes. I agree with that entirely. We've been discussing for over a year now in various fora why the CA infrastructure is so broken; there was a wonderful panel at financial crypto last year with a chap from Mozilla having to defend himself against a room full of annoyed people. Why is it that security APIs are almost unfixable? Some of us have looked at that a lot at Cambridge.

Well I think we understand that in these cases the interface has become unmanageable because of economic and political failures. There's asymmetric information, there's other externalities, there's conflicts of interest, and there are governance failures at scale. Now up until now we've talked about security economics, but when you start talking about large scale-governance failures, that gets you into the realm of politics. So I wonder if there are any ideas we can pinch from leafing through a few books on political theory.

A bit more background: a couple of things that we've done in the last five years. The failure of PIN entry device tamper resistance: it turned out that devices that were certified to be secure weren't, and a couple of bad guys got access to a warehouse in Dubai where PIN entry devices paused to catch breath on route from the factory in China to the distribution chain in Europe – and put wicked electronics in them. They got caught, they got arrested, and they should have been tried last October. But they got off because the banks would not bring evidence against them. The certification regime is still as broken as ever, nobody has the incentive to fix it; just pretend that things are secure when they're not.

Then there's the No-PIN vulnerability, which we talked about a couple of years ago; one bank tried to fix it and then abandoned the fix. Two weeks ago I was at a Payment Systems Economics Conference in America and the chap from the European Payments Council was speaking. So afterwards I asked him, "Well what about all these EMV vulnerabilities, when are you going to do something to fix them?" He'd been talking about how the EPC would help governance and the payments base. No, he didn't want to know. He didn't even want to discuss the topic; he said, "that's the banks' problem, not our problem".

So this tends to convince us that economics and politics are often too hard.

Another of the inputs to this thinking was a wonderful talk that I heard Eric Rescorla gave at Indocrypt 2011, last December. He said, why are all the fixes to

B. Christianson et al. (Eds.): Security Protocols 2012, LNCS 7622, pp. 146–160, 2012.
© Springer-Verlag Berlin Heidelberg 2012

TLS, in his words, "stone knives and bearskins"? You've still got all these attacks like Bleichenbacher's attack, and Klima's attack, which should have been fixed by moving to another ciphersuite with OAEP. Instead they fixed it by messing around with error messages. MD5 collisions – dealt with by sequence number randomisation rather than moving to SHA256; BEAST, well don't even ask! And even things that were anticipated well in advance, like AES, for which plug-and-play design provision was made, they're still not there on almost half of the servers on the Internet. What's happening is that you've got two sided effects which are so serious and the scale is so large that you end up having to do one-sided hacks. There just aren't the appropriate control points where you can win, and challenge, and contest what's been done at the moment.

OK, so where do we get into politics? Suppose you have a benevolent monarch who could mandate upgrades. This is presumably how you would do TLS if you had a world government. A world government would just say, TLS 1.0 is evil, and as of the 1st July anybody caught using it will be dragged off in handcuffs. Now the problem that we have is that many of the failures of protocols, APIs, and security architectures, result from lobbying. A good example here is the expansion of the CA universe from three firms to 600 firms, which led to all the problems that we had with Komodo, and Diginotar, and others. And the problem we have here is that if you had a world government then the world government's court would be absolutely chock full of lobbyists, and the place would be even bigger than DC and there would be even more lawyers, there would be even more corporate officers, and there would be even more shining parties and grand lunches. And the lobbyists would tout the mark 2, right? Because lobbyists operate best where there's a concentration of power. So the insight is that this is the crypto equivalent of "power corrupts", and "absolute power corrupts absolutely". So if the W3C really could dictate protocols then you would see it starting to rot in the same way that the national capital of any powerful country starts to become infested with the lobbyists.

So what sort of governance evolution might we expect in the protocols world? What sort of stuff gets done in politics to stop governments rotting, to see to it that countries persist, not just over a generation or so, but over centuries? Are there any ideas that we can pinch?

Well when you read through your primer on political theory you see that human governance systems have tended to evolve through a number of different models. There are dozens and dozens of these, and there are different political theoreticians who have put forward different taxonomies, but wherever you look you can find some rather interesting and suggestive ideas. For example, as soon as we have animal husbandry or agriculture, you see the rise of chiefdoms where hunting bands would coalesce into a larger unit and come under the control of one particular guy and his family. And this is, if you like, early ARPANET, run by a guy in California, or local sysadmins at your local computer laboratory. There's a boss sysadmin who is in effect the chief of that particular chiefdom, and who resolves all problems.

And then of course you get kingdoms when these start to scale up. I remember one of the first email systems I used was Prestel, about 25 odd years ago, and you end up with proprietary systems that have a bit more real interface to other users. Now if you go back to the 16th century there were certainly individuals who travelled in England, and Spain, and France, and so on, and there were certainly individuals in the mid-1980s who used more than one system, and I've used CompuServe as well as Prestel, but the only way you could ship stuff between them was by downloading it to your home computer and then uploading it to the other system.

What happens when things come together into a big empire? Well there's the Confucian system where the idea is that you have stability from hierarchy. You also get meritocracy, you get lots of really bright vice-presidents, and assistant vice-presidents, and so on, running the organisation. You've got loyalty to the organisation and bosses, and you promote social harmony by means of personal relationships.

Sandy Clark: What Virgil talked about?

Reply: Well it's reminiscent of the last Silicon Valley firm that may shortly be doing an IPO – athough I've never seen Facebook discussed in the context of being essentially a Confucian system of organising the world! I don't know if our Chinese guests will have any comments on that at question time. Anyway you start looking at politics and protocols, you can look at early democracy. Democracy emerged in Athens when they had a series of revolutions following a pattern where a good king would be followed by his son a bad king, there'd be an uprising, and the leader of the uprising would become the new good king, his son would be a wastrel, there'd be an uprising, and so on. And people said, well surely there's a less expensive way of changing the government than having a civil war every two generations, so that they got the idea that we put little pot shards together and decide things that way. Bulletin boards, multi-user dungeons, and so on, are run, or were run, using citizen democracy of the kind of that we hear written about in Athens where every citizen would gather together in the Agora and business would be done there. Enlightenment? Well perhaps the Internet, and Usenet, connecting everything together, trying to run things on a rational basis, without perhaps as much experience at the beginning as we now have. Industrial Revolution, you can talk about web commerce, and TLS, and so on. Maybe PGP could be described as being a Chartist sort of movement.

OK, so what do we see as the players now? Well, how do we, as a practical matter, fix bad rules and replace rotten institutions in the online world nowadays? Well the first thing you notice is that emergent multi-nationals fix local failures. This has been happening of course since the 19th century, but in our particular world, you see for example, Google trying to fix the CA problem by simply being aware of every certificate that's ever been seen anywhere in the world, and applying appropriate rules to try and detect attacks. You see Facebook trying to fix the problem of passwords by combining passwords with surveillance and other combinatorial techniques to crack down on large-scale spam. There is another series of approaches where there's a community of peer players. For example, the 20-odd, or thereabouts, transit providers that we used to have until two or three years ago, more or less peers, and the chief geeks would meet at Nanog and cause the world to work, at least at the BGP level, very much in the same way that 20 fishermen at a Turkish fishing village would meet in the tea house and decide, "we will have the following fishing patches for next year, and they will rotate in the following manner."

And then of course there have been many attempts by nation states to get involved, most of which have been false starts. There is now the possibility that something might come along if DNSSEC starts taking over from traditional TLS CAs as the way in which you stake your claim to your domain, and it's also beginning to be looked at as a very plausible way to manage keys for BGP SEC that some people are starting to look at. Now if each top level domain can run its affairs as it sees fit, then the various national domains, .uk, .de, .pk, and so on, can in some sense get what we want or deserve. If they decide that they're going to knock out a domain if somebody for example has a website that says something rude about Kamal Ataturk, then they're perfectly entitled to do so, and that website can migrate to .de, or .uk, or .london, or .google. There's some interesting competition when you start seeing local authorities and large corporations wanting their own top level domain, as is now starting to happen. So perhaps this isn't quite the key role for nation states online, because nation states aren't going to be very good at competing with companies. Companies are better at writing software. But if you've got an arrangement like this with a hybrid corporate/nation-state approach to managing group trust at the top level, then at least you start to get the private and social interests reasonably well-aligned, unlike in the world of CAs at present where things are basically a race to the bottom.

OK, so how can we cut through this and try and figure out some first principles that might guide us? Well we've all read Rousseau and his social contract from the time of the Enlightenment. But the question when you start talking about a social contract is how is the choice made, how do people consent to the contract? And of course the mechanism we've got to do that is the election, and there are various methodological questions that you can raise about elections: Arrow's impossibility theorem and so on.

A minimal view comes from Karl Popper. Popper simply says that you shouldn't expect anything more from an election than the fact that it's a bloodless coup; when people get fed up with the rascals in power they can throw the bums out and get the other lot of bums in without actually having to have thousands of dead people in the streets. It's simply a pure reincarnation of the idea that the ancient Athenians had two and a half thousand years ago. An objection to Popper's idea was a nice article a year or so ago by Michael Portillo, saying that without political parties you can't get the breadth and the depth for a real run at it, because in order to be a credible government in waiting, you have to have enough people together, have sufficient diversity of experience and skills, and enough staff to come up with credible position papers on all sorts of issues of interest to various interest groups. And so in practice, when you look at any real democracy, it's a means of swapping out one layer of an existing government, for a government in waiting.

In other words, I might put it this way: there's a contestable layer, which is typically the Legislature, and in America also the Executive, which supports political parties that are alternative governments. And then it's got one or more permanent layers in the civil service and in the judiciary, and how I've heard this described by a distinguished lawyer is that, although there's nothing in the machinery of a state that is fixed forever, the whole point is that some of the wheels turn at different speeds. And so if you do get a sudden rush of blood to the head, as a number of countries did after 9/11 for example, there are still sheet anchors that stop the thing being pulled too far off course. These end up in things like constitutions.

Can we apply this insight to problems like we have with TLS, or for that matter which we have with the security APIs? In the case of TLS' slowly changing layers, unfortunately the layers which rot, the things that are difficult to change because of the way TLS is designed, are things like ciphersuites, which are supposedly pluggable in theory, but turn out to be not pluggable in practice. And so the thing that we would like to be able to replace on a contestable basis is very, very hard to replace on any basis at all. So the crypto/comsec layer ends up having the flavour of a constitution, and in order to change it you've got to get an awful lot of people, Mozilla, Apache, everybody else, to collaborate over a long period of time, just like if you're changing the US constitution, you've got to organise over a long term, and get lots and lots of different States bought into the process. So in effect, the crypto/comsec layer has become kind of constitution for this part of the world. It should never have been designed that way; that was just really, really dumb.

So where is the contestable layer? Well given that we've got 600 CAs, and that most of them are incompetent, and some of them are corrupt, you would certainly hope that this long distance trust layer that they give could be ripped out and replaced by a different load of rascals, and that may in fact turn out to be the case.

But here we come to the interesting bit. To change something like that you have to do an attack. Because if you're going to replace CAs with DNSSEC then in effect DNS is going to sign a cert saying, the following key is a good key for the website of sainsburys.co.uk, and I know I'm not an SSL cert, I'm something else altogether, so I'm an evil intruder, but trust me, I'm a good evil intruder! In other words, you are an acceptable attacker. And similarly if you're going to bootstrap BGP SEC not with proper certs that come from ARIN or whatever, but by DNS stuff, then somebody has to take a decision, or there have to be mechanisms put in that DNSSEC certs can be used to provide keys for BGP SEC.

Now if you've been around the protocol scene for 10 years or so this might remind you of something: the chosen-protocol attack. This is an idea of Bruce Schneier's based on an earlier idea that Peter Landrock brought here to the Protocols Workshop in 1996. It's as follows: if banks get customers to sign transactions then you design a protocol to attack that underlying protocol. So if a bank protocol says, a customer wants to buy 10 gold coins, the bank says "sign X" which was a hash of "I hereby wish to buy 10 gold coins and charge the account number so-and-so", the customer then signs it and the transaction is done. So what the Mafia do is they design a protocol so that when somebody wants such and such a naughty picture, it says "Prove your age by signing X", and he signs X. And of course by running these back-to-back, the poor punter can end up authorising stuff out of his bank account. So in general, if you've got a protocol, you can fashion another protocol to attack – as a general proposition. So it seems that in order to do democracy online, in order to contest an existing protocol, you basically have a mechanism whereby you put together a chosen-protocol attack, and this raises the question of what meta-mechanisms or what controls there might be around this.

Now let me give you a second example, which is very topical. It's a firm in Germany that's been going now only five years or so, Sofortüberweisung it's called, which means "instant payment". It has been causing an awful lot of bother for the German banks. Rainer Böhme and I sat down in January and tried to buy, if memory serves, a ticket from KLM from Hamburg to Amsterdam, or something like that. So we ordered the ticket, and the KLM website said, do you want to pay with a credit card, and pay an extra 4.90 Euros, or do you want to pay with Sofortüberweisung and then there is no charge. So of course you click on Sofortüberweisung, and it then puts up this screen here which says, "put in your name, put in your bank sort code, put in your account number, put in your address". And then you go to the next page and it says, "You're now going to be charged a total of a 180.62 Euros, so there's some more bank information that's required". And it then says, "Put in your PIN." This particular bank, that's what's required; other banks it's a PIN and a TAN, a one time code that's required. And this is of course all at Sofort's bank, and there's nothing deceptive about it. It says "Login bei ihrer Bank" – "login at your bank", and it's got all the little certificates, and decals, and Verisign trusted, and . . .

Matt Blaze: Well I did this.

Reply: Well, millions of people are, these guys have landed over 3% of the online payments market, now this is serious stuff. And what's actually happened is that so far as seeing a man-in-the-middle attack on your bank, which is here, OK, so your bank with this slightly dowdy and crufty website ask for these login details, and these are immediately relayed to you by a very much more swishy and "authentic looking" website run by Sofort bank.

And the magic difference is that Sofort is a lot cheaper to the merchant. Buying with a credit card typically costs 2.5%, plus perhaps a little bit more. Sofort charge .75% plus 10 cents, so the merchants are starting to fall in love with them. And this is basically how it happens, straightforward middleperson attack, it relays the authentication dialogue, and if it works it goes into your bank account, and they put in software which understands all the 300-odd banks in Germany, and now they're working in Switzerland, and Austria, and the Netherlands, and they're coming to Britain real soon now. And so they can check whether you've got the available credit, or cash, or whatever, and they just do a credit transfer to pay for the purchase. Boom!

Now the interesting thing here was that the German banks first of all tried to stop this by technical measures. They put up captchas and stuff like that, and Sofort basically won that fight because they had better programmes, zero captcha solvers faster than the 300 banks between them could actually put up effective captchas. Tells you something about banking IT, but there you are! So what the banks then did was to get the lawyers and haul Sofort into court saying, "the defendant is a wicked person because he's inducing our customers to break the terms and conditions of their contract with us." And what happened then was astounding – because the Federal Competition Authorities went along to the court and they said to the judge, "Well we actually like these Sofort chaps, you know, they're bringing some much needed competition into a very, very cartelised payment business." "Oh", said the judge, "thanks! Case suspended!" And so now there's at least one German bank setting up its own service of this kind, and of course there's Barclays setting up PingIt in the UK, although that works with direct debits rather than middleperson attacks, so the ethical issues, if you like, don't arise. But it's a very, very interesting case to watch, because here you basically have to have the chosen protocol attack in order to bring competition into a market, which the competition authorities thought was overdue.

Frank Stajano: Does Sofort accept the liability if your account is then hacked?

Reply: Well go and look at their pages, they say basically that nobody's ever lost money by shopping with us, it's satisfaction or your money back. And so there's an open question about whether there was some runaway fraud, but so far it would make everybody good. Quite possibly if there were just one or two incidents they'll pay up, but even that's open, in effect.

Phil Brooke: Presumably the banks that have been defrauded will just say, now you gave your credentials to this lot, and maybe transferred liability

Reply: Well there's an interesting question here because if Sofort are going to end up playing the same role as Visa and MasterCard in the payment system in Europe, then you could argue, and in fact I have argued, that you should regulate them in the same way. And similarly if Barclays take over much of the mobile payments scene in the UK, because they've got a good product and get it to market better, then again, you should look at them in the same light. Now Sofort may have started off as a start-up, but they've now got a proper bank in their group with a banking licence, and so it's difficult to run the trust argument in any very direct way. It may be better to say that if what you're worried about is truth in advertising, consumer protection, deposit insurance, and so on, then you should regulate these things directly on the whole industry in a transparent and neutral way, rather than jumping on one particular provider because the incumbents say, "Help he's stealing our breakfast! Please regulate him."

Phil Brooke: I'm thinking more of the incumbents, who or use Sofort as an excuse to beat their customers with.

Reply: Well that may very well happen, but we'll have to wait to see. And perhaps the reactions of regulators in different EU countries will be different, because it has been historically in the cards business.

Sandy Clark: I remember last year or the year before when you and Steven Murdoch had spoken about the problems with Chip and PIN, and one of the things that I remember is that the UK laws did not protect the consumer because it was argued that you had a PIN and if somebody could break your account therefore you didn't take care of your PIN, and so you were responsible. So if you're typing your credentials, which include your PIN, into somebody else's webpage they're sending you, that has nothing to do with your bank, isn't that therefore your responsibility if something happens to your details, or if you end up losing money?

Reply: Well if you remember I think the Workshop before that we talked about Verified by Visa, and Verified by Visa was basically an exercise whereby the world's banks trained all their customers to enter their banking credentials at merchant websites. So they sowed the wind with VBV and they reaped the whirlwind with Sofort. So are you going to lose any sleep about that?

Sandy Clark: I'm a US citizen and so $50 is the most they can charge me.

Jonathan Anderson: The bank could still say, "you've had a fraud on your account Mr Anderson, we see that you've used Sofort UK in the past"; just because Sofort can't be done for incitement doesn't mean that the bank is required to ignore the fact that I've given my PIN to somebody.

Paul Syverson: Some criminal organisation — Sofort.

Jonathan Anderson: Yes, exactly — desperate criminals!

Reply: So this will depend, it will vary from one country to another. In Germany this seems to have died down, but in the Netherlands apparently the banks are making a lot of PR against Sofort and telling their customers not to use it. Of course the customers ignore that for the most part.

Joseph Bonneau: Is Sofort just arbitrage, that the banks could cut out by lowering their rates if they really cared about it?

Reply: The banks have a similar mechanism, a Giro payment mechanism, but it's crufty, and it tends not to be well integrated. It's used, for example, by travel agents in Germany, whereas if you go to the airline directly you end up with Sofort, and the charge is actually lower than Sofort, because it can be as low as .3%.

George Danezis: But there is a more fundamental argument, that the banks are making their money from merchants. When they think of merchants, they think High Street merchants. The online business is not big enough to change that despite by the fact that the High Streets are getting empty, and the shops are closing, and everybody is shopping online. But of course none of their executives are going to accept that that business model is dead, and it's worthwhile just supporting very streamlined online transactions. I think that's the key element here in what will bring their business down.

Reply: Well I think that Sofort do well because it's a company full of geeks, and the average bank is a company full of guys in suits who lend money to property developers.

George Danezis: I don't know, when it comes to the stock market they're very good at getting geeks, so won't they have to look for systemic reasons?

Reply: But small savings and loan banks in obscure states in Germany? it's not Silicon Valley. Paul.

Paul Syverson: So I was very intrigued in the earlier part of your talk where you were drawing analogies to democracy, and the regime change, and CAs as I guess the government, leaders, politicians, and what have you, and you were looking for, I thought, a stand-in for what allows us to stably move from one regime to another, and you started to talk about that. But, I mean, these guys are still all approved by Verisign and all that, so it seemed to be that they were part of that same old guard, as it were, in that respect. Did I miss something?

Reply: Well I first pointed out that we may very well see DNSSEC taking over from the current swamp of SSL CAs. Now since that hasn't happened yet, but it's just something that's being talked about, I thought, let's look at a case where you actually have a challenge on the basis of a chosen protocol attack. And that's exactly what's happening here in the case of Sofort. Now if I can return to my last slide, which shows the conclusion. And it's this: If you're going to contest the policy, the governance of a nation, with ballots rather than bullets, then one of the things that you need is a loyal opposition, and that is a problem that many countries have had in Asia and Africa, and Latin America, and elsewhere, that even if the dictator has become tired of office and thinks he might very well retire and spend some of his stolen billions, if there isn't a credible opposition party to come in and maintain law and order so that his stuff doesn't get stolen, and his family don't get murdered, and so on, then it becomes difficult to hand over.

What we've got in countries like Britain and America, and so on, is a set of two or more political parties who have been in turns in and out of power, who know what the games are, what the rules are, and you've got a relatively stable structure, and you know what the fixed parts are, and what the more rapidly moving parts are of the constitution. So the loyal opposition is a fundamental concept here. This is Conservatives versus Labour versus Lib Dems, it's not the Socialist Workers Party. Now my point here is that to contest a protocol you similarly need a loyal attacker. Now if you had some bad man in Moldova doing a middle-person attack on the Berliner Sparkasse, that's a completely different business from if you've got Sofort bank doing a middle-person attack on the Berliner Sparkasse, that's my point. And then the difficulty is how do you tell between the two. Do you have a meta-mechanism whereby you say, these people here are loyal attackers, and these people here are rascals who need handcuffs put on? Now how do you go about expressing and doing that kind of discrimination? Do you do it in the technology; do you do it in the platform; do you do it with architecture; do you do it with mob appeals to the user saying, "please all of you press this button, go to this website and press this purple button?" How do you do it?

Sandy Clark: That would be?

Matt Blaze: Yes, I can't help but think that you came to an example of a chosen protocol attack that involved an increasingly obsolete industry of traditional banks, and their revenue model being threatened by an upstart. Where have we seen that before, in protocols, and in technology of communications? Well the reporting in motion picture industries come to mind. What we see is a steady stream of incredibly bad behaviour, that at some point either becomes more reasonable or ends in a nuclear explosion, and assaulting of the earth left behind in order to protect the business model. So, is that ultimately what you get without a loyal attacker?

Reply: Well this is the question that I come to here at the end, who's going to assess the attacker's loyalty? Now the interesting case about Sofort is that in Germany it was the court, the banks went to court, the government intervened, and they lost. End of story. Right? So you have a relatively well-managed and peaceful transition from an old, oligopolistic, duopolistic regime, to a new more open and contested one, and that's purely in the public interest. So in DNSSEC it may be nation states implicitly if you end up with it being the nation states which licence most of the top-level domains – which in turn then certify much of the namespace. Joe?

Joseph Bonneau: Is the question, how you assess the attacker's loyalty, or how the existing protocol determines whether to fight or to accede to it?

Reply: Well it may be a complex mix of technology and policy. So here, for example, in the last point: who else, apart from a court with competent jurisdiction, can decide whether an attack was to be allowed to proceed, or whether the attacker was to have handcuffs put on. It could be the big platform vendors – firms like Google and Microsoft, and even perhaps Facebook, are in a position to say, "Attack X is not tolerable – we won't put up with it, we will plaster these bad guys with lawyers and tie up all their assets" or they could turn round and say, "This is a nice innovation – we will support it in the next release of the browser." So there's a decision there being taken by a private sector actor.

Another possibility is to say that any attack is lawful if it's done by a big company. An attack is lawful if it's done by a company that can afford to employ ten or more lawyers, if you want a simple rule of thumb. This is, if you like, the Lexmark case, do you all know of the Lexmark case? Lexmark is a company that sells printers, and they sued a company called Static Control Components, which did cryptanalysis of, and replication of, the chips that they used to control access to ink cartridges, and they lost. The judge ruled in effect that in the USA at least, in this type of market, it's a free-for-all for cryptologists. The printer company can hire the best cryptographers to make the best security chips they can, and the ink cartridge re-filling companies can hire the best cryptanalysts they can find to try and break that cryptography so that they can get access to those markets.

So do you simply say that any respectable company is going to be deemed to be a loyal attacker? This is perhaps the Milton Friedman free-market approach dealing with this problem. Do you instead, perhaps give some credence to competition authorities, as happened in the German case? That would be DG COMP generally in Europe; you've the Federal Trade Commission in America.

We could be really old-fashioned here: we've got this lady in Westminster, the Queen, to whom politicians profess loyalty, and who will act as a tie-breaker and a referee in the case if there's a hung parliament. Do you have to have some external referee? Is that desirable or useful, it's probably not implementable, probably doesn't scale, but these are the sort of ideas we perhaps have to start thinking about.

George Danezis: So to me all of these confusions go around the main issue: there is no such thing as security, there is security for the banks and security for me, and actual protocols embody both to some extent: there is some for me and some for the bank. So in this particular case, Sofort act on my behalf so there isn't criminal intent, and there is no actual criminal action, because they act as my attorney as much as my browser that renders the website of the bank when I do the detail, it's just a conduit to perform a transaction that I wish to perform.

Reply: Yes, they're acting with my mandate. There is still a truth in advertising issue but that's the detail.

George Danezis: Right, so in that case really the security system is valid only insofar as the bank, and the banking sector has embedded in their security system links to protect your business model, and that was part of the aim of their protocol. And it is not the job of the court to enforce their monopoly through the technical artefacts they have created to protect that monopoly, by not allowing me to use an attorney, potentially referring your real attorney to do my business. So to some extent this really comes down to the basis of what is competition, what is intent, and all that stuff.

Sandy Clark: But with security you have to have liability as well.

Reply: Right. Paul?

Paul Syverson: Yes, so two questions, one is, I'm wondering how in this picture of top level domains and stuff, weird things that aren't even using the protocols at all like .onion addresses fit in, and the other, whether that's a loyal attacker, or whether that's just out there. But also in all of this I seem to get lost a little bit; sometimes it sounds like what you're talking about is transitions of loyal opposition inside of an existing structure, and then sometimes it sounds like you're seeking for a move from feudalism to democracy, and those are different sorts of transitions, and you seem to jump back and forth, and I'm not quite sure which you're going for.

Reply: Well I'm sure there will be all sorts of different types of transition. The main point that I'm trying to make with this talk is that it is not enough for us to think about the engineering or the economics of security, we have to start thinking about the politics as well. And when trying to analyse serious real-world problems, whether it's the challenge to the card brands posed by Sofort or PingIt, or whether it's the challenge to the SSL ecology posed by DNSSEC, that many of the useful concepts that we can import and play with, may be concepts from political science.

Jonathan Anderson: I think that maybe there's an over-emphasis on the actions and the qualities and the properties of the attacker, because I think the main thing with changing government with ballots instead of bullets, it's not that ballots are cast, it's that when ballots are cast the people who are currently in power are willing to say, "let me collect my things", if they go the wrong way. And so similarly it's not so much that you've got a much better protocol, and you behave nicely in the way you try to replace the protocol, or it's not so much that Sofort plays nicely or not nicely with the banks, the issue is the commercial actors which cease to exist: effectively you have to kill them to remove them. They're not so happy to say, "let me collect my things, maybe I'll get to move back into this nice house in a few years".

Joseph Bonneau: There's sort of an analogy, which is that companies, they pull out of certain markets if there's too much price competition and they don't think it's profitable anymore, and that's basically the equivalent of saying, we've been beaten by rules that we accept.

Paul Syverson: Or the judge says, "Too bad."

Joseph Bonneau: Yes, but they were basically saying, we were not beaten fairly, we were beaten by a process we don't accept, and it required a judge to say, no, this is a legitimate coup.

Jonathan Anderson: So the equivalents would be if the banks said, "you know what, we're not very good at this whole online thing, so we'll sit back and just let the other guys have it".

Joseph Bonneau: They have done that for some things. Banks don't do everything they've always done: they have outsourced some stuff and said, "Other people can do it better than we can."

Reply: Well why don't they just go to Sofort and give them 10 billion Euros for the company and then set it up as being the service contractor for the Giro credit system. And there's all sorts of ways in which they could have finessed it, but the way they appeared to be finessing it is that some of the more entrepreneurial banks will set up competitors to Sofort, so you'll end up instead of having 300 banks in the Internet payments business, you might end up in Germany with half a dozen payment services providers, some banks and some non-banks.

Jonathan Anderson: Right, so that's actual competition.

Reply: So it's normal business evolution. And it's an interesting case history because it's not just the breaking of a cartel in the commercial sense, but it's also the overthrow of, if you like, a protocol eco-system, which is the subject matter of these workshops. And the example that I was able to find — it's a done thing rather than something that's just starting, as is the case with DNSSEC. But perhaps once we start looking around we can find other examples, other analogies to use.

Frank Stajano: The interesting thing is that Sofort doesn't actually offer any technical benefit over what the bank would do itself: it's just an aggregator, and it allows you to do a payment from your bank account, which if the bank wanted to let you do, you can technically do, because Sofort just relies on what you can do from your account anyway. So if the bank wanted to undercut Sofort it could just say, "do it from your account"; it's your account anyway.

Bruce Christianson: And we will only charge you the same as Sofort.

Reply: Yes, but you know what an enormous amount of innovation there is in our world by companies who hire a decent usability engineer, so you end up not having to retype your account number and the merchant's account number five different times. And also what Sofort gives you is instant confirmation that the sale has gone through, which you don't get from Giro credit.

Frank Stajano: No, but Giro credit is the alternative to doing the payment, the BACS equivalent, from your own account. Sofort uses a human API on which it types, which you could use yourself if only your bank integrated that.

Reply: As far as I understand it – one would have to check the details of this with Rainer – you get instant certainty of payment, which people set a lot of store by. I suspect what's happening is that you're paying Sofort, and once Sofort knows that it's got the money, it pays the merchant, and because the merchant trusts Sofort, this means you can get immediate confirmation that, "Yes, you are flying to Amsterdam next Sunday, and your booking number is such and such". Whereas if you paid Giro credit then you might have to wait three days for a confirmation.

Frank Stajano: The way I'm paying, you wouldn't pay Giro credit, you would pay the airline from your bank account.

Reply: That's what I meant, by Giro credit.

Bruce Christianson: But the point that Sofort allows you to correlate two transactions and make them tie up, that's the service promise.

Frank Stajano: Yes, well if the bank wanted to behave like that and just cut out the middleman, it could make them one transaction.

Reply: Well nobody's questioning that for a second. We're dealing with the economics and politics, not the engineering, and if the banks do not possess capable software engineers and usability engineers, then that may cost them a lot.

Frank Stajano: My point was simply that all this clever engineering of Sofort was for interfacing to all the 300 banks, but if each individual bank said, I'm going to undercut Sofort, they could do it without any of the effort that Sofort has put in, maybe just one tenth.

Reply: Well sure, as a theoretical matter, maybe not as a practical one, given the staff they've got. But that isn't fundamentally the point of this talk. Virgil.

Virgil Gligor: Coming back for a moment to the loyal attacker, it turns out that most major companies do have loyal attackers – they're called security researchers – whom they actually pay for exploits. They have stables of loyal attackers. And of course they have the power to change their own systems, and their own protocols. A bigger problem appears with the government having a role in it, because the government doesn't own any piece of software, so the question is, how would we legislate this loyal opposition by government as opposed to just private bodies which already have the loyal attackers?

Reply: Well by loyal attacker I mean attackers who can put together a competitive eco-system, and then push it forward as a credible opposition to the one run by the incumbent. And I suppose the way I would suggest the protocols community deal with this is that we don't always have to think in terms of using the word "attacker", we might perhaps want to use the word "incumbent", and the word "challenger", because that's more neutral in judgemental terms. And if we're going to assume that all the players in this space will be proper registered companies who employ lawyers, and who therefore at least believe that they're acting lawfully, then using judgemental terms like "attacker" is perhaps misleading.

Virgil Gligor: In some ultra sense I think that competition does that, so for example, whatever Microsoft feared the most, namely competition in the Internet business, has happened, there's Google. Whatever Google feared the most has happened, is Facebook. So the word competition sort of comes through the normal competition processes.

Jonathan Anderson: It also comes through things like consumer rights, because if Google wasn't able to sue Microsoft to say, "give us the specification for Word so that we can import it into our online doc thing", then that competition can't really happen.

Virgil Gligor: So I think the larger point that Ross is making is that while this thing happens it does happen slowly, very slowly, and consequently we fall between the cracks, and we will have periods of time when we get unresolved security problems, and unresolvable security problems.

Reply: Well the other point, one of the other points that I'm trying to make with this talk is that political science and theory of constitutional law point us to the idea of having some parts of the constitution that are contestable, namely the legislature — and in America also the executive — and others which move very much more slowly: the constitution itself, the Supreme Court, and so on and so forth. Now when we are designing protocols that we hope will be deployed on a global scale, then we should actually think about which parts of the protocol ecology should be contestable, and which should be very much more slow moving.

Now this isn't going to be static over time. We have trouble with TLS because of all the rubbish crypto that most of the world's browsers and servers are using, but now that we've got things like AES and SHA256, and SHA3 coming along, the crypto there is within spitting distance of being able to be put finally to bed? But we still have to think carefully about which parts of the engine are likely to accumulate cruft and need to be challenged and replaced over time. And perhaps that means anywhere where security economic forces can cause featuritis, and feature creep, and growing complexity, as has happened in some parts of the SSL world.

Virgil Gligor: Right, but also an alternative may be just get rid of that infrastructure, maybe we can come up with something more clever than DNSSEC — which has been around by the way for about 17 years, 16 years, with no traction — or something more clever than PKI.

Reply: Well there's your opportunity to put in a draft proposal to the DHS and get some people working on infrastructure 3.0.

Virgil Gligor: Tough, because there are people who just love DNSSEC.

Reply: Right, so we're done.

Usability Issues in Security

Yuko Murayama[1], Yasuhiro Fujihara[2], Yoshia Saito[1], and Dai Nishioka[1]

[1] Graduate School of Software and Information Science, Iwate Prefectural University,
152-52, Sugo, Takizawa-mura, Iwate 020-0193, Japan
{murayama,y-saito}@iwate-pu.ac.jp,
D.Nishioka@comm.soft.iwate-pu.ac.jp
[2] The Medical Department, Hyogo College of Medicine,
1-3-6 Minatojima, Chuo-ku, Kobe City, Hyogo 663-8501, Japan
yfuji@hyo-med.ac.jp

Abstract. Usability issues in security have been discussed such that users could use the security tools easier. On contrary we presume another aspect of usability issues in security; an interface which causes a slight disturbance and discomfort so that a user would be aware of security threats and risks. The idea is that we should not feel Anshin to be secure. Anshin is a Japanese indicating the sense of security. We need a risk-aware interface to notice an insecure situation so that we would install security countermeasures. It is a warning interface for the insecure situations. We show how we could implement such an interface in a mail system to prevent users from sending email messages to incorrect destination addresses.

Keywords: the sense of security, security, trust, user survey, warning interface.

1 Introduction

Human interfaces have been researched in terms of usability [1]. From e-commerce and trust viewpoints, Stephens gives design elements, such as page layout, navigation, and graphics which affect the development of trust between buyers and sellers in e-commerce [2]. Pu also reports that how information was presented affected trust building in user interfaces [3]. According to Riegelsberger, Sasse and McCarthy, affective reactions influence consumer decision-making [4]. Whitten and Tygar pointed out that user interfaces in security systems would need special interfaces [5]. They took the Graphic User Interface (GUI) of a version of the Pretty Good Privacy (PGP) system as an example, claiming that users would not adopt the system due to its poor user interface even though the system was secure.

On contrary, we presume another aspect of usability issues in security — an interface which causes a slight disturbance and discomfort so that a user would be aware of security threats and risks [6][7]. The idea is that we should not feel Anshin to be secure. Anshin is a Japanese term which is composed of two words:

B. Christianson et al. (Eds.): Security Protocols 2012, LNCS 7622, pp. 161–171, 2012.
© Springer-Verlag Berlin Heidelberg 2012

An and Shin. "An" is to ease, and "Shin" indicates mind. Anshin literally means to ease one's mind [8][9][10]. We use the term for the sense of security in this paper.

Quite often, users are unaware of such security threats; therefore, they do not take any countermeasures. We need a risk-aware interface for a user so that the one would take security countermeasures. It is a warning interface for the insecure situations. We show how we could implement such an interface with an email system to prevent users from sending email messages to incorrect destination addresses, so that we could prevent information leak.

This paper reports the result from a user survey on discomfort feelings and the application of such an interface for a mail user agent (MUA) to prevent users from sending messages to incorrect destination addresses. Moreover, we tried and classified the subjects according to their perception of discomfort so that we could possibly implement a warning interface which adapts personally to each one of those individuals. Finally we show how to identify to which group an individual user could belong by means of the seven questions from the questionnaire, whose factor loadings to each factor was the highest.

The next section presents related work on interfaces. Section 3 reports on our user survey on feeling discomfort in computer use. Section 4 reports on our preliminary experiment with a prototype system in which we implemented such a waning interface to a mail user agent. Section 5 describes on classification of the subjects into groups, and Section 6 discusses on grouping towards adoptive warning to an individual user. The final section gives some conclusion and presents future work.

2   Related Work

Human interfaces have been researched to avoid human errors in safety engineering. For example, a dynamite system is designed so that one cannot blast so easily; the one needs to press two different switches simultaneously to initiate an explosion. This sort of design has been recommended in military [11]. One cannot start operating a microwave without shutting the door [12]. Natural gas has no odor, but for a safety reason unpleasant odorant is added so that one can detect gas leaks [13].

Such interfaces have been used in the electronic space as well. When a user tries and executes incorrect operations on a computer system, the one would get a warning message asking whether the one would proceed or not. The problem is, however, the user might get used to answer "yes" only to proceed without being fully aware of the warning message.

We presume that we could draw user's attention to warning messages by applying the interface which would cause discomfort. Sankarapandian et al. [14] suggested an interface to make the user aware of the vulnerabilities caused by unpatched software. They implemented a system which showed annoying graffiti on the user's display along with a description of the threat. The user can clean such graffiti by applying necessary patches. Egelman et al. [15] conducted an experiment on the rate to avoid the damage caused by phishing; the experiment was based on a C-HIP (Communication–Human Information Processing) model [16] in which the interface warns users about vulnerabilities. They reported that the user responses to a warning varied according to the type of interface used. Raja [17] implemented a personal firewall with a physical security metaphor. The result of their experiment showed that the safe behavior would be increased with an interface.

3 Questionnaire Survey on Feeling Discomfort in Computer Use

We tried and investigated the factors causing discomfort when one used a computer system, firstly by collecting the elements which would cause discomfort to users, and secondly by identifying the factors of discomfort by a questionnaire survey and factor analysis [18]. We collected discomfort elements using two methods, viz. a literature survey [19] [20] [21] [22] [23] and a preliminary survey. In our preliminary survey, we asked subjects for comments about situations and events which caused them to feel discomfort.

We conducted a questionnaire survey in order to measure the degree of discomfort caused by each discomfort element. We prepared forty six questions based on the results from our preliminary survey. We asked subjects to rate each discomfort element. The rates included five ranks: from calm (zero points) to acute discomfort (four points). We have provided details of this survey [24].

We collected three hundred and ten data. In total, as subjects we had one hundred forty six men and one hundred sixty four women of the second-year, third-year, and fourth-year undergraduates from four different departments. The mean age of the subjects was approximately 20.38. Most subjects had completed the course on computer literacy and used a computer daily. We conducted an exploratory factor analysis using the maximum likelihood method. We made the initial analysis with the maximum likelihood method and a promax rotation. Three high factor loaded items in each factor are shown in Table 1. The seven factors include thirty eight items in total and explained 56.1% of the total variance. We present seven factors that contribute to discomfort feeling as follows.

Factor 1: *Time consuming* which consists of eleven high factor loading items related to looking for things that are difficult to find or to input information using a keyboard or a mouse.

Factor 2: *Information seeking* which consists of eight high factor loading items related to a situation in which a user is attempting to find information that is difficult to locate.

Factor 3: *Message* which consists of seven high factor loading items related with messages that interrupt a user's activity.

Factor 4: *Unexpected operation* consists of five high factor loading items related with a system malfunction that is unexpected or unintended by a user.

Factor 5: *Difficulty in seeing* which consists of three high factor loading items related with the sense of sight given by a physical aspect.

Factor 6: *Time delay* which consists of three high factor loading items related with waiting time and system delay.

Factor 7: *Noise* which consists of three high factor loading items related with the sense of hearing given by a particular sound.

Those seven factors include thirty eight items in total and explained 56.1% of the total variance. Moreover, the internal consistency of each factor was as follows: Cronbach's coefficient alpha = 0.867 for Factor 1, 0.842 for Factor 2, 0.771 for Factor 3, 0.731 for Factor 4, 0.757 for Factor 5, 0.699 for Factor 6, and 0.649 for Factor 7.

Table 1. Examples of question items and their factor loadings for the factor

(three high factor loadings items in each factor)

Item	Factor Loadings
Factor 1 (Time-consuming)	
Q45 You look for a particular window out of too many windows.	.745
Q46 It is hard to find software or files you are looking for.	.655
Q43 Your texts are transformed with the auto-correct function.	.644
Factor 2 (Information-seeking)	
Q21 You are not sure whether the information on a website is accurate or not.	.803
Q22 It is hard for you to see information on the website due to its background color.	.707
Q20 You see advertisements displayed on the website.	.663
Factor 3 (Message)	
Q09 You get a system message on a display to ask you whether you would like to update some software or not.	.699
Q13 You try and start a prohibited operation and get prevented from doing so. (e.g. restricted operation)	.602
Q28 You get a system message suddenly to ask you whether you would like to update some software or not.	.580
Factor 4 (Unexpected operation)	
Q17 You set up a LAN cable correctly but cannot connect to the internet.	.681
Q08 A computer restarted unexpectedly while you were using it.	.591
Q18 You get connected to the internet from time to time.	.562
Factor 5 (Difficulty-in- seeing)	
Q32 You need to read too long messages on a web page.	.830
Q31 You read texts in too small font size.	.675
Q33 You need to keep scrolling to read a document.	.450
Factor 6 (Time-delay)	
Q01 It takes so long to boot up a computer.	.801
Q16 It takes so long to get an access to and display a web site.	.536
Q02 It takes so long to shut down a computer.	.481
Factor 7 (Noise)	
Q27 When you heard sounds or music unexpectedly.	.702
Q14 You heard suddenly aloud noise from a pair of speakers or through a headset.	.534
Q26 You come across a website which makes too much user of Flash.	.425

3.1 A Preliminary Experiment with a Prototype System

The purpose of an interface causing discomfort is to help the user be aware of risks; however, the interface should not discourage a user from using it. Sending an email message to an incorrect destination address could result in private information leakage. Lieberman and Miller [25] have developed a system to show the photograph of a recipient on the message. To give a face as an external cue, let the user be easy to notice when you enter the wrong address.

We tried and implemented an interface with some factors of feelings of discomfort for a mail user agent (MUA), which would give a warning if an incorrect address were specified by a user. We have developed add-ons of Thunderbird 2.0[TM] using XUL and JavaScript[TM]. When the user tries to send an email message to the address that is similar to the one that she has ever sent. In the message screen, when a user inputs a destination address, if it matches with the criteria such as the address to which the user seldom sends, the address in a specific domain and the address similar to other addresses, the system displays the warning by the factor, *Difficulty in seeing*. As shown in Fig. 1, this interface provides some sort of discomfort to the user when she attempts to send a message to an address that is similar to the one that she has previously sent an email message to. Such discomfort may include a change in the text size or in the color of the text and background of the incorrect address. We have provided details of this experiment [26].

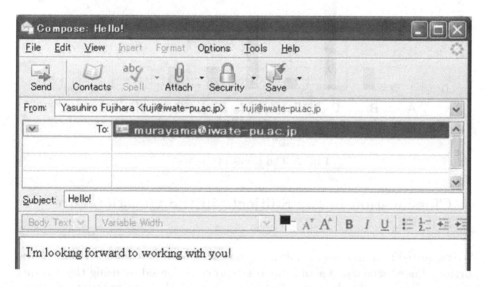

Fig. 1. An example of an interface causing discomfort

In order to evaluate the effects of this interface, we compared the frequency of incorrect sending between using an interface causing discomfort and no warning interfaces. We conducted the experiment with ten university students who majored in computer science. The tasks of sending an email to a designated address were conducted thirty times for each interface. We have registered addresses in the address book, which appear similar to the addresses designated in the tasks in order to mislead the subjects when they use the auto-complete function in the "to" field. The subjects were instructed to send each message within 45 seconds so that they would be in hurry and might specify incorrect addresses easily.

Fig. 2 shows the frequency of sending to incorrect addresses. The number of times of incorrect addressing was reduced by the use of the interface. The mean of the number of times with the warning interface was 2.1 times, whereas the one without the warning interface was 3.7 times. However, the effect by the interface varied according to each subject.

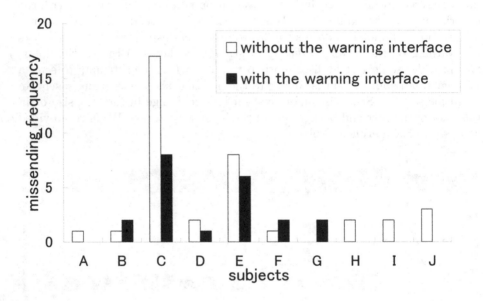

Fig. 2. The result of the task

4   Classification of the Subjects in the Questionnaire Survey

We conducted a preliminary experiment on the warning interface. Although the portion of users who could avoid threat scenarios increased by using the warning interface, it appeared to have no effect on some users. We assumed that one of the reasons is the difference in perception of discomfort among users. On the basis of data from a previously described questionnaire survey, we classified subjects according to the perception of discomfort. We analyzed the factor scores from the previous factor analysis by hierarchical cluster analysis with the WARD method and squared euclidian distance (seuclid). The number of clusters was four based on information criterion (BIC(3)=1245.64, BIC(4)=1243.28, BIC(5)=1273.31). The relationships between the groups and factors are shown in Fig. 3. The result of one-way analysis of variance showed that there are significant differences in all groups (p<0.001). We present the characteristics of each group as follows.

- Group 1 constituted 26% of the subjects in the questionnaire survey. The subjects in this group had high factor scores for all factors. It is considered that the application of discomfort would be effective. In addition, it is possible that a strong level of discomfort would not be required.
- Group 2 constituted 27% of the subjects. They had low factor scores for all factors. It is considered that they do not perceive as discomfort on all factors. The effectiveness of the interface causing discomfort is expected to be minimal. If an interface is to be provided for this group, a strong level of discomfort would be required. Compared with other factors, a higher factor score was shown for factor 7 (*Noise*); therefore, the use of this factor should be considered for this group.
- Group 3 constituted 29% of the subjects. They had low factor scores for factors 6 (*Time-delay*) and 7 (*Noise*). It is considered that the effectiveness of warning interfaces using these factors would be low.
- Group 4 constituted 18% of the subjects. They had high factor scores for factors 4 (*Unexpected-operation*), 6 (*Time-delay*) and 7 (*Noise*). It is considered that warning interfaces using these factors would be effective.

The result of the cluster analysis shows that a more effective interface can be provided by dividing users into groups. We conducted one-way analysis of variance to examine the properties of subjects. The results of the analysis are shown in Table 2. The gender and major were significant (p<0.05); however, a multiple comparison (Tukey HSD) revealed no significant differences between any combinations. In this survey, all subjects were university students, and we could consider that there were no major differences between their properties. However, based on these results, we cannot contradict the relationship between the properties and groups.

5   Discussion

Reinecke and Bernstein [27] developed a system in which the interface is selected automatically using properties based on the cultural background. An adaptive interface was provided according to a user model based on five dimensions such as "Power Distance", "Individualism", "Masculinity", "Uncertainty Avoidance" and "Long Term Orientation". For estimating the dimensions of each user, they applied the relationship between dimensions and residence history from Hofstede's survey [28]. Accordingly, if the perception of discomfort was decided based on a user profile, it would be possible to provide a warning interface customised to a particular user.

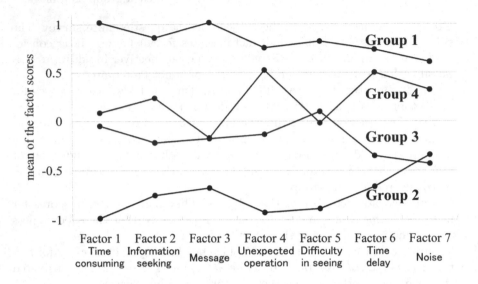

Fig. 3. The relation between groups and factors

Table 2. Relationships between the properties and groups

Properties	F-value	P-value
Gender	2.881	.036*
Age	0.277	.842
Major	3.495	.016*
Grade	0.293	.830
Computer usage time	2.108	.099
Frequency of Internet shopping	1.182	.317
Experience of computer being infected by a virus	2.541	.057
Experience of computer not running smoothly	0.738	.530
Experience of problems such as information leakage	0.876	.454

We conducted a discrimination analysis on each factor based on responses for items with the highest factor loadings. The standardized coefficients of the functions are shown in Table 3 and the discrimination results are presented in Table 4. From the responses to the seven items, 74.2% of cross-validation data could be accurately classified. This result leads to our warning interface that it is possible to for users based on their response to a small number of questions. It should be added that by generating more accurate questions, the number of questions required for analysing the groups can be further reduced.

Table 3. Coefficients of the canonical discriminant function

	Function 1	Function 2	Function 3
Q45 in factor 1	.378	-.174	.418
Q21 in factor 2	.289	-.033	.239
Q09 in factor 3	.429	.444	.507
Q17 in factor 4	.445	-.400	-.355
Q32 in factor 5	.337	-.402	.070
Q01 in factor 6	.427	.162	-.612
Q27 in factor 7	.284	.666	-.230

Table 4. Result of discrimination

		Discriminated groups				
		1	2	3	4	total
	1	66	0	4	11	81
	2	0	66	15	3	84
Original groups	3	2	9	70	9	90
	4	10	2	15	28	55
	total	78	77	104	51	310

6   Conclusions

This paper reported a warning interface for computer systems and presented we could possibly provide the users with an adaptive one according to individual perception of discomfort. The results from the questionnaire survey on feeling discomfort in computer use revealed that subjects can be divided into groups on the basis of their reaction to the respective discomfort factors. Moreover, we could identify to which group a user would belong with several questions.

Since all test subjects in our survey were university students, there might have been few differences in their properties. In addition to the property "major" for which a significant difference could be ascertained, an analysis of eight items allowed us to accurately evaluate the groups with a probability of 76.1%. Further investigations are required regarding the properties of the subjects.

As future work, we need to implement each different warning interface to a group as well as to investigate the effectiveness of such adaptive warning interfaces. Moreover, since smart houses are constructed with home networking, the application of such interfaces could be used so that security and safety incidents such as gas leak could be reported in an electronic way, perhaps to a house owner on trip or a house security and safety service provider located remotely.

Acknowledgements. This research has been supported by Grant-in-Aid for Scientific Research (B) from the Japanese Ministry of Education, Culture, Sports, Science and Technology (MEXT). We appreciate all the comments and discussion at the Security Protocols Workshop.

References

1. Nielsen, J.: Usability Engineering. Academic Press (1993)
2. Stephens, R.T.: A framework for the identification of electronic commerce design elements that enable trust within the small hotel industry. In: Proc. of ACMSE 2004, pp. 309–314 (2004)
3. Pu, P., Chen, L.: Trust building with explanation interfaces. In: Proc. of the 11th International Conference on Intelligent User Interfaces (IUI 2006), pp. 93–100 (2006)
4. Riegelsberger, J., Sasse, M.A., McCarthy, J.D.: Privacy and trust: Shiny happy people building trust?: photos on e-commerce websites and consumer trust. In: Proc. of the SIGCHI Conference on Human Factors in Computing Systems (CHI 2003), vol. 5(1), pp. 121–128 (2003)
5. Whitten, A., Tygar, D.: Why Johnny Can't Encrypt: A Usability Evaluation of PGP 5.0. In: Proc. of the 9th USENIX Security Symposium, pp. 169–184 (1999)
6. Fujihara, Y., Oikawa, H., Murayama, Y.: Towards an interface causing discomfort for security: A user survey on the factors of discomfort. In: Proc. of the Second IEEE SSIRI 2008, pp. 173–174 (2008)
7. Fujihara, Y., Mukai, M., Kanamori, Y., Murayama, Y.: An interface causing discomfort to prevent users from missending e-mail messages to incorrect addresses. Poster and Demonstration Paper Proc. of IFIP TM 2012, pp. 9–12 (2010)
8. Murayama, Y., Hikage, N., Hauser, C., Chakraborty, B., Segawa, N.: An Anshin Model for the Evaluation of the Sense of Security. In: Proc. of the 39th Hawaii International Conference on System Science (HICSS 2006), vol. 8, p. 205a (2006)
9. Murayama, Y., Fujihara, Y., Nishioka, D.: The Sense of Security and a Countermeasure for the False Sense. In: Christianson, B., Crispo, B., Malcolm, J., Stajano, F. (eds.) Security Protocols 2011. LNCS, vol. 7114, pp. 205–214. Springer, Heidelberg (2011)
10. Malcolm, J.: The Sense of Security and a Countermeasure for the False Sense (Transcript of Discussion). In: Christianson, B., Crispo, B., Malcolm, J., Stajano, F. (eds.) Security Protocols 2011. LNCS, vol. 7114, pp. 215–222. Springer, Heidelberg (2011)
11. Norman, D.A.: The Psychology of Everyday Things. Basic Books (1988)
12. International Electrotechnical Commission: Safety of household and similar electrical appliances — part 2: Particular requirements for microwave ovens (MOD IEC 60335-2-25) (1996)

13. U.S. Department of Energy: Natural Gas (2012),
    http://www.fossil.energy.gov/education/energylessons/gas/
14. Sankarapandian, K., Little, T., Edwards, W.K.: TALC: Using Desktop Graffiti to Fight Software Vulnerability. In: Proc. of ACM CHI 2008, pp. 1055–1064 (2008)
15. Egelman, S., Cranor, L.F., Hong, J.: You've been warned: An empirical study of the effectiveness of web browser phishing warnings. In: Proc. of ACM CHI 2008, pp. 1065–1074 (2008)
16. Wogalter, M.S.: Communication–Human Information Processing (C-HIP) Model. In: Wogalter, M.S. (ed.) Handbook of Warnings, pp. 51–61. Lawrence Erlbaum Associates (2006)
17. Raja, F., Hawkey, K., Hsu, S., Wang, K.C., Beznosov, K.: A Brick Wall, a Locked Door, and a Bandit: A Physical Security Metaphor for Firewall Warnings. In: Proceeding of Symposium On Usable Privacy and Security (SOUPS 2011), pp. 122–131 (2011)
18. Oikawa, H.: A study of a causal structure model for a discomfort interface. Master's thesis, Iwate Prefectural University Graduate School (2008) (in Japanese)
19. Ramsay, J.: A factor analysis of user cognition and emotion. In: Proceedings of the SIGCHI Conference on Human Factors in Computing Systems (CHI 1997), pp. 546–547 (1997)
20. Awad, N.F., Fitzgerald, K.: The Deceptive Behaviors that Offend Us Most About Spyware. Comm. of the ACM 48, 55–60 (2005)
21. Takahashi, K., Nakatani, M., Nishida, S.: Information Presentation from the standpoint of a sense of security. In: Proc. of HIS 2002, pp. 289–292 (2002)
22. Tsuji, K., Okuda, T., Takahashi, K. and Ito, T.: Analyses of the discomforts aroused by stimulus sentences with reference to effects of modality and gender. The Japanese Journal of research on Emotions 3, 64–70 (2005) (in Japanese)
23. Hagiwara, H.: Sensory Aversion Degrees for Adolescents. Bulletin of Junior College of Shukutoku 45, 89–113 (2006) (in Japanese)
24. Fujihara, Y., Murayama, Y.: A user survey on the interface causing discomfort for warning. In: Matrai, R. (ed.) User Interfaces, pp. 21–34. INTECH (2010)
25. Lieberman, E., Miller, R.C.: Facemail: Showing Faces of Recipients to Prevent Misdirected Email. In: Proceeding of Symposium On Usable Privacy and Security (SOUPS 2007), pp. 122–131 (2007)
26. Fujihara, Y., Kanamori, Y., Mukai, M., Saito, Y., Murayama, Y.: A preliminary experiment on a warning interface causing discomfort for sense of security, Anshin. In: Proceedings of the International Workshop on Infrastructure Assurance, pp. 69–75 (2010)
27. Reinecke, K., Bernstein, A.: Improving Performance, Perceived Usability, and Aesthetics with Culturally Adaptive User Interfaces. ACM Transactions on Computer–Human Interaction 18(22), Article 8 (2011)
28. Hofstede, G.: Culture's Consequences: Comparing Values, Behaviors and Organizations across Nations, 2nd edn. Sage Publications (2001)

Usability Issues in Security
(Transcript of Discussion)

Yuko Murayama

Iwate Prefectural University

Good morning. Last year I was supposed to attend the workshop, but I'm from North Japan and due to the disaster I couldn't make it, so this year I'm very happy to be here. I will talk a little bit about our work on Anshin trust, and then I will introduce our research on a warning interface causing discomfort for risk awareness.

Traditional research on security would expect that the user would feel secure with secure systems, but how can you be sure people feel secure when you provide them with a secure technology? English is not my mother tongue, but I looked up the word security and it has many aspects. In system security, they are working on the technology aspect, but what was missing was the sense of security; so this is a study on how a user of secure technology feels.

So I introduce a Japanese word, Anshin, well it could be Chinese as well. Anshin is composed of two characters. "An" means no fear, and "shin" is you

are wary, so Anshin literally means you are free from being wary, so you feel very comfortable or something like that. State government used quite a lot of this word, they would like to create an Anshin world in Japan; it's not happening now but they want it. So we tried to measure Anshin quantitatively, to deduce the factors which make you feel Anshin, or what makes you feel secure. This is our motivation.

Most research targets the provision of a good secure system so that the user would feel Anshin. But if you have a not-secure system, the user should feel uncomfortable, or insecure, or something like that; that could be the secondary (or maybe primary?) target of research. The problem is, if the system is secure, and the people do not feel Anshin, they don't use it, so we have a usability problem, whereas if the system is insecure but the people do feel Anshin it's a security problem. So that is how things are.

The related concepts are security, safety, reliability, and dependability. Security deals with a psychological threat, which would be caused by the intention from a deceiver, whereas for safety and reliability the researchers used to work

B. Christianson et al. (Eds.): Security Protocols 2012, LNCS 7622, pp. 172–180, 2012.
© Springer-Verlag Berlin Heidelberg 2012

on hardware safety and hardware reliability, such as something like a mean time between failure rate, and the threat would not be intentional. However those people in reliability need to deal with software and networked software, and naturally they have to think about the security as well. So nowadays they call the area dependability. And what is trust? Trust has been researched for many years in sociology, philosophy, psychology, many areas. However, in Information Science it has started being researched only in the 90s, so it's quite new in our area. According to papers by Camp[1] and Hoffman[2], trust is composed of many areas, like safety, security, usability, reliability, privacy. Most of those areas deal with user's feeling, so Anshin actually is a set of those user's feelings in each area. At the moment we are only working on the sense of security, but we would like to work on the sense of privacy, sense of safety, reliability, and all that.

According to our definition, Anshin is the emotional part of trust. Actually so far trust has been studied only in the cognitive part. In 1985 Lewis, a psychologist, identified there are two aspects of research in trust[3]. One is the cognitive part, which is usually done, and the other part is emotional trust, so he is the one who identified the emotional part of trust for the first time. For cognitive trust most papers suggest three factors: competence, benevolence, and integrity of the trustee, though many papers have added others.

Yamagishi is a Japanese sociologist who has been working on Anshin; he has a different view from ours. What he suggests is that Anshin is for a traditional society like Japan in which we are xenophobic; we are comfortable in our own community, but we are not comfortable if someone came from the outside to our community, and we just exclude them. That is a community with Anshin in which you don't need trust. According to his recent book[4], Japanese are poor at processing trust, because we didn't need it. But nowadays the society is getting global so we need to process trust. The community of trust is something like the world: you are surrounded by many deceivers; even your neighbour might deceive you. If you have such a risk you need trust.

In the trust research community in Information Science they say if there is a risk you need trust, if there is no risk, you don't need trust. So this is how trust should be. We started to identify what would make you feel secure. So we had many sets of user subjects. We used a psychological way of research, so a lot of user surveys, and statistical analyses, like factor analysis. So the most recent, we redesigned the questionnaire, and did a survey using a webpage. The problem with our previous survey was that we used a questionnaire which was created based on feedback from people with security knowledge, like computer

[1] Camp, L.J.: Design for Trust, in Trust, Reputation and Security: Theories and Practice, LNAI 2631, Springer (Berlin) 2003. Available at:
http://ssrn.com/abstract=627610
[2] Hoffman, L. J., Lawson-Jenkins, K. and Blum, J.: Trust beyond security: an expanded trust model, Communication of ACM, Vol. 49, No. 7, pp. 94–101 2006.
[3] Lewis, J. D. and Weigert, A.: Trust as a Social Reality, Social Forces, Vol. 63, No. 4, pp. 967–985 1985.
[4] Yamagishi, T.: Why did Anshin disappear from Japan? (in Japanese) Shueisha International 2008.

science students, and our previous work on the Anshin factor for people without information security knowledge used the same questionnaire. So we needed something else: this ELM Model, from psychology[5]. Suppose you have information, a commercial message about a car, you would like to buy a car and you have a good knowledge of the car, so you have a motivation, and you have knowledge. Then you would decide whether you accept the first message or not by yourself. That is the central route. However, if a person is not interested in buying a car, nor, he or she has no knowledge of the car, he or she would process whether to accept that message or not with the peripheral route. The peripheral route is where you wouldn't assess that message directly, but you would decide according to whether you trust that company, or, you trust something, you know; I trust this company so I will try it. So you wouldn't look at the message itself, but you decide things based on the trust in someone else.

So for the people without particular knowledge of security, because people would decide these things according to this peripheral route, we need to identify what makes them have this sense of security. It's different from those like computer scientists. So we made a new questionnaire based on incorporating brainstorming, and the KJ method. KJ method is a technique to compile a huge amount of data, invented by a Japanese anthropologist[6]. You need to process so much data, so this is how we did it. With the new survey with a new questionnaire we came up with four factors; three are identical to the results from the previous survey, but on the fourth, reputation of the company from a third party or whatever, this is the new factor we have found. This is our work on Anshin.

Now I have to talk about the usability issues. Because if the system is insecure, the user needs to feel insecure. We tried to identify what sort of interface makes them feel insecure. So that is such an interface to cause discomfort. Interface in security has been researched in different ways. According to Tygar[7] PGP interface is so bad people didn't use it very much, and others observe that in e-Commerce, if the interface is good, people will feel it more trustworthy and they will use it. Our work is a little bit different because we are not seeking for usability but the disusability for this risk awareness. The idea is that if you have a gas leak you first smell, however, gas itself originally has no smell, it's just for risk awareness that people put a bad smell in it. So we thought, we can use this sort of thing on a PC, or on the Internet, or interface, so that's our motivation. Because my colleague is a statistician, and from a psychology background, so we used the same sort of technique we used on Anshin research.

If you have this sort of interface you will feel insecure when you are insecure. So we had a user survey, what makes you feel discomfort when you are using PC or whatever. So we asked both computer science students and others, in total

---

[5] Elaboration Likelihood Model (Petty and Cacioppo 1981).

[6] Kawakita, J., The KJ method — A scientific approach to problem solving, Technical report. Tokyo: Kawakita Research Institute (1975).

[7] Whitten, A. and Tygar, D.: Why Johnny Can't Encrypt: A Usability Evaluation of PGP 5.0, Proceedings of the 9th USENIX Security Symposium, pp.169–184, 1999.

300 students, and found numerous factors that make a user feel very uncomfortable when they are using a PC. So we tried to implement this just for a test, and because we are using undergraduate students to implement, it was easier to implement the colour factor where the system has provided you with some message with a different colour.

So the problem we addressed was this: have you ever sent an email to a different person that has a similar email address? I have many times. I asked the secretary to bring us tea, we had a guest, so we had tea, but what happened was I sent this message to a manager of a company because they had a similar address. I had such errors many times. Auto-complete and if a person is in hurry or in panic — if you have an email from someone, "Your paper has been accepted, but you need to register in two days" or something — you're going to rush. So that sort of situation, you will easily make a mistake. And different windows, well so many windows on one display, and you are doing different work simultaneously, there is a good chance for you to make an error.

So we just tried to make an interface, a warning interface, like if you put this destination address, to which usually you don't send, it will give you a warning, or something. So we made it, and did some evaluation. So that's the end of my talk.

Sandy Clark: Right before you spoke, we'd been having a discussion on seatbelts and airbags, and whether or not they were really useful. And one of the things that Bruce brought up was that a study in New Zealand showed that people would actually drive safer if they perceived themselves to be more at risk, so the idea of putting a spike and not allowing you to have a seatbelt would cause you to drive safer[8].

And I'm wondering what about false Anshin, what about the "padlocked" logo on a webpage that makes someone feel secure when they really aren't.

Reply: I'm running this project on false Anshin at the moment, and we haven't come up with a conclusion yet because it is difficult to test, but in ACM CHI I think, two years or three years ago there was a paper on driving that, in a navigation system, they tried to input false information. So the information is correct in 90%, and 70%, 60%, they tried to reduce the rate. What happened was drivers would drive slower and slower when they don't trust the navigation.

Sandy Clark: But everyone tends to trust their GPS and drive off a cliff into the water.

Reply: Maybe.

Sandy Clark: And the other thing I'm wondering is, it might be interesting to test how long it takes people to get acclimated to the change of colour or to the warning signs, and start ignoring them.

Phil Brooke: There's a study which reported an anti-phishing toolbar which tried really hard to grab the user's attention, to the point of taking over much of the screen. It gradually expanded to alert them that they were about to go and do something a bit dumb. They found they had to put very big warning banners before people would actually take notice, users tried to get through it

---

[8] See LNCS 7114, p 216.

even when it's taking over 50% of their screen space. And it's the habituation that I click through, whatever.

Sandy Clark: So it would be interesting to test just how long it takes. Because I find now with Chrome, when I think I'm going to one site and it's kind of actually going to somewhere else, Chrome just stops everything, it says, are you sure you want to do this. And once or twice I've actually thought about it, like, you know, I don't want this, I have to type in my mail password, I'm going to my hotel's registration.

Phil Brooke: But most people are just going to go, get that out of my way.

Reply: Yes, that's right.

Bruce Christianson: I think the difference is between putting up boxes that people know they have to click through, and changing the ambience.

Phil Brooke: Yes, but how long does it take for this ambience to just be blocked? You have to keep changing this ambience to keep ...

Bruce Christianson: But it's the equivalent of suddenly noticing that all the street lights are out, and most of the people around you are walking very large dogs on long leads.

Phil Brooke: After a short time people become comfortable with a change in their environment, so do we need to change the environment frequently?

Sandy Clark: Yes, because you have to feel at risk, you have to not have a sense of Anshin in order to behave in a fashion that would keep you secure.

Jonathan Anderson: But you don't actually have to make people feel scared all the time.

Sandy Clark: Yes you do.

Jonathan Anderson: What you need to do is present information about actual risks in a way that can be salient. Apple's mail program does something like this: you can set a mode where if you email somebody outside your organisation (that's maybe a silly policy, but basically if an email address doesn't match your configured regular expression) then it comes up as red when you type it in.

Reply: The problem with this sort of interface, if it's too much people just wouldn't use it anymore.

Jonathan Anderson: Right, but if there's a subtle little cue that people can choose to ignore, or choose to pick up on, you're still in a much better position than if you're either being paternalistic and saying, this is a bad thing you shouldn't be doing it, or else not presenting the information so no-one will feel unsafe.

Sandy Clark: But we tend as security people to agree that users are a problem and we're not going to be able to fix the users, so we have to fix the user interface, right. And what we talked about with the whole idea of seatbelts and airbags is that people behave in a more risky fashion if they *think* they're more secure.

Reply: Yes, you always need to have some sort of amount of risk, you want to feel it, if it's too safe you want to act in a more risky way, something like that.

Jonathan Anderson: But I don't think we need to start changing UIs to scare people, the problem is we need to stop using them to make false promises, because the goal is always, oh eCommerce will be safe, you should keep your credit cards online. In order to make people feel safe and secure and want to do this, you have to make all these wishy washy promises about how everything is secure. Whereas if we're just a bit more realistic and honest in saying, the online world is a scary place and sometimes bad stuff happens, but you should probably use it anyway.

Sandy Clark: No, because then people would blame their government, you're supposed to take care of us.

Jonathan Anderson: Well no, because actually I was just going to say that this is a very interesting contrast. At least in the US you have this duality going on where on the one hand, with respect to spending your money, everything is safe, you can throw your money at anything, it will stick, and the right thing will come back, and it's all great. But if you drive around Washington you see these big signs that tell you there's an accident ahead; but when it doesn't tell you there's an accident ahead, what it says is, "report suspicious behaviour", you know, be constantly fearful, people around you are ready to jump on you, blow you up with something. But it's OK to give them money.

Bruce Christianson: Well the thing I like about your approach is that it sees security and usability as two sides of the same coin. And who was it who wrote that paper[9] where they basically said security and usability are both about trying to predict what the user might legitimately want to do? That seemed to me like quite a good way of looking at it.

Paul Syverson: Thinking about the users in Tor, one of the motivating things that you hear all the time is that usability is a security property, you know, stop thinking about it as usability and security, usability defines whether or not the system is secure, it's part of the security.

Jonathan Anderson: And if you have a computer and never introduce anything into it, or connect to anything, it's pretty secure, but yet it's not really useful.

Bruce Christianson: Bob Morris was once asked if he could secure somebody's computer, and he said, yes, took a pair of pliers out of his pocket and he cut the power cord on it.

Todd Andel: Yes, that's right. There's some research going on at Tufts University, I think is very applicable, not on trying to warn users, but they're looking from the attacker perspective, what can I do before the user gets suspicious? I would think it's related, because they were trying to key on from someone messing around the system and, you know, the users go about their normal business. And in their research they're using sensors of brainwaves to start "seeing" suspicion, so I think it's probably a very related topic to this[10].

---

[9] Aligning Security and Usability: KP Yee, IEEE Security & Privacy Magazine 2(5), 2004.

[10] Hirshfield et al., Brain Measurement for Usability Testing and Adaptive Interfaces: An Example of Uncovering Syntactic Workload in the Brain Using Functional Near Infrared Spectroscopy. Proc. ACM CHI 2009 Human Factors in Computing Systems Conference, (2009).

Reply: We have a little experience with ten subjects: six of them felt something was wrong, but they kept sending email without any change. Only four realised with this interface and they changed the address. So maybe people wouldn't bother, even when they have noticed.

Jonathan Anderson: This is something where a computer can in fact help us, so the e-mail interface says, I notice you're emailing Ross, and Joe, and Frank, but it's not the Frank that you usually email at the same time as Ross and Joe, did you maybe mean this other Frank. And you can do that sort of profile in a helpful way.

Reply: And in the other related work according to them they put a picture of the people who you are sending, so you will be sure to whom you are sending.

Sandy Clark: So maybe that's the answer, you're not scaring a person, you are providing them with different choices.

Bruce Christianson: But it's almost like putting up the wallpaper, you know, the faces of people you're sending to, stuff in the background, so that people can say, oh, that's not right.

Paul Syverson: And activate a different part of your brain.

Sandy Clark: Yes, not the fear part, but the, oh wait, this doesn't look right part.

Paul Syverson: This adversary study thing sounds interesting to me. We usually think of an adversary looking at the usability and, you know, putting up a phishing site, so trying to look secure when they're not really. But one of the techniques used by certain censoring countries when they're trying to censor the use of the Internet, they don't actually shutdown, for example, the Tor network, or encrypted communication, they just degrade its performance. So the idea is it works, but it doesn't work very well, and the insecure stuff works much better, so it's an attack on the usability. They make security less usable, well it's just as maybe usable but less pleasant, and so people just switch over to the thing that can be monitored and blocked.

Bruce Christianson: It's interesting that the English word secure actually has a similar entomology to Anshin: *se*, meaning without, and *cure*, meaning care, so it literally means careless, without concern.

Paul Syverson: I like the confusion of careless versus without worry!

Bruce Christianson: Well exactly, there's a wonderful quote from Shakespearean times: "the only way to be safe is never to be secure"[11].

Todd Andel: I think the overall solution is if we can figure out how to get the gas smell into the user interface we'll be fine.

Reply: Because that way anybody knows the risk. The problem with security is hardly anybody understands the risk.

Phil Brooke: I don't think it's quite that simple. The reason the gas leak problem works is that it's unusual, you don't walk around the streets and smell gas, if you smell gas if it's unusual, it's unpleasant, and people go, that's a gas leak, that's the problem.

Paul Syverson: Whereas computer interfaces are safe all the time.

---

[11] Francis Quarles, see LNCS 7114, p 215.

Bruce Christianson: And all the gas smell means is that someone is cooking.

Phil Brooke: Well this is what I was getting at, because you can use discomfort to tell the user there's a problem, but how much do you need, how fast do you need to change it?

Paul Syverson: Because if you get accustomed to it then you start to ignore it.

Feng Hao: But there's another issue about false positives, if you have the gas smell you know for sure something is wrong. But the difficulty with usability is that the system makes the decision for you, and if you've got a few false positives then people get annoyed and they just turn off.

Reply: Or repeating this sort of interface with a different practice. As Paul identified the regulation of speed, there is a time delay factor, if it's so slow people will feel something is wrong.

Paul Syverson: Yes, we usually think of that as, how can we design our secure system to not have that problem, but I thought what was interesting in this case was we found that as an instance of attacking the system, and that it was more effective than if they just blocked it people would get annoyed and they would try to get around it. But if you just make it annoying then people get annoyed at the secure system not at the attackers.

Sandy Clark: Which is what's happened with the little pop-up "do you really want to do this?" because people are just going "OK".

Paul Syverson: One of the best lessons like that I remember is this story about some system where they had to make sure that there was actually an operator sitting at the console periodically before committing to something. So there was a separate galvanically connected button that you would press separately to indicate you were there. After they were using this system they asked some of the operators, oh what is that button for, and they said, oh, sometimes the system clogs up and we hit this button and it clears it out, and that's what they thought, they thought it was clearing a clog.

Jonathan Anderson: So at the risk of going on a bit of a tangent (because we don't like to do that sort of thing here), if you're talking about increasing discomfort, there was somebody at MIT recently who was thinking about how to encourage people to be greener, and she built a little cilice thing like in the Da Vinci code that presses into your legs, and the more electricity you used the tighter it squeezes and it hurts. And then as you turn the lights off you get more relief.

Frank Stajano: There was something that was done about ten years ago by Steve Mann from the University of Toronto who used to walk around with the camera around his eyes, and he said, he wanted something that would give him a painful disconnect, it gave him an electric shock when he didn't have Internet connectivity. And that was something that was him making a point, if you deny me access to the network now you are torturing me.

Jonathan Anderson: I don't know if you can use electric shocks in a user interface.

Frank Stajano: Well his point was not to train himself, it was more in the spirit of what Ross once did called the perjury trap: you do something which would be a pain for you, but you do it to deter other people from doing something bad to you.

Ross Anderson: The idea there was that you would want to prevent a court from ordering you to decrypt something, for the sake of argument, so you would arrange that you could only decrypt if you not only put in a password but put in a declaration under oath that you were doing the decryption of your own free will. And therefore if a court ordered you to do this decryption it would be ordering you to commit perjury, and the courts aren't supposed to be able to order people to commit perjury.

Frank Stajano: It's exactly isomorphic to that, you would do something to your own disadvantage, not for the sake of it but to prevent other people from doing something that is seen as bad towards you.

Ross Anderson: I've since come across research literature under the behavioural economics field about how people create all sorts of difficulties for themselves in doing certain things in order to counter their tendencies towards addiction; for example to give up drinking at lunchtime as a matter of policy, because it is just too easy to go down the pub and have a pint, and then another one.

Usable Privacy by Visual and Interactive Control of Information Flow

Shah Mahmood and Yvo Desmedt

Department of Computer Science,
University College London,
United Kingdom
{shah.mahmood,y.desmedt}@cs.ucl.ac.uk

Abstract. With over 2 billion people using the Internet and over 800 million people registered on the popular social networking website Facebook, one problem that is widely discussed in the media and extensively researched in academic circles is that of ensuring privacy of the users. Privacy has been defined as the "individuals right to control information about themselves", but this right is hard to enforce if one does not understand the flow of information. In this paper, we suggest that in order to bring privacy enhancing protocols into life, for the user, we need to visualise the information flow from the user to the Internet and vice versa. This would help users better understand what information they are sharing with whom and disable any undesired flows, with a mouse-click or a finger-tap, before it is too late.

Keywords: Security Protocols, Privacy, Security, Information Visualisation, Information Flow.

1 Introduction

The level of human connectivity has reached its unprecedented horizons with over 2 billion people using the Internet [3] through their desktop computers, laptops, netbooks and smart phones. The complexity of Internet browsers on these devices is increasing with the advent of new applications, always pushing the previous boundaries. Firefox alone has thousands of plugins for varying functions. Network games are getting more and more popular. Facebook, the popular social networking website, now has over 800 million users [9], and Google search is used by over 1 billion people per month [8]. More than 7 million applications or websites are integrated to Facebook. Users interact with more than 900 million objects including pages, groups, events, etc. All this results in an enormous amount of flow of information.

Social networks along with other web services have been criticised for breaching the privacy of its users. There has been a vast number of initiatives to educate the users so that they do not provide excessive amount of personal information online. Facebook privacy consciousness has been echoed in this reply by President Obama when a school student who wanted to become the President of the

B. Christianson et al. (Eds.): Security Protocols 2012, LNCS 7622, pp. 181–188, 2012.

United States asked him for advice. He replied, "Be careful about what you post on Facebook, because in the Youtube age, whatever you do will be pulled up again later somewhere in your life ..." [1].

The advice by President Obama is applicable to a much broader audience as there is no shortage of stories about employees being sacked due to their Facebook postings [15], students being suspended, users being robbed [14], etc.

Despite all the emphasis on user's awareness, researchers have noticed a dichotomy in the actual behaviour and perception of privacy by users, where in some cases users have been found to sell their private information to super markets for a loyalty card worth a few pounds after a year of regular grocery shopping[1][5,10]. It would not be fair to consider this dichotomous behaviour as a reflection of the lack of users' desire to protect their privacy. Acquisti and Grossklags [4], rightly point towards the bounded rationality and limited working memory of the users for this dichotomous behaviour, but, they do not provide any solution to the problem. In this paper, we propose a solution to the problem identified by them. Breach of privacy occurs only when a user's information flows to an object (system or another user), outside the expected and desired set of objects. A user can avoid such flow of information only when he understands the flow. Indeed, with ever increasing complexity and sophistication of technology, even experts fall victims of being unable to understand the flow of information, e.g., Lewman of the Tor project mentioned that he was under the impression of being connected to a remote server using Tor and logged into the service, only to later find out that the connection was direct and not through Tor [11]. Even experts need sniffers e.g., tools like Wireshark to get a better insight into the low level flow of information. Although these tools are useful, they provide a view at a level too deep for the non-geek.

The world of computer technology has evolved from stroking the keys to point and click, and recently to touch and tap. Users need a more graphical and interactive view to better understand the currently obscure world of communications up and down the stack. This is the focus of the paper. First, we propose a more user friendly, graphical and interactive view of the flow of information to help users better decide what information they want to share and who they want to share the information with. Then, we explain the advantages of the graphical and interactive view for users and service providers, where service providers may use the view to identify any vulnerabilities with ease. Finally, we show that the graphical interactive view of information will help with user's trust in the use of technology, which could boost the user base for a service provider.

2   Graphical and Interactive View of Information Flow

We propose a graphical and interactive view to bring to life, the currently user-obscure flow of information. Facebook, in January 2011, offered users to opt-in to secure browsing [16]. Prior research has shown that users are reluctant to

---

[1] The first author regularly shopped for his groceries using a Tesco's loyalty card for 13 months only to receive GBP 7 worth of coupons.

make changes to the default settings [12]. Normally it is too cumbersome for the user to search into all the options and visualize the impact of switching between them. It will be much easier for the user if they are provided with a view as shown in Figure 1. With this user friendly view, users will be encouraged to change from their current settings to another without making too much extra effort.

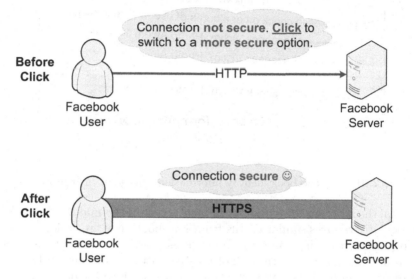

Fig. 1. Easier, graphical and interactive switch to secure browsing

In December, 2011, Facebook founder Mark Zuckerberg's photos were leaked by a relatively simple, presumably accidentally found, vulnerability in Facebook protocols [2]. The vulnerability was exploited if a user reported a victim's display photo as nude. Facebook followed by sending more photos of the victim, even from his private albums to ask the reporting party to verify, if they were also nude. It took Facebook the leak of the personal photographs of it's founder, to fix the bug, which would have been far easier to identify and rectify if the protocol was visualised as shown in Figure 2. The vulnerability was fixed after the leak.

Facebook, by default, emails notifications about almost any activity relevant to the user including any friend requests received, friends commenting on the users' wall, any photos of the users tagged, any new message for the user on Face-book, etc. These email notifications contain links to the activity on Facebook. Phishers also send users emails with links seemingly coming from legitimate sources, but actually directing the user to the attackers pages. These attacker

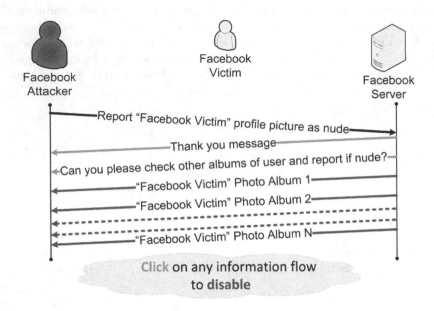

Fig. 2. Helping Facebook identify information leakage in their protocols

pages steal their victims credentials or launch a man-in-the-middle attack. When users regularly receives similar emails from Facebook they are easier to fall victims to phishers claiming to be Facebook. It is possible to turn off these email notification and thus reduce the risk of phishing attacks, but currently the user needs to search into several levels of options by first clicking the downward pointing arrow in the top right corner of the Facebook page, then clicking on "Account Settings" from the pull down menu, followed by clicking the third option in the left side labelled "Notifications", then clicking on "Facebook" under the "All Notifications" in the center of the page and, finally unchecking the desired notifications. It will be much more user-friendly if the flow was represented as shown in Figure 3 and the deactivation would be graphically possible with a click.

When Google+ was launched, one aspect that was widely appreciated, and marketed as a privacy feature, was the concept of circles. A user could divide her social network contacts into different circles and share content on a circle by circle basis. Though Facebook termed all the user's social network contacts as "Friends", there was a possibility of classifying users into lists [13]. Google+ circles were appreciated more than Facebook lists (which were widely unknown to users) due to its graphical and interactive un-usability. In real world, relationships with people change with time, i.e., some people get closer and others get emotionally distant. It is hard for users to keep on reflecting such relationship changes in our social network presence. A better way would be to visualize information flow on the basis of each update, as shown in Figure 4. The picture on

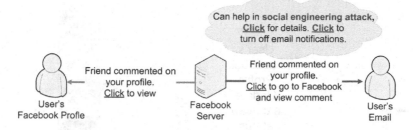

Fig. 3. Identify possible flows of information that may aid in social engineering attacks

the left is that of the user who is updating his Facebook profile. The information is flowing, shown by the directed arrows, to the list of those friends[2], shown on the right, of the user with whom the information is currently being shared, each represented by a thumbnail picture. Some of the pictures may be uploaded recently and not recognizable by the user, for additional information e.g. name, etc., the user can move the pointer over any of the arrows or pictures. Clicking on any of the arrows will disconnect the flow of that particular information to the specific person and save the user from regretting the sharing of private and embarrassing information described in the study by Wang *et al.* [17].

These were only a few examples where the graphical and interactive view of information flow can be considered as a more usable means of ensuring user's privacy. In practice, the visual and interactive view may identify many currently obscure leaks of information.

3   Advantages of Graphical and Interactive View of Information Flow

The use of graphical and interactive view of information has several advantages including the following:

Countering Limitations of the Working Memory. The human working or operant memory is limited [6]. When a user logs into a social network or provides information on any other website, he is psychologically distracted in many ways. These distractions make users less conscious about privacy. With a graphical flow of information available, a user can be reminded of what information is being shared and with whom. It will bring back the concern about privacy into the working memory.

Countering Bounded Rationality Problem. Human rationality in decision making is limited by the amount of time they have to make a decision, the amount of data, the arrangements of data, cognitive limitations of the mind etc [7]. Decision makers should not be expected to make optimal decisions in a

---

[2] These are actual Facebook profile photo thumbnails of the first author's friends, who have kindly agreed to the use of their photographs.

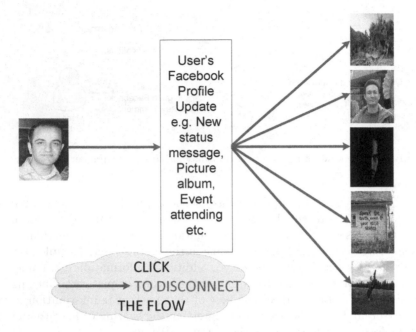

Fig. 4. Visualising Facebook updates and providing users with interactive control

complex scenarios, in a limited time. When a user visits a website, he should not have to spend hours reading the privacy policy, understanding the technical jargon, getting aware of all the parties with whom the information will be shared, etc. A more graphical representation of her information flow can put him in a better position for quick decisions.

As a Protocol Verification Technique. The graphical and interactive view of information flow can help privacy experts, allow service providers testing unit to identify leaks of information, e.g., in scenarios like Figures 3 and 2.

Transparency and User's Increased Trust in the System. Using graphical representation of information flow, users will feel more in command of their private data. This will build their trust and confidence in the system giving them better control when sharing information with circles of their trust.

4   Future Work

To test the empirical impact on users' behaviour, we would implement a Firefox extension that provides the outlined framework of graphical and interactive view of information flow protocols. The extension will be interfaced with Facebook to control data within the social network and also with Wireshark for real time connection monitoring. This real time visual flow of information will provide a user with a better understanding of the information they are sharing. The extensions will be distributed amongst participants and their feedback gathered to provide evidence of the impact on user's decision making.

5   Conclusion

In this paper we proposed a more user friendly view of information flow protocols. This, according to our hypothesis, will aid users to counter for the limitations caused by bounded rationality and limited working memory of humans. We expect the view will result in better privacy practices and will narrow the gap between the perception and behaviour regarding privacy. Moreover, the tool can also be used as an aid for detecting information leakage by service providers.

Acknowledgements. The authors would like to thank Ross Anderson, Bruce Christianson, James Malcolm, Frank Stajano, Matt Blaze, Virgil Gligor, Paul Syverson, Sandy Clark, Jonathan Anderson, and Mauro Conti for their comments about the paper. The first author would also like to thank UCL for financial support through UCL's PhD studentship programme.

References

1. Obama advises caution in use of Facebook. Associated Press (September 8, 2009)
2. Facebook bug sees Zuckerberg pictures posted online. BBC (December 7, 2011)
3. Internet World Stats (2011), http://www.internetworldstats.com/stats.htm
4. Acquisti, A., Grossklags, J.: Privacy and rationality in individual decision making. IEEE Security & Privacy 3(1), 26–33 (2005)
5. Anderson, R.J.: Security engineering - a guide to building dependable distributed systems, 2nd edn. Wiley (2008)
6. Baddeley, A.: Working memory. Science 255(31), 556–559 (1992)
7. Berger, P.L.: Models of Bounded Rationality, vol. I-III. The MIT Press, Cambridge (1982)
8. Efrati, A.: GM signs Google apps pact, in initial step toward cloud. The Wall Street Journal (November 2011)
9. Facebook. Facebook Statistics, http://www.facebook.com/press/info.php?statistics
10. Gross, R., Acquisti, A., John Heinz III, H.: Information revelation and privacy in online social networks. In: WPES, pp. 71–80 (2005)
11. Lewman, A.: Tor: Onion routing. UCL Computer Science, Information Security Seminar Series (January 11, 2012)
12. Mackay, W.E.: Triggers and barriers to customizing software. In: CHI, pp. 153–160 (1991)
13. Mahmood, S., Desmedt, Y.: Poster: preliminary analysis of google+'s privacy. In: ACM Conference on Computer and Communications Security, pp. 809–812 (2011)
14. Michael Henderson, D.L., de Zwart, M., Phillips, M.: Will u friend me? Legal Risks of Social Networking Sites. Monash University (2011)

15. Monkovic, T.: Eagles employee fired for Facebook post. New York Times, March 10 (2009)
16. Naraine, R.: Facebook offers https browsing, but not yet by default (2011),
http://www.zdnet.com/blog/security/facebook-offers-https-browsing-but-not-yet-by-default/8009
17. Wang, Y., Komanduri, S., Leon, P.G., Norcie, G., Acquisti, A., Cranor, L.F.: I regretted the minute I pressed share.: A qualitative study of regrets on Facebook. In: SOUPS (2011)

Usable Privacy by Visual and Interactive Control of Information Flow (Transcript of Discussion)

Shah Mahmood

Department of Computer Science, University College London, UK

I'm here to discuss our work about usable privacy through visual and interactive control of information flow. I have done this work in collaboration with Professor Yvo Desmedt at UCL. We will first talk about the importance of users' privacy, then discuss the reasons that current privacy mechanisms are failing and following that we will discuss our new proposal for a visual and interactive control of information flow.

Today, the Internet is used by over two billion people. Facebook claims that 845 million people are actively using their social network. Over one billion searches take place on Google every month. According to Google Search, "Facebook privacy" is over 28.91 times more famous or infamous than "Iraq war". Users' sharing of personal data online, has lead to embarrassment, for example, in the case of Congressman Weiner. In another incident, students from the University of Oxford were suspended because of the photos they posted on Facebook. Alexander in Malaysia was imprisoned because he expressed his atheist views on Facebook. In many other examples users have lost their employment because they shared some personal data online.

This led to campaigns of awareness, numerous heated debates in media and academia. One student who wanted to become the US President asked President Obama for advice; the President's reply was, "Be careful about what you post on Facebook, because in the YouTube age, whatever you do will be pulled up again later somewhere in your life ...". This indicates the importance of users' privacy in the enormously connected world of social media.

These awareness campaigns have certainly had their impact, even if not to the extent one may desire. People are becoming more private according to recent research by Dey et al.[1]. Researchers have also noted the dichotomy in user behavior: users claim that they respect their privacy, they want their private information to be kept secure, not to be leaked, but still they trade their information for a loyalty card. I personally signed for a Tesco club card and used it for 13 months only to get £7 after regular grocery shopping for the entire duration. So, I valued my grocery information at £7 for 13 months. To experimentally test users' dichotomic behavior we performed a targeted friend attack using Facebook. We sent friend requests to 595 strangers, 370 of which were accepted. Another 3969 users requested to add us. Strangers were willingly falling

---

[1] Ratan Dey, Zubin Jelveh, Keith W. Ross: Facebook users have become much more private: A large-scale study. *IEEE PerCom Workshops 2012*: 346–352.

B. Christianson et al. (Eds.): Security Protocols 2012, LNCS 7622, pp. 189–198, 2012.

for our honeypot. Further details about our work can be found in our IEEE PerCom paper[2].

James Malcolm: Can you tell us a bit more about that second point, how did you do that?

Reply: That is a very interesting question. For the first 99 days we blocked the option of other people requesting to add us. We requested to add 285 targeted users in these 99 days. The requests were sent from a pseudonym. Using this user account we liked the posts by our targets on publicly visible Facebook pages and groups, to create a bond with them. After 99 days we allowed everyone to send us friend requests. For the initial stage we targeted users with a large number of Facebook friends and those who were more social. Thus after the 99 days we already had established a bond with the friends of our targets, who were by then our Facebook friends.

Matt Blaze: Did you do that manually?

Reply: Yes, all this was done manually without the use of any crawlers or bots.

Matt Blaze: Did you make any intelligent comments that a bot would have failed to make?

Reply: No, we only liked our targets' posts and did not make a lot of intelligent comments.

Paul Syverson: As you blocked the users at first, did you attempt to create a club where the users were initially not cool enough to get in and then you let them in?

Reply: This is exactly what we did. Google+ tried that and failed, but we succeeded.

Jonathan Anderson: Do you also have a hundred million friends like Google+?

Reply: Well, we did not manage to have that many friends and it would not have been possible on Facebook with a user's maximum limit of having 5000 friends. However, we managed to have approximately 4300 friends. After the experiment, we deactivated the account without collecting or saving any personal and identifiable data.

Let us come back to our discussion about today's topic. Acquisti and Grossklags[3] showed that users' dichotomous behaviour regarding their privacy might be because of human beings' bounded rationality and limited working memory. They only provided empirical evidence of the problem without any solutions. Here, we will discuss some possible solutions.

Lewmann of the Tor project, during his talk at UCL, discussed how he was deceived by the system's complexity into connecting to a remote server directly instead of using Tor. This is only one example out of the countless incidents where even an expert finds it difficult to be certain about their privacy practices. No

---

[2] Shah Mahmood, Yvo Desmedt: Your Facebook deactivated friend or a cloaked spy. *IEEE PerCom Workshops 2012*: 367–373.

[3] Alessandro Acquisti, Jens Grossklags: Privacy and Rationality in Individual Decision Making. *IEEE Security & Privacy 3(1)*: 26–33 (2005).

one, including experts, can afford to use sniffers at all times to monitor every packet, in detail, leaving their computer to the Internet or vice versa. This room is full of security and privacy experts, but how many of us actually analyze every single packet? We do not and we cannot. In this case, when experts find it impossible, what is the solution for the non-expert user?

Although there is no single universally agreed definition of privacy, we would consider it to be the "right of an individual to control information about themselves". Now, if a user can not understand the flow of information, how would he be able to control it? This makes the privacy problem a problem of information flow. In such a case, what should we do?

Our solution is to provide users with a visual and interactive view of the information flow. When users were unable to do relatively complex calculations without any tool, in a limited time, we invented calculators. When traders needed tools to aid them in decisions for their high frequency trading, we invented models for algorithmic trading. Now, when we as humans are bounded in rationality and are constrained by our limited working memory, which makes us unable to make the optimal privacy decisions, we once again need tools to provide us with decision support. We have proposed two mathematical models to aid us with such decision support[4].

We need to provide users with a visual view of the information. They cannot sit and use Wireshark to do deep packet inspection for every incoming and outgoing packet. The world of computers has evolved from stroking keys to point and click, touch and tap, and voice recognition. Users need to be provided with easier view of information flow, they cannot and should not be expected to understand the underlying technical complexities.

Yuko Murayama: A researcher once told me that it is hard to create a commercial film for a cryptographic technology because of the difficulty to explain its functionality to a common user, i.e., what this technology provides them.

Reply: Is it hard, or there's a lack of incentives for the thing to be made, because even the evolution of the mobile phone was hard, but Steve Jobs came and caught the idea, he made the iPhone look better. So can't we catch the idea of providing visual privacy and ease of access to users.

Jonathan Anderson: Well the trouble is that the only people using the current model who are in a position to do it are the people who will never have an incentive to do it, because you have to have complete visibility of the network in order to do information flow visualization, you can't do it from the edges, you have to be in the core. And the people who run the core don't want you to be privacy salient.

Reply: At the edge on your own network you could control the flow information from/to your local machine. Similarly you can control the view of your information on social networks in the cloud.

---

[4] Shah Mahmood, Yvo Desmedt: Two New Economic Models For Privacy. *ACM SIG-METRICS/ Performance Workshop on Privacy and Anonymity for the Digital Economy (PADE)*, 2012.

Jonathan Anderson: All you see on your local network is everything that's leaving your computer, so all you see is that everything is gone, is that the only visualization you can do?

Reply: Yes, you can see the visual flow of information from your computer and the interactive part of the model ensures you can visually discontinue any flows, e.g. using a point and click.

Competition changes privacy practices of companies. Just consider the improvements in privacy practices by Facebook after Google+ came into competition: its settings became better, it started giving the option to use HTTPS, its "lists" which were not visible became visible in the profiles of users. So, if competition is there, we think the incentives will be created for a network.

The business models of many websites today are based on the revenue generated from advertisements, so if advertisers could benefit from a more transparent system, the service providers would have incentives to help transparency.

Sandy Clark: Advertisers don't benefit at all from privacy, advertisers make their money from mining information about you.

Reply: Well, some prior research has shown that a more transparent system gains a user's trust, which leads them to sharing more data, which could actually be more useful for advertisers.

Sandy Clark: What about the fact that privacy prevents advertisers from mining information about you that is what they need for targeted marketing?

Bruce Christianson: Actually, what the advertiser wants to do is to target advertising to the people who are likely to buy it. They don't necessarily want to know who those people are at the time those ads are placed, if they could just be assured that the ads were going to the right people, and that a proportion of those would make contact with them, they would be satisfied.

Jonathan Anderson: Again, the problem is that, you may have diminishing returns, where segmenting people into 20 categories gets you 90% of the way in terms of targeting value, but there's no reason not to be as intrusive as you can; even if it only gets you another 1% value it does get you something.

Bruce Christianson: At the moment advertisers do it because they can, they've got no incentive not to do so and they have got no disincentive to avoid it.

Jonathan Anderson: I can't imagine what the disincentive would be aside from something like regulation. I mean, I can't imagine a scheme in which the advertiser says, "we're in a position to mine and get more information but we choose not to because it would be a big risk, or it would be more expensive to us somehow." I don't see how that's going to happen. I wish it would.

Sandy Clark: If you were the company who decided to get slightly less information, you're then putting yourself at a competitive disadvantage.

Reply: As Bruce said earlier, the advertisers are interested in targeting their buyers, not necessarily who they are, so if we remove the lemon market effect and bring in transparency, users will be more aware of what data about them is shared and will enable them to control it.

Jonathan Anderson: No, because the users do not choose.

Sandy Clark: No, the advertisers are the people who want to sell you something and they want to know to whom to market. Even if a tiny bit of information gives them a competitive edge, they will attempt to acquire it.

Reply: If I have to choose between Google+ and Facebook, and Google+ gives me the clean information flow and everything, then I will surely go for Google+.

Matt Blaze: So are we talking about the flow of information from my computer, or from something in the cloud?

Reply: Both.

Matt Blaze: Right, I think with my computer, I at least have a chance of trusting that visualization, even if I don't know how to write the software provided, but for something in the cloud I have to actually trust that the cloud provider: (1) knows how to write the software, and (2) is being honest with me about it.

Reply: We have to trust the system, and if there is transparency we are going to trust it more.

Bruce Christianson: There's two separate arguments here, one is the user, one is the advertiser. To the user we're saying, we won't let advertisers mine your data, but we will allow advertisers to target you if you've indicated you're willing for us to do that. To the advertiser you say, you can't.

Matt Blaze: Well that's what they're telling you, that's the interface. What actually happens is unclear.

Bruce Christianson: Yes, it is unclear.

Matt Blaze: I find it interesting that we don't even know what this is worth. It is instructive that you cannot go to Google and say, how much do you make off of me, can I write you a cheque for that amount, or maybe a little more than that amount and have you not mine my data. They won't even tell you what the number is let alone accept the cheque.

Bruce Christianson: This is an experiment in cyberspace: you say to the advertiser, "won't let you strip-mine us, but we will allow you to target and pay us by results."

Ross Anderson: Isn't that an interesting and very feasible experiment because you could instrument users to find out what ads they click on, you can participate in the options to find out what the price is, and you could certainly, to within reasonable asymptotic find out what particular users tend to be worth. Perhaps there are competitors like that which already do this.

Jonathan Anderson: So there is some visualization that already happens in that some of the large advertising firms will show you a little icon and an ad and you can click to ask, "why am I seeing this", and they'll tell you, "it's because we think that you are interested in cars". They won't tell you how they got it, and you won't get complete information flow, but the only reason you have that even is because companies got spooked by the threat of regulation, and they're so scared of regulation that they decide, "we better do something so we don't get regulated."

Ross Anderson: Well, again, one could build a tool that would filter the 30 to 50 URLs that come off a webpage nowadays and alert people to the predatory behavior of advertisers.

Sandy Clark: Ghostery already does that. It is a Firefox plugin which shows you every single advertiser that is looking at you at that moment, and you can click whether or not you want to block.

Ross Anderson: What's this plugin named?

Sandy Clark: It's called Ghostery.

Virgil Gligor: So I wonder if you could say something about what you mean by information flow. What are the ends of the information flow and could I ever set my default as no information flow?

Reply: The ends of the information flow are from a source to a destination, e.g. from your computer to Facebook or from Facebook to your friends. Yes, you can block the information flow, in which case there is no communication.

Virgil Gligor: Can you set specific rules?

Reply: Yes, you can have specific set of rules. If we consider the example of a firewall, you can have a set of rules, e.g., we would not allow x, y and z to avoid intrusion to the system. The same concepts could be used for privacy. If someone is accessing my full-name you may allow it, but if my date of birth is going to leave my computer stop it.

Frank Stajano: But if they want to send your date of birth they could obfuscate it in a way that would go past your filter, if they wanted to.

Reply: If they wanted to, yes, they could be given a warning.

Frank Stajano: The alarm will occur with a little delay and there are so many ways to obfuscate data.

Reply: That is true, the system will have its limitations.

Frank Stajano: If they have any channel they can always do enough steganography that is going to go past the filter.

Reply: Yes, I agree with you. The idea to offer Google the amount of money they earn from advertisements from your use, in return for them not targeting you was given by Larry Page a few years ago. He wanted a scheme where users could opt out of advertisements for a certain fee. However it was never practically adopted. Service providers should be given economic incentives towards a more transparent model. For example, if one service provider provides you with a transparent service while another an obfuscated one, then you as a rational user would go for the transparent option. This creates an economic incentive for the obfuscated provider to become more transparent to regain their customers. This pattern of providing more transparent service to gain strategic advantage will continue till the system reaches its Nash equilibrium, which in this case would be when all providers are equally transparent (at least in the users' view).

Jonathan Anderson: Who is the customer in that scenario? Competition only works if I get to choose, but the people who are actually doing the buying are the advertisers; they're not going to ask, "who is more a privacy preserving?" I don't get to choose which ad network serves the ad that's on my screen. I get to choose Facebook or Google+, but I don't choose that based on information flow, I do that based on who's there. Well, maybe *I* choose Google+ because of information flow, but I'm not most people.

Reply: Yes, but we can affect information flow in there, we can visualize the flow of information as shown in the next scenarios in these social networks where you can choose it in an easier way, e.g. of which network provides you a better view. You can make applications for Facebook — writing an application for Facebook is not that hard — for a complete flow of information visualized.

Sandy Clark: Part of the problem is that we're not the drivers for this; as Jon was saying, certainly in the US we don't own the information about ourselves.

Reply: No, you are the input provider, if you stop providing input, advertisers will never pay for the service. It is you who is driving the system, it's not the advertiser, the advertiser is there only because of you. If you leave the system, then the system is worth nothing. It should not be a small number of people who realize this, but a large enough number to impact the decisions of service providers.

Sandy Clark: Well, if I leave the system, I will be denying myself access to tools that I need for research and online shopping.

Jonathan Anderson: Why don't we see the scenarios.

Reply: Yes, let us look at the scenarios now. The first scenario shows the complexity for a user opting to use secure browsing on Facebook, currently involving several tiresome steps. Prior research has shown that users rarely change their default. One reason for such a behavior is the obvious complexity of these systems.

Sandy Clark: Isn't there also the assumption that they set up the default way that is the best way for you, and that implies that the default way would be secure because of course this company cares about my security?

Reply: I don't think there's anything secure in this way of using it. It's more of a pain, it's like writing the privacy policy in an obfuscated way so that no-one understands what the company does.

Sandy Clark: I absolutely agree with that.

Todd Andel: I think most people would believe that.

Sandy Clark: The assumption is that it's set up in the way that's best for you.

Jonathan Anderson: Really, does anybody actually trust Facebook?

Todd Andel: No, in general, the general public does not, and I don't think anybody in this room does.

Bruce Christianson: Operationally, yes.

Jonathan Anderson: No I don't think so, I think that there is a huge amount of distrust over Facebook.

Frank Stajano: No, there's a subtle thing, which is that you don't really know how it works, and therefore you think, if you are going to change things and you feel incompetent, you're going to break them, and you're going to be at fault, it's going to be your fault that it doesn't work. So you say, "well I don't know what's happening, and I'm not sure it's very good, but at least it's not my fault."

Sandy Clark: I am less at risk if I follow defaults.

Jonathan Anderson: I'm still in the warranty or something.

Bruce Christianson: We need to know how we're using this T word. Very often we trust Facebook not because we think they're warm and cuddly and wholesome, but because we have no choice. We feel we have no choice about who you trust any more (like Bob Morris once said).

Reply: Yes, but if you have one unique selling point and another company comes and uses more transparency as a selling point, don't you think it could drive some customers of Facebook away.

Bruce Christianson: What I would very much prefer is to say, I will use this other company because I don't have to trust them, I can see that they're doing what I want.

Sandy Clark: Yes.

Reply: That is why there is a lot of research that shows that transparency increases the use or the trust of users. So if you give them transparency the network is going to benefit from users' use, more advertisers are going to come, although they won't be able to steal your information in the negative ways as they do now. We propose to use a more abstract and transparent view for changing this setting towards being more secure.

Jonathan Anderson: But to answer your question, "don't you think if you made a service that was more transparent people would switch": no, I do not think that people would switch to a more transparent, more secure better service, because people choose their social network based on the network effects of who's already there. There are a few people, maybe only a few of the 100 million on Google+ who would choose something that is slightly, marginally better. Most would say, "I am going to leave Facebook and go to this other thing not because of a better alternative but because Facebook has done something really irritating." To go back to Ross' point, they have to get the attitude where people want to say, "throw the bums out (and let's get in another set of bums)."

Bruce Christianson: So we need to make managing your personal information fashionable.

Ross Anderson: Well this is probably what's going to undermine Facebook if anything does, the fact that it's no longer cool once your parents are there you've lost interest, or whatever.

Jonathan Anderson: Or you go to Instagram and then Facebook says, "ah, not so quick," and pull you back in.

Matt Blaze: Facebook has to do something irritating and invasive to stop people from what they are doing now.

Jonathan Anderson: Every 18 months or so, Facebook does something that users get up in arms: "this is outrageous and I'm going to leave".

Matt Blaze: And then the stock price goes up.

Jonathan Anderson: And then they back off a little bit, and then they do it more quietly later. But if there was actually a viable alternative that was sitting there ready to go at the moment when everybody was outraged, if there was a loyal opposition[5], as there were, that people actually could credibly switch to, maybe there's a chance. But Facebook has to do something really bad for people to switch.

Sandy Clark: I use Google+ for the same reasons that you do you, but my husband, my brother, my nephews, are all on Facebook, so I'm not in their social network and they're not in mine.

Reply: I have an account on Google+ and Facebook. I use Facebook for my work, but I don't use Google+ because it's not transparent, it's about the same as Facebook, in fact it is much worse because Google has much more power: it has my search, it has my email, it has my Facebook account, my Google+ account, it has everything, so combining all these threats, it's a much bigger problem than Facebook. Why should a user trust Google+? We are comparing the wrong parties: we want to compare a transparent versus Facebook, not Google+ versus Facebook. It's two evils that we are comparing; we want a lesser evil.

Sandy Clark: What if I switch to a more transparent social network and I can't get my family to switch, period.

Reply: You will: once you switch another person, it's a party thing, it's a networking thing. Once it starts falling they will lose. Where did Orkut go, where is MySpace, why did Facebook come into the market after MySpace? Because they offered easier usable service to the user.

Sandy Clark: No, because all the college kids were using it.

Jonathan Anderson: It was a generational change.

Reply: So do you think that the users will remain the same forever, there is no change for the better going to happen again?

Jonathan Anderson: No, I'm very hopeful and optimistic: my PhD work is on building an alternative architecture to Facebook. I hope that people will switch from Facebook, but I'm just saying that it is not as simple as building something that is technically better, or that provides more transparency or usability. There is a political dimension to it.

Reply: That is very true, transparency is not the only thing, but it could be one of the selling points. Coming to the other scenarios. Facebook by default emails the notifications of almost everything into your email, this could start with a social engineering attack where an attacker could send you an email that looks like Facebook sent it, you click on the link, and enable all known phishing attacks or relaying attacks. But if you use it in a more graphical and visual view of this it's very easy to just block those abstractions. Coming to scenario 3, Zuckerberg's photos were leaked in December 2011, and the protocol was very simple: it was to just report one of the photos as nude and then Facebook used to send all the photographs from the private album of the user, and you got all the properties. But with a visual view they could debug such problems very easily.

How many people remember who is on their circles in Google+, do you remember who is on your which circle? How many friends do you have on Google+?

Jonathan Anderson: I just needed it to communicate once.

---

[5] Ross Anderson, these proceedings.

Reply: Well if you look at the normal college students, or the generation that you are talking about, they have 500 to 600 friends on average, do you think they will remember who is on what list?

Jonathan Anderson: Well this is the reason to have lists, you build an abstraction so I don't *have* to remember everybody who is in my Cambridge Computer Lab circle. That's why I made the circle.

Reply: Yes, but if you put them in a friend circle, your friends keep changing, some get closer, some go apart, how are you going to manage that? One can see the evolution from a good friend to a better friend or an enemy. The current lists, or circles do not show the flow visually, that is what we here emphasize on. So it is giving you more transparency than the current system. With this technique, we are countering the limitations of working memory, you don't need to remember everything, you are seeing, visualizing everything at that point. It's about bounded rationality so you don't need to do all the calculations in your mind: the calculations are done for you, giving you a description. Mathematical models or economic models can be used at the backend. It could be used for protocol verification. It could be used for transparency for increased trust in the system. We are going to implement a Firefox plugin which will use Wireshark at the backend to provide users with a visual and interactive view of their data to and from their computer. The graphical abstraction will enable a user to better understand how these systems work and what data of theirs' is accumulated by the service providers, ISPs, and governments.

Sandy Clark: I think that would be really useful.

Sense-And-Trace: A Privacy Preserving Distributed Geolocation Tracking System

Eyüp S. Canlar[1,2], Mauro Conti[3], Bruno Crispo[4], and Roberto Di Pietro[5]

[1] Sapienza University of Rome, Italy
canlar@di.uniroma1.it
[2] VU University Amsterdam, The Netherlands
escanlar@cs.vu.nl
[3] University of Padua, Italy
conti@math.unipd.it
[4] University of Trento, Italy
crispo@disi.unitn.it
[5] Roma Tre University of Rome, Italy
dipietro@mat.uniroma3.it

Abstract. The capabilities of modern smartphones pave the way for a new collaborative usage of this technology. Several researchers already envisaged to use this technology for distributed sensing purposes. In particular, one of these purposes focuses on tracing devices (people) movement. Current solutions for distributed tracing (either based on information provided by the mobile nodes, or collected by the surrounding network) have some limitations: e.g. accuracy, privacy, cost of deployment, and cost of operation.

The aim of this paper is to highlight the open problems of distributed geolocation tracing and to propose a solution for some of the current problems. In particular, we propose Sense-And-Trace (SAT), which is a system that makes use of collaborative sensing to collect information about other mobile nodes with the final aim of tracking potential target nodes. In SAT, information is collected in a way such that the privacy of nodes that voluntarily collaborate is preserved, and the information of the mobility of a node is disclosed only to the authorized entity (e.g. a law enforcement agency with the appropriate permission). Our solution can be seen as an enhancement of the classical "neighborhood watching" concept, with fine-grained mobility information automatically-collected through the devices carried by humans.

1 Introduction

Contemporary smartphones are equipped with several sensors, such as: GPS, accelerometer, compass, microphone, camera, and proximity meter. These sensing capabilities, together with the fact that smartphones are currently widely distributed, pave the way for a new usage of this technology: for distributed sensing purposes, as already been envisaged by several researchers [2,8,20,14,6].

One of the usage of this distributed sensing capability is in tracking the movement of the devices in a geographical area (e.g. a metropolitan area), with the

B. Christianson et al. (Eds.): Security Protocols 2012, LNCS 7622, pp. 199–213, 2012.

final aim of tracking people carrying those devices. From a high level point of view, current mobile device tracking systems periodically update an authorized entity about the current position of a mobile device. In this context, we can identify two types of mobile device tracking system, namely: i) *handset-based*, and ii) *network-based* mobile device tracking systems [23,13]. The handset-based mobile device tracking systems relies on the geographic location (geolocation) information provided by the mobile device which is the "target" of the tracing. Network-based mobile device tracking systems compute the position of the target based on its distance from network infrastructure elements (e.g. base stations, access points, beacon nodes), which are not mobile. The most well known example of a network-based tracking system is the system used by cellular phone network operators, namely cell tower triangulation. The network operator knows the exact position of its cell towers. The network operator computes the relative position of the target mobile device using its distance to three or more cell towers.

Motivation and Open Problems. Both handset-based and network based solutions have limitations. In fact, in handset-based solutions, the target might not always be able (or willing) to provide the sensed information. Also, the target might provide the system with false information. As for network-based solutions, they are not very accurate (e.g. triangulation error ranges from $200m$ to $1000m$), and also they need a significant deployed infrastructure and/or cooperation from different entities (e.g. telco operators). Furthermore, in some specific circumstances (e.g. rural area, natural disaster, or terrorist attack) there might not be any deployed infrastructure available.

Researchers also tried to design hybrid solutions [16,19,11] to increase the quality of network-based solutions: the coarse information gained from the network infrastructure is refined with information provided by the target device itself. However, hybrid solutions also combine the disadvantages of both types of systems. Hence, there is still need for a tracking system that (all at once):

- it is distributed (does not rely on availability/information provided by the network infrastructure);
- it does not rely on the information provided by the target mobile device;
- it is cheap and easy to deploy and maintain;
- it preserves the privacy of the devices (users) that voluntarily participate as *witnesses*. In particular, the ideal system should: i) disclose information only to the authorized party, and ii) only about the user for which the authority requested information.

Contribution. In this paper, we discuss the open problems in distributed tracing solutions. Then, we address some of these problems proposing Sense-And-Trace (SAT): a system that makes use of collaborative sensing to track mobile devices within a geographic area, and for a given period of time. The tasks we consider in our collaborative sensing systems are: i) data acquisition, and ii) querying.

Our solution is inspired by the "neighborhood watching" concept. In fact, in the SAT system, neighbor nodes collaborate to achieve a common goal, which is to track the movements of a potential target mobile device. Indeed, SAT just improves the accuracy of traditional "neighborhood watching" by adding the capability of having fine-grained and automatically-collected information. Hence, the security protocol become "embedded" in the life of humans carrying mobile wireless devices.

Outline. The remainder of this paper is outlined as follows. Section 2 reports the related work in this area. Section 3 presents the system model we consider and the assumptions we make. Consequently, in Section 4 we introduce our proposed solution: Sense-And-Trace (SAT). Section 5 provides a discussion about the properties of our proposed solution. Finally, in Section 6 we present our conclusions.

2   Related Work

There are two categories in the work related to location tracking of mobile nodes. The first category introduces systems that track mobile nodes within a closed environment, like in a building (indoor tracking) [12,19]. The second one deals with geolocation tracking of mobile nodes outdoors [16,24,3,11,20,4].

Let us start with discussing the related works about indoor target tracking. In [12], the authors propose the *"MoteTrack"* system which is a decentralized approach to radio frequency based indoor location tracking. The MoteTrack system computes the location of a mobile node based on the Received Signal Strength Signature Indication (RSSI) from a network of beacon nodes spread throughout a building. In contrast to other known solutions for indoor tracking, the MoteTrack system is decentralized and does not rely on any back-end server. However, this system requires additional infrastructure (network of beacon nodes) to work properly. Furthermore, preserving the privacy of the traced mobile nodes is completely out of the scope of MoteTrack.

In another work [19], the authors propose *"FindingMiMo"* which is also a decentralized indoor mobile node tracking system. In contrast to the MoteTrack system, FindingMiMo does not require the availability of beacon nodes to track mobile nodes. Instead, the FindingMiMo system makes use of the available WiFi access points to track a lost mobile node. More specifically, in FindingMiMo the target mobile device logs WiFi channel conditions. When the user looses her device, she tries to find it back using another "chaser" device. The chaser compares the logs it receives from the lost device with the WiFi channel conditions it is sensing. In this way, the chaser backtracks the path that the lost device has followed to the place it is currently located at. However, the FindingMiMo system still relies on the availability of existing infrastructure. Furthermore, also this system does not take privacy into consideration.

Other research focused on location tracking of mobile nodes in an outdoor environment. In [16], the authors propose *"Adeona"*, which is a privacy preserving decentralized system to locate and trace stolen or lost devices. Adeona consists of a client-side and a distributed storage. The client-side periodically collects location information. Then, the client-side performs some cryptographic operations on the collected location information, to make it anonymous and un-linkable. The client-side uploads the location updates to the distributed storage on pseudo-randomly determined times to overcome potential timing attacks. In contrast, the distributed storage is based on an open source distributed storage system OpenDHT [15], whose nodes run on PlanetLab [5]. Only the owner of the lost or stolen system can decode the location updates from the distributed storage. As said, this system relies on the cooperation of the mobile devices it is tracking. However, in the case that a thief applies counter measures (i.e. power off device immediately, erase and reinstall software at home), then the Adeona system fails to track the target device. Moreover, as of 1 July 2009 OpenDHT was taken down from PlanetLab. So, the Adeona system is not operational anymore.

Another outdoor approach [3] proposes to accurately detect the location of a smartphone combining data from two sensors. The first sensor is the camera integrated in the phone. The other sensor is the GSM modem of the smartphone. More specifically, the first step in this approach is computing the geolocation. This system computes the location by querying (i.e by sending an AT+CSQ [10] request) the GSM modem for the RSSI. In the second step, the smartphone sends a set of pictures of its surroundings to a server. The server uses Content Based Image Retrieval (CBIR) to analyze and match the pictures with known landmarks. Then, the server computes the more accurate geolocation of the smartphone by using a *time-forwarding algorithm*. In the last step, the server sends to the smartphone the geolocation as computed in the previous step. Unfortunately, also this work did not consider privacy. In fact, anybody that can gain access to the server is able to track any smartphone involved in this system.

The contributions exposed so far rely on the cooperation of the tracked device. As well as on the fact that the tracked device provides the tracking system trustworthy information. However, in [24,25], the authors make the observation that malicious smartphone users can make their devices send falsified geolocation information to get illegitimate access to resources or provide bogus alibis. To overcome this problem, the authors propose *"APPLAUS"* which is a privacy preserving location proof updating system. In APPLAUS, Bluetooth enabled mobile (neighboring) devices generate location proofs, and it updates this to an untrusted server. An authorized verifier can query and receive location proofs from the server. The APPLAUS system makes use of statistically changing pseudonyms to guarantee the location privacy from every party. A drawback of the APPLAUS system is that it makes use of a centralized component, namely the untrusted server. When this untrusted server is unavailable due to DoS attacks, or hardware malfunctions, the system is useless.

Everything we discussed so far was related on how we can track a mobile node in either a centralized or decentralized approach. For the decentralized options it is also interesting to see how many sensor nodes we need, to track a mobile node in a given geographic area. To find an answer to this question, the authors of [9] conducted a simulation study. More specifically, in this study the authors assume a malnet (i.e. a malicious network consisting of smartphones, routers, and other WiFi enabled devices). The nodes of this malnet cooperate to track a specific mobile node. The results of this study show that a small number (some 10%) of mobile devices can track the majority of users, during a significant fraction of their travel. Based on their research, the authors draw the following conclusions: i) in the current situation, voluntary networks with perceived benefits can probably achieve the usage rate necessary to track individual movements, and ii) the ubiquitous deployment of 802.11n in smartphones would make it possible for a malnet to track the geolocation of a specific mobile node.

Finally, we want to note that none of the above systems succeed in providing a robust distributed privacy-preserving trustworthy geolocation tracking system, which is the target of our research.

3   System Model and Assumptions

The main components of the SAT system model are: i) the *nodes*, ii) a *Distributed Data Store (DDS)*, and iii) a *Data Collector (DC)*.

The nodes are personally-owned mobile devices (e.g. smartphones, or tablets). These nodes are distributed over a geographic area (e.g. metropolitan area), and they move within this geographic area as their owners travel. They communicate using their short range radios (e.g. Bluetooth or WiFi). Furthermore, they can pinpoint their own geolocation (e.g. using GPS, AGPS, or WiFi Location Service) using their embedded hardware.

In the SAT system model, we have two types of nodes: i) *sensor nodes*, and ii) *target nodes*. The sensor nodes voluntarily participate in SAT i.e. they run an application to scan their environment, and log that other wireless devices are in their communication range. The sensor nodes store their logs on the DDS using any data packet service. That is by using a mutually authenticated TCP connection either via a WiFi access point that the sensor node has access to, or by using the cellular data service (e.g. UMTS or HSPDA).

In contrast, target nodes do not have to voluntarily participate in the SAT system. This is not surprising considering that target nodes are the objects that the SAT system wants to track. To clarify this consider the following: an individual involved in criminal activities does not want to be tracked, because its geolocation might incriminate its involvement in a criminal event. Even in this case the SAT system is able to track the target nodes, because it does not rely on any (geolocation) information provided by the target nodes. A final important note is that in this system model a node can be, at the same time, a sensor node and a target node.

In this system model, the DDS is a distributed database. More specifically, parts of the database (containing the geolocations of target nodes) are stored on multiple computers within a network. These multiple computers can reside at the same or at different geolocations. In any case, the DDS falls under the administrative domain of one authorized organization.

Furthermore, in this model the DC is the only authorized entity that can track the movements of target nodes. In addition, the communication between a DC and its DDS runs over a secure communication channel (e.g. private local area network, VPN, or SSL/TLS). We also have to note that the entity type of the DC depends on the use case scenario of the SAT system. For example, if we use the SAT system for surveillance purposes (e.g. tracking the movements of suspects), then the DC is a *Law Enforcement Agency (LEA)*. Another use case scenario is that of tracking lost or stolen devices. In this case, the DC would be the legitimate owner.

In Figure 1, we illustrate an example SAT system, where $W_0, W_1, \ldots, W_5$ are sensor nodes, and S is the target node. The arrows between several components illustrates the communication links, and the messages (i.e. GLMs) that they exchange over these links.

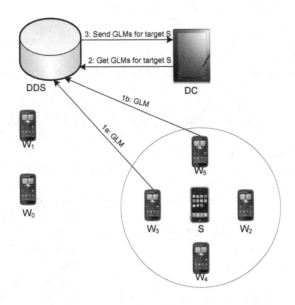

Fig. 1. Overview of our solution

We also make the following explicit assumptions for the SAT system model. Similar to [9], we assume that both type of nodes (sensor and target nodes) have their short range radios enabled continuously. Moreover, as in [17,24,25], we assume a *Pseudonymous Public Key Infrastructure (PPKI)*. In which, the trusted *Certificate Authority (CA)* acts as an authentication and authorization service for the sensor nodes, DDS, and DC. For this reason, the sensor nodes, DDS, and DC have to register with the CA. As a result of the registration, the DDS and DC receive a public/private key pair. On the other hand, during the registration phase the CA preloads each of the N sensor nodes W_i (with $0 \leq i \leq N-1$) with M pseudonyms $\{P_{i,k}\}_{k=1}^{M}$. For each one of these pseudonyms, the CA also preloads a public/private key pair $<K_{P_{i,k}}, K_{P_{i,k}}^{-1}>$ (with $1 \leq k \leq M$), and an associated public key certificate $sign_{CA}(K_{P_{i,k}})$ signed with the private key of the CA. We also have to note that the CA is the only entity that can link the real identity (e.g. BSSID or BD_ADDR) of a witness W_i to one of its M pseudonyms $\{P_{i,k}\}_{k=1}^{M}$. Finally, we assume that SAT replaces the source addresses, required by the underlying communication protocol, with the pseudonyms [22,17]. This is done as a counter measure for the localization attack as described in [22].

Below we provide an overview of all notations used in this paper in Table 1.

Table 1. Notation used in this paper

Notation	Description
W_i	A sensor node
S_j	A target node
$\mathcal{W}$	The set of all sensor nodes
$\mathcal{S}$	The set of all target nodes
N	The number of sensor nodes (i.e. $|\mathcal{N}| = N$)
$x\|y$	x concatenated to y
$A \xrightarrow{(m)} B$	An entity A sends a message m to another entity B
L_n	The geolocation of a node n
I_n	The identity of a node n
$P_{W_i,k}$	kth pseudonym of W_i
$\{P_{W_i,k}\}_{k=1}^{M}$	The set of M pseudonyms associated with W_i
$<K_{P_{i,k}}, K_{P_{i,k}}^{-1}>$	The public/private key pair of an entity A
$E_{K_A}(m)$	Encrypt message m with public key K_A of an entity A
$D_{K_A^{-1}}(m)$	Decrypt message m with private key K_A^{-1} of an entity A
$Sign_A(m)$	Sign the message m with private key K_A^{-1} of an entity A
$Verify_A(m)$	Verify the signature of the message m with public key K_A^{-1} of an entity A
$G_{GLM_{T_x}}$	A group of at time T_x concurrently created location logs

4   Sense-And-Trace

In this section, we introduce our solution: *Sense-And-Trace*. We start with giving a brief overview of our system (Section 4.1). Then, we provide the algorithmic description of our solution (Section 4.2).

4.1   Overview

To describe the overview of our system, let us assume a real use case: a surveillance scenario. In this scenario, the DC is a LEA, and it manages and operates a DDS. This LEA deploys a SAT application to collaboratively track any suspect S_j within a given geographic area GA. The LEA distributes this SAT application via application markets, like Google Android Market, Apple App Store, etc. Individuals voluntarily download and use this application to help the LEA in tracking the movements of suspects. This collaborative behavior might be encouraged via incentives (e.g. the users that aids in capturing a criminal gets a financial reward, or gets a tax reduction). We assume that N individuals in a given geographic area GA downloaded the application. In other words, this means we have a collaborative sensor network with N mobile sensor nodes (e.g. witnesses $W_0, W_1, \ldots, W_{N-1}$) in the given geographic area GA.

Now we have set the use case scenario, we continue with providing a brief overview of how SAT works on the witness side. First of all, a witness W_i needs to start the SAT application. After this, the SAT application periodically senses its environment for any S_j. In other words, each W_i checks whether S_j is within its communication range. When a S_j is indeed in the communication range of a W_i, then this W_i logs the presence of S_j in a GLM and stores it on the DDS. We provide the exact details of the GLM in Section 4.2.

In contrast, the LEA has to do the following to track the movements of any S_j. First of all, the LEA needs to query its DDS for all GLMs associated with a specific suspect S_j. After receiving this query, the DDS responds by sending all the GLMs associated with this S_j to the LEA. The contents of these GLMs provide the LEA a history of all the geolocations visited by S_j. So, using the contents of the GLMs, the LEA reconstructs the movements of S_j.

To clarify the above, let us consider a concrete example. More specifically, the situation is as illustrated in Figure 1. So, in the specific geographic area GA, we have six witnesses, $W_0, W_1 \ldots W_5$, and one suspect S. These six witnesses cooperate with the LEA to track the movements of S. As illustrated in Figure 1, S is in the communication range of W_2, W_3, W_4, and W_5. Consequently, W_0 and W_1 are not in the communication range of S. Equally important to note is that W_2 and W_4 are in the communication range of S. However, they do not collaborate with the LEA to track S because they have not started their SAT application.

In the initial situation we sketched above, only W_3 and W_5 sense and log the presence of S. Then, both witnesses (W_3 and W_5) create their respective GLMs. As a final action, they upload the GLMs on to the DDS (Arrows 1a and 1b in Figure 1).

As the suspect S moves within GA, it moves out the communication range of some witnesses, and into the communication range of other witnesses. This movement of S caused a new situation (illustrated in Figure 2). In this current situation, W_0 and W_1 are in the communication range of S. In a similar way as in the initial situation, both of these witnesses (W_0 and W_1) create and upload the GLMs (Arrows 1a and 1b in Figure 2) to log the presence of S.

Finally, when the LEA queries the DDS (Arrow 3 in Figure 2), it will receive four GLMs (Arrow 4 in Figure 2). After analyzing the contents of these GLMs, the LEA observes that S was first in the vicinity of W_3 and W_5. The LEA also observes that S moved from this initial position to a geolocation in the vicinity of W_0 and W_1.

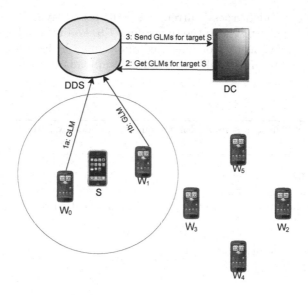

Fig. 2. The suspect S moved to vicinity of W_0 and W_1

4.2   Protocols

The SAT system uses two main protocols, namely the *"Geolocation Logging Protocol (GLP)"* and the *"Geolocation Tracing Protocol (GTP)"*. A witness W_i running the SAT application makes use of the GLP to log the presence of suspects S. Whereas, the DC runs the GTP to reconstruct the movements of a suspect S within the specified geographic area GA. Below we provide the details of both protocols.

Geolocation Logging Protocol (GLP)
Let us start the discussion of the protocols with the GLP (detailed in Algorithm 1). This is the protocol that the SAT application runs on behalf of its witness W_i to log the presence of potential suspects. After a witness starts the SAT application, the GLP periodically (i.e. every *timeOut* period of time) checks whether there are suspects in its communication range (line 1–4). For the sake of this discussion, let us assume a specific suspect S_j. When S_j is within the communication range of a W_i, then the GLP logs the presence of S_j in an encrypted log denoted as *"Location Update (LU)"* (line 6). This LU contains the following pieces of information: i) the current (i.e. kth) pseudonym $P_{i,k}$ of a witness W_i; ii) the identity of the suspect I_{S_j}; iii) the current geolocation of this witness L_{W_i}; iv) the Received Signal Strength Indication $RSSI$; and v) the timestamp TS. Furthermore, these pieces of information are encrypted with the DC's public key $K_{P_{DC}}$.

This protocol uses the LU to construct the GLM message as follows. First, the GLP creates a message by concatenating the necessary pieces of information together, namely: i) this witness' current (i.e. kth) pseudonym $P_{i,k}$, ii) the identity of the sensed suspect I_{S_j}, iii) the timestamp TS, and iv) the location update LU. Then, the GLP signs the concatenated message with the kth private key of the witness $K^{-1}_{P_{i,k}}$ (line 7). Finally, this protocol uploads the GLM to the DDS (line 8).

Algorithm 1. Witnesses sensing for potential suspects within their communication range

---

1: $timeOut = \Delta$
2: **while** $true$ **do**
3:     **if** Δ seconds passed **then**
4:         populate S with all wireless devices in communication range
5:         **for** each item in S **do**
6:             $LU = E_{K_{DC}}(P_{i,k}||I_{S_j}||L_{W_i}||RSSI||TS)$
7:             $GLM = sign_{W_i}(P_{i,k}||I_{S_j}||TS||LU)$
8:             $W_i \xrightarrow{GLM} DDS$
9:         **end for**
10:    **end if**
11: **end while**

Geolocation Tracing Protocol (GTP)

The DC uses the GTP (as detailed in Algorithm 2) to trace the movements of a specific target node S_j within a geographic area for a specified period of time. The DC provides the GTP with the required parameters, namely: i) the identity of a target node I_{S_j}; ii) the starting date and time for the trace T_{start}; and iii) the ending date and time for the trace T_{end}. GTP starts by using these parameters to construct and send a request to the DDS (line 1). On its turn, the DDS returns all GLMs associated with S_j with $T_{start} \leq TS \leq T_{end}$ (line 2). For each returned GLM, this protocol does the following. First, it verifies the signature of a GLM (line 4). Then, assuming that the signature is correct, the GTP decrypts the encrypted part (i.e. LU) of the GLM and adds it to the set of all decrypted GLMs $\{Dec\_GLMs\}$ (line 8 and 9). In contrast, if the signature is not correct for a specific GLM, then GTP discards it. In what follows, the GTP sorts $\{Dec\_GLMs\}$ in a chronologically ascending manner (line 13). After this, the GTP uses a time interval Δ to group several GLMs together. For each one of these GLM groups $G_{GLM'_{T_{x+\Delta}}}$, the GTP does the following. First, it computes the estimated geolocation of S_j (line 15). In practice, this can be done using one of the already proposed positioning algorithms (e.g. triangulation, trilateration, multi-lateration) as described in [1]. Then the GTP updates the time line that illustrates the estimated geolocation of the target node at a specific time T_x with $T_{start} \leq T_x \leq T_{end}$ (line 16).

Algorithm 2. The DC queries its DDS for the geolocation data of a specific suspect

---

INPUT: ID_{S_j}, T_{start}, and T_{end}
OUTPUT: $visitedGeolocationsTimeLine$

1: $DC \xrightarrow{I_{S_j}||T_{start}||T_{end}} DDS$

2: $DDS \xrightarrow{\{GLMs\}} DC$

3: **for** each item GLM_l in $\{GLMs\}$ **do**
4:    $signOK = Verify_{W_i}(GLM_l)$
5:    **if** $!signOK$ **then**
6:       discard GLM_l
7:    **else**
8:       $GLM' = P_{i,k}||I_{S_j}||TS||D_{K_{W_i}}(LU)$
9:       add GLM' to $\{Dec\_GLMs\}$
10:    **end if**
11: **end for**

12: $interval = \Delta$
13: $\{Dec\_GLMs\} = sort(\{Dec\_GLMs\})$
14: **for** each group $G_{GLM'_{T_x+\Delta}}$ of concurrent GLM' **do**
15:    $computeEstimatedSuspectLocation(G_{GLM'_{T_x+\Delta}})$
16:    $update(visitedGeolocationsTimeLine)$
17: **end for**

18: $return\ visitedGeolocationsTimeLine$

---

5   Discussion

In this section, we analyze our proposed solution by discussing the following points: i) feasibility; ii) communication overhead, iii) deployability and costs; and iv) privacy preservation.

Feasibility. The feasibility of this system depends on the community participation rate. As a matter of fact, researchers showed that a WiFi based community sensing system needs to achieve a community participation rate of 10% to track the movements of any individual within a metropolitan area [9].

To achieve the necessary community participation rate, our proposed system can either deploy a reward based scheme, or solely depend on voluntary participation. A reward based scheme could be as simple as giving a fixed price for the provided sensor data. Another option could be that the government could grant tax reductions to individuals that provide sensor data, which are of importance for the government. However, this topic—deserving a line of investigations on its own—is out of the scope of this paper.

Another approach is that individuals voluntarily participate to the systems to achieve a common goal. This approach has been proved to be successful in several other initiatives [18,21]. Considering this, it is not hard to see that community sensing systems that are used for the common good (e.g. security, safety) of a community would easily achieve the necessary participation rate.

Up to this point, we discussed feasibility in terms of community participation rate. Now, we discuss technical feasibility in terms of: the short range radio technologies, and their characteristics (e.g. communication range, device discovery).

In contemporary mobile devices there are two ubiquitously available short range radio technologies, namely Bluetooth and WiFi. Our proposed solution can use either one of these technologies.

The communication range of these technologies has the biggest influence on the performance of our proposed solutions. In fact, having a bigger communication range decreases the necessary community participation rate [9]. Bluetooth has a communication range of 10 meters as opposed to the 100 meters of WiFi. This implies that Bluetooth needs a higher community participation rate (i.e. $>> 10\%$) as opposed to WiFi (i.e. 10%).

The other characteristic that we want to discuss is device discovery. In Bluetooth, during the inquiry phase a master device broadcasts inquiry packets to discover neighboring devices. This inquiry phase lasts on average 5 seconds [7]. In contrast, the WiFi passive scan procedure lasts on average of $50ms$ for each channel [7]. For 11 channels, this means that the WiFi passive device discovery phase lasts for $550ms$. This implies that WiFi is suitable to track fast moving targets (e.g. cars), and Bluetooth is more suitable to track static or relatively slow moving targets (e.g. pedestrians, cyclists).

Communication Overhead. The readers might have noticed that the protocols as described in Section 4 suffers from communication overhead. More specifically, the GLP makes witnesses to create and send GLMs for every wireless device within its communication range. As a consequence SAT can potentially flood the network. To overcome this problem, the SAT system should reduce the volume of GLMs send to the DDS. One solution would be to use a probabilistic mechanism in the GLP to reduce the amount of generated traffic. However, this solution has the potential risk of not logging a wireless device that the DC might be interested in tracking. A solution that does not have this problem and reduces the volume of GLMs send to the DC is: a system in which the witnesses only track target nodes that the DC is interested in. However, providing the details of such a system is out of the scope of this paper.

Deployability and Costs. Unlike some other systems, we do not need to install additional hardware to trace the movements of a target mobile device. Our proposed system solely depends on the information provided by the mobile devices owned by the voluntary participating individuals. This means that for our system to work, we do not have to explicitly deploy anything. In addition, due to the fact that everything we need is personally owned by the voluntarily participating individuals, there are also no high costs involved in deploying and using this system. This makes our proposed system easily deployable and not expensive.

Privacy Preservation. As a final point we discuss how effective the SAT system is in preserving the privacy of the witnesses. To do this, we first have to clarify what we consider being possible for the adversary. For the sake of this discussion, we assume a global passive eavesdropper. This means that the attacker, possibly colluding with malicious nodes, is capable to overhear all the messages exchanged within our system. However, the attacker can not modify and/or inject messages.

First of all, let us look at what information is transferred in clear text when transferring a GLM to a DDS. The unencrypted part of the GLM contains the current pseudonym of a witness, the identity of the target mobile device, and the timestamp of when the target node was observed. From these pieces of information, the eavesdropper can not learn the real identity of the witness. This because the pseudonym is a temporary identifier that changes over time. Only the CA is able to associate a given pseudonym to a real identity. However, the CA only reveals this association to an authorized third party. The timestamp and the identity only reveals when a specific device was observed. So, it does not reveal where this specific device was observed. This shows that our system preserves the identity and location privacy of the witness mobile devices. Furthermore, our system also preserves the location privacy of the target mobile device from the global passive eavesdropper.

6   Conclusion

In this paper, we presented Sense-And-Trace (SAT): a privacy preserving distributed geolocation tracking system. In contrast to other proposed solutions, SAT does not rely on: i) proprietary infrastructure, ii) on the availability of existing infrastructure, or iii) on geolocation information provided by the target device. The SAT system tracks the movements of a target mobile device using geolocation information provided by (voluntarily participating) neighboring mobile devices (witnesses). Furthermore, the SAT system preserves the privacy of the witnesses, and only discloses information about a specific target mobile device to an authorized third party.

In the future, we want to to perform a simulation study to evaluate the SAT system in terms of: i) effectiveness, ii) power consumption overhead, and iii) privacy preservation under several attack scenarios. Based on the results of the simulation study, we want to develop a forensic suspect tracking system based on the idea presented in this paper.

References

1. Al-Kuwari, S., Wolthusen, S.D.: A Survey of Forensic Localization and Tracking Mechanisms in Short-Range and Cellular Networks. In: Goel, S. (ed.) ICDF2C 2009. LNICST, vol. 31, pp. 19–32. Springer, Heidelberg (2010)

2. Amin, S., Andrews, S., Apte, S., Arnold, J., Ban, J., Benko, M., Bayen, R.M., Chiou, B., Claudel, C., Claudel, C., Dodson, T., Elhamshary, O., Flens-batina, C., Gruteser, M., Herrera, J.C., Herring, R., Hoh, B., Jacobson, Q., Iwuchukwu, T., Lew, J., Litrico, X., Luddington, L., Margulici, J., Mortazavi, A., Pan, X., Rabbani, T., Racine, T., Sherlock-Thomas, E., Sutter, D., Tinka, A.: Mobile century using gps mobile phones as traffic sensors: A field experiment. In: Proceedings of the 15th World Congress on Intelligent Transportation Systems (2008)
3. Anisetti, M., Ardagna, C., Bellandi, V., Damiani, E., Dller, M., Stegmaier, F., Rabl, T., Kosch, H., Brunie, L.: Landmark-assisted location and tracking in outdoor mobile network. In: Multimedia Tools and Applications, pp. 1–23 (2011)
4. Biagioni, J., Gerlich, T., Merrifield, T., Eriksson, J.: Easytracker: automatic transit tracking, mapping, and arrival time prediction using smartphones. In: Proceedings of the 9th ACM Conference on Embedded Networked Sensor Systems, SenSys 2011, pp. 68–81. ACM (2011)
5. Chun, B., Culler, D., Roscoe, T., Bavier, A., Peterson, L., Wawrzoniak, M., Bowman, M.: PlanetLab: An Overlay Testbed for Broad-Coverage Services. SIGCOMM Computer Communication Review 33, 3–12 (2003)
6. Consolvo, S., McDonald, D.W., Toscos, T., Chen, M.Y., Froehlich, J., Harrison, B., Klasnja, P., LaMarca, A., LeGrand, L., Libby, R., Smith, I., Landay, J.A.: Activity sensing in the wild: a field trial of ubifit garden. In: Proceedings of the Twenty-sixth Annual SIGCHI Conference on Human Factors in Computing Systems, CHI 2008, pp. 1797–1806. ACM (2008)
7. Ferro, E., Potorti, F.: Bluetooth and Wi-Fi wireless protocols: a survey and a comparison. IEEE Wireless Communications 12(1), 12–26 (2005)
8. Herrera, J.C., Work, D.B., Herring, R. (Jeff) Ban, X., Jacobson, Q., Bayen, A.M.: Evaluation of traffic data obtained via gps-enabled mobile phones: The mobile century field experiment. Transportation Research Part C: Emerging Technologies 18(4), 568–583 (2010)
9. Husted, N., Myers, S.: Mobile location tracking in metro areas: malnets and others. In: Proceedings of the 17th ACM Conference on Computer and Communications Security, CCS 2010, pp. 85–96. ACM (2010)
10. European Telecommunications Standards Institute. AT Command Set for 3G User Equipment (UE). In: Digital Cellular Telecommunications Systems (Phase 2+);Universal Telecommunications System (UMTS), volume ETSI TS 127 007: 3GPP TS 27.007 version 5.2.0 Release 5 of Technical Specification (2002)
11. Kusý, B., Balogh, G., Sallai, J., Lédeczi, Á., Maróti, M.: inTrack: High Precision Tracking of Mobile Sensor Nodes. In: Langendoen, K.G., Voigt, T. (eds.) EWSN 2007. LNCS, vol. 4373, pp. 51–66. Springer, Heidelberg (2007)
12. Lorincz, K., Welsh, M.: Motetrack: a robust, decentralized approach to rf-based location tracking. Personal Ubiquitous Comput. 11, 489–503 (2007)
13. Minch, R.P.: Privacy issues in location-aware mobile devices. In: Proceedings of the 37th Annual Hawaii International Conference on System Sciences - Track 5, HICCS 2004, vol. 5. IEEE Computer Society (2004)
14. Paulos, E., Honicky, R.E., Goodman, E.: Sensing atmosphere. In: Proceedings of the 5th ACM Conference on Embedded Networked Sensor Systems, SenSys 2007 (2007)
15. Rhea, S., Godfrey, B., Karp, B., Kubiatowicz, J., Ratnasamy, S., Shenker, S., Stoica, I., Yu, H.: Opendht: a public dht service and its uses. In: Proceedings of the 2005 Conference on Applications, Technologies, Architectures, and Protocols for Computer Communications, SIGCOMM 2005, pp. 73–84. ACM (2005)

16. Ristenpart, T., Maganis, G., Krishnamurthy, A., Kohno, T.: Privacy-preserving location tracking of lost or stolen devices: cryptographic techniques and replacing trusted third parties with dhts. In: Proceedings of the 17th Conference on Security Symposium, SS 2008, pp. 275–290. USENIX Association (2008)
17. Krishna Sampigethaya, Mingyan Li, Leping Huang, and Radha Poovendran. Amoeba: Robust location privacy scheme for vanet. *IEEE Journal on Selected Areas in Communications*, 25(8):1569–1589, 2007.
18. SETI@Home. SETI@Home Project Website, http://setiathome.berkeley.edu/
19. Shin, H., Chon, Y., Park, K., Cha, H.: FindingMiMo: Tracing a Missing Mobile Phone Using Daily Observations. In: Proceedings of the 9th International Conference on Mobile Systems, Applications, and Services, MobiSys 2011, pp. 29–42. ACM (2011)
20. Thiagarajan, A., Ravindranath, L., LaCurts, K., Madden, S., Balakrishnan, H., Toledo, S., Eriksson, J.: Vtrack: accurate, energy-aware road traffic delay estimation using mobile phones. In: Proceedings of the 7th ACM Conference on Embedded Networked Sensor Systems, SenSys 2009, pp. 85–98. ACM, New York (2009)
21. Wikipedia. Wikipedia Project Website, http://www.wikipedia.org/
22. Wong, F.-L., Stajano, F.: Location Privacy in Bluetooth. In: Molva, R., Tsudik, G., Westhoff, D. (eds.) ESAS 2005. LNCS, vol. 3813, pp. 176–188. Springer, Heidelberg (2005)
23. Zhao, Y.: Mobile phone location determination and its impact on intelligent transportation systems. IEEE Transactions on Intelligent Transportation Systems 1(1), 55–64 (2000)
24. Zhu, Z., Cao, G.: APPLAUS: A Privacy-Preserving Location Proof Updating System for Location-based Services. In: Proceedings of the 30th IEEE International Conference on Computer Communications, IEEE INFOCOM 2011 (2011)
25. Zhu, Z., Cao, G.: Towards privacy-preserving and colluding-resistance in location proof updating system. IEEE Transactions on Mobile Computing, 99(preprints) (2011)

Sense-And-Trace: A Privacy Preserving Distributed Geolocation Tracking System (Transcript of Discussion)

Mauro Conti

University of Padua, Italy

This is joint work with Eyüp Canlar, my PhD-Student, who is also in the room, and whom I thank for preparing the slides. Bruno Crispo and Roberto Di Pietro also contributed to this work.

What we are trying to do is not yet mature. We are trying to design a protocol to trace people, or devices, or people that are carrying devices, in a privacy-preserving way. It seems like a contradiction, and somehow probably it is a contradiction, but I will make it more clear which privacy we want to preserve, and what we mean by tracing devices or tracing people. So I will just introduce the problem and discuss related work in this field. Then I will briefly describe what is our current approach to make this distributed tracing, and then conclude the talk.

There are several scenarios where it is useful to trace the position of devices, like smartphones, tablets, or whatever mobile device, and/or trace the position of the people that are carrying those devices. And this might be important for several reasons like, for example, we lose our device and we want to retrieve it, or we want to locate missing children by tracking their toys. But the kind of application we are more interested in are the ones related to forensics and surveillance. So, we want to trace the movement of a potential suspect, or provide the location proofs for possible alibis. For example: I was here giving this talk so I didn't commit a murder somewhere else.

In the literature there are basically two main classifications we can make of the possible solutions to trace the devices, or the people that carry devices. The first type of solution is handset-based: we rely on the information that that specific device provides to the system, and in particular, that it makes use of GPS, WiFi location services, assisted GPS, and these kind of things. The limitations are that we need the specific device and the specific person to be willing to provide their information. And of course, if it is a malicious guy, he might provide fake position information. The other type is network-based solutions, where the tracing of a device or a person is not made by relying just on a specific device but by relying on information that we can collect thanks to infrastructure like beacon structures or other type of nodes that are in the neighborhood. So there are already some solutions, but not all them are designed to be privacy-preserving. They are designed with different targets in mind. For example, MoteTrack and FindingMiMo are solutions designed to trace a lost or stolen device. The first one in particular makes use of beacon nodes that send out a signal, and this signal is sensed by a smartphone, for example, and based

B. Christianson et al. (Eds.): Security Protocols 2012, LNCS 7622, pp. 214–222, 2012.
© Springer-Verlag Berlin Heidelberg 2012

on the RSSI, the signal strength indicator, they can build a map of the current situation; and if a device is lost, by sensing the environment and sending this information to the infrastructure, we are able to locate the device. And a similar approach is used by FindingMiMo, which chooses WiFi access points and other environmental radio signals.

There is also another interesting recent solution that tried to locate the position of a device based on the information that you get from the accelerometer. These kinds of solutions are particularly interesting because they can work indoors. And there are other solutions more suited for outdoor applications which were designed with privacy in mind. So in this case I want to keep trace of my own device, but in a privacy-aware way. For example, in this solution the idea is that my smartphone will keep on tracing my position and publish this position in some encrypted way somewhere. If I need to retrieve my smartphone, I need to get access to that specific database, where only I am authorized to get the position of my smartphone. And APPLAUS is a similar system. It also tries to fix the problem that a malicious user might want to provide a fake position. So if I want to now give to the system a fake position for my smartphone, if I don't get any proof from the external environment, and I am the only one claiming my position, I could do that. So what APPLAUS does is ask for the neighborhood nodes to send a proof of the position of this specific device. I want to give to the authorities some proof that now I am here, and it's not enough that I send a message from my phone to the authorities; instead I ask your device to give me a proof that you can see me in your network, and then I will send this information to the network.

All these solutions have limitations, in particular most of them are based on the handset-based solution, so everything is based on what my device does. If I'm not willing to send my position, then my device will not ask for proofs. So what we are trying to design is a geolocation tracing system that does not rely on geolocation information that is directly provided by the potential suspicious person, that wants to trace a suspicious device, and that does not require any extensive deployment of additional infrastructure, or software. And it is privacy-preserving. With this we mean that our aim is to design a system that minimizes the privacy sensitive information that we give away. I mean, the *other* privacy information: for example, if there are witnesses sensing the position of a node, we do not want to disclose the position of the witnesses (up to a point). Of course at a point when there is an investigation, and there is an order from the court where the law enforcement agency is authorized to access some specific information, then part of the information is disclosed, but still this should be kept as small as possible.

Frank Stajano: So in this problem statement does the target provide anything? It doesn't provide geolocation; does it cooperate in any way, or is it done completely without any cooperation from the target?

Reply: We expect some passive cooperation of the target device. For example, if you are going to trace my phone, then you don't need my phone to actively participate in any protocol. However, we do assume that my phone works in a standard mode. So it does not do anything specific to avoid a tracing mechanism. So I use the Internet, I connect to the access points, I use Bluetooth and whatever.

Matt Blaze: So it doesn't rely on special geolocation information, but you're still part of a network?

Reply: Yes, I am still part of a network.

Phil Brooke: It is going to have to be registered with a cell network, isn't it?

Reply: Yes.

Frank Stajano: But the fact that the target does not cooperate means that the attack (if we called the geolocation an attack) can be directed at anyone.

Reply: The tracing?

Frank Stajano: Yes.

Reply: Yes, we indeed talk about a potential suspect, because the idea is that we trace everyone. If there is an investigation about a specific person then some information about that specific person is disclosed, and possibly a small amount about the witnesses of who traced that person.

Frank Stajano: So, when you say privacy preserving, you mean a kind of self-restraint? There's nothing in your protocol that preserves the privacy of anyone?

Reply: Yes, we tried to design the architecture in such a way that the privacy of the people participating in the distributed tracing is preserved. We also assume that there are different entities in the system, and each single entity can not trace anyone on its own.

Frank Stajano: I understand.

Matt Blaze: So I notice absent from your problem statement is that the tracking cannot be detected by the target? Why is that not part of your problem statement?

Reply: Yes, it can be included, I mean, it works, so the target will not detect that we are tracing him. The only assumption that might be feasible is that the target nodes still use the phone in a standard way, and this might not be the case if it is really a malicious person.

Matt Blaze: The scenario I'm thinking of is that, at least in the United States, the cellular providers, the mobile providers, will ping mobile phones on request of law enforcement. With the standard software in your mobile phone, this will be transparent to the end user; but if I have modified firmware or software in my phone I could detect that it's being pinged in a way that is different from its normal operation. Would that be included in your solution?

Reply: What we thought at the beginning of this problem statement is that we don't want any private company, like AT&T, to actually trace people. We are OK if the federal government has the authority to trace anyone, even in the past, but we don't understand why AT&T should keep a storage.

Matt Blaze: Well AT&T has to trace me because they have to know where my mobile is in order to route calls to it. So they are tracing me already.

Reply: So fine, they need to know where you are now, but they don't need to keep the storage of the old history of your moves.

Eyüp Canlar: It's just the cell that they need to know to route calls. Not a specific position. I mean they only need to know the cell that you're located at. However, the cell size could be something like 1 km.

Matt Blaze: Well only in the worst case. I mean, there are also micro cells that could locate me to a particular house, or even a particular room.

Eyüp Canlar: Yes, but how deployed are the micro cells?

Matt Blaze: In urban areas they're heavily deployed.

Paul Syverson: And of course when we say they must, that's in the existing technology, right? Some of us have designed cellular phone communication protocols where they don't know where you are.

Matt Blaze: Sure, but if our problem statement involves completely replacing the Internet, or cellular infrastructure, we're not likely to get much out of it.

Reply: Yes, so the idea is that we don't want private entities like AT&T to keep storage of all of our positions for the last ten years, and then in case of an order from the court then they can disclose this. Because if still they have this information, they might use it, right? Without any agreement with other institutions, right? So we will try to design a framework where this is not possible, and the only authorities that are authorized to store our historical position are these law enforcement agencies, and this architecture is owned by the government.

OK, so basically this is our way of bringing the protocol to life by embedding protocols in human life. We want to design a solution that is completely distributed on our smartphones. For example, the protocol runs also thanks to the people's life, and people's movement. And we do this by extending the known concept of neighborhood watching. We heard that in Washington DC people are asked to report suspicious activities. We also saw the warning on this projector saying "if you see this projector outside an educational room, then you have to report this". These are some well-known concepts, and we can improve on this kind of approach by providing a tool that is going to be very powerful, because we know that now everyone has a smartphone, and the smartphone has a lot of sensors. So we would like to design a distributed tracing mechanism leveraging this concept and implement it in a distributed way on people's mobile devices.

And of course we need also an incentive to have people reporting all this information. So why should I keep on tracing you, and keep reporting this to the Police? I might not care about this. I mean, why should I consume my battery, and use my computation resources? I might be selfish and not want to participate. So we also need a system where there are actually incentives to do this. But you probably already heard about, for example, an car insurance discount where if you give away your privacy and you store something that traces always the position or acceleration of your car, they will grant you a discount on the car insurance. So we might think that in order to implement this mechanism there will be some incentives. For example, if you participate in this distributed tracing protocol, then you will have a discount on taxis, or this kind of things.

Our general approach is that everyone can act as a potential witness by down-loading a specific application, and obtaining a set of pseudonyms. We assume there is a certification authority where everyone can register, and obtain a set of pseudonyms, and each pseudonym is used only for a given time interval. And this pseudonym is used by a witness to report information about some suspect that he's observing. So the idea is basically this: we trace everyone, and then if there is an investigation they will take care of which kind of people they want information about. Assume we want to trace this device, and there are a set of witnesses in this area, and in this specific time slice. For example, these wit-nesses are sensing the environment, and what they sense are, for example, MAC addresses, or RSSI, BSSID, or all the possible ways to identify a specific device. And here we need a specific behavior: the target shouldn't behave in a particu-lar way to counterfeit his identity, or at least, its physical identity like BSSID. So, we collect this information, and we send this information to the distributed data storage. In this way the distributed data storage is not able to reconstruct anything about a specific node, and also it is not able to reconstruct the position of the witnesses.

Jonathan Anderson: Is that a centralized distributed data store?

Reply: We need to make it distributed, for resiliency, to avoid single point of failure, but even if it is centralized it shouldn't be able to trace the position of nodes.

Jonathan Anderson: So there will be one of these per cell tower per network, how many of these things are there?

Reply: We didn't think about how many. We cannot assume it's a centralized entity, but we thought of making it distributed to avoid single point of failures, to have more resiliency to possible attacks to a single node, and these kind of things.

Jonathan Anderson: Because that's also just more places that the Police have to go: if there are 100 of them they have to go to 100 and say, do any of you guys have information about this phone we're tracking?

Reply: Yes: if you are authorized to collect this information then you contact those 1000 data storage centres and then say, do you have any information about this?

Matt Blaze: So the witnesses know who S is?

Reply: OK, in this specific description we assume they do, but we can con-sider these are potential witnesses, so everyone traces everyone.

Matt Blaze: OK. But I only send the messages back if the S is on the list of track nodes?

Reply: To know if this is an actual person to be traced?

Matt Blaze: Yes.

Reply: What we have in mind is that we trace everyone.

Matt Blaze: OK, and you're always sending that back to the DDS?

Reply: Yes. Of course we can imagine mechanisms to compress this informa-tion, or to do this in a probabilistic way, so that not everyone is always traced.

Matt Blaze: So basically everybody is both a W and an S?

Reply: Yes. And everyone sends information about the neighborhoods that senses a given time interval to this distributed storage. And this is sent encrypted with a private key of the pseudonym, of this specific pseudonym. So this is done because if you want to trace a specific subject then you can retrieve the information of that specific subject, and you can prove these messages. I mean, you can verify who signed this information, but this doesn't disclose more information than the time slice for which the pseudonyms have been used. So this is the idea. So in this way we collect this information. When there is a law enforcement agency that has the authority to actually query some information, it will ask for all the specific positions, for example, of a specific subject. After retrieving this information, he has to collaborate with the certification authority to decrypt all the messages, and in this way we can trace a specific subject while only partially disclosing information about witnesses. And this is the second step where we retrieve the information.

We still have several issues, so probably this protocol is not yet perfect, and we didn't implement it and simulate it, so we don't have much research on this, but it is a problem we want to address. Issues include, for example, how exactly we want to detect a specific target; we might use the WiFi ID or the Bluetooth ID, or it might be useful to use the RSSI, or other kinds of information to identify a specific node. And we want to make it privacy preserving, so that we preserve the privacy of witnesses, and of course also the privacy of potential suspect until there is an order from the court to trace that specific node.

Matt Blaze: But then, if everything is being collected, tracing can be done retrospectively. You can get information before the order was issued. A judge not only has the ability (or whatever the legal authority is) to say "from this time forward you will be traced"; but also to go back in time.

Reply: Yes, because you can access all the previous storage.

Matt Blaze: Because everybody has done this potential S.

Reply: Yes, of course. We can think of a way to optimize this mechanism, because probably it involves a lot of communication, and a lot of energy consumption. That would be the challenges to be fixed, and optimized. But yes, the idea is that everyone traces everyone, and everything is logged, and when there is an order from the judge we disclose information about that specific person, and partially about the witnesses. If you have to prove that I saw you today in this room, and I signed this information, when you verify my signature you know that I also was here today. But if that pseudonym is used only for four hours then, OK, you disclosed my position for four hours, but if I'm not the target of the investigation, this is limited to these four hours.

Phil Brooke: Why would someone want to install it on their phone?

Reply: Because you have discount on taxis.

Eyüp Canlar: Not only that. Even neighborhood watching, why are we doing it? Because it's good for all of us as a community.

Bruce Christianson: And you get 10% off your insurance.

Eyüp Canlar: That's also a good incentive; but still, if a murderer is walking around you want him to be caught, right? So that's a good incentive as well.

Reply: What about car insurance discount? There are people installing this device to get significant car insurance discount, right? So if you are helping the Police to make it even cheaper, like to carry out an investigation, then it might be of benefit for the community if you participate, so you might be willing in the first place.

Sandy Clark: And the other inspiration might be that they were tracking information anyway, and this would be a way to ensure a tiny bit of privacy.

Reply: Yes exactly, because currently Telco operators, are anyway tracing everything about our position, right?

Phil Brooke: How do you get enough weight of installations for it to be effective?

Eyüp Canlar: The paper in CCS explained that you need to have a 10% participation rate to follow everybody in a metropolitan area.

Sandy Clark: So you'd have to say like all New York City is going to do it this way.

Reply: Yes; what they reported in that CCS paper (though I don't remember the way they measured the quality of tracing) was something like: if you do distributed sensing like this, and if 10% of nodes are collecting information about the network, then that is enough to trace people.

Eyüp Canlar: They were talking about second-by-second tracing.

Matt Blaze: Are the responses from the witnesses delivered in real time, or are they sent back later?

Reply: We can think that this can be given in real time, but if we are scared about timing attacks, or other kind of things, then we might also postpone sending this information for a while.

Matt Blaze: I'm thinking in terms of the context. I'm familiar primarily with location tracking as used by the US law enforcement. When an investigation is active, on the targeted phone they want typically high resolution in time (pings of the phone) so they can tell, for example, that their target is moving now, or has moved very recently. For the real timing data, once they've decided to start tracing, as they currently use it requires real time updates of location. It seems that that creates a fundamental trade-off: either you have to deliver information about everybody back to the data store in real time (which could overwhelm the network: it might not scale up); or you have to be able to turn on real-time tracking for particular targets, in which case you're revealing the fact that a particular target is being traced. So that may be a very difficult trade-off as the system that you're describing scales up.

Phil Brooke: It's more granularity you're actually going to want. In practice, minutes delays are likely to be an issue for law enforcement for media tracking the same person's stuff, but if you've got an hour's delay it's utterly useless because you just send officers to the wrong location.

Matt Blaze: Right, exactly.

Phil Brooke: So you might have some granularity, which might be small enough that it doesn't ruin the timeliness of the application.

Reply: Sure, there are ways we can tune the general idea, and also input. You were talking about something like: "OK, from now on I want to trace a specific person", but then with that kind of system you cannot go back in time. You could use both systems if you want to run an investigation. Another thing you can do is to optimize this mechanism: if the Police know, for example, that someone was here today, then they might ask all the devices in Cambridgeshire area to trace everyone more often.

Jonathan Anderson: To turn it around a little bit suppose that, instead of the Police, I am a member of an organized crime syndicate. Am I going to be able to tell who was witnessing against me in order to either challenge the veracity of their testimony, or to reduce their incentive to provide the testimony?

Reply: OK, how can you do that?

Jonathan Anderson: No: my question (a serious question) is a sort of a dilemma. Either you're telling the person "yes, it was this phone over here that witnessed against you", or you're not going to tell them, in which case they'll reply "well, how do we know that the firmware of that phone wasn't hacked? How do we know that in fact that this is accurate testimony? I can't challenge it!". So the question is: do I in fact know who witnessed against me or not? That's the first thing, and then one of those two problems must be addressed.

Reply: No, the idea is that the witnessing is passive. Your device is talking with the access point, and just eavesdrop, and after half an hour I report this information to the authorities.

Jonathan Anderson: No: when it comes out in a court case later and they tell me "you were here on that day", I ask: "how do you know?" "because we have all these testimonies on these phones!". At that point, will I get to see which phones they are? Will my lawyers get to inspect their firmware? Will I get to send my friends around to break their owners' legs?

Matt Blaze: But we need to be careful not to abstract this as computer scientists too often do. In actual national law enforcement cases, and I'm speaking with a very heavy US bias, this is used as intelligence, not as evidence. This data is used to tell them where to follow you around, where to send the surveillance teams to look for you; as a substitute for physical surveillance, not as a form of evidence in and of itself. Because trackers have other limitations as evidence: they tell you where the tracker is, they don't tell you where the person was.

Frank Stajano: I agree entirely with your objection, in fact I was going to make a similar one. But then, to support what Jonathan said, this objection has to be fed back to the beginning where one slide said "and I'm going to use this as an alibi". Then the same thing would apply to anyone who's using the database.

Matt Blaze: Right.

Reply: That is a different approach.

Jonathan Anderson: In that case it's more an alibi finder service. You say "I was here; whose phones were also here, and do any of you remember me?"

Reply: Getting an alibi is different from tracing someone else in a passive way.

Sandy Clark: The only question I have is: how do we spoof this? I want to pretend to be somewhere I'm not.

Reply: This is one of the partially open challenges. We might say "trace that MAC address" but you might maliciously change it, so that's why at the beginning of the talk I made the claim that the target doesn't do anything particular not to collaborate with the protocol. We do not need active participation and we don't need to interact with the traced node, but we also assume to some extent it behaves normally.

Matt Blaze: My sense is that the cheap objection for law enforcement to this as a solution to their tracking problem is if it is detectable that a particular target is being traced. I think that, for this to be acceptable from the law enforcement point of view, you're going to have to address the trade-off between overwhelming it with too much data about everybody all the time, versus being able to particularize it to a particular target, and then have the identity of who is being traced become detectable, which they will not want.

Sandy Clark: There's another problem too: if this is an app that people download to be a witness, and I'm going to join a witness group, why don't I create a witness app that gives the wrong information deliberately, so that can I frame somebody?

Reply: Yes, this another open point. We should assume that there is something like a TPM on your machine, and the app that you are installing is our app which is trusted, and so on.

Sandy Clark: And then all you need is some particular quorum of fake witnesses try to say, yes I was here at this time, when I really wasn't, or to say, this guy, my enemy was here at this time.

Reply: Yes, but then the social aspect we think will play a role, because if your position is reported always by the same set of witnesses that might sound strange.

Sandy Clark: But my association would normally be by the same set of witnesses, because I hang around with the same people, and I go to the same places.

Reply: Fine, it's OK that you always hang around with the same people, but don't you meet other people?

Sandy Clark: Demosthenes and I are still searching.

Am I in Good Company?
A Privacy-Protecting Protocol
for Cooperating Ubiquitous Computing Devices

Oliver Stannard and Frank Stajano

University of Cambridge Computer Laboratory
15 JJ Thomson Avenue, Cambridge, CB3 0FD, United Kingdom

Abstract. A portable device carries important secrets in encrypted form; to unlock it, a threshold secret sharing scheme is used, requiring the presence of several other devices. We explore the design space for the protocol through which these devices communicate wirelessly, under the additional constraint that eavesdroppers should not be able to recognize and track the user carrying these devices.

1 The Problem

The user carries a device, the Pico [11], containing important secrets (authentication credentials for all of the user's accounts) that must not be disclosed to attackers. The memory of the Pico is encrypted with a key that the Pico periodically forgets and reconstructs, through k-out-of-n secret sharing [9], from the shares it receives via short-range radio from other devices, the Picosiblings. The Picosiblings are meant to be physically bound to the user more tightly than the Pico itself, so that the Pico can equate the proximity of the Picosiblings with the proximity of the Pico's owner.

Assuming that the secret has already been split into n shares and that the devices have already been suitably initialized, what protocol should they use to communicate? The protocol must offer the following properties (from the original Pico paper [11]):

- The Pico can ascertain the presence of any of its Picosiblings in the vicinity.
- Each Picosibling responds to its master Pico but not to any other Pico.
- At each ping, each Picosibling sends its k-out-of-n share to the Pico, in a way that does not reveal it to eavesdroppers.
- An eavesdropper can detect the bidirectional communications between Pico and Picosiblings but not infer identities or long-term pseudonyms.
- The Pico can detect and ignore old replayed messages.
- The Pico can detect and ignore relay attacks (e.g. with Hancke-Kuhn [3]).

Our attacker model is essentially Dolev-Yao [1] as far as messages go (the adversary can overhear, intercept and modify all traffic) but with the added twist that the attacker may also capture the Pico (while it is in a locked state) and some

B. Christianson et al. (Eds.): Security Protocols 2012, LNCS 7622, pp. 223–230, 2012.

of the Picosiblings (fewer than k). We assume the adversary *cannot* capture the Pico while it is unlocked and that the adversary *cannot* capture more than k Picosiblings.

The main goal of the attacker is to unlock the Pico: if this happens, it's game over. Another goal of the attacker is to recognize an individual user from the overheard messages between Pico and Picosiblings: since the Pico and the Picosiblings are strongly tied to an individual, this ability might be used to violate the individual's location privacy.

We believe the problem is hard enough that we don't want to optimize prematurely: we won't add extra constraints before we have found at least one correct solution. Once we have one, though, additional nice-to-have properties would take into account the physical constraints on the ubicomp devices, in particular the very limited energy available to each of the Picosiblings[1].

1.1   Timing and Storage Details for the Pico

This subsection gives some background about the lifetime of the shares and of the shared secret but is not essential to understand the protocol between Pico and Picosiblings.

The high level protection goal is that, when the Pico is away from its Picosiblings, it becomes locked in a way that prevents an attacker from retrieving the authentication credentials, even if the attacker can totally dismantle the Pico and read every bit stored in it. This is achieved by encrypting all[2] the non-volatile memory of the Pico with a master key that is securely erased when the Pico is locked.

Since the protocol described in this paper (communication between Pico and Picosiblings) is what allows a locked Pico to reconstruct its master key, it must obviously be allowed to run even while the Pico is locked. Therefore, if it needs access to any persistent state, that state cannot be part of the memory that gets encrypted under the master key; that state will instead be available to an attacker who captures a locked Pico.

We assume that the hardware architecture of the Pico ensures that, if the attacker captures an unlocked Pico, it is not feasible to extract the master key or the shares from the Pico before they are securely erased. Discussion of how to achieve that is outside the scope of the present paper but we envisage using a Hardware Security Module[3] or perhaps techniques similar to those pioneered by TRESOR [6], whereby keys are only ever stored in processor registers rather than in RAM. We may also wish to encrypt the RAM itself, as suggested in various cryptoprocessor designs such as Kuhn's TrustNo1 [5].

We define system parameter T_1 as the maximum time interval that the Pico will remain unlocked once it is no longer in range of at least k Picosiblings.

---

[1] In an ideal world they'd be so parsimonious with energy that they could be implemented as passive RFID tags.

[2] Well, almost all—see next paragraph.

[3] Such as the TPM (trusted platform module) chip featured in many modern laptops.

We expect it to be in the range between a second and a minute: the exact value will have to be tuned with user testing. It needs to be short for security reasons, but not too short for usability and power consumption[4] reasons.

The Pico requests a share from each of its n possible Picosiblings, staggering the requests so that each Picosibling is contacted in succession at a definite time depending on the Picosibling's number[5]. The cycle time is set so that the interval between successive requests for the same share is shorter than T_1 by some margin.

Once share s_i is received, the Pico loads the share's countdown timer[6] with the value T_1. If the shared secret is not there and at least k shares have a non-expired timer, the shared secret is recomputed. If the same share is received again before the countdown timer expires, the timer is reloaded to T_1; but when the timer eventually expires, the share is securely wiped and the shared secret is recomputed using the remaining available shares, or securely wiped if fewer than k shares remain.

2   A First Attempt

With disregard for computational costs and power consumption concerns, we first propose a solution based on public key cryptography.

The protocol between the Pico and each of its Picosiblings consists of a ping from the Pico and a pong from the Picosibling.

The Pico has a key pair for each of its Picosiblings: $k_{1,j}, k_{1,j}^{-1}$, with j ranging over the Picosiblings. Each Picosibling too has a key pair: for Picosibling number j it will be $k_{2,j}, k_{2,j}^{-1}$.

The ping message, from Pico to Picosibling, means: "hey, Picosibling j, are you there? If yes, please send me your key share s_j." It consists of a random nonce r, signed by the Pico with its private key $k_{1,j}^{-1}$ so that the Picosibling can verify its provenance and encrypted under the Picosibling's public key[7].

$$\text{Ping for Picosibling } j, \text{broadcast by Pico}: \quad E_{k_{2,j}}(S_{k_{1,j}^{-1}}(\text{"ping"}, r))$$

Note that the so-called "public" key $k_{1,j}$ isn't actually public: it is only known to the Pico and to Picosibling j, so nobody else can verify that signature.

---

[4] Shortening T_1 increases the minimum frequency of pings from Pico to Picosiblings and therefore increases the radio communication costs.

[5] This allows the Picosibling to go to sleep most of the time except when it expects a transmission from the Pico. This assumes that the Picosibling has a continuously-running clock, and that running the clock has negligible cost compared to turning on the radio for listening. We need to address the issue of clock sync between the Pico and the Picosibling, especially in case we also allow the Picosibling to be switched off completely, clock included.

[6] This is only a conceptual description—the implementation does not need to keep a separate countdown timer for each share so long as the effect is the same.

[7] This protocol plays it safe but is potentially redundant; while we do want to protect the integrity and source authenticity of the nonce r, it is not clear that we need to protect its confidentiality.

On receiving a ping message, Picosibling j verifies the signature[8] using the Pico's "public" key $k_{1,j}$. If the signature matches, the Picosibling proceeds. If it does not match, the Picosibling ignores this message.

Having recognized a valid signature, Picosibling j composes a pong message by concatenating the received nonce r with its share s_j, signing the lot with its private key $k_{2,j}^{-1}$ (so that the Pico can verify its provenance) and then encrypting the signed message under the Pico's "public" key $k_{1,j}$.

$$\text{Pong from Picosibling } j: \quad E_{k_{1,j}}(S_{k_{2,j}^{-1}}(\text{"pong"}, r, s_j))$$

Here the encryption is necessary, to prevent eavesdroppers from learning s_j, but it could be argued that the signature is redundant, given that no other principal is supposed to know the Pico's "public" key $k_{1,j}$. If we explicitly treat this "public" key as a secret known only to the Pico and to Picosibling j, then the $k_{2,j}, k_{2,j}^{-1}$ key pair of the Picosibling is no longer necessary: the Pico knows that the message came from Picosibling j because no-one else could have encrypted it under $k_{1,j}$.

At this point one wonders why $k_{1,j}$, if it's shared only between the Pico and Picosibling j, should be a "public" key instead of a symmetric key. More on that in section 3, but meanwhile here is a major vulnerability that already kills this first attempt.

2.1   Attack

Assume the attacker records the traffic between the Pico and a sufficient number of Picosiblings. Later, the attacker captures the locked Pico. Having extracted $k_{1,j}^{-1}$, which by hypothesis is unencrypted even in the locked Pico[9], the attacker decrypts a previously recorded pong from Picosibling j and recovers s_j. Provided that the attacker could record the traffic with at least k Picosiblings, he or she now has at least k shares and can recover the master secret that unlocks the Pico. Game over.

3   A Symmetric-Key Ping-Pong Protocol

We switch to symmetric keys, not to save energy (though that's always nice) but primarily to be able to renew keys in order to defeat the previous attack. Now the Pico shares a symmetric key $k_{3,j}$ with Picosibling j, which is used for

---

[8] Clearly there is the possibility of what Stajano and Anderson [12] called a "sleep deprivation torture" (battery exhaustion) attack against the Picosibling, by forcing the Picosibling to verify bogus signatures. Under our stated assumptions we won't worry about it until we have a solution to the main problem.

[9] Otherwise the locked Pico could not run this protocol to obtain the shares that allow it to unlock itself. Thus the $k_{1,j}^{-1}$ keys, for all j, are only protected by whatever modest tamper resistance we can add to the Pico, so we must assume that an attacker with unsupervised physical access to the Pico will be able to retrieve them.

Encrypt-then-MAC in both the ping and the pong. However, after every ping-pong, the two parties renew this symmetric key by hashing it: this stops the previous attack because the key that the attacker finds in the Pico cannot be used to read past messages. A counter c_j is included next to the random nonce r so that the two parties can stay in sync with the number of hashes of the key even if some messages get lost in transit.

The protocol still consists of only two messages, a ping and a pong, followed by a local hash computation at both ends:

$$\text{Ping for Picosibling } j, \text{broadcast by Pico}: \quad EtMAC_{k_{3,j}}(\text{"ping"}, r, c_j)$$

$$\text{Pong from Picosibling } j: \quad EtMAC_{k_{3,j}}(\text{"pong"}, r, c_j, s_j)$$

$$\text{Both (with appropriate sync)}: k_{3,j} := h(k_{3,j})$$

Why Encrypt-then-MAC [4] rather than just MAC in the ping and just Encrypt in the pong? As with the previous protocol, we wish to preserve the integrity of the nonce r, which justifies the MAC in the ping. But this time we also have a good reason for *encrypting* the ping: we want to hide the counter c_j from the eavesdropper, who might otherwise use it to correlate pings from the same Pico to mount a privacy attack. As for the pong, we wish to protect both the confidentiality and the integrity of the share s_j.

3.1 Attack

Although we stopped the previous attack, a more elaborate variation of it still applies, although it is a little harder to mount for the attacker.

The attacker steals the locked Pico, extracts all its keys $k_{3,j}$ and counters c_j, extracts a copy of the encrypted non-volatile memory, then *returns* the Pico and hopes the victim will continue to use it without noticing the tampering. If so, the attacker records the future traffic between Pico and k different Picosiblings, decrypts it using the extracted keys and recovers k shares and hence the master key that decrypts the extracted memory image. Game over again. With this countermeasure we can stop the attack towards the past but not the one towards the future.

We can't even tell the user: "if you lose your Pico, redo all your secret sharing before using it again", because the user can't easily tell whether he "lost" the Pico. If he just left it in his room *and found it there when he returned*, how does he know that the attacker didn't come and image it and then left it there? This can be seen as a distant relative (same social setting, different technical steps) of Rutkowska's "evil maid" attack [8].

It would appear that a sensible countermeasure against this attack is to make the Pico tamper-evident[10], although security then dangerously depends on the user always inspecting the seal with sufficient care.

---

[10] Which is much less demanding than tamper-resistant, and thus not unreasonable.

4   Reset

A related design issue came up while implementing simulations of these protocols: when and how can a user reset the Pico or the Picosiblings to their factory default state? Can the attacker do the same? If yes, is there any advantage in doing so?

In the context of the general problem of resetting unattended devices to factory default, we [10] previously distinguished between the simple but effective Big Stick Principle ("anyone with physical access to the device is allowed to take it over") and the more elaborate Resurrecting Duckling security policy model, in which the mother duck can order the duckling to commit seppuku[11] but where the duckling device must be sufficiently tamper resistant to prevent a third party from doing the same.

In the Pico paper we said the Pico can be reset by invoking seppuku from the unlocked state. So this is a case of Resurrecting Duckling in which the Pico is the duckling and the mother duck is any cloud of k or more Picosiblings[12]. Therefore, only someone who holds enough Picosiblings can reset the Pico.

How about resetting a Picosibling itself to factory default? We don't want an infinite regression of duckling pairings, so we make the Picosiblings obey the Big Stick Principle. We could have a physical reset button on the Picosibling, for example, which would make it forget its association with its Pico. The Picosibling is thus subject to denial of service (adversary pressing the reset button and cancelling the security association, causing the Picosibling to stop working as intended), but it is anyway because someone with physical control over it could equally easily just smash it to pieces. Besides, if the adversary has physical control of the Picosibling, what worries us much more than denial of service is the possibility that, with enough of them, he might extract the share (or just use the Picosibling as is) to unlock the Pico.

5   Re-pairing Attack

Another attack, which is independent of the ping-pong protocol, consists of stealing the Pico from the victim while it is still unlocked (grab-and-run style theft) and then, before T_1 expires, re-pairing k new (blank) Picosiblings to the stolen Pico. Then the attacker can keep the Pico unlocked indefinitely and extract all its secrets.

This attack is, technically, outside our attacker model, because the Pico is captured while unlocked; however it is also relatively easy to prevent.

One possible countermeasure is to ensure that the process of adding a new Picosibling takes longer than T_1, so the operation can't be completed without being in the aura of k already-paired Picosiblings to keep the Pico unlocked.

---

[11] Seppuku is the ritual suicide of the samurai. In this context it means, essentially, that the duckling will reset itself, forgetting any existing security associations and preparing to be taken over by a new master.

[12] We gloss over the business of the additional special shares like the biometric and the remote server [11].

Another possible countermeasure is to ensure that changing the set of Picosiblings requires the two special shares (where the biometric share in particular is used to indicate explicit user consent).

The two countermeasures could even be combined, for good measure.

6 Related Work

The most comprehensive work about this problem space is Peeters's PhD dissertation [7], published a couple of months after this workshop, which addresses related issues in much greater depth and provides much more elaborate, robust and mathematically verified solutions than the protocol we sketched here. On the security side, it offers a method for storing shares on devices (like the Picosiblings) that do not offer secure re-writable storage; the main requirement is that the devices be able to store, in tamper-proof secure storage (such as a PUF [2]), an immutable factory-defined private key. On the privacy side, it offers a privacy-protecting mutual authentication protocol, efficient enough to be usable with RFID tags and capable of supporting multiple readers. Unfortunately, though, it does not appear easy to combine these two useful but independent primitives into a single solution that would offer the benefits of both.

References

1. Dolev, D., Yao, A.C.-C.: On the security of public key protocols. IEEE Transactions on Information Theory 29(2), 198–207 (1983)
2. Gassend, B., Clarke, D., van Dijk, M., Devadas, S.: Controlled Physical Random Functions. In: ACSAC 2002: Proceedings of the 18th Annual Computer Security Applications Conference, p. 149. IEEE Computer Society, Washington, DC (2002) ISBN 0-7695-1828-1
3. Hancke, G.P., Kuhn, M.G.: An RFID Distance Bounding Protocol. In: Proc. IEEE SECURECOMM 2005, pp. 67–73 (2005), http://www.cl.cam.ac.uk/~mgk25/sc2005-distance.pdf
4. Krawczyk, H.: The Order of Encryption and Authentication for Protecting Communications (or: How Secure Is SSL?). In: Kilian, J. (ed.) CRYPTO 2001. LNCS, vol. 2139, pp. 310–331. Springer, Heidelberg (2001)
5. Kuhn, M.: The TrustNo 1 Cryptoprocessor Concept (1997) (manuscript), http://www.cl.cam.ac.uk/~mgk25/trustno1.pdf
6. Müller, T., Freiling, F.C., Dewald, A.: TRESOR Runs Encryption Securely Outside RAM. In: USENIX Security Symposium. USENIX Association (2011), http://www.usenix.org/event/sec11/tech/full_papers/Muller.pdf
7. Peeters, R.: Security Architecture for Things That Think. Ph.D. thesis, KU Leuven (June 2012), http://www.cosic.esat.kuleuven.be/publications/thesis-202.pdf
8. Rutkowska, J.: Why do I miss Microsoft BitLocker? (2009), http://theinvisiblethings.blogspot.co.uk/2009/01/why-do-i-miss-microsoft-bitlocker.html
9. Shamir, A.: How to Share a Secret. Communications of the ACM 22(11), 612–613 (1979), http://securespeech.cs.cmu.edu/reports/shamirturing.pdf

10. Stajano, F.: Security for Ubiquitous Computing. Wiley (2002) ISBN 0-470-84493-0
11. Stajano, F.: Pico: No More Passwords! In: Christianson, B., Crispo, B., Malcolm, J., Stajano, F. (eds.) Security Protocols 2011. LNCS, vol. 7114, pp. 49–81. Springer, Heidelberg (2011),
    http://www.cl.cam.ac.uk/~fms27/papers/2011-Stajano-pico.pdf
12. Stajano, F., Anderson, R.: The Resurrecting Duckling: Security Issues in Ad-Hoc Wireless Networks. In: Christianson, B., Crispo, B., Malcolm, J.A., Roe, M. (eds.) Security Protocols 1999. LNCS, vol. 1796, pp. 172–182. Springer, Heidelberg (2000),
    http://www.cl.cam.ac.uk/~fms27/papers/1999-StajanoAnd-duckling.pdf

Am I in Good Company?
A Privacy-Protecting Protocol
for Cooperating Ubiquitous Computing Devices
(Transcript of Discussion)

Frank Stajano

University of Cambridge

My name is Frank Stajano and this is work done with my brilliant undergraduate student Oliver Stannard. I am very proud of his work. He is doing his final project on an aspect of what I presented last year, namely Pico.

As background: it used to be OK to use passwords for user authentication when you had to remember one or two reasonably short "things". But nowadays it's a different situation: you have to remember a gazillion different passwords and you are being told that they have to be all different, that they have to include special characters, uppercase, lowercase, numbers and symbols, and they have to be long enough otherwise they can be brute-forced, and they can't include anything like your pets or relatives because they can be looked up on Facebook, and you cannot write them down, you have to change them every three months, and so on, and so on. So on usability grounds it's no longer OK to use passwords, and a variety of researchers have been offering solutions to improve on that situation. And I did too: last year I presented Pico[1], which is a solution from the "something you have" category. It's a token that remembers all your credentials, hence its name: Pico della Mirandola was a guy with a fantastic memory and this Pico has a prodigious memory that can remember all your credentials. The credentials are not really passwords anymore, they are key pairs—but I won't be describing Pico today, you can just read last year's paper; this was just to put this year's problem into context.

And this year's problem is as follows. If my primary directive is that I promise users that they will not have to remember any secrets for authenticating, then I have a problem when my token is lost or stolen: how do you link the token to the actual human user? Normally most existing authentication tokens use a PIN, but the PIN is again something you have to remember, and you fall back into many of the problems you had before, except perhaps that you remember only one secret that is then your proxy to all the others. But I promised that I wouldn't make users remember secrets, so I had to find some other way of authenticating the user to the token (never mind the token to the rest of the services).

Another thing that I wanted to provide with the Pico was the feature of *continuous authentication*. If you authenticate by typing your password, for example, the system knows that at that moment you were there (perhaps); but,

---

[1] See LNCS 7114 pp 49–97.

B. Christianson et al. (Eds.): Security Protocols 2012, LNCS 7622, pp. 231–241, 2012.
© Springer-Verlag Berlin Heidelberg 2012

after that, there's a growing window of uncertainty about whether you are still there, or whether you're now away, you went to the toilet or something and left your laptop behind. The system knows that you typed the password at some point and there is a trade-off between the convenience of not having to retype it every five minutes, and the vulnerability of having perhaps several hours in which someone else could be using the computer that you once authenticated to. Continuous authentication is a feature that Pico provides between itself and the verifiers, but we want to have something similar between the user itself and the Pico too. So, instead of unlocking the Pico with a PIN, we unlock it by sensing the presence of other electronic gadgets that are intended to be even more closely tied to the user than the Pico itself is. For example, here you have a young subject with a nose piercing, ear piercing, and watch, and belt, and cell-phone, and all of these things could be equipped to talk to the Pico. And here you have a slightly older character who might be wearing a wig, and dentures, and a tie, and glasses, and shoes, and all these things could also be equipped with RFID-style Picosiblings that might talk to the Pico.

The Pico is then going to sense this cloud of radio proximity signals from the Picosiblings, and when it finds that there are enough nearby it will feel comfortable. "Am I in good company? Am I in company of the devices I know that have been paired with me? Then I will unlock myself; otherwise I will lock myself." I am of course hand-waving over a number of things, all mentioned in last year's paper. There are two special items that I also consider as additional potential shares in this k-out-of-n secret sharing system that reconstructs the Pico's master key out of the shares provided by the Picosiblings. One of them could be a live biometric: it could be that your Pico looks at your retina, or your iris, it could be that the Pico takes fingerprints, a scan, something that is more closely coupled to you than just holding the token, and which would mean more trouble for the bad guy if he also had to copy that. Not impossible to overcome, just one more hurdle. And another special item is to have an additional share on a network server that's controlled by you: the Pico has to talk to the server in order to get that extra share, and the advantage is that, unlike all the other Picosiblings, if you lose the Pico, this is a share you can revoke! You can go back to your server and say: now stop sending your share, if the Pico asks for it, because the Pico is outside of my control. And you could give it greater weight in the k-out-of-n scheme. This secret sharing scheme within a cloud of small mobile devices reminds us of something that Yvo Desmedt and colleagues presented some ten years ago called "T^4", for "Threshold Things That Think"[2]. This was the general picture of what I described last year.

Oliver's final year project was about producing a simulation of the interaction between the Pico and the Picosiblings—an in-computer simulation with different programs talking to each other. He's had a crack at this list of specifications that were in my paper last year. What should the protocol between the Pico and the Picosiblings look like? These were the requirements I set out. First of all, the whole point is that the Pico can find its Picosiblings if they are nearby.

---

[2] In Symposium on Requirements Engineering for Information Security, 2001.

How many must be nearby? k-out-of-n means that you can have n very large, for example, 20 Picosiblings that you have paired in your Pico. You might own 20 pairs of shoes, but today you're only going to wear one; so your k could be this pair of shoes you have today, and these glasses, and this watch, so k is 3 in this case, and tomorrow you can wear different shoes and it still works. You have a big n, but potentially a much smaller k, which lets you select the things you want. Then of course there's a number of additional problems: what do you do with the $n - k$ things that you leave at home? Could people grab them from your home? Is your home secure enough? And so on. We are not going to worry about that today: we have enough on our plate with trying to find a protocol for communication between the Pico and the Picosiblings.

So the Pico can find its Picosiblings if they are nearby. The Picosiblings will respond only to the Pico that they are paired with, not to anybody else who asks the same question, because if they did that then you would have a location privacy (traceability) problem, which we also want to address. The Picosiblings send their share (each Picosibling holds a share) without revealing it to eavesdroppers. The eavesdropper can see the traffic between the Pico and the Picosiblings, but cannot infer a long-term pseudonym for the identity of who's there, otherwise this would cause a traceability problem again. We want to have protection against a replay of old messages, and we also want to have distance-bounding protection against relay attacks, for which we may plug in an existing solution such as Hancke-Kuhn.

What is our attacker model here? We have a Dolev-Yao case of "the attacker can do anything to the messages" as far as communication between the Pico and Picosiblings goes, but in fact it's even worse, because we allow the possibility that the attacker also *steal* the Pico. In that case, at least we say they will steal it while it is locked—they are not allowed to steal it while unlocked. I shall describe this more precisely later, but you already have an intuitive idea of what this means: when it's near the Picosiblings it is unlocked, when it's away from the Picosiblings it is locked; and, when it's locked, nothing that is on the Pico itself can be used. So the attacker can capture the Pico while it is locked, and can also capture some of the Picosiblings, but not k or more, otherwise they would own more than the threshold and they would be able to unlock the Pico immediately. From a security viewpoint, the game is won by the attacker if they unlock the Pico; but also, from a privacy viewpoint, the attacker wins if they can recognise the individual from the traffic between the Pico and the Picosiblings.

As soon as I mentioned that the Picosiblings are an RFID-like device, then people will observe that they have a small processor, a small reserve of energy and you can't run complicated computations on them; well, we're not worrying about that for now. It's hard enough just to get all these properties (I don't even know if we *can* ever get all those properties) before we worry about this, so: no premature optimisation. Once we have a solution for the primary requirements, we'll worry also about making computations simpler for the Picosiblings.

I'm going to give a little background about how the secrets are stored on the Pico, and on how the Pico and Picosiblings schedule their communication.

The locked Pico is supposed to be resistant to an adversary who takes it apart, and probes its hardware and looks at all the bits in it, and therefore it has the "moral equivalent" of full disk encryption (even though of course it doesn't have a disk): its whole storage (except for what is needed for bootstrapping) is encrypted under some master key, and this master key is not stored in the locked Pico, which is why the Pico is secure when locked. And there's a number of technologies we could be using for supporting this: we could have some kind of trusted module chip; there was an interesting project, Tresor, presented at last year's Usenix Security, where the authors were doing encryption while holding the keys only in the registers of the processor rather than in RAM; and TrustNo1 is an architecture presented by Markus Kuhn some 10–15 years ago in which everything, including the RAM, is encrypted. Anyway, so we assume that we are erasing the master key securely whenever the Pico gets locked, and we could do it with one of these mechanisms or possibly others.

Once the Pico is unlocked it remains unlocked so long as it's in range of at least k of its Picosiblings. But when it is no longer in range it will lock itself (after waiting for a while to provide some hysteresis, to avoid bouncing between locked and unlocked on an edge case). When it locks itself the master key is wiped, and all that you can get out of the Pico is the encrypted version of the storage.

Feng Hao: If the master key is erased, how do you actually recover?

Reply: You recover the master key by this k-out-of-n secret sharing with the shares . . . [that are in the Picosiblings].

Feng Hao: But I thought that is encrypted by the master key!

Reply: No, I am not making myself clear enough. The master key is reconstituted by secret sharing with at least k shares, of which each of the Picosiblings holds one, and these shares have to be fed back into the Pico for reconstructing the master key. Now, as in a normal full-disk-encryption system, "full" isn't strictly true because you need something to bootstrap and run the encryption and so on. Thus here, too, the claim of "full" encryption is not quite true because you still need, in clear, the part that talks to the Picosiblings to get the extra shares. But, once you get the shares from the Picosiblings and you reconstitute this master key, then you can access the rest of the Pico storage, which is the part that contains the credentials for authentication to the services. Does this make sense?

Feng Hao: Yes, so the shares are not encrypted.

Reply: The shares are in the Picosiblings, the shares are not stored in the Pico other than temporarily. The Pico continuously cycles through all its Picosiblings trying to see if each of them is there, and it says: "Are you there? If you are, please give me your share." And the Picosibling gives its share, and the Pico only keeps that share for a limited time, after which it wipes it out. So, as the Pico get a share s_i (where the subscript relates to having received it from Picosibling i), there is a kind of countdown timer for that particular share, which means "I've got it now, and it's now 59 seconds old, 58, 57, . . . and when it gets to zero I erase it". And when I erase it I say: "do I have enough shares left (k or more) to reconstitute the secret?" If yes, I am fine; otherwise I lock the Pico because there aren't enough shares. This is the clearest way I can find to explain what happens, although Oliver implemented it more efficiently without having to keep track of a separate timer for each share.

Ross Anderson: But, if the Pico itself doesn't keep the secret long-term, then surely it's not a matter of the Pico storing things temporarily in the siblings, but the siblings storing their shares temporarily in the Pico?

Reply: The siblings do store their shares temporarily in the Pico, yes: each share is stored for a time T_1 and then erased. If the attacker captured the Picosibling it would contain a share, and this is why our attacker model says you can steal some Picosiblings so long as it's fewer than k, otherwise you would reconstruct the master key that way.

With that said, this is an initial attempt at a protocol for talking between Pico and the Picosibling. The Pico has a key pair but, as was the case in the first presentation yesterday[3], public doesn't really mean that you broadcast it to everyone, it's just communicated to a specific Picosibling. Similarly the Picosibling has its own key pair of which the Pico has the public part, and this pair is different for every Picosibling.

Jonathan Anderson: Is there a reason why it needs to be public key encryption? I mean, if you're talking about a computer in my dentures, can we do the same thing with symmetric crypto?

Reply: Well, perhaps we could, but we are not going to optimise for energy usage here before we have a working solution. If we can do something better later by simplifying it, then so much the better; but we are not going to start by looking for the most economical solution, we're just going to start for a solution that might work, and it's not even a given that this one might work. So let's take things in steps.

James Malcolm: Where does the key in the Pico come from? I thought all the keys in the Pico were erased.

Reply: Yes, well, OK; to reduce confusion, let me try and list all the things that I call keys. There is the master key for the Pico which encrypts the rest of the storage of the Pico. Inside that encrypted storage there are keys that talk to the verifiers (the stuff that we are not talking about today but that we discussed last year: when you authenticate to a verifier remotely, your credentials are key pairs that are protected by this master key). Then there are even more keys that are used for the communication between the Pico and the Picosiblings: these are the parts that are in the "unencrypted bootloader" space [because you need to access them before you had a chance to reconstitute the master key that decrypts the rest of the storage].

James Malcolm: So it's whole disk encryption, but actually you're reducing the amount of "whole"?

Reply: Yes! As I said earlier, when I say *full* disk encryption it's never truly full because you need to run some (unencrypted) bootstrapping code that will decrypt the rest before you can get in. Here it's the same: you need something

---

[3] See Andel, these proceedings.

that's unencrypted (the keys for communication with the Picosiblings) so you can get the shares to decrypt the master key. These are *not* keys that Pico uses to authenticate to the real verifiers. The core item that goes across from the Pico to the Picosibling is a random nonce. The Pico is saying: "Are you there? Please send me your share." It could say just that, but then this would be subject to replay. To prevent that, this question is augmented with this random nonce by the Pico. It's integrity-protected by signing it, and it's confidentiality-protected by encrypting for the Picosibling. It could be argued that we don't really need to have it confidentiality protected. Do we need it integrity-protected? Yes, otherwise someone else could pretend to be the Pico to elicit a response from the Picosibling (privacy attack). The Picosibling then replies with its share, bundled together with the nonce from the Pico and signed with the private key of the Picosibling, and then encrypted for confidentiality with a key of the Pico; and here confidentiality is necessary otherwise an eavesdropper would learn the share, obviously.

Ross Anderson: So you're assuming that the Pico can at some time be captured?

Reply: Yes.

Ross Anderson: This protocol assumes that you can never have more than $k - 1$ Picosiblings captured at any time during the history of the Pico, because middleperson attacks can be mounted at arbitrary times to record the shares from the Picosibling?

Reply: Yes. If you could, at any time in the history of the world, capture an aggregate of k or more Picosiblings, then, after extracting the secret from each of them, you would have the master key.

Ross Anderson: So if you wanted to have a world in which the threat model was that you could only capture up to k Picosiblings *in any one time period*, then at the end of each time period you would have to refresh the Pico's private key.

Reply: I would have said: redistribute the master key, re-share the secret.

Ross Anderson: You could either re-share the secret, or you could change the main public/private key pair in the Pico so that it discarded the old key pair, and thus old encrypted shares could no longer be decrypted.

Reply: But if the adversary has captured, in history, a total of k or more Picosiblings, and has extracted the shares from them, he doesn't actually care about the traffic any more because he knows the shares and it can reconstruct the master key.

Ross Anderson: I was thinking of an attack where an active attacker, using close-in RF for example, captures or forges a number of these protocol exchanges, and therefore comes to own a number of shares encrypted under the Pico's key $k_{1,j}$.

Bruce Christianson: And then it captures the Pico, which contains the keys to unlock the captured traffic, and now he can read the shares.

Reply: Yes: you are anticipating the attack I was about to present in the next slide. The attacker records lots of traffic containing communications with k

or more Picosiblings and then captures a locked Pico. Since, as James observed, the keys for communication with the Picosiblings cannot be protected by the full disk encryption, then they may be extracted by physical probing of the Pico, and if you have those keys then you can read back all this traffic, including the shares sent by the Picosiblings. And so if you have listened to exchanges with at least k distinct Picosiblings you can then reconstitute the master key of the Pico, and so that's a win for the attacker.

Feng Hao: Why do you say an attacker can decrypt part of the traffic, it depends on the key chain protocol, right? If the protocol is for secrecy then you capture the device and get all the private keys, but the sessions in the past should still be secure, so if you get a key exchange protocol with that property, then the attacker shouldn't be able to decrypt past traffic even though he has captured the current keys from the Pico.

Reply: OK, you are absolutely right. If the messages are sent in the primitive way that I showed, then having the keys and having the traffic is enough to decrypt the latter with the former. If I did something smarter like you are suggesting then, even with the knowledge of the current keys you might not be able to read past traffic. And we have done something, to be shown next, which is maybe a less sophisticated way of doing what you just said. This time we use a symmetric key instead of a public key, but we keep hashing it every time the exchange works. The Pico sends a random number (and a counter, maybe, to help me re-synch across lost messages here—since we are using radio we must assume that we are going to lose messages at some point) and the Picosibling sends back something, encrypted under this shared key, that contains the random number, the counter, and the share; and then, once this has worked, both of us are going to produce a new version of the $k_{3,j}$ by hashing, and so if you capture my Pico you see my current $k_{3,j}$ which will be used for all the next exchanges, but you don't see what I used in the past for the messages that you captured previously. This is just a skeleton, of course; it would need something to not lose sync between the two parties.

This new version addresses the previous attack, which is based on past traffic, because the key that's found inside the Pico will only decrypt future messages. Do we have a threat of someone attacking the future messages, then? Unfortunately yes. What could happen is that the attacker steals the locked Pico, reads all it contains, and then returns it, and the user of the Pico *doesn't realise* it has been stolen and imaged and then keeps using it. And then at that point the attacker has the $k_{3,j}$ that's going to be used for the next message that it captures, so it can learn that Picosibling's share s_j at the next ping response. And this is similar to what's known as the "evil maid" attack on an encrypted laptop: you are in your hotel, and you leave for dinner, and then your maid, while you're away for dinner, images your hard disk and perhaps puts a new bootloader in the hard disk that captures your password and sends it to her; then, although you use the computer as usual, the bad guys can retrieve the password that you typed in yourself and decrypt the image they took of your disk.

I don't see an easy way to stop this other attack. Even the (obviously unusable) countermeasure of telling the user that they should re-key their system every time they lose control of it, can't possibly work, because they never know whether they did lose control or not. I mean: have I lost control of my other computer while I'm giving the talk right now? Is anybody messing around with my bag under that chair over there while I am in front of the audience, sometimes looking at the screen, and trying to remember what my presentation was about?

Matt Blaze: The usual answer to this is tamper resistance.

Bruce Christianson: Or tamper evidence.

Reply: Is this the best we can do?

Paul Syverson: What about using proactive secret sharing? So that, when you're updating the threshold secret, the shares are always being updated, and the old ones don't affect the new ones.

Reply: Isn't this something that would also have the problem of the previous fix, that it will stop the attack for past traffic already recorded but not for future traffic?

Bruce Christianson: If the image is exact then the evil maid can do anything that the Pico can do.

Paul Syverson: I guess it depends: if you've completely broken the stuff in the past then, yes; but assume you were worried about shares being compromised in attacks, but not all of them. If the adversary has broken a threshold number of shares then you're stuffed, but the whole idea of proactive secret sharing was that eventually somebody will have broken into older things, but they don't do them all at once, and so if they break some now and some later you're preserving the same secret but the shares are changing all the time.

Reply: So you're offering a solution for the problem that Ross highlighted earlier: if the bad guy breaks three shares now and then another three shares later and eventually they add up to k, in the old scheme he's broken the system, but with proactive secret sharing he hasn't.

Paul Syverson: Right, yes.

Matt Blaze: I think without tamper resistance you're screwed. Why should my evil maid stop at imaging my Pico? My evil maid is going to replace my Pico with one that has firmware or software that the adversary is controlling, or maybe a back channel for the adversary to send them everything that it's doing in the future.

Sandy Clark: And that's already documented! People travelling to hostile environments on government business right now are warned never to let their electronic devices out of their sight even if they're showering, because the *batteries* are Trojans! The evil maid will come and replace the battery in something that you left sitting on the back of a counter while you're in the shower, and then you are compromised.

Paul Syverson: But still, is the threat model right? There are people who have to worry about that, but I think a lot of the things that Frank was talking about are more commonplace. Somebody opportunistically grabbing your device because later they're going to use it to try to steal stuff from you, OK; but they're probably not going to have *Trojan batteries*!

Matt Blaze: But imaging my device and loading custom firmware on my device are not terribly different from each other.

Reply: I'm interested in the asymptotic boundary of where we can go: can we do *anything* without eventually relying on tamper resistance? If the answer is no, then there's little point trying to be too elaborate.

Ross Anderson: Well, even *with* tamper resistance there are limits. People who work in senior positions are given Blackberries that communicate by means of Bluetooth to other similarly sized devices that contain crypto, and the failure model is that people put both of them in the same pocket of their jacket as they use them both at the same time.

Virgil Gligor: Maybe we'll come full circle and use passwords again!

[ALL LAUGH]

Bruce Christianson: But the question is, how difficult would it be to make the Pico sufficiently tamper evident than the user could tell if it had been read?

Sandy Clark: Right, because I think tamper resistance is futile, but tamper evidence is useful.

Feng Hao: If I use this kind of device as a password to my gmail account, if one day I lose the secret, I will lose everything, so presumably you have some disaster recovery mechanism, maybe a secret bit of piece of paper in a safe somewhere; and, if you have proactive secret sharing, that simply cannot be changed. And so you have a very difficult problem!

Reply: In last year's Pico paper I said I'd use a forcing function to ensure you took back-ups of your Pico. Recharging and taking a back-up are two actions that are inseparable, therefore every time you recharge (and you're going to recharge because otherwise it doesn't work) you are also taking a back-up. I thought it was a neat solution but, on giving the Pico talk in three continents, I've been challenged on various points including this one. I think the only proof is building a prototype and then having to tie all the ends together. If you use proactive secret sharing to fix that attack, then would the back-up still work? You have to go full circle and build one and see if you've addressed all the objections and attacks and if all the countermeasures still work when they're applied together. You need the equivalent of some kind of regression testing. And I can't in my head work out if all the answers I give to individual objections (which are all valid) compose into something that still works consistently. That's why I really want to build one.

Sandy Clark: What I find interesting about Pico is that I think it's going to change the threat model. Passwords allow for remote attacks, whereas if you authenticate with an actual physical device then the attack has to be physical. So then, are you safer or are you more in danger? If someone wants to steal your money then they'd have to mug you and cut off all of your Picosiblings!

Reply: The advantage of this scenario is that it's not so scalable: you have to be really targeted by the bad guy for it to happen.

Dylan Clarke: On a less extreme theme, assuming people were using Picosiblings regularly, if somebody wants to steal my laptop, they're going to steal my glasses and my shoes as well.

Sandy Clark: And cut off your earring and your nose piercing.

Ross Anderson: So then you need nanites in your blood, so you no longer need to have a blood transfusion.

Sandy Clark: Yes, and then you need a certain quorum of blood, you don't need all of it but you need some of it.

Ross Anderson: Well in that case, the feat is what they do in Rio, they take you at gunpoint to a slum, and sit you down at a computer and get you to empty your bank account.

Sandy Clark: But how about that other discussion that we had? Could you lie? Could you reveal a fake Pico, a "duress" one that would you let you take out a certain amount of money but not all of it?

Jonathan Anderson: Your left eye is the real biometric and your right eye is a duress biometric.

Dylan Clarke: Or one piercing sends out a signal when it's remote.

Reply: Good fun! Well, in the interest of time, I'll skip ahead to the re-pairing attack. The attack is that the guy steals the Pico while it's still unlocked (and this is actually outside the threat model that I mentioned before, because I said it could only be stolen while it was locked). But if the attacker does steal it while you are using it (someone just grabs it and runs), what do you do? If he runs faster than you he could then re-pair it with blank Picosiblings he bought in the shop, and then he becomes the master of that Pico. We thought about this and came up with two suggestions. The simpler one is to ensure that the procedure for adding a Picosibling takes longer than the expiring time for the existing cloud because it needs to decay, and therefore the attacker will not be able to re-pair it with his own new ones before the Pico locks itself again.

Sandy Clark: Unless you walk around with blank ones and just stand close enough to somebody.

Reply: Yes. So the other thing that we said, which could be done independently or together, is to ensure that, when adding a new Picosibling, the procedure for changing the pool of shares also requires you to access the two special shares, which are the network server and the biometric. This works well if the biometric can be taken as an indication of explicit consent from the user, which somehow depends on the specific biometric. If you have to slide your finger on a reader, you'll be aware that you're doing it, whereas if the biometric consists of scanning your iris it could be done with a concealed camera so it's not a great indication that you consented. All ideas we are throwing around.

This is the stage we're at. As you see, it's very unfinished, and we are still looking for something that we could consider a satisfactory solution; but, besides a solution, we're still looking for more attacks, because it's important to understand the attacks before writing up a final solution. Any more comments?

Jonathan Anderson: I do worry slightly about your "we'll worry about power consumption later" comment, because something like that can be the difference between whether this is possible or not possible to do. And if you leave power consumption to the very end then you may find yourselves designing a protocol that can't possibly be implemented in anything realistic like a device that will go in my glasses, or in my dentures, or in my pipe.

Reply: I agree with you there; on the other hand, if I start without a clue of how any protocol at all would ever solve this problem, how am I going to have a chance of making one that would work in my glasses? Maybe if I get one working when I have fewer constraints, I might have to throw it away to do a new low-power one that works in my glasses, but at least I've got a clue about how I solved the non-power-related security problems.

Jonathan Anderson: But mightn't it be more interesting if you ended up with a protocol that, even though it didn't have all the properties that you initially thought you might like, had *some* of those properties (that are obtainable in a realistic energy scenario) but it additionally showed that to get the other properties you need to upgrade to something that also involves higher power devices?

Reply: That would be a fair way of proceeding. On the other hand, methodologically I prefer to start from my actual requirements, not from the things I'm going to get because that's what can technically be done with today's technology.

Paul Syverson: Of course, in a future scenario where these devices are in fact all embedded in you, then a simple power replenishment comes from eating!

Matt Blaze: Wait a minute, I've got a certain amount of discomfort with your saying "well, let's worry about making this part of it practical later" because everyone in this room has spent a significant part of their careers pointing out the errors of the people who say "well let's worry about security later"; and now we're saying "let's worry about power management later".

Paul Syverson: Yes, but the difference is he is presenting academic research and stuff, and we're criticising people who have deployed systems.

Matt Blaze: Right, that's true, but we're also saying, here's the security protocols to put in your deployed system.

Reply: Let me defend my position, then.

Matt Blaze: No, I'd rather make up what your position is. I know you're not actually proposing a real system; but, if you were...

Paul Syverson: We know you're saying something reasonable, but he finds it much easier to attack his own version.

Matt Blaze: My comment makes much more sense if you had said something different.

Virgil Gligor: On that note, I think we are ready for lunch.

Stayin' Alive:
Aliveness as an Alternative to Authentication

Jonathan Anderson and Robert N.M. Watson

University of Cambridge Computer Laboratory
{jonathan.anderson,robert.watson}@cl.cam.ac.uk

Abstract. Authentication protocols attempt to discern whether or not a user is who she says she is based on what she has, is or knows. In many situtations, however, such as protecting Wikis from robots and Distributed Hash Tables from sybils, identity is less important than liveness: it's not *who you are* that matters, it's whether or not you are alive. We propose extensions to the Kerberos authentication which allow systems to test whether or not they are interacting with a real person, optionally disregarding their identity. We demonstrate how such extensions could be used to support realistic user interactions with requiring shared definitions of global identity.

1 Introduction

Last year, one of the authors of this paper attempted to contact a professor at a notable US university in order to arrange a lunch appointment. This professor had — perhaps out of an attempt to avoid spam — created a system by which one could not e-mail him unless one had demonstrated their ability to receive e-mail by submitting their own (publicly accessible) e-mail address into a Web form and replying to a generated single-use address. This system may be effective at blocking spam, but it is also effective at dissuading legitimate would-be corresponders and collaborators from initiating conversation.

Disregarding this particular implementation, there is an insight to be gained from this situation. Sometimes, e.g. when attempting to fend off unsolicited mass e-mail, it is not important to know whether or not a potential correspondent's identity corresponds to a unique name within a global namespace; the important thing is whether or not that correspondent is really there at all. When controlling access to a Wiki, we do not need to know the name or government-issued ID number of a contributor, we would simply like to know that edits come from a real person. We may also like to know that a long string of thoughtful, well-researched edits have come from the same person, but that knowledge does not require a globally-agreed-on notion of the user's identity.

Today, many websites attempt to use CAPTCHAs to distinguish anonymous users from anonymous bots. This approach is not applicable to other networked services such as mail servers, anonymous FTP servers or distributed hash tables since the CAPTCHA protocol executes within the context of a Web session.

B. Christianson et al. (Eds.): Security Protocols 2012, LNCS 7622, pp. 242–250, 2012.

Outside of the Web context, existing authentication and authorization tools are a poor fit for the general case of networked services.

In this paper, we propose extensions to the well-known Kerberos suite of tools that allow users to establish communications channels by demonstrating liveness without requiring *a priori* agreement on globally-unique identities. Our extensions use a new security protocol primitive called *unboxing*, and we demonstrate how traditional attacks against authentication protocols only exist in a *denatured* form.

2   Kerberos

The Kerberos protocol [4,5,6], a simplified form of which is depicted in Figure 1, provides authentication and authorization for networked services such as file servers and SMTP servers. Kerberos allows security-sensitive authentication logic to be separated from the "business logic" of servers.

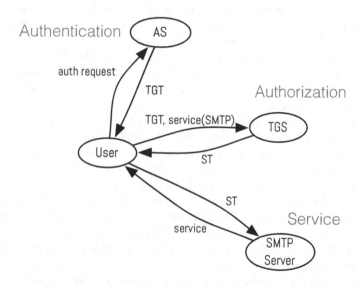

Fig. 1. Kerberos v5 protocol

For instance, let us consider a scenario in which a user Bob wishes to avail of services (e.g. a mail delivery queue) provided by an SMTP server. Rather than implement its own authentication service, the SMTP server relies on a centralized Authentication Service (AS) to authenticate Bob. Bob first communicates with the AS, proving knowledge of a secret key derived from a password, and is granted a cryptographic Ticket-Granting Ticket (TGT). Bob can then reveal the TGT to a Ticket-Granting Server (TGS) in exchange for a Service Ticket (ST). This ticket is a packet encrypted under a key shared by the TGS and the Service Server (SS), i.e. the SMTP server in our case. The ticket certifies the

SS that Bob's identity has been verified by the AS and provides a session key which Bob and the SS can use in support of their confidentiality and integrity requirements.

A simplified model of the exchange between Bob and the AS is:

$$\texttt{KRB\_AS\_REQ}: B \xrightarrow{\quad B,A \quad} A \tag{1}$$

$$\texttt{KRB\_AS\_REP}: B \xleftarrow{\quad TGT=\{B,k_{BT}...\}_{k_{AT}},\{k_{BT}\}_{k_B} \quad} A \tag{2}$$

$$\texttt{KRB\_TGS\_REQ}: B \xrightarrow{\quad B,S,TGT,S,\{B,t\}_{k_{BT}} \quad} TGS \tag{3}$$

$$\texttt{KRB\_TGS\_REP}: B \xleftarrow{\quad \left\{ ST=\{B,k_{BS},...\}_{k_{TS}},k_{BS} \right\}_{k_{BT}} \quad} TGS \tag{4}$$

$$B \xrightarrow{\quad \{T,...\}_{k_{BS}} \quad} S \tag{5}$$

in which B and S are the names of Bob and the SMTP server, t is the current time (to demonstrate freshness), k_B is Bob's "reply key" (generated from Bob's password) and k_{XY} is a symmetric key used for communication between principals X and Y. Using this protocol, Bob can demonstrate knowledge of his password to the AS without having to reveal it to the SMTP server, both Bob and the SMTP server can know to whom they are speaking and each server can focus on the one clear function for which it has been designed: authentication, authorization or delivering mail.

In the vanilla Kerberos protocol, message 1 can be replayed by an attacker, inducing the AS to send the attacker a `KRB_AS_REP` message. This message does not reveal any key material, since keys are encrypted under k_B and k_S, but such a replay could aid a known-plaintext attack on k_B, which is usually based on a user-chosen password. In order to prevent such an attack, the AS can require "pre-authentication" data to be sent as part of the `KRB_AS_REQ` message. This data can be as simple as the current timestamp encrypted under k_B (to demonstrate knowledge of Bob's password-derived key), but it can also be an arbitrary multi-round challenge-response protocol between a client-side plugin and a server-side plugin.

Kerberos solves an important problem: it allows a trusted third party to be leveraged by clients and servers to set up secure communications with mutual authentication. This neatly fulfills the requirements of mail *relays* that only forward mail for known users, but it fails to address the mail *submission* problem: an SMTP server delivering mail directly to local recipients does not need to be able to authenticate mail senders, but it will use authentication as a proxy certification that the sender is a real user and not a spam bot.

We propose a Kerberos extension to support the direct validation of "aliveness" claims as well as — or instead of — traditional authentication. This extension uses existing spaces in the Kerberos protocol intended for preauthentication data to carry the results of an interactive Turing test approximation, allowing services to be accessed by users not on the basis of *who* they are, but *whether* they are.

3   Liveness Extensions

Using the existing Kerberos preauthentication framework [2] and plugin APIs, we propose to extend the user's interaction with the AS according to the communication graph depicted in Figure 2. We introduce additional messages into the initial Kerberos authentication exchange, adding a demonstration of *aliveness* via some instantiation of Turing's *imitation game* [8].

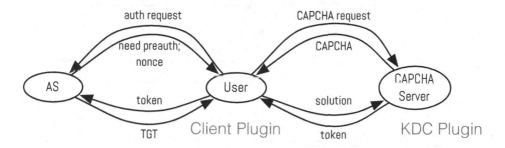

Fig. 2. Proposed Kerberos extensions

3.1   Notation for Human Readability

Security protocols typically use a curly-brace-and-subscript notation to indicate that a message is encrypted, e.g. $\{B, k_{BT}, t\}_{k_A}$. In the protocol that follows, we introduce a new notation for messages that are not encrypted, but are rather encoded in a form that can be easily decoded by humans but is less easily decoded algorithmically.

The most common form of such a message is the CAPTCHA [1], but other forms of "human computation" are possible. The creator of the CAPTCHA, Luis von Ahn, denoted a *human algorithm game* which is easy for humans but hard for computers by a one-way function, $G(x) = y$ [9]. We define *human decoding* as a human algorithm game in which x is an encoding of information — such as a CAPTCHA — that can easily be decoded by humans but not computers. We will denote such a message with the notation $[x]$ and expect that a human can trivially decode $[x]$ to x.

3.2   Protocol

Our complete protocol with "liveness" extensions to Kerberos is depicted in Figure 3.

In the initial communication between Bob and the authentication service Alice, Bob requests a Kerberos Ticket-Granting Ticket (TGT) from Alice for the server S using the identity "anonymous". Alice replies with a standard Kerberos error code KDC_ERR_PREAUTH_REQUIRED which specifies that Kerberos authentication must be preceded by a "pre-authentication" step, which in this case is an interactive proof of aliveness to a CAPTCHA service.

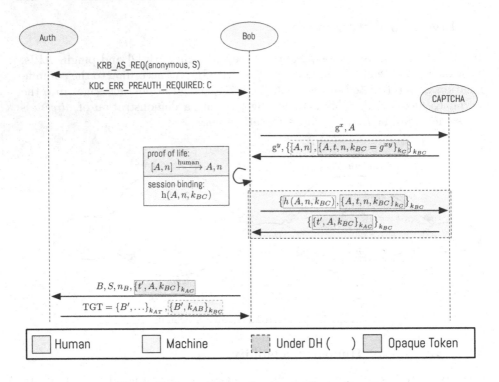

Fig. 3. Kerberos "pre-authentication" via aliveness

Bob's interaction with the CAPTCHA server consists of two round trips which convey a challenge and response within a Diffie-Hellman–negotiated channel that binds the response to the session key.

Bob begins his interaction with the CAPTCHA server by initiating a Diffie-Hellman exchange (g^x) and providing the name of the realm A to which he would like to authenticate. This name will be included in the token which the CAPTCHA server eventually provides to A in order to prevent one *aliveness token* from being spent at multiple sites.

The CAPTCHA server replies with the second half of the Diffie-Hellman exchange (g^y) in the clear and a user-decodable challenge $[A, n]$, as well as a state cookie. This cookie contains the name A, the time t that the challenge was sent, the nonce n that the challenge was generated from and the negotiated session key k_{BC} being used to protect communications between Bob and the CAPTCHA service. The use of cookies allows the CAPTCHA server to be stateless apart from a replay cache.

The challenge $[A, n]$ sent to the user contains both the name of the Kerberos authentication realm and a dictionary word generated from the random nonce n. An example of such a challenge is depicted in Figure 4,

Bob's response to this challenge consists of C's state cookie and a cryptographic hash of three elements: the name A from the challenge, the word n from the challenge and the session key k_{BC} being used to communicate with the

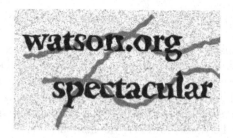

Fig. 4. A user-decodable CAPTCHA: $[A, n]$

CAPTCHA server. The session key is included in order to bind the response to the channel over which it is given, mitigating the middleperson attack described in Section 4.

Finally, the CAPTCHA server gives Bob a token $\{t', A, k_{BC}\}_{k_{AC}}$ that Bob can present to A as evidence that he solved a CAPTCHA for service A at time t'. This token also contains the session key that Bob negotiated with the CAPTCHA service; A can use this key to bootstrap a new shared secret k_{AB}. The rest of the protocol run is standard pre-authenticated Kerberos with one exception: as well as granting Bob a Ticket-Granting Ticket (TGT) and performing a password update to k_{AB}, A must also assign a new pseudonym B' which can be used to identify this particular "anonymous" user in the future.

At the conclusion of this protocol run, B possesses a Ticket-Granting-Ticket (TGT) in the name of an anonymous user who was believed to represent a real, live person at time t'. Such a user might now be granted limited access to a public FTP server, temporary access to an SMTP server for the purposes of mail delivery (but not mail relay) or rate-limited access to an IRC server or a Wiki. Without explicitly naming a user, our Kerberos realm has established a secure communications channel with "that user". If the user fulfils the traditional Kerberos security assumptions (e.g. not revealing secret keys to anyone), there can be continuity in future communications between the unnamed user and existing Kerberized infrastructure.

4   Denaturing a Middleperson Attack

denature, v. /dɪˈneɪtjʊə(r)/ /diː-/ (Oxford English Dictionary)

1. *trans.* To render unnatural. Obs.
2.
    (a) To alter (anything) so as to change its nature; e.g. to render alcohol or tea unfit for consumption.
    (b) *Biochem.* To modify (a protein) by heat, acid, etc., so that it no longer has its original properties.

Since Bob shares no long-term secrets with the Authentication Server (AS), the AS cannot set up a confidential channel between Bob and the CAPTCHA server.

Thus, an active adversary Mallory can launch a middleperson attack between Bob and the CAPTCHA server.

After inserting himself, however, Mallory is unable to exploit his position in the conventional way. We refer to this as a *denatured* attack: the new assumptions implicit in anonymous "authentication" render the original properties of the attack unfit for use. The attack exists, but it no longer has its original properties.

Mallory is able to "steal" Bob's CAPTCHA by not forwarding it, but rather solving it himself. If he does, however, he has effectively carried out a Denial of Service attack against Bob but has not breached Alice's security policy: to Alice, one unknown anonymous user is as good as another. If, on the other hand, Mallory forwards the CAPTCHA to Bob, Bob's solution does not help Mallory to authenticate himself, since it is bound to the session key k_{BM} and Mallory needs a solution bound to k_{MC} in order to acquire a "CAPTCHA solved" token. Thus, Mallory has exactly the same power to authenticate to Alice whether or not he is attacking Bob: this is a *denatured* middleperson attack.

5   Related Work

The Kerberos network authentication protocol [5,6] is based on an earlier authentication protocol by Needham and Schroeder [4]. These protocols allow users to receive authorisation tokens from a trusted authentication and authorisation server. These tokens can be presented to networked services such as file servers and mail servers, proving to those servers that the user has the right to use them without revealing the user's password to them. Kerberos relies on a strong notion of user identity, although primitives have been introduced to deal with some degree of anonymity.

Zhu, Hartman and Leach's RFC 6112 proposes anonymous credentials for Kerberos [10]. This would allow users to be granted tickets that identify them only by realm, not personal identity. These tickets provide a natural expression of the "identity" expressed by the above aliveness extensions: they identify an identity that it believed by a particular AS to have some property, which in our case is to *be alive*.

RFC 6112 would also allow users to obtain tickets from a TGS without any authentication whatsoever that prove nothing about the ticket bearer's identity. Lacking any authentication, this protocol cannot prevent automatic ticket harvesting; a Sybil-prevention feature such as that afforded by our liveness extensions would be a natural fit for this part of the RFC.

Holt and Seamons' Nym is a pseudonymous credential system that allows users to convert pseudoname tokens into TLS client certificates [3]. For instance, a user could request a pseudonymous token from a server that enforces a "one token per IP address" policy. This token can then be exchanged for a client certificate that is accepted by a service such as a Wiki. The aliveness extensions that we propose applying to Kerberos could fit equally well into the Nym framework: the token service is agnostic towards the policy that it enforces. Indeed, the authors of Nym observed that tokens might be earned by solving CAPTCHAs or puzzles;

what our extensions add is the specific cryptographic protocol that should be used to earn the token.

Tsang *et al.*'s Nymble is a larger system for providing credentials that are unlinkable by default but linkable when the credentials are misused [7]. Nymble includes a pseudonymous credential acquisition phase, but the focus of the work is elsewhere: blacklisting pseudonyms. As with Nym, Nymble could benefit from the inclusion of our aliveness protocol in its credential acquisition phase.

6   Conclusion

The Kerberos protocol and its existing extensions provide a useful service: given a trusted third party, clients and servers can authenticate each other and set up secure communication channels. The protocol is a natural fit for services such as mail relays that only provide service to users who are known to the system administrator according to a pre-arranged unique name. It is a less natural fit for services that are offered to anonymous users: in Kerberos, authorisation requires authentication.

We have extended Kerberos, using an existing "pre-authentication" framework and plugin architecture, for scenarios which the existing model does not fit well: services such as chat systems or Wikis that do not necessarily require a globally-unique username but do need to know whether or not the user is alive. The protocol uses a technique and notation called *unboxing*: an analogue to encryption that is trivial for humans but difficult for machines.

The protocol is secure against eavesdropping by a passive adversary and indifferent to active attacks: there are no pre-existing shared secrets to steal and a middleperson cannot impersonate the authenticating user. A middleperson can authenticate themselves to the server instead of the client he is attacking, but the attack is *denatured*: rendered unfit for use and without its original properties. The server is indifferent to which anonymous user is currently connected; the only property it is required to verify is that the connected anonymous user is alive.

Our protocol allows network services to be provided to anonymous-but-alive users. User authorization is not done on the basis of *who* one is, but *whether* one is.

Acknowledgements. We would like to thank Paul Syverson, Matt Blaze and Ross Anderson for helpful comments and questions during the workshop at which this protocol was presented.

References

1. Von Ahn, L., Blum, M., Hopper, N.J., Langford, J.: CAPTCHA: Using Hard AI Problems for Security. In: Biham, E. (ed.) EUROCRYPT 2003. LNCS, vol. 2656, pp. 294–311. Springer, Heidelberg (2003)

2. Hartman, S., Zhu, L.: A Generalized Framework for Kerberos Pre-Authentication. RFC 6113 (April 2011)
3. Holt, J.E., Seamons, K.E.: Nym: Practical Pseudonymity for Anonymous Networks. Technical Report 2006-4, Internet Security Research Lab (ISRL), Brigham Young University (June 2006)
4. Needham, R.M., Schroeder, M.D.: Using encryption for authentication in large networks of computers. Communications of the ACM 21(12) (December 1978)
5. Neuman, B.C., Ts'o, T.: Kerberos: an authentication service for computer networks. IEEE Communications Magazine 32(9), 33–38 (1994)
6. Neuman, C., Yu, T., Hartman, S., Raeburn, K.: The Kerberos Network Authentication Service (V5). RFC 4120 (July 2005)
7. Tsang, P.P., Kapadia, A., Cornelius, C., Smith, S.W.: Nymble: Blocking Misbehaving Users in Anonymizing Networks. IEEE Transactions on Dependable and Secure Computing 8(2), 256–269 (2011)
8. Turing, A.M.: Computing Machinery and Intelligence. Mind 59, 433–460 (1950)
9. von Ahn, L.: Human Computation. Technical Report CMU-CS-05-193, Carnegie Mellon University, Pittsburgh, PA (2005)
10. Zhu, L., Hartman, S., Leach, P.: Anonymity Support for Kerberos. RFC 6112 (April 2011)

Stayin' Alive: Aliveness as an Alternative to Authentication (Transcript of Discussion)

Jonathan Anderson

University of Cambridge

I'll start as I often do with an obligatory handwave towards the theme of the workshop. This isn't so much about bringing protocols to life as a protocol that says whether or not you are currently alive, and this is based on some thinking I've been doing with Robert Watson. The title is "Stayin' Alive: Aliveness as an alternative to authentication", because sometimes authentication is not the property that you actually want.

Here is the problem: I'm going to call it the lunching cryptographers problem. We have a computer scientist in a new town, he's there for a conference, and he says, "there's another computer scientist in town who I'd like to chat with, maybe we could grab lunch together." The trouble is, they each have their own personal mail servers that they use, but they don't like spam very much. So they both have Kerberos set up so that you can't just email them directly, you have to get tokens first[1]. One person must authenticate to the other, so they can't speak to each other unless one trusts the other. This seems very unsatisfactory: what we'd really like is to have two mutually suspicious parties enter into a conversation without one having to say, "I am in a position of authority to give you tokens, but not vice versa".

One conventional solution to this sort of problem is a trusted third party. If both parties share keys with this third party, they can negotiate a key to share between them, but we don't really like that solution very much. In a lot of cases, we're not really interested in an absolute sense of identity: passport numbers and the like. What we really want to know is that this isn't a spammer who's bugging me, it's actually a person, and then if we converse and this real person says interesting things, then maybe they're somebody worth having lunch with.

We see a similar problem when we're dealing with Wikis: we want to stop — or at least rate-limit — defacement, so when people spam Wikis we try to stop them with things like CAPTCHAs that ask, are you actually a real person? This could also be called the Cambridge Admission Protocol. Here's Alice: Alice is a very clever student somewhere outside the UK who would like to come to Cambridge. She wants to talk to the Board of Graduate Studies, and the Board of Graduate Studies is trying to decide, do we want to make Alice a student here or not? How should this be done? Does the Board of Graduate Studies really need to inspect Alice's passport at this point? I would contend no. The Board of Graduate Studies doesn't actually care who she is in an absolute sense,

---

[1] This is inspired by real life events, though no names will be given.

B. Christianson et al. (Eds.): Security Protocols 2012, LNCS 7622, pp. 251–258, 2012.
© Springer-Verlag Berlin Heidelberg 2012

defined by some global identity that's vetted by a trusted third party, what they actually care about is, is this a real person? Then they can start a conversation, and then through that conversation, the applicant sends a research proposal. Then we ask them some questions and they answer, and that leads us to think that they wrote the research proposal, and it carries on from there. So there are many situations in which we don't actually care about authentication so much as we care about aliveness, just being alive.

A brief word about the notation. On this slide we have a very conventional sort of notation: you have a secret, it's encrypted under some key, and then you can decrypt it and get the secret out if you have the key. This is something a computer can do, it's a very mechanical thing. We're proposing, as an analogue to this encryption notation, a generalisation of the CAPTCHA concept: an un-keyed function that is easy for a human to do but hard for a machine to do. We represent this with square brackets. This would be an excellent point for somebody in the audience to jump in and say, "no, we're using square brackets to indicate this other protocol construct in our work, and readers will be con-fused"... but nobody is jumping in, so very good. We'll use this square-bracket notation to represent something that a human being can easily remove, a box, as it were, but that isn't so easy for a machine to do. This could be a CAPTCHA image, but it could also be a natural-language sentence with complex grammar that is difficult for a machine to parse.

We also propose a new technical term: to *denature* an attack. In some cases, because we're trying to translate a new concept into an existing paradigm of authentication, there will be attacks that technically work, but I'm going to claim that at least one of these attacks is *denatured*, rendered unnatural. We've changed its nature, like denatured alcohol in the Prohibition era, modified it so it no longer has its original properties. So yes, technically there is a middleper-son attack, but I'm going to argue that it doesn't matter, because it's not a middleperson attack as we commonly understand understand it: it doesn't have the significance that it usually has.

I'll jump right into the protocol. We start with Kerberos because Kerberos is a system that is commonly used to provide authentication services for lots of things like mail servers, and you could imagine adapting Kerberos for all kinds of things. You could imagine adapting Wikis and things to use Kerberos. Here's an overall view of Kerberos: you talk to an authentication server, you produce an authorisation request, they can come back and say, "actually I want stronger authentication, I want pre-authentication", which usually involves something like encrypting a timestamp under a key derived from your password. They say, "ah, I think you are who you say you are", then you get a ticket-granting ticket, and you can bring that to a ticket granting server, which may or may not be the same computer. You then say, "I want to talk to the SMTP server", and he says, "OK, you've got a ticket that I think is allowed to do that", so you've got authentication, then authorisation, and then you've get a ticket that you can actually present to the SMTP server.

We're going to modify this protocol a little bit with Kerberos' plugin architecture: we introduce a new kind of pre-authentication. We're going to have a token that we can bring to a CAPTCHA server — and I say "CAPTCHA server" in the philosophical sense, it can be any kind of human computation — and solve a CAPTCHA. We then get a token back that we can use to prove that we are — or are collaborating with — a person: an anonymous person, but a human being.

So the protocol looks a bit like this. Bob wants to talk to some server, so he goes to its authentication server and he does a normal-ish Kerberos initiation: he says, "I'm an anonymous person, and I want to talk to this server S". The auth server says, "OK, I need you to do some pre-authentication for me, I need you to talk to this server C". So Bob talks to server C and starts a Diffie-Hellman: here's a value of y^r and I am trying to authenticate to server A. The CAPTCHA server does the other half of the Diffie-Hellman and gives Bob a boxed (human-solvable) parameter that contains A's name and a nonce. There's also a cookie, some data for the CAPTCHA server, just to keep the CAPTCHA server stateless, and it includes a timestamp for freshness. At this point Bob, because he is a human, is able to un-box this parameter get parameters A and N. In this case A might be a second level domain and N gets translated into a dictionary word.

Bob then calculates a CAPTCHA solution, which is a hash of the boxed parameters and the Diffie-Hellman–negotiated key that we're currently using. That binds the solution to the current session, for reasons I'll describe in a little bit. He sends that back to the CAPTCHA server, under the negotiated key, as well as the cookie that contains all the information the CAPTCHA server needs to check that the solution is correct and fresh. At this point the CAPTCHA server gives Bob a token encrypted under a key shared between the auth server and the CAPTCHA server. Bob can't read this token, but he presents it to the auth server as evidence of pre-authentication and the Kerberos protocol continues as normal. Like the standard protocol, the auth server can provide Bob with a new key to use for authentication from now on. So the key that Bob negotiated with the CAPTCHA server is used to bootstrap a new key with the auth server, and then Bob and the auth server have a normal Kerberos-type relationship. At the end of this protocol, Bob ends up with a new identity, and this identity is some anonymous person, we don't really know who he is, but we believe that he was actually a person at time t and he can prove that he's still this particular anonymous person by using k_B.

From then on we can use that to upgrade into a more formal relationship. Alice talks to the Board of Graduate Studies, proves that she's a real person, then they ask her to send in a research proposal. The proposal is interesting, so they ask her to send in her forms. Eventually they decide to admit her, so they upgrade her to alice@cam.ac.uk: we have an upgrade path for anonymous Alice to get a real identity.

Now you may be saying, "wait a minute, you are doing Diffie-Hellman, you have no pre-shared secret, we could do a middleperson attack, a ha ha ha, your whole system is broken!" Well I'd like to try and convince you that it's not broken, the attack is *denatured*: it exists, but it doesn't mean what a middleperson attack normally means.

On this slide, Bob talks to an authentication server, then he goes to the CAPTCHA server, but it's actually a malicious CAPTCHA server, Mallory. In this picture, Mallory wears a British black hat: it looks a bit like a Trinity College porter. So Bob starts doing the Diffie-Hellman with Mallory while Mallory starts a Diffie-Hellman with the real CAPTCHA server. The real CAPTCHA server gives Mallory a cookie and a puzzle, which we assume Mallory can't solve by himself, so he forwards it to Bob. Bob gives Mallory his solution: a hash of the name A and nonce N from the CAPTCHA server's boxed puzzle, together with the Diffie-Hellman–negotiated key that Bob is currently using. If Mallory tries to pass this through to the CAPTCHA server, the server will notice that the solution is wrong because it was expecting the hash to include k_{MC}, not k_{BM}. That's just the wrong answer, so Mallory is busted.

Now that's all under the assumption that Mallory is unable to perform human computation and solve CAPTCHAs. Let's try again, assuming that Mallory colludes with a human being who can unbox these puzzles. In that case we do the same thing: Mallory talks to the real CAPTCHA server, which gives him a puzzle to solve, parameters to unbox. If Mallory passes the puzzle on to Bob, Bob will construct an incorrect solution like before, but that doesn't matter to Mallory because Mallory is now able to solve the puzzle himself with the aid of his colluding human. But at this point, I'm going to claim that the attack is *denatured*, because what has happened? Somebody talked directly to the CAPTCHA server, and that somebody established that he was a person who was able to solve a puzzle at time t. Neither the auth server nor the CAPTCHA server actually care who did this: it's not like Bob has a pre-existing identity that Mallory is attempting to use. If Mallory is now able to claim to be an anonymous person because Mallory solved a CAPTCHA, well, that's fine: you're claiming to be any particular person, just **a** person. From Bob's perspective this is annoying because his pre-authentication didn't happen, but it's actually just a denial-of-service-attack: Bob is unable to communicate to the real CAPTCHA server. So as far as Bob is concerned it's not man-in-the-middle, it's denial-of-service, and as far as Mallory is concerned, well, he had to get a human into the loop in order to solve a puzzle that proves that... a human solved a puzzle. So that actually seems fine.

You're all very quiet; I guess I'm not winning the Roger Needham award!

Ross Anderson: I suppose if all you're doing is bootstrapping off a CAPTCHA incident, then you can put other things in the CAPTCHA incident with which you could bind them, for example, the perjury trap mentioned earlier. So then all you know is that you're speaking to someone who declares under the penalties of perjury that he's not logging on under coercion. But we won't know who's not logging on under coercion, so in this case it could be the spook who's logging on perfectly voluntarily to do the planned attack on your system rather than the user whom you do not want to be coerced.

Reply: Right, and so in that case you know that it's an anonymous person who either isn't being coerced, or doesn't mind lying, but it's definitely not somebody who isn't being forced by somebody who cares about perjury, yes.

Any other questions?

Matt Blaze: Well I'm trying to figure out what the property is that this has, and map that to a set of properties I can use. The example you had before this is that Alice wants to go to Cambridge and Cambridge has the very high standards of only accepting humans as graduate students. So Cambridge's admissions department is now satisfied that it was talking to a human when it engaged the conversation, but Alice is still left in the cold here. So we don't seem to have actually...

Reply: How is Alice still left in the cold, sorry?

Matt Blaze: Because she didn't get to talk to Cambridge.

Reply: Oh, you mean in the middleperson case?

Matt Blaze: Yes.

Reply: Right, well if you assume that Mallory is capable of pretending to be the CAPTCHA server, if he's doing a DNS attack or something then you're not going to talk to the real server anyway. So it's true that this doesn't provide availability.

Matt Blaze: All we've done is prevented the attacker from stealing Cambridge's CAPTCHAs.

Reply: That is true. So, I call the Cambridge Authentication Protocol in slight jest, the thing where it originally came from was somebody who had this really vigorous and zealous spam policy where he wouldn't give you his email address. You had to go to a webpage and provide some address that he could send a token to, and then that token could be used to generate a one-time email address, and that would bootstrap a conversation. And this seemed kind of annoying because it involves a lot of going back and forth, but also because it's saying, I have to give you my email address, what if I'm not happy to give a real email address? If you don't actually care who I am, why can't we just initiate a conversation in which you can logon to my SMTP server, but you're not going to be sending much spam because you are considered an anonymous *person*, so you can request delivery to me but that's all. If you want to have a mill full of people solving CAPTCHAs, fine, but you only get to spam me once for every CAPTCHA that gets solved. Also, those CAPTCHAs can't be re-used: you can't take my CAPTCHA and use it to prove human-ness to Bruce, you have to commit to talking to Bruce before you get the CAPTCHA.

Matt Blaze: OK, so I'm just trying to get my head around this; I'm not suggesting that this isn't useful, but in that motivating example, Alice and Bob, or whoever the two lunching cryptographers are, both want each other to solve a CAPTCHA, and we want some solution in which both sides end up doing it. And then when we got to the Cambridge admissions example, Cambridge is a server, and it can't solve CAPTCHAs, it only wants people who want to come in to solve CAPTCHAs. So are we coming to the bilateral one?

Reply: Right, so that was a unilateral protocol where somebody has established an anonymous identity. Then you could imagine doing the mutual distrust thing by saying, "if you do the same thing for me over there then we can bootstrap a two-way communication channel" and nobody had to trust anyone initially with a real email address. But yes, this is the one-way case; for Cambridge this makes sense because we assume that it's easier for Alice to authenticate Cambridge then for Cambridge to authenticate anybody who wants to apply. But when you have the lunching cryptographers thing, you use this to bootstrap something else.

Matt Blaze: Right, but one of them has to go first.

Reply: Yes, somebody has to go first, but nobody had to give out their real email address, nobody had to give an identifier that could be used to spam them.

Ross Anderson: So from the point of view of the economics I think it would be preferable to have an anonymity service rather than an anonymity protocol for the simple reason that so many things you want in real life is to know that the person you're talking to now is the same person you talked to two years six months ago, when they deposited some money in the bank. And if you really prove liveness in one instance you only get a small part of that potential volume.

Reply: This is part of why we have this "anonymous at time t" identity: after the initial conversion, one party can prove that they are the **same** anonymous person that participated in that conversation. Without requiring real names, you can prove that you're the same anonymous person; you can upgrade the temporary key by exchanging long-term public keys, but you can prove ownership of that original identity while remaining anonymous.

So the thing about the anonymous identifier service: that's sort of what the CAPTCHA server does. What you don't want is for someone to solve one CAPTCHA and get a token that can be presented in parallel to everyone in the world who cares about aliveness. Instead, you went to this CAPTCHA server, which could be run by reCAPTCHA.org or someone, committed to a party that you wanted to aliveness-authenticate to and received a token than says "this token was given to someone who wants to talk to you and who was alive at time t".

Paul Syverson: There are various systems which have been designed along the lines of what Ross was just saying, there was Nym, and Nymbler, and blagger, and in all of them, you sign up completely anonymously, and then you have a pseudonym, and their main motivation was the one you gave, people are putting stuff into Wikipedia, and you don't want to limit yourself to authenticated users, but you want to be able to revoke people's ability to put new stuff in easily. And so you basically had pseudonyms, and if you have a pseudonym then you just go in for free, and the assumption is it takes a little bit of work to get another pseudonym, and there's various ways to do that. But they seem to capture a moderate amount of what you are trying to do, only somebody has already built them.

Ross Anderson: I suppose what I was hinting at is that, if you had a more biometric way of checking that the person you're talking to now is the person you were talking to 13 months ago, that would be more consilient with how we've come to operate as humans in that we're good at recognising faces even if we forget names.

Sandy Clark: Facial recognition software is nowhere up to recognising faces the way that humans can. I went to the Casino Conference with the person who's doing facial surveillance work, and there is nothing available commercially.

Reply: Some of it's getting pretty good in the laboratory though.

Ross Anderson: Talk to Feng about his thesis work on irises, and tying cryptographic keys to iris scans.

Reply: So I'm not familiar with Nym, I don't know if it includes this aspect of also demonstrating the property that this is not just this is a pseudonym, but it was believed to be a real person at a certain time. Part of what we're trying to do here is to tie into a plugin architecture. At first I thought, "let's actually build the thing for Kerberos", then I looked at the Kerberos source code, and I said, "maybe let's just describe the protocol". But this is something that you could actually incorporate into your setup so that you could use it on your mail server tomorrow — if we actually wrote the plugin — so it ties into lots of things. Lots of Wikis have CAPTCHAs, but the CAPTCHAs aren't bound to the context in which they're used, and therefore can't be used to prove that you have a particular attribute. But I will look into these, thanks.

So we have this notation that we think could be a useful thing, the idea of humans un-boxing something as an analogue to machines decrypting something, and hopefully this protocol is somewhat useful.

Is that it then?

Michael Roe: Just a quick observation, as far as I know no-one has yet tried extending Proverif, all those kind of formal verification tools to include CAPTCHAs, and you could presumably write some kind of formal guarantee that says, the attacker can't cause a protocol failure without the attacker running this thing that causes work, but I've never seen anybody...

Reply: I did go to a talk a month ago of somebody who is trying to model security ceremonies in Coq, I think, and where security ceremonies are superset of protocols, and it's end-to-end from human brain to human brain, as opposed to from host to host, and it includes primitives like "the person can read this off-screen", "the person can type this into that machine" and then they tried to verify that some protocols work the way we think they do. It seems like that's particularly interesting because then you could ask, "in order for this protocol to work the way I think I do, how much ceremony is required?"

Matt Blaze: Yes, I can't help but be reminded, tangentially, of the authentication in the AT&T Clipper phones in which to do a Diffie-Hellman, the hash of Diffie-Hellman is displayed on each end, and then you read the hash to each other, and confirm they match. You haven't established who it is you're talking to, but you're establishing that if there is someone in the middle they are able to perform human voice generation of the appropriate hash code.

Sandy Clark: Unless you recognise the voice.

Matt Blaze: Over that you could not recognise the voice, it's such low bandwidth that you couldn't recognise yourself, but it had the flavour of what you're doing.

Reply: Well in that case I guess you could man-in-the-middle in the active sense.

Matt Blaze: If you have a team of operators in your man-in-the-middle station.

Reply: Well, then you could actually listen to communications from one to the other, whereas in this, if you man-in-the-middle then you just break ...

Matt Blaze: Well it's solving a different problem, it's only similar in flavour, it's not the same.

Bruce Christianson: It's ultimately a question of what service you're trying to provide.

Paul Revere Protocols*

Paul Syverson

Naval Research Laboratory, USA

Abstract. At the start of the American Revolution, Paul Revere designed one of the most famous covert signaling protocols in history. Though incredibly simple, it has interesting features that we explore in this paper. We also consider the use of Paul Revere protocols in covert computer communication. The Sleeping Beauty problem is a heavily researched puzzle in the theory of probability that previously only had counterintuitive descriptions and complex analyses. Representing it using Paul Revere protocols in covert computer communication provides a clear, natural explanation and simple resolution of this problem.

1 Introduction

The first armed conflicts of the American Revolution against British rule were the battles at Lexington and Concord Massachusetts on April 19, 1775. As is perhaps typical at the outset of a war, the atmosphere just prior was charged with anticipation. On orders to disarm rebels of their arms stores in Concord and arrest the leaders, particularly Samuel Adams and John Hancock, the military governor sent out patrols on April 18 to inquire after Adams and Hancock as well as to monitor any messengers who might be reporting on movements of the British Regulars (soldiers) garrisoned in Boston. For more than a week before, the rebels had been anticipating military action. The different and increased actions of patrols that day indicated that something was imminent.

Amongst other events of April 18, Paul Revere gave an order to signal the rebels in Charlestown upon the movement of the British Regulars from Boston. The signal was to be of lanterns shown from the steeple in the Old North Church, the tallest building in Boston and in the North End, thus visible across the Charles River. The famous poetic rendition of the protocol from Longfellow was "One if by land, and two if by sea." This was to indicate whether the troops were coming by boat across the Charles River or over the then narrow isthmus connecting Boston to the mainland. There was an elaborate and multiply-redundant alarm and announcement system that the rebels used in events leading up to the war, but in this paper we focus only on this simple protocol (and others we study and devise that are similar to it).

Unlike most security protocols, the Paul Revere protocol (PR) does not employ cryptographic concealment of the message sent nor steganographic hiding of a message within other communication. It was meant to be entirely covert,

---

* The rights of this work are transferred to the extent transferable according to title 17 U.S.C. 105.

B. Christianson et al. (Eds.): Security Protocols 2012, LNCS 7622, pp. 259–266, 2012.

and the message was simply encoded. It might seem that there is thus nothing to be analyzed. But there is more here than is immediately apparent.

First note that the signal is of one or two lights. This can be seen as an optimal choice. The receiver could not know whether a message is coming or not. Thus, one could not use zero or one lights since there is then no way to differentiate no sending of a message at all from the sending of a zero. Alternatively we might think of one light as functioning simply to indicate a message is being sent, the other (or its absence) then conveying the message. This is then the minimum necessary. But besides thus being an efficient use of resources, using the minimum served a security function. Being seen to send a message at all was very risky, possibly fatally so. Thus the message was shown only briefly, and using just one or two lanterns may have been a safe choice as well.

2   How Many Messages Fit in a Bit?

There has been controversy since at least the 1800s over who was in the steeple signaling with the lanterns, Robert Newman or Captain John Pulling. Fischer [3] gives a compelling argument that the circumstances indicate that it was actually both men acting together, while Thomas Bernard kept watch below.[1] This naturally gives rise to considering the protocol as comprised of two messages of one light each, rather than a single message of either one or two lights.

Besides any coordination question, this might also raise questions for the Regulars if they should have occasion to afterwards capture a single man with a lantern and question him. Even if they know the protocol, if he refuses to speak or won't say anything beyond admitting that he held up a lantern, this won't tell them whether the signal was one or two.[2] Alternatively, the man might have been killed when captured but be seen to be in possession of a lantern. Then the uncertainty might be between no message sent, or one, or two.

Note that the uncertainty for the adversary in this case could hold if they knew the protocol specification of one if by land, two if by sea, but did not know whether one man or two were involved in sending the messages, or if they only expected one man and did not know whether he had held his lantern aloft once, twice, or not at all. Though there is every indication that they acted together with full knowledge of each other, we could easily imagine a protocol in which the two signalers were not told or able to observe whether the other signaled or not, specifically to complicate what could be learned if either should be compromised. For example, they could each have been given separate instructions by a superior. At the appropriate time, they could arrange to be within hearing, but not view of each other, e.g., at windows on either side of a chimney. They could then say "Ready. Set. Now." to each other and then follow their individual instructions about whether or not to hold up a lantern. Along with the simplest possible covert signaling protocol, in this case we would have the simplest possible threshold-secret protocol.

---

[1] Though I have used many sources for historical statements made herein, I primarily rely on [3].

[2] Thanks to Henry Corrigan-Gibbs for first suggesting this possibility in discussion.

For the Regulars, however, it was generally clear at that point that rebels in Boston were aware of their actions. The most important part of the sent message they would want to prevent and/or detect may be simply the indication that the Regulars were on the move. Any message at all would have conveyed that much, but in our alternative PR protocol involving two signaling principals able to synchronize while keeping the half-bit each may have sent private from the other, the message sent could not be revealed by a captured man. Not only is there uncertainty between "Land" and "Sea" if it is known the captured man showed his light; there is also uncertainty between no message being sent at all and "Land" if it is known that he did not. (This seems to be almost a dual of the following question first given to me by Bob Morris at a SPW long ago: Can one determine which of three switches controls a single incandescent bulb that is out of sight in an adjacent room if one can put the switches in any combination of on and off one wants but is permitted only a single opportunity to enter the room and observe the bulb? For those not familiar with this classic, the answer is left as an exercise to the reader.)

Let us leave the question of what an eavesdropper might learn and consider the uncertainty of the intended receiver in Charlestown. There are several sources of uncertainty for our Bob across the river from Alice. The channel does not guarantee delivery. As Fischer observed, Revere called the lights "lanthorns" after the use of paper-thin slices of cow-horn to cover the sides. "These primitive devices emitted a dim, uncertain light." (op. cit., p. 99) This could have made it hard to see one or both lanterns being raised. To send a message require Alice and Bob to synchronize: he must be receiving at precisely the moment she sends. But their synchronization is not guaranteed in this setting. It is thus unclear whether no signal indicates nothing to tell or synchronization failure between them. Also, the lights might have been shown in succession or at least not held up exactly simultaneously from start to finish. Indeed, though no doubt written for dramatic intent[3] rather than to underscore this possibility, the Longfellow poem says of Paul Revere in the relevant passage:

> And lo! as he looks, on the belfry's height
> A glimmer, and then a gleam of light!
> He springs to the saddle, the bridle he turns,
> But lingers and gazes, till full on his sight
> A second lamp in the belfry burns.

The synchronization issue creates the potential that any of no message, "Land", or "Sea" could be received when "Sea" is sent—even if the channel is clear and the signal is strong.

If we ignore the possibility of no message being received, and simply consider that a 1 will be received with certainty but that a 2 will be received with probability p and a 1 with probability $1 - p$. we obtain Golomb's Z-channel. Variants

---

[3] There are many well-known historical inaccuracies and embellishments in Longfellow's poem, which was written largely to serve as inspiration to Northerners in 1861, as the America South was on the verge of seceding from the United States, rather than as a historically accurate document.

of this where the amount of time to send a signal is what distinguishes which of two messages is sent have also been examined as covert signaling channels. Analysis of these channels assume that specific messages can be sent repeatedly, allowing the communicants to compensate for noise in the channel. In our case of an optimal one-off signal, this is not possible and the assumptions underlying analyses of channel capacity, etc. do not apply—whether for Golomb's analysis of the Z-channel or for covert timing channels [6].

3   Updating Paul Revere: A Rebel Meets a Princess

We have already considered expanding the original Paul Revere protocol to a threshold-secret variant, not by changing what is sent at all but simply by allowing that the lanterns might be held by two people who coordinate but do not know whether the other held a lantern aloft or not. We now consider applying the basic protocol structure to more modern covert signaling contexts.

As already noted, in the setting of the original use of the PR protocol it is likely that conveying "The Regulars are on the move." was as important or more important than the specific "Land" or "Sea" message. But in other settings the interaction between Alice and Bob may be accepted as unavoidable, and the goal of their adversary is to make sure that Bob can infer as little as possible from observing Alice's activity. For example, in a multilevel secure system, Alice (High) may share a resource with Bob (Low). Typical covert-channel security in this context is to prevent or limit what Bob can know about other High information. Thus, if there is a High file with "Land" or "Sea" written in it, the goal of Alice would be to signal which to Bob, while the adversary's goal would be to prevent that. Of course standard access control rules will prevent such things as Alice writing a 1 or a 2 to some file Bob can read. But if she can cause something to occur in the system either once or twice, she can covertly convey the same thing. It may not be practically possible to prevent Bob from detecting such occurrences when they happen, but if the system prevents him from keeping track of whether it was a single or double occurrence, this would seem to have the same practical effect.

What Bob can learn under precisely such restrictions has actually been extensively studied, not in the theory of covert communication but in a philosophical thought problem in reasoning about probability, the Sleeping Beauty problem:

Once upon a time, Sleeping Beauty was forced to participate in a bizarre experiment. Deranged researchers planned to put her to sleep for an extended period. Their next actions depended on the results of a fair coin flip. If it landed heads, they would wake her up once during her sleep and would then give her a potion that wiped any memory of having been awakened. She would then stay asleep until the end of the trial. If the coin landed tails, they would perform the same experiment, except they would wake her twice during the trial instead of once, wiping her memory after each encounter. (For convenience of exposition these awakenings are said to happen on Monday and/or Tuesday.) Upon her first awakening, what probability should she attach to the coin having landed heads?

One obvious answer to the question is 1/2. She believes the coin is fair. So she believed the probability was 1/2 before going to sleep. She knows the protocol. So she already knew she would be woken up and has thus learned nothing new upon awakening. So she should assign the same probability as she did before she went to sleep.

Another obvious answer is 1/3. If this experiment were carried out over and over again, only 1/3 of the times when she woke would the coin have landed heads. Any awakening is basically indistinguishable from any other. So the probability of heads is 1/3.

This is the Sleeping Beauty problem as first set out by Elga [2]. (It was first named the "Sleeping Beauty problem" by Stalnaker in describing unpublished work of Zuboff.) It is in essence a Paul Revere protocol where Sleeping Beauty is prevented from keeping track of whether she has seen one or two occurrences. And, if there is a way for Sleeping Beauty to correctly answer the question with a probability different from 1/2, then it would seem to imply that it is not adequate in the multilevel-secure covert signaling example above to prevent Bob from keeping track of occurrences. If she is able to say correct things about the value of the coin flip then she must be reflecting this even though she does not know whether she has been awakened once or twice.

So what does the literature say about the problem? It is part of a larger research area on updating probabilistic beliefs in agents with imperfect recall. The literature on the problem is unevenly (but significantly) split between "halfers" and "thirders". (Note that the above two are not the only arguments for the halfer or thirder position even just as sketches, but we will not examine most of them.) The literature also includes those who simply argue against one of the positions [9], or discuss various aspects but take no single position themselves. Much of it examines various rationality principles, such as van Fraassen's reflection principle [1,5], reasoning about oneself and one's own state, or questions associated with axioms of probability, for example, countable additivity [8]. What all the accounts mentioned have in common (and in common with others as well) is that their accounts involve the revision of beliefs as Sleeping Beauty moves to a new state through time and/or learns about her state, e.g., learning that it is Monday. They also involve the fantastic story of complete memory erasure. Halpern does present a multi-agent system analysis of the Sleeping Beauty problem that indicates uncertainty arises not so much from imperfect recall on Tuesday as from the asynchrony that at the moment of considering the question on Monday, Sleeping Beauty does not know what day it is [5]. Nonetheless, he still retains the basic fantastic story and analysis of belief change over time. Arguments relying on fantastic assumptions are hard to judge because, when they lead to surprising conclusions, we are left wondering if the conclusions are any less fantastic even in contexts where such assumptions don't apply. It is thus preferable to avoid them if the same basic points can be made without them.

Based on this concern, Neal [7] constructs another problem with essentially the same uncertainties and probabilities but without the fantastic memory erasure. His problem, the Sailor's Child, involves decisions by a sailor about whether to have children and with whom based on a coin flip and a committed but un-known written statement in a book. The question is then for a child attaching a probability to the possibility that s/he has a step sibling in another city. The Sailor's Child problem avoids the fantastic. But it does not avoid a bizarre, con-voluted, and unlikely enough story that one may also wonder what intuitions for that situation can tell us about assigning probability when bizarre assumptions and intentions are not in effect. Notice however that, for computing systems, intentional resetting of recent memory while still retaining all prior knowledge is not fantastic but rather standard.[4] Thus, looking at covert communication via a Paul Revere protocol may be beneficial to our understanding of the Sleep-ing Beauty problem and not just the other way around. We now set out the connection between the two in more detail.

4   Sleeping Beauty Channels

Consider a system with a single discrete channel. At any given time, a bit is sent on the channel or not. The system is initialized with all values set to 0. The system takes the result of a fair coin flip at t_{Sunday}. If heads, it places a 1 on the channel at t_{Monday} and a 0 on the channel at $t_{Tuesday}$. If tails, it places a 1 on the channel at t_{Monday} and also at $t_{Tuesday}$. Times can be taken to reflect the obvious ordering implied by the subscripts, although this is not actually significant. A receiver, SB, reads the channel whenever a 1 is sent on the channel and stores the value, but it is only permitted to store the single bit. It is not permitted to access or store the current value of the system clock at the time the bit is stored or to retain what the previously stored value was once a new value is stored. It also does not read the channel when the value sent on it is 0. After $t_{Tuesday}$ the system halts and all values are reset to 0. The storing of a 1 corresponds to waking Sleeping Beauty on the corresponding day.

Given that her stored value is a 1, what is the probability that the coin was heads? The fraction of times the coin is heads when the observed value is 1 will tend to 1/3 the more times the experiment is run. Thus, expected value of heads given a 1 across all runs is 1/3. Potentially there is a backwards channel. If Sleeping Beauty could signal to her High collaborator that she will guess the coin is tails, and if he can set the number of tails awakenings to be as described above, then he can cause her to be right about the value of the coin on 2/3 of the awakenings that occur in a repeated experiment. But we have not been given that this is a repeated experiment, and the only uncertainty would seem to be due to the fair coin flip itself. Whether she is woken once or twice is determined

---

[4] There is at least one account prior to ours that captures the relevant probabilities with appeal to neither the fantastic nor the bizarre. Groisman [4] provides an account in which an automated device places one green ball in a box if a coin lands heads and two red balls if the coin lands tails. On his account, the answers of 1/2 and 1/3 are correct respectively *under the experimental setup of coin tossing* and *under the setup of wakening* (removing a ball from the box). This account is not fantastic and not bizarre, but I personally did not find it very illuminating either.

once the coin is flipped. And she knows only that she is awakened; by design she does not know how many times. Is this enough for her to learn anything about a High value?

To help resolve this, we consider different ways that one could create the distribution of an unfair coin starting with a fair coin. (These are in a way complements to the famous von Neumann algorithm for creating a fair coin distribution from an arbitrarily weighted coin.)

The conceptually simplest way to create the unfair-coin distribution would be to physically alter the fair coin so as to affect its propensities for heads and tails. If this is done so as to make the coin weighted towards tails at two to one odds, then it seems clear that even for a single trial, the probability of heads is $1/3$. But in the Sleeping Beauty problem the coin is not physically altered. The distribution of reporting on coin flips is what is changed.

Suppose whenever the fair coin comes up heads, a secondary (fair) coin flip is made. If the secondary coin flip is heads, then a heads is noted. If the secondary coin flip is tails, then the initial heads is ignored (i.e., nothing is recorded), and another trial is begun. If the primary coin flip is tails, this is recorded and another trial begun. In this setting the expected fraction of heads in a series of trials will again trend to $1/3$. This seems more like the Sleeping Beauty scenario than the weighted coin does: Here the coin is fair. Sleeping Beauty knows the protocol. And even though it is just the distribution of recorded coin flips that is changed, we can easily see that if the experiment is only run until she is given one result (awakened a first time), the probability that the fair coin is heads in that case is $1/3$ (since $\sum_{n=1}^{\infty} 1/4^n = 1/3$).

We have now reflected a distribution with a two to one ratio in favor of tails based on a fair coin flip, but note that this comes from omitting results from the distribution not adding them, as in Sleeping Beauty problems. So construct a standard Sleeping Beauty series in the obvious way: If the coin flip is heads, record a heads. If the coin flip is tails, record two tails. The sequence of recorded coin flips will also tend towards a distribution of $1/3$ heads and $2/3$ tails.

So is there a Sleeping Beauty channel that can pass probabilistic information about secret values to Sleeping Beauty? There is no ordinary covert channel in the sense of a way to cause Sleeping Beauty to have different observations or actions depending on a High value. The situation is constrained so that her observations are always indistinguishable. In the scenario with the secondary coin flip, however, the probability that a guess of tails is correct about the first recorded coin flip is $2/3$. And by varying the algorithm for what is recorded according to secondary coin flips, this probability can be made arbitrarily high. Thus, there is a backwards channel: if Sleeping Beauty conveys her intended guess to a High insider, he can arrange that she is correct about that with arbitrarily high probability, even though the value about which she is guessing is what the result of a single fair coin flip is.

But note that no amount of adding values to the series of recorded coin flips can affect the probability of the first recorded coin flip. In the standard Sleeping Beauty scenario, if she conveys an intended guess of tails, she will either be wrong about this once or right about it twice. And each of these possibilities is equally likely, given the fair coin. Because this protocol does affect the distribution, if the experiment is repeated she can be right about the value of coin flips 2/3 of the time. So there is a backwards probabilistic channel in this still weaker sense. But, unlike the previous scenario, she cannot gain even probabilistic information about any particular coin flip.

In the original Sleeping Beauty problem (or our covert signaling representation of it above) being woken doesn't correlate in any way to the probability of being heads for any single trial. Thus, in the original Sleeping Beauty problem she should refuse to answer the question until she is told how many times the experiment is run. She cannot tell which trial she is in if there is more than one, but she should answer 1/3 if she is told the experiment will run for more than one trial, and she should answer 1/2 if she is told that it will only be run once.

5   Conclusion

In this paper we have examined what is perhaps the simplest protocol ever devised for covert communication. Though its designer, Paul Revere, was an amateur at protocol design, it was optimally secure and efficient and was effective in critical real-world use. We also showed how a minor change, simply removing an implicit communication between the message senders, transforms this into the simplest threshold-secret protocol. Finally by considering Paul Revere protocols in the context of modern covert computer communication, we were able to resolve and explain in a natural way the Sleeping Beauty problem, a basic question in probability theory that had previously depended on counterintuitive assumptions and appeal to abstract principles about self awareness, countable additivity, and updating of beliefs.

References

1. Arntzenius, F.: Reflections on Sleeping Beauty. Analysis 62(1), 53–62 (2002)
2. Elga, A.: Self-locating belief and the Sleeping Beauty problem. Analysis 60(2), 143–147 (2000)
3. Fischer, D.H.: Paul Revere's Ride. Oxford University Press (1994)
4. Groisman, B.: The end of sleeping beauty's nightmare. British Journal for the Philosophy of Science 59(3), 409–416 (2008)
5. Halpern, J.Y.: Sleeping Beauty reconsidered: Conditioning and reflection in asynchronous systems. In: Gendler, T.S., Hawthorne, J. (eds.) Oxford Studies in Epistemology, vol. 1, ch. 5, pp. 111–142. Oxford University Press (2005)
6. Moskowitz, I.S., Greenwald, S.J., Kang, M.H.: An analysis of the timed z-channel. IEEE Transactions on Information Theory 44(7), 3162–3168 (1998)
7. Neal, R.M.: Puzzles of anthropic reasoning resolved using full non-indexical conditioning. Technical Report 0607, Dept. of Statistics, University of Toronto (August 2006), retrieved from http://arxiv.org/abs/math/0608592v1
8. Ross, J.: Sleeping Beauty, countable additivity, and rational dilemmas. Philosophical Review 119(4), 411–447 (2010)
9. White, R.: The generalized Sleeping Beauty problem: a challenge for thirders. Analysis 66(2), 114–119 (2006)

Paul Revere Protocols
(Transcript of Discussion)*

Paul Syverson

Naval Research Laboratory, USA

All right, saving the worst for last. I guess, keeping with the theme, this is not (well in a sense it is) about bringing protocols to life: in this case it's more bringing history to life. I'm going to be describing an actual protocol that was quite significant in history. Some people may know about it. This is a poem that describes the events. This is something that American schoolchildren for many generations, or decades, were forced to memorize after it came out. I was actually, I think, after that period: I don't remember ever having to memorize this (and my school did keep things around for a long time: we were still having air-raid drills when I was a senior in high school in 1976). But in any case I didn't have to memorize this.

It's about Paul Revere's ride. And the relevant part is here in the second stanza:

> He said to his friend, "If the British march
> By land or sea from the town to-night,
> Hang a lantern aloft in the belfry arch
> Of the North Church tower as a signal light,

And then the famous line was:

> One if by land, and two if by sea;
> And I on the opposite shore will be..."

So he was waiting for the signal, and then he's going to go raise the alarm. What was this alarm about? There were a lot of things going on, and then there was a lot of confusion amongst the Whigs (who were the American rebels at the time). They were expecting the possibility of some sort of military action fairly imminently. Some of the leaders amongst them, Adams and Hancock, had already absconded out of town to Lexington, expecting things might not be looking so good. The Regulars (which were the soldiers) were definitely attempting to keep their actions covert. The descriptions say that when they were mustering they left the barracks from the back, and they were supposed to wrap their gear and things to keep it from clanking.

But Boston in 1775 was kind of a small town, so people very quickly figured out what was going on. The rebels knew about the expedition by the time it was going out, and also the Regulars knew that everybody in town knew. So that was

---

* The rights of this work are transferred to the extent transferable according to title 17 U.S.C. 105.

B. Christianson et al. (Eds.): Security Protocols 2012, LNCS 7622, pp. 267–275, 2012.
© Springer-Verlag Berlin Heidelberg 2012

OK. But not only were they trying to keep it quiet, they were also trying to keep it contained—and I'll come back to that in a minute. The expected targets of this military expedition? There were two things. One, it was thought they were going after Adams and Hancock, who were some of the big leaders. They were off in Lexington. And not too far from Lexington was Concord, and there was an arms store there that people thought was going to be captured (possibly).

There are a lot of commonly held beliefs about this, which are wrong. You'll notice in the Longfellow poem he says, "If the British march", and the famous thing (I think that there was actually a movie with this title) "The British are coming, the British are coming" which is supposedly what he said when raising the alarm. But he never said that. At that time nobody was thinking that these were headed towards two separate countries. They were rebelling inside their own country against some things that they weren't happy about—their government. So they were all British. The Whigs didn't think "we're not the British". That was a later historical reconstruction.

Also, Paul Revere was not on the other side. They were signaling the Whigs in Charlestown, and actually the guy they first sent out was captured; he never made it. Revere actually rowed across the Charles, and, when he left town, he already knew that this was underway. (There were some interesting astronomical things going on: there was a full moon, and actually it is suspected that the shadowing actually helped protect him. Anyway I'll get to that.) And then there was another guy, Dawes, who went out through the blockade at Boston, which I'll come back to. One thing I wanted to note was, this wasn't just some sort of one-off protocol that they came up with. There was an elaborate signaling system. There had been earlier alarms and things, and there was quite a bit going on in terms of trying to propagate the information out throughout the Whigs when things were amiss.

So what is all this stuff about "by land or by sea"? How can you go some place either by land or by sea? It might not be apparent. The white part on this map is what Boston looks like (more or less) today. It's been filled in quite a bit from then. The brown part is the shape of the land in 1775. So, when Dawes had to go out there was a blockade here. This was the width. It was a very narrow isthmus, and so he had to get through without appearing suspicious. And that was why Revere went across the river. This was the Charles River, and you can't actually even see on this map the part of Charlestown that existed back then. It was just up here off the map. And the Old North Church, as it was called, was at the time the tallest building in Boston, and therefore it would be visible across the way. So that's what they were doing.

And so what about this protocol? It's interesting: first of all, there's no feedback. They're doing something securely but no feedback, one-way. You can ask Matt and Sandy[1]; trying to do something about security without feedback is a tricky thing, and they can tell you about that another time. Also it's optimal: because you couldn't just send out a single signal; that's only going to work if you're just saying "now" or something like that. You need two, one to basically say, "the message is

---

[1] Or see LNCS 7114 pp 336–358.

coming", and then another to differentiate. It's actually a little bit more subtle because it wasn't that one was for one of these and the other for the other. They can be mixed together—I'll come back to that too in a bit. And this optimality wasn't just good efficiency: it was also a security property. If you were caught doing this, up there signaling people across the way, you were likely going to get killed. So the signal had to be covert to protect the sender: they could only hold it up for a very brief time, and the less chance that they were seen the better their chances of not getting killed for doing this. In fact there were two guys up there, and one guy in the street watching things happen.

Now I was talking about this to a guy named Henry Corrigan-Gibbs, and he noted to me (and there's no evidence that this happened at all but I was thinking about it) that you could actually do this as a secret sharing construction. (By the way, there was a big debate: I read some of the 19th century literature about whether this guy [Robert Newman] or this guy [Capt. John Pulling] did it. And the most compelling thing turns out to be that they both did it—but I'm not going to go into that in the interest of time). So you could imagine that maybe both these guys go up the steeples, and maybe they're on either side of a chimney or something. Each one is going to hold up a lantern, possibly, but neither one knows whether the other one is, and this amounts to a secret sharing protocol because now the people on either side don't see each other's message. But now, if you don't know whether the other guy held up the message or not, then you're kind of in a nice position: if one guy is captured and he held up his lantern, well you don't know whether one lantern was held up or two. And if he didn't hold up his lantern, then you don't even know whether a signal was sent or not.

Frank Stajano: If you are a lantern bearer and you don't know what the other guy is showing, how do you know what you are supposed to show to signal the intended message?

Reply: I'm assuming in this case that the protocol is that they were each told separately whether or not to hold up their lantern.

Frank Stajano: So there was a master guy who told them, "now you do this, you do that"?

Reply: Yes, but they don't know about the other one. This is just a little aside: interestingly, even in this very minimal, simple, tiny protocol you could have a form of secret sharing going on that would help protect things.

Bruce Christianson: They're briefed before they actually climb the tower?

Reply: Yes, right. So this is optimal, which is nice. But the problem with optimality is it doesn't leave a lot of room for error. This is a little bit further down in that same poem, it's fairly long. (I should point out also, as I said, there's lots of mistakes. And as history, Longfellow's poem is crap. But he was also writing in 1860: the U.S. had another crisis brewing, and he was aware of that. A lot of this had to do with inspiration. And as inspirational poetry it was great. So the fact that the history wasn't perfect, I think he could be forgiven for that.) But in any case, as we see later in the poem, he's saying that Revere sees the light and he springs to his saddle. But then he turns back, and he sees another one before taking off. Well, what if he didn't turn back? Or what if one of these two guys was out of sync with the other? There is easy potential for problems. And in fact these lanterns were called lanthorns because they were covered with cowhorn, which is a dim thing. And you could easily imagine there's various ways that that would be a problem.

Matt Blaze: I always thought that they just go up and they leave the lanterns there. They don't?

Sandy Clark: That's what I thought too.

Reply: No, no. Well OK, I wasn't there myself, but my understanding from reading the history is that it was actually very brief, because you wanted the guys on the other shore to see but you didn't want any of the Regulars down in the street to notice.

Matt Blaze: No, but I mean, "someone left the lanterns on again".

Sandy Clark: The picture that went along with the poem was of this tower with two lanterns in it.

Reply: Well that tower actually burned down. The one that's in the North Church was rebuilt in the 1800s.

Matt Blaze: Yes, because of all of those lanterns!

Reply: So the question is, what if you can't be sure about this? And in fact there's been some analyses of, not the same thing, but some related things. Golomb's Z-channel, so named by the shape, was a heavily researched and analyzed covert signaling channel in probability theory: when you're not sure if a message might be sent cleanly or it might not be. This is actually a little bit messier than that because you might not see anything. So you actually have the possibility of two being received, or one, or nothing, and I would have no idea what sort of probabilities to attach to this. But that's OK, because I'm not going to look at the analysis this way anyway. Because I'm going to instead look at something that helps us get a little bit of a handle on probabilities of a very similar problem. This is actually the problem I was thinking about first, and then it occurred to me that this related to the Paul Revere thing. And then I started to think about Paul Revere. But actually the causal order in myself was that I was thinking about another problem first: a strange thought experiment people do to reason about probability and belief updating.

The story goes like this. Sleeping Beauty is taking part in some weird experiment in which she's put to sleep on Sunday night, and a fair coin is flipped (sometimes it's flipped later, I don't care). If the coin comes up heads, she's woken up on Monday and she's asked, "What is the probability that the coin was heads?" If the coin is tails, the exact same thing happens except that, after she's asked on Monday night, she's put back to sleep and her memory is wiped. She has no memory of being awoken. And then she's awoken on Tuesday in the same sort of closed room so she can't tell Monday from Tuesday, and she doesn't know the days. And she's asked the same question, "What do you think the probability of heads is?" And then Wednesday she's woken up, and the experiment is over. So the question is, what should she say when asked, "What is the probability that the coin is heads?"

So one obvious answer is 1/2. Well she knew it was a fair coin on Sunday. She hasn't learned anything new: She knew she was going to be awakened. She got no new information, she knew a priori the probability was 1/2. Nothing has changed, so the probability should be 1/2.

Another obvious answer is 1/3. There's various analyses to do this. I'll just give a quick one. If you did this experiment over and over again, 1/3 of the time that you're woken up, the coin would be heads, 2/3 of the times you are woken up the coin would be tails. So obviously the answer should be 1/3 just from the statistics.

This is actually a problem that has an extensive literature—there's maybe twenty, thirty papers on this.

Bruce Christianson: I'm presuming that Sleeping Beauty is a Bayesian? Or not?

Reply: There are several Dutch book analyses of this. Most of the literature is to deal with belief updating: if you learn something new, what are proper principles for updating your beliefs when you've got new information? Or whether this is new information, and principles of rationality for that. I can't remember the details now but somebody showed that one answer or the other actually violated countable additivity in some way. And there's even a quantum mechanical analysis that I ran across. So I mean, there's a lot of stuff on this.

One thing that at least a few people have noted, is: wait a minute, her memory is wiped!? (I didn't know... I was thinking that didn't have anything to do with computer security before. Well in Frank's talk[2] that turned out to be an issue, you could actually be doing that for somebody). But there is at least one person who said, well look, you have these weird thought experiments, where you're wiping people's memories...

Matt Blaze: But you're actually only wiping her memory of the last couple of days, right? You're not wiping her memory of how many sides a coin has?

Reply: No, correct, you're not wiping other memories.

There's this problem, though, with these philosophical problems where you do weird science-fictiony things. Who knows how should you judge that? So Neal actually came up with a variant where the probabilities work out the same, but you don't create a science fiction story. I won't go through it carefully, but in this one there is a sailor who is involved with women in two different ports. They each want to have a kid with him, so he of course—what else do you do?—decides on a coin flip that, if it's heads he's going to have one child, if it's tails he's going to have two children. But then, based on this same coin flip... he has this book, which he's never looked in, called *A Sailors Guide to Ports*, and he's going to have a child with the woman whose city name appears first in the *Sailors Guide to Ports*. And then, at some point later, a sailor's child wants to know "what's the probability that I have a sibling". And he goes through and shows that basically the probabilities work out the same as in the Sleeping Beauty problem. And OK, yes, fine, so it doesn't involve fantasy per se, but it's still a weird, contorted, confusing philosophical construct. So I was thinking, maybe there's a simpler way we can think about this.

---

[2] Stajano, these proceedings.

Frank Stajano: There's additional probability involved here from having sex with them, after having chosen with whom.

Reply: I'm not going to go into details on *that*, the Sailor's Child example. But I thought: what if you were just thinking that Sleeping Beauty has a friend in the experiment and he's going to signal to her? The only mechanism, the only visible thing is: he can set the number of times she's going to be awakened, if tails. You know, heads once, but, they can agree to this. This can be communicated in the open to her ahead of time. So he could set it to be 20, or whatever. And at first blush (and actually my analysis here is different from what's in the pre-proceedings paper), it would seem that, if she's woken a million times, when she's woken up it's almost always tails. And so even if she just says that it's likely to be tails all the time, that seems to be true with high certainty. I want to unpack that a little bit and think about it.

One question is: what do we know about covert channels when there is an uncertainty about receiving things? Daryl McCullough looked at this at Computer Security Foundations back in 1988. And he had what he called half-bit channels. You can see it's somewhat similar in notion. He had two kinds. There's the positive half-bit channel, where if you get a signal, then that's really a signal. But in absence of a signal, maybe there was no signal—maybe they meant to send zero but maybe it just didn't arrive. You don't know. And then you have a negative half-bit channel where, if you didn't get a signal, that's because there was no signal: there's no accidental non-sending (or something like that, I'm not really sure how to say that). But if you received a signal, it could be noise, or it could be real.

And this made me think that you can have an implicit channel. Suppose the Trojan knows that she's going to say heads with probability p. And you can't change that, it's set ahead of time. But if he could go back and then arrange the coin flips—he can arrange the High information—so that the Low answer is correct, then even though there was not a channel in the traditional sense, it still seems pretty clearly an illicit flow. What Low thinks about that High information will in fact be correct, even though it was made correct for her based on what she was going to say. So I started to unpack that a little bit. They almost seem to be the same.

I identified at least three cases. In one case you could have the Trojan actually arranging the outcomes of the coin flips. So he's setting whether heads or tails match what she thinks. Alternately he could actually filter when to send to her, so that the proportion of the messages that are sent match what she's going to say. So then, if the Trojan didn't send half the time when the coin is heads, then this would match. And again, that seems fairly clearly to be giving her information. But in the Sleeping Beauty problem as described, if he's just arranging so that when the coin does come up tails you just send out a bunch of times, then she will in fact be right about the distribution of tails along there. But that's not really going to tell her anything about the coin flip at any given time, so it seems like thinking about it in this way helps make it really obvious that the right answer is 1/2.

The other thing I thought about this is that all this weird memory wiping is perfectly natural in a computing environment. It's called a discrete memoryless channel: you send something through and then there's no memory. Certainly with a computing device we can have this situation, it could be memoryless. So, Heads you send a ping, tails you send two pings. And then this goes through, and all she's seeing is a series of pings. And again, pretty clearly, any time she's seeing the pings the distribution is going to be such that 2/3 of the time if this is run over and over again, it's going to be due to tails. Nonetheless for any given flip of the coin, she's not going to be able to know. What this is really capturing is that she can't tell when one experiment begins and the next one ends. But again, it seems fairly obvious that the probability is 1/2.

And so looking at this, I got a couple of surprising take-aways out of looking at this work. The first one is that we always think "You don't want amateurs designing your security protocols. That's always a formula for disaster." And we have here at least one good counterexample. This was quite successful. In the end the Whigs won the war and all, and the alarm did get out. So that was kind of surprising. Now I'm used to getting lessons for computer security out of philosophy. (I know a lot of people don't, but I find this happens all the time.) But this lesson was sort of surprising to me because, you would think if you effect the probability that Low is correct about a High value, that would seem clearly a covert information flow—a problem that you would want to rule that out. But I think that what the Sleeping Beauty problem shows you is that you can set up the protocols so that Low is right more of the time than would otherwise be, about the High value, and yet somehow Low doesn't learn anything about the High value. And that was interesting to separate that out, because that was not at all expected. The second one is that this was doubly surprising. One, because I'm not used to getting lessons for philosophy out of computer security. But that's in fact what happens here, because this thing about wiping memory that seemed to be such a weird thing isn't not even worth blushing at, here, in the computer security context. And the other thing was of course that you need that answer to the Sleeping Beauty problem. It became clear from the computer security perspective in a way that was murky with all these weird convoluted stories.

Jonathan Anderson: The lesson for computer security from philosophy, isn't that just copying from Low to High? I mean, you know what Low is going to say so you arrange High to be what Low would have guessed.

Reply: So you could say that this is writing up. But I guess it depends what you're concerned about. In some sense you're writing up. We usually say that writing from Low to High is OK. But Low is telling you effectively: "in the future I am going to choose this value", and then I set up my High values in the computer. I mean, as an example, if Low picks a cryptographic key and then says to High, "when you are responsible, when you have control over the random number generator that's going to generate this key, I'm going to pick this key. You won't be able to communicate to me. But I'm going to pick this key, so make sure that's what you enter in there." That seems problematic. So I agree that it should be OK to write from Low to High, but it's writing from Low to High in a very problematic way.

Jonathan Anderson: In that particular case, isn't it more the integrity that you care about? Because you are using something untrusted to protect something trusted, so you don't want to be reading your encryption keys from somebody who's Low?

Bruce Christianson: Then just swap Low and High.

Jonathan Anderson: Yeah, Biba would fix that. I guess I'm saying that, for keys you care about confidentiality, but you also care about integrity, because you don't want Low messing around with your random number generator.

Reply: No, I disagree, because Low is not messing around with the random number generator here. Low is communicating to High, which is fine. And then you have a malicious High source, which is not supposed to be able to muck with the random number generator, but if they're both trusted at that level, and in fact it has access and is able to do it, it compromises integrity.

Matt Blaze: Low is rewriting the firmware of High.

Bruce Christianson: Well, threats always come in pairs, and the question is: Is Low learning stuff about High that they shouldn't know, or is High corrupt and shadowing Low? And the question is how do you tell those two cases apart.

Reply: Usually we have a notion that writing up is fine and writing down is not. But it depends what you're writing up. And I don't mean this just from an integrity perspective here. This is a secrecy point. If you can tell somebody what you're going to be thinking in the future, and then they can arrange it, that's as if there was a flow. If the secret is actually something which is not a random value (a coin flip or something), but rather "the president's motorcade will be going down this street", then you can't change that. But then again, maybe you can: I'm Low, and I will say, "I'm going to decide that the president's motorcade is going down Sydney Street." And then if High has control over the schedule for where the president's motorcade is going to go, and he changes the schedule of the president's motorcade (so he in fact *does* go down Sydney Street), that's just as bad as the covert flow down. And it's basically the same thing even though we like to pretend that the causal order has to go from High leaking to Low.

Frank Stajano: But it requires a cooperation from High that isn't there.

Bruce Christianson: Yes, but the point is that High has not written to Low, and therefore nothing which was put into the system to detect writes from High to Low will discover enough.

Jonathan Anderson: Yes, but if you have an integrity policy which says "critical information, stuff that ought to be random shall only be derived from things that we trust and have good reason to believe are actually random", then you say, well which of the streets will we pick to drive the limo down?

Bruce Christianson: Well now you have the same problem of whether High and Low would interchange.

Jonathan Anderson: Yes, so it's integrity instead of confidentiality.

Reply: Right, but the point is: usually if you want to say "Low cannot affect the random number generator, but Low can still write up to High", then Low can write up to High. And then if one High process can talk to another one, you're separating it out. So I mean, if you want to put that all together, then yes, Low is compromising the integrity of the whole thing. But usually the way we put it is: it's fine if you get Low information up to High and look at that, and do things.

Jonathan Anderson: As long as you don't make High decisions based on that information.

Reply: No, that's not true, that's supposed to be OK.

Matt Blaze: It leaks information when High's computations have side effects that Low can observe. It's the motorcade going by that's the problem.

Ross Anderson: Well, the fundamental assumption here is that there's bad software at High, because if all the software at High is perfectly specified and correctly programmed, you won't need Bell-LaPadula in the first place.

Reply: Right, that's the whole point of multi-level security, the idea that they might have a Trojan horse at High who can signal to Low. And the thing that Low finds out in the future in fact was due to a Trojan at High. But it wasn't that High was manipulating some variables that Low could observe, that we didn't think (we should probably invoke Earl Boebert's definition of a covert channel here, but maybe I'll save that for after, the one about burning down the barn in a manner surprising to the officials). But in any case, you don't have the High process manipulating things that are then later observable by Low. Rather you have the High process manipulating things that he knows Low is going to say. So it kind of turns the usual causal relations upside down.

Matt Blaze: But it has been pointed out that Bell-LaPadula stops being useful in real computer systems, because real computer systems aren't useful unless they have externally visible side effects that are able to act as a channel from High to Low.

Reply: Right, we go back to the example somebody brought up earlier about Bob Morris saying, "Can you secure this system?" And then you cut the power and say yes.

Matt Blaze: Yes I know exactly how to do that.

Reply: Yeah, I know how to make a secure brick, but yes, yes, exactly.

Jonathan Anderson: If you reverse the way the causality flows, you need to switch. If what you cared about was confidentiality, then when you flip the causality around you need to care about integrity.

Reply: Right, but the surprising piece is: people don't usually think about flipping around the causality. They don't think about mucking around with High so that when Low comes to a decision it will be the right decision. They usually think about trying to cause Low to have a right decision, that's why it's interesting.

Bruce Christianson: We'd focus on trying to stop High from holding the lantern up where we can see it.

Reply: Right, and I only came to that by thinking about this Sleeping Beauty thing, where I was thinking whether you could in fact signal someone.

The Last Word*

Tim Wilson: What precautions do you personally take against eavesdropping?
Bob Morris: Well, first of all, I try never to say anything of significance.

---

* Extract from a talk given by Robert Morris at the University of Hertfordshire during the early days of the Security Protocols Workshop.

Author Index